Contradictions of School Reform

Critical Social Thought
Edited by Michael W. Apple, University of Wisconsin, Madison

Also published in the series:

Contradictions of School Reform

Educational Costs of Standardized Testing

Linda M. McNeil

CRITICAL SOCIAL THOUGHT SERIES • MICHAEL W. APPLE, EDITOR
ROUTLEDGE • NEW YORK AND LONDON

Published in 2000 by
Routledge
29 West 35th Street
New York, NY 10001

Published in Great Britain by
Routledge
11 New Fetter Lane
London EC4P 4EE

Printed in the United States of America on acid-free paper.

Library of Congress Cataloging-in-Publication Data

McNeil, Linda M.
    Contradictions of school reform : educational costs of standardized testing / Linda
McSpadden McNeil.
       p.   cm. — (Critical social thought)
    Includes bibliographical references and index.
    ISBN 0–415–92073–6 (hard) — ISBN 0–415–92074–4 (pbk.)
    1. Education—Standards—United States. 2. School improvement programs—United
States. I. Title. II. Series.
    LB3060.83.M38   2000
    379.1'58'0973—dc21   99–048312
                                                         CIP

To my mother,
Oleta Kelley McSpadden

and the memory of my father,
Thomas Willard McSpadden

gratefully.

Contents

PART III

The "Perverse Effects" of Legislated Learning

Acknowledgments

Our schools exist for the children. I hope that this book helps shed some light on what they see when they go to school each day and what they need when they are there. To the extent that I have succeeded, I owe a great debt to the teachers who welcomed me into their classrooms and who talked freely about what it means to teach in times when children's needs are so great and the public's will to support schools so limited, when the problems are so complicated and the hopes for a quick, cheap fix so seductive. The official reports of the "impact" of state policies rarely include teachers' voices; this book is my attempt to add their voices and those of their students to the record.

I am grateful as well to the principals and central office administrators of the school district, particularly the personnel of the research and evaluation office whose curiosity about teaching and learning in the magnet schools prompted them to lend their approval to the extended field observations in schools. High school students continue to welcome me into their classrooms and into their confidence. They have much to tell us about what they hope to learn and be and why they are often afraid that being in school does not always make much sense. That they are so invisible in many of the reform debates and policies makes it essential that the "indicators" not be the final public word on their school experience.

Funding for the years of data collection was provided by a grant from the Office of Educational Research and Improvement of the U.S. Department of

Education. A Mellon Fellowship and the support of the Rice University Center
for Education provided invaluable support for data analysis and writing time.
The Brown Foundation, Inc. has been a faithful supporter of our work with
teachers in urban schools and of my research. I am grateful every day for their
confidence that schools can be good places for children and for their leadership in the funding community on issues of schooling and children. The interpretations herein reflect my own analysis and not that of the U.S. Office of
Educational Research and Improvement or other funding organizations.

Being a visiting scholar at the Stanford University School of Education
came at a critical time in the analysis; for extending that opportunity, I am
particularly indebted to Larry Cuban and Nel Noddings. Michael Kirst of the
Stanford School of Education faculty was willing to discuss how things worked
"behind the scenes" of Ross Perot's reform effort. Conversations with Elliot
Eisner and a group of Stanford graduate students helped maintain a humanistic, non-technicist view of the curriculum at just the time I was working
through the data on the state's protocols on teaching and testing.

We are like our students in that we thrive when someone cares for us and
cares about our work. I am indebted to those colleagues whose writings teach
and inspire and whose caring helps sustain both my inquiry and my vision.
Maxine Greene, Patricia Albjerg Graham, Jacqueline Jordan Irvine, Herbert
Kliebard, Catherine Lacey, Mary Metz, Nel Noddings, Jeannie Oakes, Maconda
Brown O'Connor, John Palmer, Hally Beth Poindexter, and William Russell are
among the many who are "in" this book through the constancy of their support. Patsy Sloan, Alice Kagi, Mary Louise Brewer, and Diane McNeil Dittrich
are among the teachers who remind me by daily example what "authentic
teaching" can be.

My colleagues in the Rice University Center for Education have given
much more personal support than I could have imagined and have taken the
findings of this work and their own expertise in urban schools as a call to create innovative programs for authentic learning for both teachers and students. I am grateful every day for their courage as well as for their friendship.
The findings reported in this book are far more clear to me, and more confi-
dently asserted, because they stand in the context of the cumulative understandings we have from the Center's collective work in schools. Ronald Sass,
scientist and global systems expert, keeps firmly grounded in advocacy for
teachers and students. He is my codirector of the Center and an incompara-
ble colleague and friend, who manages to maintain optimism even in the face
of the direst stories from schools. Angela Valenzuela has taught me well to lis-

ten to the silenced voices among the children and their communities; her tough mind and gracious spirit have been invaluable to my students and to my work. Patsy Cooper, Bernie Mathes, and Margaret Immel, all of the School Literacy and Cultures Project, have given us a deeper understanding of children and of the kinds of teachers they need to nurture their fragility and resilience as they grow. Through Cultural Conversations, Connie Floyd teaches us deeper ways to consider racial identity formation and its centrality to teaching and learning and, in so doing, has aided my analysis of the racial issues in the magnet schools. Elnora Harcombe, through the Model Science Laboratory Project, has shown us, and the nation, what urban teachers can become when a community invests in their learning; her helpful readings of this manuscript have been instructive, her friendship a great gift. In the "Ways of World-Making" seminars of the Asia Outreach Project, historian Richard Smith brings teachers into ways of knowing that help open a wider world for them and their students, just as his inimitable teaching inspires in them a different kind of work.

My goal of using this book to give voice to teachers has been greatly inspired by the Center's School Writing Project, which for more than ten years has helped teachers find their voices as writers and in turn create among their students communities of readers and writers. Marvin Hoffman, founding director; Sharon Smith, Sheila Whitford, Terri Goodman, Priscilla Fish, and many other teacher leaders of School Writing Project have my profound respect and gratitude for every time I have heard a child, often in a desperately under-resourced school, say "since I became a writer. . . ." Doris Rodgers Robins, along with Barbara Reed, has helped break down the de-skilling effects of local school policies by linking teachers to their national colleagues through the Coalition of Essential Schools. Cheryl Craig, in her work with teachers and principals, Wallace Dominey and Cylette Willis, in science education, Randy Hanson, and Amanda Lehrer Nash have joined the Center more recently; they have my gratitude for the new ideas and programs they have added to the Center's work in urban schools. None of us would have been able to undertake any of these endeavors if Linda Bachrach had not been passionate in helping build the financial base of the Center; she taught the philanthropic community about children's possibilities and about their need for strong teachers. Vice Provost for Research and Graduate Studies Jordan Konisky has given the Center strong support and advocacy. Debra Gamble, our administrator, Catherine Crawford, program director, and Brenda Tristan, staff assistant, make sure that all of this creativity and innovation stand on a steady base. I am indebted to them not only for all they do for the Center but also for assuming extra duties during the completion of this book. Laurie Hammons brought a very professional level of attention to the details of the manuscript; Laurie, I thank you.

I am grateful to my students in the Rice Teacher Education Program and to the students who have shared in the research seminar. Among them, Ann Piper, now a teacher, provided valuable assistance to this research. My colleagues in the Department of Education, Meredith Skura, Joe Dan Austin, Lissa Heckelman, Roland Smith, Myrl Carlson, and Olga Trejo, have all helped make this work worthwhile.

I am very much indebted to Lorrie Shepard for analyzing the economic costs of the TECAT; that study countered the public relations messages and enabled others to begin to look behind the rhetoric of standardized "reforms." George Madaus, too, merits thanks; the investigations he, Walt Haney, Al Beaton, and their colleagues have undertaken into the economics of the testing industry are much needed and all too rare.

Michael Apple has changed our field, altered our ways of seeing schools, pushed our thinking about schools and society. The issue of *education and power* is, by his efforts and his support of many others', no longer the province of esoteric social critics, but a central part of the lexicon of theory and practice in education. By his own writings and by his generous efforts to help critical scholars find each other, he has broadened the audience for critical scholarship and has deepened the collective potential of the work. I am pleased that this study of the negative consequences of standardization in education will be read as a part of the Critical Social Thought Series, in the context of the growing body of writings on the convergence of increasing pressures to commercialize and de-democratize public education.

Heidi Freund of Routledge has shepherded the book by attending to both its contribution to critical scholarship and its potential to help parents better understand whether their schools are serving their children well.

I am grateful to Tom and Sal McSpadden, Judith Schoenherr, Bill and Barbara Jordan, Joyce and Rob Quinn, Margaret Sass, Dan and Sharon McNeil, and Gordon and Mary Cosby, and Liz and Larry Kuo for reasons they each know well.

To Kathryn and Carrie, my gratitude for all you are and all you are becoming. See you on the Mesa.

And now that the book is complete, I find that I am left with no words to say adequately what most needs to be said: to say thank you to Ken McNeil for making this all possible. His continued belief in the project and in me has been a gift. In the courtroom his deep knowledge of complex organizational behavior and his strong sense of justice are visible to all; in this book, they stand just out of sight, but invaluably so.

My father was a petroleum engineer with a major oil company for more than thirty years. It was from him that I learned to be skeptical of bureaucratic power. He was an inventor and a creative craftsman in a corporation that permitted only the Inventors to invent. He ignored the organization chart and went on inventing anyway, designing new tools, securing patents for new instruments to detect and deter corrosion and, later, crafting new gadgets for woodworking. He was eager to read this book because he had followed the Perot reforms with great interest and with no trust at all in the quick fixes Perot's standardization plans claimed. He had seen people try to "engineer" an oil well from an air conditioned office five hundred miles away; why would anyone want to run schools that way? We miss his wit and good sense, his insatiable curiosity, the things he made. This book is dedicated to his memory and to my mother who, along with him, has been a rock of steady support for our family.

L.M.

1999

Series Editor's Introduction

The news about schools is grim, we are told. We are constantly reminded that schools are supposedly failing. Our children are not being prepared to meet the challenges of the present or the future. Our educational system is inefficient and ineffective, with poor test scores and even worse discipline. Our teachers are poorly trained academically and are more interested in pay than in meeting the needs of our students and our economy. The knowledge that is taught is "dumbed down," or it fails to uphold traditional moral standards. These and other charges are constantly leveled at schools and teachers. The solutions that have been proposed are varied—and sometimes contradictory. But all agree that major reforms are needed.

In school systems throughout the nation, one of the major elements of reform has been the development of "standards." Proponents of standards believed that these would ensure quality education, particularly since they would allow for testable results that would enable comparisons to be made between schools and across districts. At times, these standards take the form of broad goals intended to guide the work of students and teachers. Yet, increasingly, they are not broad at all, but extremely narrow and reductive. Given the immense amount of time and money we are spending on the development of local, state, and national standards and of tests to measure whether or not we have succeeded in reaching them, it is remarkable that very little is known about what their effects are, especially in those schools populated by students whose achievement historically has been quite low. What happens in those states and cities where the rush to standardize the curriculum and measure its success through standardized testing has been the strongest? Who benefits from this? Do such things as standardization and high-stakes testing really improve the schooling of the least-advantaged children? Do they improve the quality of teaching and curricula? Granted, holding teachers' feet to the fire of standardized teaching, curricula, and testing gives us a sense of security, but is there a significant downside? It would be deeply ironic if these supposed reforms actually made the situation worse rather than better. Because of this, it is absolutely essential that we ask critical questions about the realities of life in schools in those places where standardization has become *the* universal answer to the deep-seated problems of education. Linda McNeil's book, *Contradictions of School Reform*, takes us inside some real schools and asks these kinds of critical questions. In doing so, she extends the reach of the democratic and critical tradition in education in important ways.

Such critical work has never been more important than it is now. Neo-liberal, neo-conservative, and authoritarian populist critics have set about "reforming" schools so that they meet the needs defined by conservative forces, not those of the most disadvantaged members of this society. For neo-liberals, markets will solve all of our problems. For neo-conservatives, only by returning to a thoroughly romanticized version of "the Western tradition" and only by instituting a form of Social Darwinist competition through ever-rising "standards" will schools be effective. And for the authoritarian populists of the religious right, only by bringing God back into the classroom can we return to order, discipline, and "real knowledge" (Apple 1996, 2000). Thus, the choices given to us are either setting the market lose on our teachers and children or instituting mechanisms of extremely tight control over schooling.

It is the latter that provides the central theme behind *Contradictions of School Reform*. The book traces the history and the effects of the intense pressure to standardize curricula, teaching, and evaluation in the United States during the past two decades. It provides powerful lessons about what can happen, especially to our most effective teachers and schools, when business models are connected to systems of tight control in education.

For many conservative critics of education, it is the very combination of models taken from the corporate sector and mechanisms of strict accountability that will provide the engine to drive educational reform in more effective directions. In essence, the assumption is that being "businesslike"—that is, bringing the procedures that supposedly have guaranteed efficiency, leanness, and flexibility in the corporate sector—will automatically bring about fundamental change in education (Clarke and Newman 1997). It is extremely interesting that given the vast wealth of models of effective school reforms, policy makers have gravitated toward those generated out of the corporate sector. While there is actually a long history of such borrowing (Kliebard 1995), what may work for issues of administrative efficiency and budgets, may be much less effective in dealing with either meaningful teacher-student interaction or the utter complexity of classroom life. After all, our children are *not* plastic masses of raw material that can be "processed" in the same way we make breakfast cereals.

Often an utterly romanticized portrayal of the business sector is used to justify these mechanisms of tight control. Yet, it is important to remember that an extremely large portion of businesses *fail*. While the financial failure of firms is important, I am also talking about other kinds of failure. The literature is filled with accounts of alienated employees who find little meaning in their work and who are constantly subjected to external controls that have little or no relevance to the way work is best organized (see Apple 1995; Greider 1997). Is this what will happen in schools? Can schools be treated as "businesses"? What is lost in the process? These are among the questions that McNeil's analysis helps us answer.

It is unfortunately all too usual that the most widely used measures of the "success" of school reforms are the results of standardized achievement tests. This simply will not do. We need constantly to ask what reforms do to schools as a whole and to each of their participants, including teachers, students, administrators, community members, local activists, and so on. Without asking these kinds of questions, we are apt to be satisfied with surface changes that offer superficially positive results while actually often making problems significantly worse in the long run.

A good example of this is the current pressure toward marketization and privatization of schools through voucher and choice plans. We are beginning to see the hidden effects of this in a number of countries. Rather than dispersing power to local communities, it seems actually to consolidate more power within the administrative structure of the school. Much more time, energy, and resources are spent on enhancing the public image of a "good school" and less time, energy, and resources are spent on pedagogic and curricular substance. Teachers experience not increased autonomy and professionalism, but intensification of their work. Schools overall paradoxically do not diversify, but become more similar and more committed to a standard and traditional (and often mono-cultural) curriculum. Finally, it is becoming clearer that the effects are exceptionally negative on poor children and children of color (Whitty, Power, and Halpin 1998; Lauder and Hughes 1999).

These issues are not limited to education in the United States, but are instead truly international. For example, during a period of time when I was living in London, one of the major daily newspapers had a headline that read, if I may paraphrase, "Radical Teachers Block Reforms." The story related how a group of elementary school teachers had become deeply upset about the use of government-mandated standardized testing to justify a return to tracking in the early elementary grades. They were convinced that these mandatory tests would have unequal effects. Rather than improving schools, the tests would have quite discriminatory results. While couched in the language of educational reform, the ultimate effect would be to put in place an even more damaging system of race and class stratification. It would actually make it that much harder to create an education that was responsive and socially just. As recent research has documented, these teachers were correct (Mentor et al. 1997; Whitty, Power, and Halpin 1998).

The fact that many of the current conservative reforms being instituted in many nations have often revivified inequalities makes it all the more imperative that we not accept unquestioningly the rhetorical claims made by politicians, conservative critics, and efficiency experts that they have *the* answer to turning our schools around. Rather than accepting the claims, what we need to do is to pay close attention to what actually happens in schools to teachers, to children, and to successful and democratic educational practices when we look behind the rhetorical artifice. This is McNeil's aim, and she is quite successful in reaching it. She details the costs that must be paid when we assume that standardizing teaching and curricula and having the tail of the test wag the dog of the teacher and the student are the major paths to improved schooling. As she demonstrates, the price we pay is not worth it when measured in the lives and futures of identifiable children and teachers.

The arguments in *Contradictions of School Reform* can be summed up in Linda McNeil's own words:

> The soundbites that seduce policymakers always emphasize claims
> of benefits, not actual costs. As documented in this book, the costs
> are great: a decline in the quality of what is taught and a new form
> of discrimination in the education of poor and minority kids. But
> perhaps the worst effect is the silencing of two voices most important in understanding the real effects of standardization: the teachers and the children.

These arguments are not simply stipulated. McNeil takes us into schools that were engaging in an education that was serious, disciplined, and meaningful to students who are among the most dispossessed. She shows what happened to these and other schools when major changes were mandated that put in place reductive instruments of standardization and control. The stories she tells may not be pleasant, but we ignore them at our risk.

This book not only adds a good deal to our understanding of what happens when reforms go awry but also it reinvigorates the tradition of critical research in education by illuminating the connections between policy initiatives and what actually happens at the level of practice in schools. In doing so, McNeil has entered into an area that has too long been left unexplored by critical educators. Critical research in education is guided by a set of broad ethical and sociocultural commitments: extending the reality of democracy to all of this society's groups and institutions, including all of its economic, political, and cultural life; eliminating the basic causes of the massive differences in wealth and power, in economic and cultural capital; investigating the ways in which education participates in maintaining these differences or may be employed to alter them; and providing important aspects of the theoretical, historical, and empirical resources to help us challenge rightist offensives and to defend the gains that have been made in schools and elsewhere (Apple 1999). *Contradictions of School Reform* is clearly within this tradition; yet, at the same time, it pushes the critical tradition back into a much closer and more fine-grained analysis of the daily realities of teaching, curricula, and testing in the schools of America.

It is crucial that we realize that there *are* alternatives to the policies and practices that Linda McNeil so powerfully criticizes. As she shows, there were schools in the city on which she focuses that were already engaged in some very effective education, especially with poor children and children of color. We can look elsewhere as well, since these schools are not alone. In *Democratic Schools*, James Beane and I have brought together descriptions of schools and their curricular, teaching, and evaluative practices that are currently having considerable success in bringing a critical and socially just education to their students and local communities (Apple and Beane 1995, 1999). Thus, our task is both critique and affirmation. McNeil engages in both. It is important that we do no less ourselves.

Michael W. Apple
University of Wisconsin, Madison
1999

Author's Preface

The setting for this book is Houston, Texas. This is extremely significant. Houston has the fifth largest public school system in the United States. More than 150 home languages are spoken by the children in its public schools.

For a simple and powerful reason, what happens in Houston can quickly affect the entire nation: Texas is the second largest state in the United States, and its political power increasingly sets the national agenda.

As this book will show, Houston and Texas have become a seedbed for some of the most extreme forms of standardization in education. As we all know, the culture of media politics can transform at lightning speed a bad idea into a popular political sound bite. And just as quickly, powerful political interests develop a vested interest in it. They often begin to scapegoat and attack any voice raised against it.

The sound bite is a simple one already recognized everywhere: "accountability by standardized testing" as the panacea for school reform. This idea is spreading like wildfire through the national debate on education. Dozens of states and many foreign countries are adopting this model with no understanding of what it does at the classroom level. It is often justified with little more than vague claims of "success in Texas." And everywhere around us teachers and parents who question these claims are scapegoated as uninformed, entrenched, or against improving education.

The sound bites that seduce policymakers always emphasize claims of benefits, not the actual costs. As documented in this book, the costs are great: a decline in the quality of what is taught and a new form of discrimination in the education *of poor and minority kids. But perhaps the worst effect is the silencing of two voices most important in understanding the real effects of standardization: the teachers and the children.*

Thoughtful people cannot allow that to happen. They need to know the historical, the true, living day-to-day classroom dynamics this standardized testing sound bite has masked. Otherwise, we cannot understand the harmful consequences they will produce if adopted on a national and global scale.

That is why this book is important. It is one of the first studies to show the detailed linkages between standardized policy reform and the true dynamics of the classrooms where our children learn. It goes beyond the scapegoating to the detailed, empirical tracing of what happens to teaching and children when standardized testing takes control of schools.

The irony is that this panacea has two great costs: it undermines quality, and it increases discrimination.

When the research that forms the basis of this book was completed, the findings presented a devastating picture of the de-skilling of teachers. During the course of the classroom observations in an urban district's highly successful magnet schools, state-level reforms were imposed that de-skilled teachers and compromised both the curriculum and the role of students as learners. The state-level reforms, under the rhetoric of ridding schools of "illiterate" teachers, put in place both standardized assessments of teacher behaviors and test-driven standardized curricula. These controls, under legislation sponsored by billionaire H. Ross Perot, applied to all schools equally, without regard to the quality of academic programs in the schools, the cultures of the children, historical inequalities of funding, or the professional knowledge level of the teachers.

As these policies were implemented, teaching in this state, and in this urban district in particular, was becoming intolerable for our best teachers, the ones the national reports say are in short supply, the ones dedicated to urban children. Standardization was driving these teachers from public school classrooms. It was threatening the career commitments of new graduates we were preparing to be urban teachers.

No one gesture, no one effort can undo the effects of a statewide mandate. But a small group of us decided to work together to begin to create alternative possibilities for supporting urban teachers. Our response was to create an organizational base from which to counter the de-skilling of teachers. With a scientist colleague, Ronald Sass (a biologist and global climate change expert), I founded the Rice University Center for Education. The Center took on the task of designing, funding, and operating programs of teacher development and research.

Contradictions of School Reform is one of three important studies being published this year by Center researchers. Together these works address our nation's most critical educational issues: persistent inequities in students' access to educational quality; the quality of teaching; and the rush to standardization. They demonstrate the harmful conditions resulting from our history of neglect and discrimination, and even more compellingly, they show the creation of new forms of discrimination arising out of increasing standardization. They also show that this does not have to be the case.

Subtractive Schooling: US-Mexican Youth and the Politics of Caring, by Angela Valenzuela (1999) documents the ways that U.S. schools create failure in Mexican American youth by teaching them in ways that subtract from their cultural identity and, as a result, their capacities to learn. Her study is based on a three-year analysis of a Latino high school where a history of scarce material resources obscures an even greater scarcity of caring for and caring about the capacity of these children to learn. *Dare to Learn: Science Teachers Accept the Challenge* (2000) is Elnora Harcombe's story of the capacity of middle school science teachers to transform both their understandings of science and their abilities to engage children in meaningful science learning when a community invests in its teachers.

These studies grew out of the Center's extensive work with urban teachers. That work was undertaken to counter the official de-skilling produced under legislation which will be described in *Contradictions of School Reform.* The Center's teacher development projects are based in innovative structures we have created in urban schools. From the Model Science Laboratory, to the School Writing Project and Cultural Conversations and our other projects, the Center's initiatives all grow out of research on teaching and learning; all predicate children's development on the intellectual and professional development of their teachers. Hundreds of teachers and thousands of children have been affected by the Center's projects, none of which provides a recipe, none of which sells a package or a set of prescriptives. There are many talented and dedicated teachers who say that they are still in teaching, and still in public schools, because of what they have learned and what they have become through the Center.

We know, then, that it is possible to teach well in urban schools. And we know that our diverse students can learn and become fully engaged in learning that opens for them productive futures. It is critical therefore that we examine those policies that work against real learning. We need to look close-up at those policy prescriptions that are de-skilling teachers, reducing their power to bring their best knowledge into the classroom, requiring them to teach a generic curriculum divorced from their children's varied experiences and devoid of a basis in child development.

In response to the standardizing reforms discussed in this book, the very teachers who had worked extra hours, and often spent their own money, to create rich curricula and creative, productive learning environments that were changing the futures of their urban children, were calling for help in finding jobs in private schools or in other states. These were teachers with choices; they had chosen teaching, in the hope of "making a difference." "Now," as one teacher said, "I am just an employee." If these teachers and others like them exited (or, less likely, acquiesced to the legislated prescription to comply with the increasingly generic and technical controls on their work), then the losses to the children, and to the community, would be far-reaching.

The urgency *then* to establish the Center, and to create a collective response to the official de-skilling of teachers, is matched *now* by the urgency to write the larger story. The preliminary analysis of the magnet schools, as written immediately after the field observations in a series of papers (see bibliography), focused on the seemingly inadvertent effects of the Perot reforms in increasing the very bureaucracy he said he had hoped to destroy. In those analyses, the dominant effect of the state mandates was described as exacerbating the exact problems the reforms were intended to correct: by increasing bureaucratic controls, these reforms inadvertently strengthened the very forces that are known to undermine teaching and learning, as teachers and students react against controls by limiting their own work. Those analyses were substantially correct for that time.

What has become increasingly clear in the years since the reforms came to be implemented is that the enduring legacy of those reforms is not merely the strengthening of bureaucratic controls at the expense of teaching and learning. It is also the legitimating of a language of accountability as the governing principle in public schools. Incipient in the Perot reforms was the shifting of control over public schooling away from "the public," and away from the profession, toward business-controlled management accountability systems. These systems use children's scores on standardized tests to measure the quality of teachers' and principals' performance and even use aggregate student scores within a school building as evidence for the comparative "ratings" of schools.

There have been several iterations of state testing and test-driven curricula implemented since the reforms begun under the Perot legislation in Texas. The TABS test was followed by the TEAMS test, and now the test is called the TAAS. The individual tests themselves are less significant than the system of controls they represent. The TAAS, the Texas Assessment of Academic Skills, is rarely referred to with any mention of the "academic." It is known by its advocates in the state government and among the state's business leadership as "the Texas Accountability System," the reform that has "shaped up" schools. It is touted as the system that holds "teachers and principals accountable." In many schools, principals' tenure has been replaced by "performance contracts," with "performance" as measured on a single indicator—the aggregation of student TAAS test scores in the school. Publicity about the "Texas Accountability System," centered around rising test scores, has generated copycat legislation in a number of states, where standardized testing of students (newly implemented or begun in the 1980s) is increasingly being used as the central mechanism for decisions about student learning, teacher and administrative practice, and even whole school quality (Heubert and Hauser 1999).

As Kliebard (1986), Cuban and Tyack (1995), and others have written, the idea of educational reform is engrained in the nation's notion of linear progress and in its attempts to engineer social policy and practice. Teachers, and those who follow educational policy and practice, know well that most reforms have a short life; teachers express the wisdom that "this too shall pass." The specific rules and prescriptions enacted under the Perot reforms did, indeed, pass. The particular test-driven curriculum was scrapped, and by the late 1990s the teacher assessment "instrument" was updated. But the institutionalizing of the locus of control over curriculum, teaching and assessment that began under the legislated reforms of the 1980s has more than persisted. It has become the basis for a tightly "aligned" set of prescriptions that not only locate the authority for educational decisions at the state level but also locate the power over those decisions in the domain of conservative business leaders.

Even more significant is that the use of a very narrow set of numerical indicators (that is, student scores on statewide tests) has become the only language of currency in educational policy in the state. Principals report that there can be little discussion of children's development, of cultural relevance, of children's contributions to classroom knowledge and interactions, of those engaging sidebar experiences at the margins of the official curriculum where children often do their best learning. According to urban principals, their supervisors tell them quite pointedly, "Don't talk to me about anything else until the TAAS scores start to go up." Teachers also report that the margins, those claimed spaces where even in highly prescriptive school settings they have always been able to "really teach," are shrinking as the accountability system becomes increasingly aligned, with teacher and principal pay tied to student scores. Even under the Perot reforms, teachers in the magnet schools (among others) were able to juggle the official, prescribed, and tested curriculum and what they wanted their students to learn. Even if they had to teach two contradictory lessons in order to assure students encountered the "real" information, many of them managed to do so in order that their students did not lose out on a chance for a real education.

A continued legacy, then, of the Perot reforms is that the testing of students increasingly drives curriculum and proscribes both teaching and the role of students in learning. This prescriptive teaching creates a new form of discrimination as teaching to the fragmented and narrow information on the test comes to substitute for a substantive curriculum in the schools of poor and minority youth. Even more serious in its consequences is the legacy of the institutionalizing of the externalized authority over schools. During the years of desegregation, there could be, and were, public discussions of the purposes of education, the role of the school in the community, the issue of who should be educated and who (and what level of legislative and judicial bodies) should govern access to and provision for education. There were even debates over what constituted a public language with which to discuss public education— the languages of equity, of academic quality, and of community values all intersected and mutually informed the highly contested decisions regarding means to break the power of segregation.

When education is governed by an "accountability system," public language or languages are displaced by an expert technical language. When educational practice and policy are subsumed under a narrow set of indicators, then the only vocabulary for discussing those practices and policies is the vocabulary of the indicators.

The Texas Accountability System can be discussed, and is being discussed, in the policy arena, in terms of its technical fine points. Policymakers and school administrators permit discussion only of such technical issues as the numbers and categories of students being tested (e.g., Can English as Second Language speakers be tested, and if so how recently after their immigration into U.S. schools?), the subjects and grade levels to be tested, the cut scores to be used as bars to graduations, the degree of movement in scores needed for principals' bonuses, the cut scores to determine promotion above third grade.

This closed system does not, however, permit discussion of the system itself, its premises, its imbedded values, its effects on children. Any effects not captured by test scores are seen as "anecdotes" rather than "data" and are therefore dismissed as inconsequential.

Behind the test scores and the technical policy debates, however, is the reality that the Texas system of educational accountability is harming children, teaching, and the content of public schooling. Even more serious is the use of the system of accountability to justify de-democratizing the governance of public schooling and, in particular, urban schools. Advocates of the accountability system now see it as a way to replace the "special interest groups" (parents, minority groups, labor groups, teachers) who have sat on or lobbied elected school boards; a strict accountability system of testing would report to a corporate governing body, through test-score data, on the performance of school personnel. (These far-fetched ideas sound improbable but are similar to those in several cities where "chief executive officers" now run big-city school systems.)

The extensive field-based research in the magnet schools uncovered the beginnings of these prescriptive reforms, as they were first being implemented, and showed unquestionably their negative effects on teaching and learning. Those effects visible at the classroom level, as serious as they were, have proven now several years later to have been the least worrisome legacy of the Perot reforms. Of more lasting harm has been the imbedding of the controls, the legitimization of "accountability" as the language of school policy, and the structuring out of the possibilities for wider public and professional discourse on the purposes of schooling for our children.

This book is the first that traces the effects of imposed standardizations from the system level into the classroom. It does so by capturing teaching and learning in a set of schools prior to the implementation of the centralized controls and then by documenting the effects of those controls on those classrooms. The study does not abstract policies of standardization, but documents the particular historical and political factors at work in a particular state, building a record of the economic and political rationales behind the policies and of the way the politicization of teaching and learning began even at that policy level to silence teachers and communities.

There are many narratives in this book, but just one central message. *The central message is that educational standardization harms teaching and learning and, over the long term, restratifies education by race and class.* To fully understand how standardization of testing and curriculum reduces children's access to a quality education, and how standardization in the long run creates cumulative deficits in the educational opportunities of our poorest children, the book takes the reader through every level of the educational system—from classrooms where teachers were teaching successfully prior to centralized, standardized reform; to the policy arena where the standardizing policies had their origins; and back into the original classrooms to document the ways standardization directly caused a watering down of what was taught. Finally, the book analyzes how these centralized policies, despite their negative impact on teaching and curriculum, have become entrenched in the ideological and political language of educational policy and, as a result, have institutionalized a new discrimination. This new discrimination is the widespread pattern of substituting test-prep materials, devoid of substantive content and of respect for the ways children learn, for the curriculum in the schools of children who historically have scored lowest on standardized tests—the poor and minority children in urban schools.

Part I of the book, The Context of Control, lays out in a chapter called "Standardization, Defensive Teaching, and the Problems of Control" what we already know about the tension between the controlling goals and the educational goals in schools. The tendency of teachers, where controlling goals overwhelm the educational purposes, to accommodate to controls by teaching an artificial "school knowledge" in order to gain compliance from their students is reviewed.

Part II of the book, Schools Structured for Learning, documents substantive, engaging, authentic teaching and learning in schools that were, from their origins, designed to be structured to support teaching and curriculum rich in substance and credible beyond the walls of the school. These are magnet schools, established to foster desegregation in a racially mixed urban district with a history of discriminatory educational practices. Chapter 2 provides the historical background that led to their establishment and offers the account of one of the first and most famous of these schools, a high school whose curriculum focuses on opening opportunities for minority youth to enter medical-related careers, a school whose curriculum therefore must be credible outside the walls of the school. Chapters 3 and 4 look closely inside classrooms at the ways teachers in schools structured in support of their academic goals can create meaningful and productive education, even for youth who historically have not been well served by urban schools. Chapter 3 describes in rich detail the Pathfinder School, where there were no boundaries between teachers' professional and personal knowledge and the knowledge they made available to their students in school. In chapter 4, students and teachers at a science and technology high school are seen to be entering into a bargain to assure that the school, despite severe resource shortages, lives up to the quality implied in its name.

Part III, The "Perverse Effects" of Legislated Learning, moves from the classroom to the origins and effects of legislated learning. The centralized reforms that imposed standardized test-driven curriculum on these and other schools in their state have their origin in the political and business arena, and not in the communities nor among the educational professionals in the schools. Chapter 5, "We've Got to Nuke this Educational System," explains the political and economic trade-offs that began with an attempt to raise teachers' pay and ended with the cynical enactment of a set of controls on teaching and learning. These controls, centered around cost accounting, began immediately to reduce the quality of the curriculum and to alienate the most educated and highly professional teachers. "Collateral Damage," the sixth chapter, returns to the classroom for a fine-grained analysis of the ways these controls harmed specific curricula, teachers, and students, the students whose learning had been so productive in the magnet school prior to standardization.

Chapter 7, "The Educational Costs of Standardization," enlarges the narrative to analyze the long-lasting effects of these controls, discussing the way the progeny of the 1980s reforms (namely, the TAAS system of testing) is being used to mask continuing inequities and to silence public and professional discourse on education.

This is a complex set of narratives. The issue itself is complex. We have not previously had this much of the story: where these centralizing policies come from; what schools were like before standardization was imposed; and what happened to children, teachers, and curricula once the standardized controls were in place. And we have not had the longitudinal story to help us understand what happens to public education when these standardized controls become institutionalized, become what many children and newer teachers, if we are not careful, will come to think of as "school."

Taken together, these layered narratives provide a vital system-to-classroom analysis of the effects of centralized, standardized controls on what is taught and learned in schools. Ultimately, they show us the effects of standardized controls on the possibilities for the "public" in public education when the language of accountability usurps developmental, cultural, and democratic discourse.

The Examiner

by F. R. Scott*

The routine trickery of the examination
Baffles these hot and discouraged youths,
Driven by they know not what external pressure
They pour their hated self-analysis
Through the nib of confession, onto the accusatory page.

I, who have plotted their immediate downfall,
I am entrusted with the divine categories,
ABCD and the hell of E,
The parade of prize and the backdoor of pass.

In the tight silence
Standing by a green grass window
Watching the fertile earth graduate its sons
With more compassion—not commanding the shape
Of stem and stamen, bringing the trees to pass
By shift of sunlight and increase of rain,
For each seed the whole soil, for the inner life

*A poem taught by Ms. Williams to her English class at the Pathfinder School. *Twentieth-Century Canadian Poetry: An Anthology*, Earle Birney (ed.), (1953), Toronto: Ryerson; also in *Mirrors: Recent Canadian Verse*, Jon Pearce (ed.), (1975), Toronto: Gage Educational Publishing.

The environment receptive and contributory—
I shudder at the narrow frames of our textbook schools
In which we plant our so various seedlings.
Each brick-walled barracks
Cut into numbered rooms, blackboarded,
Ties the venturing shoot to the master stick;
The screw-desk rows of lads and girls
Subdued in the shade of an adult—
Their acid subsoil—
Shape the new to the old in the ashen garden.

Shall we open the whole skylight of thought
To these tiptoe minds, bring them our frontier worlds
And the boundless uplands of art for their field of growth?

Or shall we pass them the chosen poems with the footnotes,
Ring the bell on their thoughts, period their play,
Make laws for averages and plans for means,
Print one history book for a whole province, and
Let ninety thousand reach page 10 by Tuesday?

As I gather the inadequate paper evidence, I hear
Across the neat campus lawn
The professional mowers drone, clipping the inch-high green.

Part I

The Context of
Control

Chapter 1

Standardization, Defensive Teaching, and the Problems of Control

Standardization reduces the quality and quantity of what is taught and learned in schools. This immediate negative effect of standardization is the overwhelming finding of a study of schools where the imposition of standardized controls reduced the scope and quality of course content, diminished the role of teachers, and distanced students from active learning.

The long-term effects of standardization are even more damaging: *over the long term, standardization creates inequities, widening the gap between the quality of education for poor and minority youth and that of more privileged students.* The discriminatory effects of standardization are immediately evident in the reduction in both the quality and quantity of educational content for students who have historically scored low on standardized assessments. Over time, the longer standardized controls are in place, the wider the gap becomes as the system of testing and test preparation comes to substitute in minority schools for the curriculum available to more privileged students. These new structures of discrimination are being generated by the controls that began in the schools documented in this study and that in the succeeding years have become the dominant model of schooling in one of the nation's largest and most diverse states, Texas. This book documents the immediate educational costs to curriculum, teaching, and children when the controls were first introduced. It then analyzes their growing power to damage the education of all children, but particularly those who are African American and Latino.

3

In the name of improving educational quality and holding schools and school personnel more accountable for their professional practice, the state government enacted a set of standardized controls to monitor children's learning and teachers' classroom behavior. These controls arose outside the educational system, derived from pressures from the business establishment to fund only those educational expenses that contributed to measurable outcomes. They were implemented from the top of the state bureaucracy, through the district bureaucracies, and subsequently imposed on schools. The controls were set forth as "reforms." The activities they mandated were to be uniform, and the means of monitoring the activities were standardized scoring instruments. In the name of "equity," these reforms imposed a sameness. In the name of "objectivity" they relied on a narrow set of numerical indicators. These hierarchical reform systems seem upon first reading to be extreme, but over time they have become the model for increasingly hierarchical and prescriptive systems being promoted as improving education. More seriously, they have legitimated "accountability" as the presiding metaphor in shifting the power relations governing public education.

The research reported in this volume did not begin as a study of the effects of state-level educational standardization. The findings are all the more powerful because, in fact, they were not expected. Nor were they sought. This research began as a search for organizational models of schooling that provided structural support for authentic, engaged teaching and learning. The research was designed to study schools in which school knowledge was credible, in which teachers brought their own personal and professional knowledge into the classroom, and in which teachers and students entered into shared, authentic study of significant topics and ways of knowing. Analyzing such teaching and learning in its organizational context could shed light on the ways the structures of schooling can enhance, rather than impede, educational quality.

Teaching and learning widely regarded to be authentic, to be meaningful to the students and to their experiences beyond school, was found in a series of urban magnet schools. As exemplars of authentic teaching and learning, the magnet schools carry special importance because their students were predominantly minority, African American and Latino. These schools had been established to be of such high quality that they would serve a city as the vehicle for desegregation through voluntary cross-city student transfers. This book was intended to document the ways that curriculum and learning are constructed and made meaningful in schools whose organizational structure subordinates the credentialing function and other procedural and behavioral controls to teaching and learning. The magnet schools proved to be schools where teachers and students, free of the constraints of the state textbook adoption list and from state and local prescriptive rules governing curriculum, co-constructed rich academic environments in a multiracial setting.

During the collection of observational data in these magnet schools, while the data on authentic teaching and learning were quite persuasively accruing, the state enacted policies meant to "reform" all schools.[1] These policies brought all schools in the state under a centralized system of prescriptive rules and standardized procedures for monitoring compliance. These exemplary magnet schools, serving racially diverse and in many cases poor students, were not exempt from the centralized controls.

As the controls were imposed, and the regulations increasingly standardized, the quality of teaching and learning at even these exemplary schools began to suffer. Teaching, curriculum, and students' roles in classrooms were transformed by the standardizations and by the categories of compliance they imposed. Within the observational data began to emerge phony curricula, reluctantly presented by teachers in class to conform to the forms of knowledge their students would encounter on centralized tests. The practice of teaching under these reforms shifted away from intellectual activity toward dispensing packaged fragments of information sent from an upper level of the bureaucracy. And the role of students as contributors to classroom discourse, as thinkers, as people who brought their personal stories and life experiences into the classroom, was silenced or severely circumscribed by the need for the class to "cover" a generic curriculum at a pace established by the district and the state for all the schools.

The magnet teachers and their students did not comply thoughtlessly with the new standardizations. Instead they struggled to hold onto school lessons that held credibility in the world outside schools, to lessons that sprang from teachers' passions and children's curiosities, to lessons that built a cumulative base of new understandings for these students, many of whom were counting on the magnet schools to open previously closed doors to college and careers. The work of resistance itself, however, took a toll on time, energies, and the activities that could not be salvaged as the controls became more tightly monitored.

Controlling Myths

The myth of such controls is that they "bring up the bottom," that they are aimed at the lowest levels of performance. The myth further promotes the idea that "good schools" will not be affected and, conversely, that any school that is adversely affected by centralized controls must not have been a "good" school. The corollary holds for teachers: if teachers are negatively affected by standardized reforms, then they must have been the "weak" or "bad" teachers in need of reforming.

The following analysis shatters the myth that standardization improves education. It challenges the widespread notion that standardization equals, or leads to, "standards." What will be clear from a close-up analysis of the effects of standardization is that, in fact, *standardization undermines academic standards* and seriously limits opportunities for children to learn to a "high standard."

The issue of the confusion between standardization and "standards" is of critical importance because increasingly scores on individual students' standardized tests of academic skills and of the mastery of subject content carry with them serious consequences both for the students and for those who teach them. "High-stakes" decisions, such as grade placement and promotion (or retention), placement in highly stratified academic tracks, and even graduation are increasingly determined by students' scores on centrally imposed, commercial standardized tests. When they are used in "accountability systems," individual and aggregate student test scores are used as indirect measures of teachers' work, principals' "performance," and even of the overall quality of the school. Such practices are highly questionable and are prompting serious scrutiny by policymakers and testing professionals of the possible misuses of student tests (Heubert and Hauser 1999).

The ethical questions raised among testing experts regarding the use of standardized student tests for other purposes such as employee (teacher, principal) performance and school quality tend to be regarded by policymakers in heavily centralized states and districts as points requiring fine-tuning and, in fact, are often used as justification for extending tests to additional grade levels and subjects to "assure that the testing is as comprehensive as possible."[2]

The Texas case is important to study and to analyze at each level of implementation because it demonstrates the wide gulf between academic "standards" and the curricular content to which students have access under a highly centralized system of standardized testing. It is crucial to understand because it provides the first opportunity to examine how issues of quality and "high standards" become so easily co-opted by the similar language—but oppositional philosophy and opposite consequences—of standardization. The "high stakes" to the students, in the use of their scores to regulate an entire system, appear at first to be merely the decisions made about them individually—their promotion or graduation, for example. The schools described in this book in some detail demonstrate that what is ultimately at stake is the capacity to provide a substantive education that is not driven by, not stratified by, and not reduced by the kinds of standardized tests being increasingly adopted across the states under the guise of "raising standards."

That standardization is harmful to teaching and learning is not a new idea. Critique of the embodiment of technical mechanisms for transforming the power relations within schools and reordering the power relations that govern the larger role of school in society is the subject of a now comprehensive body of theory (Apple 1979, 1995, 1996; Apple and Oliver 1998; Beyer and Apple 1998a; Freire 1970, 1985, 1995; Giroux 1983, 1996; Greene 1978; McLaren and Gutierrez 1998; Sarason 1971, 1996; Wise 1979; Wrigley 1982; and others). Such critical scholarship, including critical cultural studies, studies in the political economy of schools, and critical analyses of pedagogy have emerged as bases upon which to examine the increasing technicizing of public education. At the macrolevel of theorizing, there is, within this body of scholarship, increased attention to and understanding of the conservative transformation of American public education through the use of technicist forms of power. In addition, fine-grained classroom studies, particularly in the area of the sociocultural linguistics and critical race studies, are documenting the linguistic and culturally subtractive effects of generic models of schooling on Spanish-dominant and other immigrant and minority children (Fordham and Ogbu 1986; Gutierrez and Larson 1994; Gutierrez, Rymes, and Larson 1995; Romo and Falbo 1996; Suarez-Orozco 1991; Valenzuela 1999).

This scholarship has been essential in creating frameworks for questioning the power relations that shape the role of the school in the larger society. In addition, through critical scholarship we have now an established tradition for examining the social and cultural origins of school knowledge, for raising questions about whose interests are served by educational institutions and whose interests and cultures are represented by the knowledge and ways of knowing institutionalized in schools. Critical studies have insisted that our understandings of schools and the educational practices within them not be limited to technical representations of the schools, their programs, or their students' performance. Our conceptualizations of the ways race, social class, social "place," gender, conflicting community histories, and competing definitions of schooling that all shape "schooling" for us are enriched by this growing literature.

Even within an increasingly complex and international body of scholarship, however, there are serious gaps. One of these is the absence of critical scholarship that carries theory into, or builds theory from, what goes on inside schools. And even more glaringly and ironically absent, given the role of critical scholarship in raising issues of power and power inequities, is the lack of up-close studies of systems of schooling. Jean Anyon's powerful book, *Ghetto Schooling: A Political Economy of Urban Educational Reform* (1997a), stands as an exception. This extraordinarily complex study examines the interrelation of race, local politics, local economics, and even the global economic forces that have over time "pauperized" urban education in a major U.S. city, Newark, New Jersey. Her study is exemplary for situating both the "problems" of urban schools and their potential to become educational for poor and minority children not merely in their internal structures ("Do they 'work'?"), but in the sociocultural contexts of their communities and in the economic and political forces beyond those communities that have over the years come to dominate the resources and political power available in support of these schools. Her analysis is especially powerful because it does not leave these forces at an abstract level, but rather concretizes particular groups, particular legislation, particular individuals' roles in the destruction and rebuilding of the civic capacity of a community to act on behalf of its schools.

Yet even this very detailed study stops at the classroom door. Its analysis of the factors inside schools that have over the years been damaged by increasingly racist and class-based resourcing of schools is descriptive of both the organizational factors (leverage over resources, teacher preparation, administrative authority) and programmatic components (availability of kindergarten, creation of alternative programs for children not well served by traditional schools). But this description and analysis are seen more from an organizational perspective and from the perspective of community constituencies working to reclaim the power to improve schools, rather than from children's experience of these and other aspects of schooling. We still have serious need of studies that not only get inside classrooms but also document from the inside out the ways increasingly differentiated power relations are changing systems of schooling and the ways those systems are shaping what is taught and learned.

It is critical scholarship, then, which gives us a lens for going beyond the appearance, slogans, and indicators, to examine the forces such as standardization that are increasingly shifting both school practice and the power relations shaping that practice. What has been missing from both the global theorizing and the microlevel studies from a critical perspective is an analysis of *how these standardizing forces play out through the system of schooling*: from the political forces shaping the policies, through the bureaucratic systems enacting the policies, to what children are taught and what they experience in the classrooms under these policy mandates. *Contradictions of Reform* provides the first such comprehensive analysis of a system of standardization and its educational consequences. It overcomes the silence in the critical literature about how standardization comes about, how the innocuous-sounding language of standardization ("high standards" and "accountability") comes to mask the reductions in academic quality, and how technical indicators ("objective measures") transform what is valued in teaching and curriculum. The analysis further fills the gap in the critical literature by situating the voices and experiences of particular teachers and students within a particular system, overcoming the tendency of global theorizing to portray a picture that, even if essentially correct, remains at such an abstract level that it lacks credibility to a broader public trying to understand its schools.

Contradictions of Reform looks firsthand at "best case" schools where teachers and highly diverse students, despite serious resource shortages, had been able within the context of a supportive organizational structure, to co-construct authentic educational experiences.

These schools are recorded here in extensive detail to demonstrate the complexity of creating and sustaining such educational programs and to give tangible evidence of the educational value to students when their classroom knowledge is credible and when the educational process involves the minds and knowledge base of the teachers and the minds and experiences of the students. The study then traces the ways standardized controls directly and negatively impact the teaching, curriculum, and role of students in those schools. These standardized controls are traced from their origins in the business leadership outside schools, through political trade-offs with the governor and legislature that silenced educators and forced them to accept a highly complex system of controls over their work in exchange for even very modest pay increments. The analysis then tracks the bureaucratic implementation of these controls, into "instruments of accountability," to measure teachers' classroom practice and the "outcomes" of children's learning. This systemic analysis, from corporate pressure to legislature to school bureaucracy to classroom, sheds new light on the harmful effects of policies that on the surface seem to be benign attempts to monitor educational quality and to assure that schools are run in a cost-effective manner. In reality these policies of standardization are decreasing the quality of teaching and learning in our schools, especially in the schools of poor and minority children. The analysis concludes with an examination of the longer-term effects of such systems of accountability; there is growing evidence that the institutionalization of standardization is widening the gap between poor and minority youth and their peers in more privileged schools.

The language of accountability seems, on a commonsense level, to be about professional practice that is responsible to the children and to the public. The language of standardization appears to denote equity, of assuring that all children receive the same education. Behind the usages of these terms in educational policy, however, is a far different political and pedagogical reality. "Accountability," as will be discussed in the last chapter, reifies both a resource dependency and a hierarchical power structure which maintains that dependency. It further undermines both the public voice in public schooling and the public role of schools in democratic life. "Standardization" equates sameness with equity in ways that mask pervasive and continuing inequalities. Taken together, the increasing use of *standardization*, prescriptive of educational programs, and *accountability*, equating educational accomplishment with outcomes measures, are restructuring public education in two critical ways. First is the shifting of decisions regarding teaching and learning away from communities and educational professionals and into the hands of technical experts following a political agenda to reduce democratic governance of schooling. Second (and particularly serious in its consequences for children in light of the success of the magnet schools in educating highly diverse students) is the restratification by class and race through highly technical systems governing the content and means of evaluation. The final chapter will show how the forms of control, which have their origins in the 1980s reforms, are now deeply entrenched and are not only reducing the overall quality of education but also dramatically widening the gap between poor and minority children's education and the education of more privileged youth.

Standardization in the form of legislated controls over testing and curriculum is an externalization of management controls arising from the bureaucratizing of schooling early in the twentieth century. Its derivations from within the organizational structures of schooling, rather than from theories of child development and learning, have traditionally signaled a separateness from teaching, learning, and curriculum. The perceived separateness between school organization and teaching and learning has been shown, however, to be misleading. Even where there are not in place formal controls over curriculum and teaching, there are, within bureaucratic school structures, imbedded controls. These bureaucratic controls are not separate from the educational purposes of schooling; rather, they play an active role in determining the quality of teaching and the nature of what is taught.

Defensive Teaching and the
Contradictions of Control

The public will to provide an education to all the citizens in a democracy carries with it issues of cost (Who will pay for such an education?) and governance (How will so many schools be organized and overseen?). It is one of the great ironies of American education that in order to provide a free public education to all its children, schools were created along the model of factory assembly lines in order to reduce the cost of schooling per child and assure millions of children of a diploma, a credential of school completion (Callahan 1962; Kliebard 1986; McNeil 1986). A school that is designed like a factory has a built-in contradiction: running a factory is tightly organized, highly routinized, and geared for the production of uniform products; educating children is complex, inefficient, idiosyncratic, uncertain, and open-ended. Historically, the two purposes of schooling, that is, educating children and running large-scale educational institutions, have been seen as separate domains. The one is aimed at nurturing individual children and equipping them with new knowledge and skills; the other focuses on processing aggregates of students through regularized requirements of the credentialing process. A bureaucratic school, or a school that is part of a bureaucratic system, is thus structured to be in conflict with itself (McNeil 1986, 3). And at the point of the tension—where the two oppositional forces intersect—are the children, the teacher, and the curriculum. How the tension is resolved will in large measure shape the quality of what is taught and learned in the school.

"When the school's organization becomes centered on managing and controlling, teachers and students take school less seriously." With this statement I summed up the analysis of schools and classrooms I wrote as the book, *Contradictions of Control: School Structure and School Knowledge.* To elaborate, I added, "They [teachers and students] fall into a ritual of teaching and learning that tends toward minimal standards and minimal effort. This sets off a vicious cycle. As students disengage from enthusiastic involvement in the learning process, administrators often see the disengagement as a control problem. They then increase their attention to managing students and teachers rather than supporting their instructional purpose" (McNeil 1986, xviii).

That earlier research study, an ethnographic analysis of the factors shaping what is taught in schools (McNeil 1986), revealed that the effects of bureaucratic controls on teaching and learning were not vague influences, but rather very concrete and visible transformations of course content and classroom interaction. That study, conducted in four high schools in the midwestern United States, revealed that behind overt symptoms of poor educational quality lie complicated organizational dynamics (McNeil 1988c). The nature of teachers' practice, the quality of course content and the level of students' engagement may not themselves be weaknesses, but may be symptoms that reflect teachers' and students' accommodations to priorities built into the organizational structure of the school.

Where teachers feel that they have no authority in the structure of the school, or where they see the school as emphasizing credentialing over the substance of schooling, they tend to create their own authority or their own efficiencies within the classroom by tightly controlling course content. They begin to teach a course content that I termed *school knowledge*, which serves the credentialing function of the school but which does not provide students with the rich knowledge of the subject fields nor with opportunities to build their own understandings of the subject.

As background for examining the authentic teaching and learning in the magnet schools, it is important to understand the very concrete ways in which teachers in the midwestern schools shaped school content in reaction to the schools' subordination of the educational goals to the goals of control and credentialing. Teachers who wanted their students to comply with course requirements often did so by reducing those requirements in order to gain minimal participation with minimal resistance. I termed this *defensive teaching* (McNeil 1986, ch. 7). Teachers who taught defensively, asking little from their students in order to satisfy institutional requirements with as little resistance and with as few inefficiencies as possible, tended to bracket their own personal knowledge from the treatment of the subject of the lesson. And they used strategies to silence student questions or (inefficient) discussions. These strategies bear reviewing because it is in part their absence from the magnet classrooms that so starkly shows the differences between teaching in a supportive organizational structure and teaching in a controlling environment.

First, teachers controlled content by *omission*. They tended to omit topics that were difficult to understand and or contemporary topics that would invite student discussion. They especially tended to omit subjects, or treatments of subjects, that were potentially controversial. Controversy, and passionate student discussion, might threaten the teacher's interpretation; interpretations that differed from the teacher's were seen as threatening teacher authority. One teacher even said he had eliminated student research papers because at a time of volatile political debate he found that students doing their own research could become "self-indoctrinated," that is, they came to their own interpretations of the subject (McNeil 1986, 172). At the least, controversy could disrupt the pacing of the coverage of the course material, causing the third-period class, for example, to lag behind the less talkative fourth-period class.

Teachers also maintained a controlling environment in their classes by *mystifying* course content. They mystified a topic by making it seem extremely important, but beyond the students' understanding. It was to be written in the notes for the test, but not understood. In economics class, topics like the Federal Reserve system or international monetary policies would be subjected to mystification; they would be mentioned but not elaborated upon, with the message that students need to recognize the term but leave the understanding of the subject to "the experts." (At times teachers also mystified topics about which *they* had little knowledge, willingly obscuring their students' access to the topic, rather than to learn on behalf of or in collaboration with their students.)

The information that was important to the content of the course, the content that teachers did want their students to learn, would be presented in the form of a list of facts (or names or dates or formulas or terminologies) to be memorized and repeated on tests. Complex subjects that were too essential to the course to be omitted (the Civil War, for example, in a history class; cell processes in biology; the effects of reagents in chemistry) would be reduced to lists and fragments of fact and transmitted by the teacher. In most cases, the lists were presented in a format that condensed and structured the course content into a consensus curriculum. One teacher explained that her job was to read the scholarly literature (in her case, "the historians") and distill the information into a list on which "all historians now agree." This *fragmentation* of course content tended to disembody the curriculum, divorcing it from the cultures and interests and prior knowledge of the students, from the teachers' knowledge of the subject, and from the epistemologies, the ways of knowing, within the subject itself. It also placed barriers between the knowledge as packaged for use in school and its relation to understandings of that subject within the cultural and practical knowledge outside schools. The origins of ideas, the shaping of interpretations, the possibility of inquiry into where this knowledge came from and how it was shaped by human experience were all absent from the curriculum. "School knowledge" was a priori what the teacher conveyed and students received to satisfy school requirements.

A fourth strategy these teachers used to control course content, and with it classroom interactions, was what I have termed *defensive simplification*. When teachers perceived that students had little interest in a lesson or that the difficulty in studying the lesson might cause students to resist the assignment, they made both the content of the assignment and the work students were to do as simple as possible. They minimized *anticipated* student resistance by simplifying course content and demanding little of students. This strategy was used when the topic was complex and in need of multiple explanations if all students were to understand; labor history might be reduced to a list of famous strikes, labor laws, management policies, and key labor leaders. The connections among these would go unexplained; they would simply be names on a list. Student assignments were reduced to taking notes on lectures, copying lists from the blackboard, filling in blanks on worksheets, and reading one or two pages on the subject. Extensive writing that called for student interpretations, for student research beyond the classroom, for engagement with text was absent from these classes—in stark contrast to the responsibilities that, as will be demonstrated, the magnet students assumed on a regular basis.

The thin academic content in these classes, surprising because these were known as "good schools," gave the impression that the teachers were undereducated in their subjects. Interviews with the teachers, however, revealed that they were well read, that they kept up in their fields, that they discussed literature and current events and new discoveries with their friends. They frequently talked with adults, in the teacher's lounge or over lunch, about complex ideas and about what they were learning from their personal reading and travels. When they came into the classroom, however, the subject they had discussed outside the classroom would be rendered unrecognizable when presented to their students as lists and facts. They rarely brought their personal knowledge, or their professional knowledge of their subjects, into the classroom (Shulman 1987); personal knowledge and school knowledge were for them quite separate. In interviews teachers explained that they feared that if the assignments (and treatment of course topics) were too complex, then students would not do the work. In addition, they feared that if students knew how complex the world is, particularly our economic institutions, then they would become cynical and discouraged about their futures and about "the system." They mistook their students' compliance for acceptance of what they were being taught.

Although most of the students in these middle-class, White schools sat quietly and appeared to be absorbing the information provided by their teachers (most of them passed the subjects), interviews with students at all achievement levels revealed that the students did not find the school knowledge credible. School was far from their only source of information; they had televisions, jobs, grandparents, and peers. They did not necessarily have sophisticated understandings of various subjects, but they knew that for some reason "they only tell you here what they want you to know." I had been in the schools for so many months before interviewing students that when we did sit down to talk, several expressed their concern that I might be taken in by the content of the lessons. They advised, "Don't believe what they tell you here," and then each would go on to tell of a school-supplied fact that was directly contradicted by a personal experience or by something learned from a job or a parent. (Some of the school-supplied information was more reliable than what they learned at their jobs or from their friends, but not having the opportunity in school to examine and to come to understandings of what was being taught, they assumed a greater credibility on the part of what they learned outside school.)

The students and teachers in these schools were meeting in an exchange to satisfy the bureaucratic requirements of schooling. The teachers recognized full well that if the school were smooth-running and few students failed their courses, then the administration would be pleased, and that any extra efforts—to develop an interesting curriculum, to assign and grade student research papers, to stay late to meet with students wanting extra help—would not only not be rewarded but also be disdained as unnecessary. The students knew that if they exerted at least minimum effort, then they would pass their required courses; if they ventured opinions and tried to start discussions, then they would be viewed as disruptive. (*Contradictions of Control* includes examples of student attempts to bring their own ideas into the classroom; one teacher lowered "class participation" grades if students tried to discuss).

In response to impersonal bureaucratic schools that emphasized the controlling and credentialing functions at the expense of the educative goals of schooling, teachers and students were engaged in a vicious cycle of lowering expectations. When teachers tightly controlled the curriculum, the students mentally disengaged; teachers saw student disengagement as the reason to tighten controls. When administrators saw teachers and students exerting so little effort, they saw the school as "out of control," and in response they tightened up administrative controls, issuing new directives and increasingly formalizing the hierarchical distances between the administration and the classroom. Within this cycle of lowering expectations, the school, for both teachers and students, begins to lose its legitimacy as a place for serious learning.

The *Contradictions of Control* schools held within them the potential for authentic teaching and learning. It was to be found not in merely changing the dispositions of individual teachers, but in breaking the cycle of lowering expectations set up when teachers teach defensively and students find school knowledge not worthy of their effort. Breaking this cycle within the traditional bureaucratic school structure, in which the credentialing and controlling processes of schooling so easily came to dominate the educational purposes of schooling, can be difficult. The teachers in the midwestern schools were not under legislated curriculum directives, nor was their pay tied to student test scores or compliance with standardized mandates. These teachers were not directly de-skilled by a regulatory context. They were participating in their own de-skilling by bracketing their personal knowledge when they entered the classroom and by using on their students the controlling practices they so resented from administrators.

One school stood out from the others as a school whose administrative structure was organized not to enforce rules and credentialling procedures, but to support teaching. That school (McNeil 1986, ch. 6) demonstrated that when the professional roles, resource allocations, and procedures of a school are organized in support of academics (rather than oppositional to "real teaching"), teachers feel supported to bring their best knowledge into the classroom. They are willing to take risks in incorporating into lessons their questions and uncertainties as well as their deep understandings of their subject. They are willing to let their students see them learning and asking questions (rather than controlling all discussion) and, in turn, they invite their students to make their own questions, interpretations, and partial understandings a vital part of the learning process. Seeing that school, where curriculum content was not "school knowledge," but was congruent with the knowledge that teachers held and with the subject as it is encountered in the world outside schools, raised the question of what other structures of schooling might foster authentic teaching and learning. Observing that school where scarce resources went first to instruction in a variety of imaginative ways, and where administrative personnel put their own time and efforts at the disposal of their faculties, raised the possibility of identifying other examples of schools structured to support educating children in ways consistent with their need to be nurtured and with their need to learn content whose purpose went far beyond building a record of grades and school credentials.

Contradictions of Control cut new theoretical ground for understanding the complex relationships between school organization and what is taught and learned. The wisdom that school administration and instruction are loosely linked domains was challenged by the clear evidence that a controlling administrative environment undermined teaching and learning by the responses it invoked in teachers and students.

The analysis presented here began with the selection of the magnet schools as counterexamples to the organizational de-skilling of teachers. These schools, as the next three chapters document, proved that schools can be organized in ways that do not put teachers in conflict with administrative purposes when they do their best teaching. They show that in a supportive environment, teachers will work alone and collaboratively to develop complex and up-to-date curricula, that they will tackle complex and controversial topics essential to their students' understandings, that they will struggle to find ways to make learning possible for all their students. The magnet schools carried many agendas as they were established and as they came to be the chief conduits to college for hundreds of minority youth in a city with a long history of discriminatory school practices. For this analysis, their benefit is in exemplifying the possibilities for authentic teaching and learning when schools are structured to foster learning rather than to process students or control them.

The success of the magnet schools in providing a substantive education for diverse urban students was jeopardized when a layer of organizational controls became state law (chapter 5). These controls, centralized and highly standardized, threatened the educational programs by imposing on the magnet school curricula magnified versions of the simplifications used by the midwestern teachers to limit their students' access to knowledge. The magnet teachers refused to be de-skilled, but as chapter 6 will dramatically record, the costs of new standardization policies fell heavily on their curricula and on their students and threatened to drive them out of public classrooms when remaining meant participating in the de-skilled teaching of "school knowledge."

The experiences of the students and teachers in the magnet schools under increasingly standardized controls raise serious questions about the purposes behind these controls. For educators, they also raise serious questions about the long-term effects of students whose entire educational experience is dominated by standardization. In chapter 7, I discuss those long-term effects, both on children and on the system of schooling. When standardization becomes institutionalized, and student testing comes to be used for monitoring "accountability" throughout a state's educational system, the negative effects fall most heavily on the poorest children, minority children whose entire school experience comes to be dominated by an attempt to raise their (historically low) test scores at any cost. I will document those effects in chapter 7, showing how standardization, when it begins to shape a whole system, in effect creates a new system of discrimination.

Part II

Schools Structured
for Learning

Chapter 2

===============

Magnet Schools:
"The Best Schools Money Can't Buy"

When the U.S. Supreme Court declared in 1954 that racial segregation of public schools was unconstitutional, the court ordered that public school districts desegregate "with all deliberate speed." As in many urban districts across the United States, desegregation in Texas school districts proceeded in a way that was neither deliberate nor speedy. Almost twenty years would pass before the largest cities would have desegregation plans in place. By that time, many Whites would have moved from racially diverse cities to mostly White suburbs. Thousands of school children would have passed through the twelve grades of public schooling before their communities—and the courts—decided who would sit together in schools, and what those schools should be like when they did.

Structuring Possibilities for Authentic Teaching

When the courts finally declared the urban district under study here a "unitary" district, that is, one whose school integration is as complete as demographically feasible, they approved a plan that used special schools as sites for voluntary racial integration, leaving the majority of the schools relatively untouched. These special schools were deemed *magnet schools*. They were to have academic programs so special and of such high academic quality that they would "draw" from racially segregated neighborhoods (and their racially segregated schools) children who would ride a bus across this large city to a school in the neighborhood of another race. In order to be sufficiently attractive to children and their parents, these schools were allowed (in some cases, required) to create distinctive academic programs, unlike any other in the city, often unique in the state. Their specialization by definition released them from compliance with regulations regarding standard course offerings. And their distinctive courses required textbooks and instructional materials not on the state's textbook adoption lists; these courses required as well an active role for teachers in designing curricula and in creating and selecting instructional activities and resources. (Developing curriculum is the usual work of teachers in schools that do not have centrally adopted textbooks and curricular prescriptions, but it becomes the exception under highly regulated conditions.) The magnet schools were designed, established, staffed, and administered as specialized schools. They had the support of the federal courts, and therefore the central administration also endorsed creating programs of academic distinctiveness and excellence for children of all three races involved in the desegregation plan: African American, Hispanic, and White.[1]

These special schools did not fully integrate the city's public schools. But they stand as models of integrated schools successfully built around strong academics. And they stand as academically strong schools where children of all races found paths to academic and career futures that would have rarely been open to them in their home schools. Their significance as research sites for this study lies first, in *their structures, which were organized to support the educational goals of the schools,* rather than to control and regulate classroom practice or process students through to a credential; second, in the potential for *authentic teaching and learning* to thrive in such an organizational environment; and finally, in the *diversity of the children* for whom such an education was intended to be both accessible and productive.

These schools were set up to counter highly contradictory, but long-standing characteristics of local schools. The first was the requirement that all schools comply with standardized regulations, from the required number of minutes for the teaching of reading to the number of hours in the school day. The second was the highly disparate funding across schools (more remarkable given the centralized regulations), which was being contested in the desegregation lawsuits as not only disparate but also discriminatory by race. To create schools of excellence, the district placed the magnets outside the traditional regulatory structure of standardized rules and standardized textbooks. This freedom from the traditional generic regulatory structure, combined with the explicit directive to create specialized programs to meet the court-ordered volunteer transfer ratios, made these schools compelling case studies for analyzing teaching practice, curriculum, and student roles when teachers in schools are not caught between standardization and teaching.

The initial question guiding the field observations was whether such organizational support for the educative goals of schooling would foster teaching that avoided the negative effects on teaching and curriculum seen to be typical in the classrooms of de-skilled teachers. Would working to create and sustain specialized academic programs that needed their expertise cause (or enable) teachers to bring their personal knowledge into the classroom, into their interactions with their students? Would the ways of knowing and the stuff of learning inside these schools be congruent with ways of knowing outside the domain of schooling?

Within the magnet school structures, as the case study chapters will richly demonstrate, teachers did not create controlling environments in the classroom in order to sustain their authority; they did not employ pedagogies that proscribed students' intellectual engagement, for the sake of efficiency; nor did they place artificial limitations on curricular content. The teachers' constructions of knowledge and of instructional approaches in these settings were no accident. Many of them had chosen to transfer to these new magnet schools precisely to escape the controlling environments of their previous schools, which were under both state and district regulations over what could be taught and what textbooks could be used (the books, usually survey texts, were actually sent from the state, so there was little flexibility). These were teachers who had deliberately resisted tendencies in their prior schools to teach regulatory requirements and who had claimed, within their own classrooms, the space to teach in ways they had felt to be authentic. Some had worked in small cohorts of teachers whose practice created an oasis of professional support for engaged and engaging teaching; these teachers knew the value of a shared collegial philosophy and welcomed the opportunity to work in a school whose whole mission, not just its margins, conformed to their notions of "real teaching and learning." Teaching in a magnet school would, for these teachers, hold great possibilities. Such a school setting, such a purposeful venture, would give them the luxury of making their students and their teaching their whole focus, without the constant pressure to fend off or work around the continual series of directives that emanate on a regular basis from the central office or state education agency. By their selection of schools and by their teaching in those schools, the magnet teachers provided a potential counterexample to the teachers who participated in their own de-skilling in response to a controlling administrative environment. Whether and how they did so, and to what effects on their students, was at the heart of the classroom observations.

The magnet schools, then, are important in this study for their organizational structures, designed to support authentic teaching and learning, and for the ways teachers were able to take advantage of those structures to break down the walls between "school knowledge" and "real knowledge." Their being magnet schools, per se, is less significant to the analysis of the effects of standardization than these organizational relations and their effects.[2] The significant organizational variable was that the inherent tension between the educative goals and the controlling goals of the school was structurally resolved in the direction of the educational purposes by virtue of the magnet schools' permission to step out of hierarchical regulations.

The Magnets, Race, and Desegregation

Because these schools had not only to educate their own students but also to be the primary vehicles for the district's desegregation compliance, it is important to consider the ways their place in that history of racial conflict helped shape their identities, both in their early years and during the observations that form the basis of the case study chapters to follow. Magnet schools were not the first solution proposed to the long history of segregation and inequality in this district. In fact, their creation came after a long and tense period of racial tension. In some cases, the proposed desegregation plans themselves added to the conflict by pitting minority groups against each other, eclipsing any attention to educational quality. That the magnet schools were ultimately successful in educating student populations reflective of the city's diversity is more remarkable in light of the drawn-out litigation and debate that preceded their formation.

With residential segregation typical and children zoned to neighborhood schools, the pattern of single-race schools in Texas cities has mirrored that across most of the urban South. By state law, cities with large numbers of Black students had to provide a separate school for them, linking statute to custom. White teachers taught White children in all-White schools; Black teachers taught Black children in all-Black schools. Latino children's schooling varied by community, with many smaller communities having dominant Latino populations and thus Latino dominance in the staff and students in the school; others were present in small numbers in predominantly White schools; still others, as their numbers increased in urban areas, attended segregated schools within large urban districts (DeLeon 1989; San Miguel 2000). And in other communities there was the expectation that Latino children would stay in school only through the first eight or ten grades.

Despite the presence of Blacks in the city from its earliest days in the 1830s, including freedmen's towns, no Black was elected to the school board until 1958. Despite the fact that Texas was a part of Mexico until well into the 1800s, no Mexican American was elected to the school board of this city until 1972.[3] White business leadership has dominated all aspects of city life throughout its history, first as a center of agricultural commerce, and later during its ascendance in petrochemicals, space exploration, and medicine.[4] This dominance has, in part, been maintained by "at-large" elections for city council, school board, and other elective positions. Without neighborhood-based district seats, minority candidates would have to run a citywide campaign for an at-large position, a dauntingly expensive challenge for any candidate not backed by the business establishment. As documented in *Free Enterprise City*, the White business elite controlled all public spending, shifting dollars from neighborhood infrastructure investments (in streets, sewers, and services such as parks and libraries) to build a highly modern infrastructure in the imposing central business district. Ethnic neighborhoods and potential civic activists were kept down, kept poor or co-opted (Feagin 1988; McAdams 1998), assuring continued business dominance. The history of discriminatory funding of schools paralleled the discriminatory funding of city services, following racial and income patterns. According to Feagin, over the years few mechanisms existed for redress; there were few workers' unions, few organized community or ethnic associations with the resources to maintain a strong collective voice at the policy table. Like the shining glass business district, a few "good" high schools carried the district's reputation; many schools in Black and Latino neighborhoods have lacked even basic supplies and equipment.

Desegregation of the schools and its implicit requirements for more equitable funding of schools and wider participation in the governance of the district were contested for many years. As various plans were proposed locally or imposed by courts, the social construction of "race" as well as the political construction of "education" were played out with much conflict, with much delay, and with little regard for the consequences for children's educations.[5] Sixteen years after *Brown v. Board*, in 1970, Federal District Judge Ben Connally had ordered the "immediate" implementation of an unpopular involuntary desegregation plan, under which integration in this district would be accomplished by construing Mexican Americans as "White" for purposes of desegregation, using them, rather than Anglos, to integrate with African Americans. As Valenzuela explains (1999, 45), this ruling "constituted an outright denial of a Mexican American ethnic minority status," and it reified the status quo, which kept minority and White children in separate (and unequal) schools. Such a plan would be unlikely to lead to a redress of the discriminatory provisioning of schools, one of the chief goals behind the rejection of "separate but equal" justifications for separate schools; separate had never been funded as equal. (Mexican American children's schools had never been provided with the resources typical of "White" schools, so the use of the "Whiteness" label only to transfer Mexican children into other, underfunded, traditionally all-Black schools, was thus an even more egregious externalizing of their cultural identity.)[6]

At the point of this pairing plan, Blacks and Mexicans joined forces to appeal the ruling to the U.S. Fifth Circuit Court of Appeals; the NAACP Legal Defense Fund and Mexican American Legal Defense and Education Fund (MALDEF) led the opposition. MALDEF's brief specifically challenged the construal of Mexican Americans as White and cited 1970 case law *(Cisneros v. Corpus Christi ISD)*, which established the legal framework to accord Mexican Americans protected minority status under the Fourteenth Amendment (San Miguel 1987, 2000), a protection jeopardized if they were to be considered "White" only for purposes of integrating schools. The desegregation plan put forth by the Fifth Circuit retained the use of Mexican American children to desegregate previously all-Black schools and further suggested a desegregation plan based on pairing a specific number of African American and Mexican American elementary schools (including only one White school in the plan) for the reassignment of students. The remedy for the segregation of high schools was to create "integrated" high schools by redrawing the skewed boundaries that had arbitrarily separated Mexican American and African American students. At this time (1970), the urban district's student population was approximately 55 percent White, 33 percent African American, and 10 percent Hispanic, with very small numbers of Asian and Native-American children. (By the mid-1980s Whites and Hispanics would each comprise around 25 percent, with Blacks numbering 50 percent; by the year 2000, Hispanics have a clear numerical majority with approximately 52 percent; Blacks stand at 33 percent; Whites at 10–11 percent and Asians approximately 4 percent.)[7] Throughout this period, the desegregation plans centered on populations counts of children per school, according to operant legal definitions of their race.[8]

While these issues of children's racial ratios and patterns of school pairing were being contested, plans were also being devised to reassign teachers in order to integrate faculties; these plans were also under the court order. Many of these crossover teachers recall the dislocations for their careers and for their students as these assignments were made; some Black teachers remember walking into empty classrooms in White schools where parents had had their children reassigned to the White teachers. The story of the many gains and losses as, once reassigned, teachers, administrators, and children began to reconstruct "school" in integrated settings, is a story that has yet to be written. The dominant issues before the courts were the ones of racial counts and the reorganization needed to balance the races across the required number of schools.

Of great concern to families was the educational quality their children would receive. Within each racial group, according to the memories of many who were parents of school children or community leaders at that time, there were fears that integration would dilute educational quality. On the other hand, there were also fears that segregation would perpetuate not only severe inequities in quality but also an entire antiquated system that would serve none of its children well. Whites feared that integration would "dilute" the academic quality in their schools (and their children's access to privilege). Blacks feared that they would lose control over their flagship schools, particularly the two high schools most noted for graduating future civic leaders and professionals; integration could dilute not only their educational quality but also the social capital that enabled them to nurture the next generation of Black leaders.

Mexican Americans reacted to the "White" designation and its implications for busing their children rather than those of Anglos by organizing a boycott of the public schools and, in some cases, establishing *huelga* ("strike") schools. DeLeon records that several thousand children were involved, including 60 percent of those who would be bused under the order to pair their schools with those in African American neighborhoods. Just as *Brown v. Board* came out of years of Black activism for equality under the law (Egerton 1994), the *huelga* boycott grew out of Mexican American activism in the Chicano movement across the Southwest, working for improved conditions for farmworkers, greater access to legal and economic opportunities, and the maintenance of Spanish language and culture, which preceded Anglo presence in this region. The Mexican-American community was divided, according to Valenzuela, along generation lines with older Mexican Americans "preferring to work through the system," accepting recognition as White or Caucasian, and pursing integration. "In contrast, the new generation was radical, vocal, and ideological. It advanced a critique of the public school system as dissuasive of the needs of Mexican American youth" (Valenzuela 1999, 47). Mexican Americans put forth twenty demands, chief among them being accorded ethnic minority status and an appeal of the school-pairing plan to the U.S. Supreme Court. Appeals brought no relief and the district was denied a stay in the implementation of the pairing of Black and Hispanic schools. The plan to pair schools avoided the massive mandatory cross-town busing of children that people of all three racial groups feared (a plan used in some other cities), but exacerbated fears that educational quality as well as cultural coherence would be jeopardized by the other plans being put forth by the courts. In addition, the years of controversy and delay had caused many middle-class families, especially Whites, to move to the suburbs. By the time the district began to implement school pairings, its "White" numbers were dropping, Blacks were anticipating losses in their own schools, and the Mexican American communities were increasingly skeptical that the desegregation remedies being put forward actually met the intended spirit of the law.

In this conflicted context, several community groups and school board members had begun searching for politically acceptable alternatives to the mandates that were alienating virtually every community group, including those dedicated to ending segregation and discrimination in the schools.

A Search for Equity with Excellence

After years of conflict in this city, magnet schools as possible solutions to the separation of educational quality from desegregation were the subject of discussion by small groups of parents and educators. Such schools seemed to offer the possibility of overcoming the resistance to both forced busing and school pairing, on the one hand, and to the so far unsuccessful attempts to promote voluntary racial transfers across the traditionally segregated schools, on the other. A local elementary school had already demonstrated the attractiveness to middle-class parents of a school with a special focus. This school created a gifted-and-talented program and advertised that students outside its attendance zone could apply for admission. The school was successful in helping retain White, middle-class families otherwise considering private schools or a move to the suburbs. This school pre-dates the magnet school policy but became the first elementary Pathfinder school[9] (see chapter 3) once the magnet system was designed. Coincidentally, a number of artists, arts patrons, educators, and philanthropists had long envisioned creating a high school for performing arts, modeled after the New York High School of Music and Art. Gore documents (1998) that plans for such a school were put forward and shelved several times, even gaining unanimous approval from an otherwise very divided school board in 1968, but that plan was not acted upon. Finally in 1972 the school board approved the creation of a "vocational" school for the visual and performing arts. The "vocational" designation would qualify the school for state vocational education funding, essential since the district did not plan to pay for equipping the school. This high school was designed to prepare students for careers in dance, music, graphic arts, and media; desegregation was not, incredibly, an explicit purpose of the school at its founding. Community response to these two schools did, however, demonstrate that families, children, and teachers of all races were eager for urban schools, which offered solid opportunities for learning. School board members committed to integration, and others less enthusiastic but resigned to some form of desegregation, began to see in these specialized schools a model for voluntary racial transfers. Later both the school for the arts and the Pathfinder elementary school would claim the distinction of being the "first" magnet school.

It would be 1974 before a racially mixed task force made up of educators, central office staff, and community leaders would put forth a plan for magnet, or specialized, schools to be the centerpiece of the district's desegregation efforts and 1975 before such a plan would be approved by the courts. It included ideas for new schools, with two as free-standing schools, and most of the rest as schools-within-schools. In addition, a number of the district's vocational high schools were reviewed for their potential to attract students of all three races, and many of them were redesignated as magnet schools. From a small number of schools at the outset in the mid-1970s, more than 100 such programs in the city's more than 250 schools were developed over the next twenty years into "magnets." The early list of magnet schools included the gifted-and-talented schools, beginning with the first Pathfinder elementary created prior to magnet status, and later adding a high school (see chapter 3), middle schools, and more elementary schools under the Pathfinder rubric. Magnet high schools mostly followed career themes: they included such careers as criminal justice, hotel management, teaching, media, aeronautics and space, science and engineering (see chapter 4), and business, as well as a foreign language magnet academy in a large traditional high school.[10] Leading to these high school magnet programs were middle and elementary magnets for the study of the musical arts, math and science, and foreign language. The district had to create a number of new school programs immediately, reconstituting a number of existing programs, adding a cross-town application process to the vocational schools, and creating a system of free transportation for transfer students, all in a very brief span of time.

The organizational support for these schools, as understood when the research that underpins this book began, included the role of the federal courts as legitimating these schools as academic programs designed to offer a specialized, quality education to children of all races. It included the role of the courts in approving the plan, including the list of magnet school programs, monitoring student enrollments and faculty by race, and monitoring the fairness of student application criteria and procedures. It included limited initial federal funding for the district, including financing an enhanced role for the district research and evaluation office to provide the courts with annual data on racial ratios. The organizational support also included the handling of all transfer applications, program applications, bus scheduling, and advertisement of the schools and the admissions procedures. The structural support also included the establishment of a magnet program staff in the central office who would oversee the creation of the programs, including approval of course listings within broad parameters that were rarely seen as regulations or directives and that were expected to differ from the generic course descriptions used throughout the city for each subject at each grade level. (Over time, personnel in this office tended to be people who had formerly taught in magnet schools.)

In addition, the status of these specialized programs as magnet schools, as essential to satisfy a court order to desegregate, gave especially those that were located within traditional schools the legitimacy to create specialized courses and activities that by definition would fall outside the general state regulations and the district's generic rules. The permission to step outside the rulebook, to step off the state textbook adoption list, to focus on particular subject areas, particular approaches to teaching, and very specific groups of students was a crucial, if intangible, component of the organizational context of these schools. It was vital to the kind of teaching and learning they came to foster. It is the key basis for their selection as schools that merit close study of the relationship between school structure and curriculum.

The policy language establishing these schools focuses on case law, racial population designations, and specialty themes. The policy language does not advocate particular kinds of pedagogies, does not discuss the relational aspects of teaching, does not explicitly address school culture or educational philosophies. Most of the decisions regarding magnet specialties came from what the press and school district came to term *practical academics*, with a focus on academic specialties that had a direct connection to sectors of the local economy. Such a focus depoliticized potential ideas for school programs (there is a notable lack of magnets around community culture and litera- ture—such as Chicano studies or dual language, or around political or his- torical studies such as Afrocentric studies or international or environmental topics). In addition, the pre-career focus was seen by many as a way to elicit donations from related local businesses and industry for the equipment and materials that would be needed to make these school programs match the expectations raised by their names.

Over time, the magnets proliferated, the school populations changed, and the role of the magnets shifted from a primary emphasis on desegregation to one of academic choice in a large urban district.[11] Nevertheless, this conflicted racial history forms an important backdrop for the highly successful and inclusive teaching that came to characterize the lead magnet schools, the ones created quickly to satisfy court orders and created by faculties who sought them out for their potential for teaching outside the microregulations of state and district.

"The Best Schools . . ."

The federal court approved the use of magnet schools to desegregate the school system in July 1975, and by the opening of school in September—five weeks later—the district was to dismantle the pairing system, redraw the boundaries of those schools to their original lines, design and staff thirty-two magnet programs, "market" the programs, and arrange for the students and teachers to transfer to those schools. These "centers of excellence," however hastily assembled, would generate voluntary transfers across historical racial divisions.[12] There has been much debate during the past twenty-plus years about whether these schools are elitist, about whether they have restratified students by class, about whether they create privilege for some students at the expense of those left behind in "regular" schools, schools which continue to vary in quality and in provisioning according to highly discriminatory pat- terns. Some of this debate is beyond the scope of this study. What is significant here is that the elegance of the names of many of these schools hides woeful inadequacies of resources. Their faculties (and students), nonetheless, have created programs of authentic teaching and learning that have opened to poor and minority students paths to university and to careers that had been histor- ically closed to them. In addition, the schools have helped retain in the city and in urban schools many families who say they otherwise would have diminished the district's tax base by moving to the suburbs. Very important to this study is that the professional environment created within these schools has helped keep intelligent and dedicated teachers in urban schools and in teaching. Every new superintendent and many new school board members have heard the elitism charge and come in prepared to dismantle the magnet system. After looking over the district and then seeing these schools, two of these superintendents—people who were completely different from each other—decided to keep and support the schools, saying, "This is all we have." These schools have served as examples of what urban schools can be, what urban children can do, and what a district should get serious about. The district has not, to date, given "regular" schools support and the freedom from regulations for the kind of teaching and learning that goes on in the magnets. Most of the magnet teachers have selected these schools so that they can teach the way they think all children should be taught. They see the schools as far from elite but as approximating in a big-city district their notion of "real school."

". . . money can't buy."

The district advertised the magnet schools as "the best schools money can't buy." The billboards and bumperstickers carrying this message had two audiences: first, middle- and upper-middle-class parents should see these schools as academically competitive with expensive private schools and therefore a reason to keep their children in public schools. Second, families who could never afford private schools should see these schools as offering their children what their family could never pay for. These are seen as "value-added schools." Except for the schools that emphasize the arts, math and science, and "giftedness," admission is generally based on a C average, good disciplinary records, and interest in attending. The fact that many children who enter these schools with no prior exceptional academic performance leave well prepared for the next level of schooling gives the district the rationale to maintain this system of schooling and gives the magnet teachers great pride for what they have created.

Authentic Teaching and Learning

The administrative support and legal permission to create attractive and academically sound special schools enabled the magnet teachers, even in this very hierarchical state system of schooling, to create learning environments where the content of schooling was not artificially processed merely to push students through to a diploma. In spite of severe resource shortages and uneven school-level administrative support, these teachers used the magnet setting to make school a place for real learning. They represent almost direct opposites to teachers who teach defensively, who bracket their knowledge of their subjects and of their students in order to satisfy the bureaucratic controls in their schools. Even when the magnet schools existed as little more than names, and were not provided with continuing resources, the magnet teachers used them as auspices for authentic teaching of diverse students. How the magnet teachers accomplished this is the subject of the three case studies to follow:

The Pathfinder high school shows what teaching and learning can be when teachers feel they can bring their best personal knowledge to the lessons and thereby enable their students to bring their own minds—their own intellectual engagement—into the classroom. The School for Science, Engineering and Technology is especially interesting because there the students played a major role in shaping the content of schooling; seriously underresourced by the district, this school was able to be productive only because the students entered into a bargain with their teachers to make it so. The MedIC magnet, a school that prepares students for future medical careers, was selected for this study because it is a school where the curriculum cannot be phony "school knowledge" useful only for passing school tests. The students move between this school and clinical rotations in hospitals; the content of their schooling must be credible outside school. Taken together, these magnet schools provide powerful exemplars of the kinds of teaching and learning that can occur when teachers are not de-skilled by bureaucratic controls. Their structures arose out of racial conflict and their communities' needs to affirm the responsibility to make schools that would afford all children a meaningful education. This organizational "permission" to think about diverse, urban children had powerful consequences once the schools took on a life of their own. Most famous among them, perhaps, was the high school that introduced teenagers to medical professions.

MedIC

Teenagers' posture is an enduring source of anguish and frustration for their parents. The faculty at the Medical Instructional Center had a cure for teen slouch: the white coat. Juniors at the MedIC high school received their white medical coats in a ceremony that was a rite of passage between their first two years of classwork and their next two years of clinical rotations through the Medical Center. On that day, they all stood differently. They walked with an air of confidence. They looked adults in the eye. They had already visited teaching hospitals, research labs, and a medical school. They had listened to guest lectures from famous doctors, from surgical nurses, from dental technicians. They themselves had seen the respect and authority accorded by the patients and fellow health care professionals in the halls of the clinics to the professionals in their color-coded uniforms. And now they had the white coat: it told everyone they saw that they had survived freshman Biology and mastered Introduction to Medical Lab Skills and Med Lab II. They knew the names of dozens of pieces of expensive equipment and had mastered their functions. They knew more than twenty kinds of laboratory flasks and tubes and the uses of each. They had surprised themselves by learning to convert to metric and memorizing the taxonomies of anatomy. They had completed the freshman and sophomore levels of mathematics, English, history, and the sciences. They might still slouch in class, but each afternoon when they boarded the bus to their assigned places in the Medical Center, the shoulders straightened.

Innovative Structures

The MedIC magnet high school is interesting for the partnership between the school district and a medical school and for its founders' explicit goals of human capital formation, growing local talent for the thousands of positions (hundreds of different job categories) needed to staff the city's world-class Medical Center. MedIC is interesting as one of only two magnet high schools with their own buildings (the arts school is the other) and no attendance zone. And it is important for its success in helping open premedical studies and medical career paths to minorities, especially Blacks. It is significant as a school that succeeds in providing many students who enter as average or slightly above average with an education that opens doors to college that would have been closed to them at their home school. Most significant for this study is that MedIC proved to be a school where the teachers created an education that was authentic, that is, credible when students took it into the workplace and into their future studies.

How they created a high school, with students who were eligible for admission with only C averages from their middle schools, that created a bridge to the complex world of the health professions is a lesson in creative finance, innovative staffing, and collaborative curriculum planning with a view to students' success beyond the school walls.

The school began as the dream of lead physicians in the Medical Center, who were watching the exponential growth of this complex of medical schools, private hospitals, governmental hospitals (the Veterans' Administration

Hospital, a public-private nonprofit hospital, and the state's cancer research and treatment center), nursing schools, rehabilitation centers, and clinics—all clustered in one part of the city. Thousands of jobs were being created (some of them invented in this medical center, where cutting-edge discoveries regularly made headlines), and to fill them meant recruiting beyond the city. The city's history as a commercial center and oil-and-gas town did not promise a workforce prepared for medical-related jobs. A high school that would generate an interest in medical careers could accomplish two goals: help create a pipeline to premedical and medical studies for minority students who typically had no such access; and help raise interest in and skills for the technical support jobs in the hospital district. The school began in what its early faculty called "the shack," a small, temporary building nested amid the huge hospitals; as it grew it was housed on the campus of an established vocational school, until later a building was built just for this school.

The planning of this school occurred at about the same time the arts school was being discussed. Both were heavily dependent on community resources beyond the school district for the planning of the programs and for the financing of specialized facilities. The myth surrounding the MedIC high school is that it was heavily financed by its collaborating medical college and by local physicians. (The picture in the front hall of the school is not George Washington, but the famous surgeon whose vision helped create the school.) In fact, an administrator at the school explained that it is the district that pays the medical college for its collaboration and assistance.[13]

Because the district's approval of the concept of the school did not include allocations for funding the special facilities, the start-up staff had to be creative in locating funding. The school needed to be equipped with microscopes, centrifuges, an autoclave, laboratory glassware, equipment for blood analysis and laboratory procedures, anatomical models, lab safety equipment, and many other technical supplies and equipment consistent with those that the students would use when they began rotating into clinics and research labs. The teacher of the Medical Labs courses pointed out the need for precision in the calibrating, storing, use, and maintenance of the equipment. She explained that this school's annual budget for calibrations and maintenance exceeded the equipment *purchase* budgets of other, even larger, high schools.

How did a district trying to create more than thirty magnet schools on short notice build and equip such a school? The answer was state vocational money. Like the arts high school, this school was proposed to the state as a vocational school and under that designation received extensive initial and ongoing funding from the state for those parts of the school most directly related to medical jobs.

The school recruited students as a premed school, a school to set a minority child on the path to becoming a doctor. Yet it solicited vocational education funds, as though its primary purpose was to train its students for entry-level jobs in the medical fields: medical technicians, licensed vocational nurses, and dental assistants. In fact, the school did both. By junior year, students were tracked into the college-prep sequence of courses or the practical, technical courses. (Both received the white coats.) The college-prep students took high-level science courses, interspersing six weeks of second-year chemistry, biochemistry, or molecular biology with six-week rotations in research labs. The most advanced students conducted independent research in those labs; others assisted on research projects of medical school faculty. The technical track students took courses in dental tech work and basic nursing skills; a six-months' practicum after graduation would earn certification as a licensed vocational nurse. (This program was later eliminated as the curriculum grew more college preparatory and less vocational.)

The split identity and split curriculum caused grief for the principal and the advocates of the school as they tried to balance the precollege reputation with the vocational realities. A long-time teacher at the school, who faithfully attended the school's alumni reunions, explained that the dichotomy was misleading. She had found that many of the students who left school for immediate technical jobs in the hospitals used that income to finance studies at the community college, after which they went to college and, in many cases, to medical school. She recalled quite a number of graduates who were not college-bound after their senior year who nevertheless years later were introducing themselves at the reunions as "Doctor." For both groups, MedIC clearly had provided a value-added education.

Med Class 101

The success of MedIC, according to many of the teachers, was its small and inauspicious start, in the shadow of the medical center with a small group of students. By the time the school became highly visible in its new building and in its role as a lead magnet school, the program had developed into not only a set of courses but also a series of experiences that would acquaint students with the profession of medical care through domains of knowledge needed by health professionals. The academic program was comprised of two strands, medical courses and traditional precollege academics. The two coexisted as almost two separate curricula, except in the interface between the advanced science courses and the senior research lab rotations.

The medical courses began with laboratory skills and introductions to the range of careers that comprise health care. The lab courses progressed from technical skills to the study of the scientific principles at work in the tests and experiments. By the second year, courses specialized, with nursing, dental, and other technical areas forming the core of study for students not anticipating college immediately after high school. For the college bound, the medically related courses became settings for applying knowledge learned in the traditional science classes.

Introduction to Med Lab Skills brought high school freshmen (just three months past eighth grade) into immediate contact with the awesome responsibility of delicate glassware, precision dials, equipment that hissed and beeped—all in a huge laboratory classroom. Ms. Holland presided over the laboratory with the focus of a brain surgeon, the warmth of a favorite aunt, and the coolness of a head nurse. Ms. Holland's guide for the content of her courses came from her direct knowledge of what these students would need to know in a medical laboratory. Her approaches to teaching carried over from her days as a teacher of medical technicians in the community college and as an instructor in a school of nursing. She brought her own expertise as a former lab director to her subject and to the professional standards she set for her students. "School lab" would not be a watered-down version of laboratory practices. From their first class at the school, then, the students saw that the standard for learning was not a cut-score on a test ("you need a 70 percent to pass") but demonstrated competence in transferring classroom skills into work on real patients' blood and tissue samples, real doctor's chart notations.

The beginning activities in the class centered on precision and care, on following precise directions, on learning to make accurate written notes. Understanding the science behind the laboratory practices was not at first emphasized. What students learned in the early weeks of the course were the professional norms of precision, of working with standard procedures and protocols, of taking pride in completeness and accuracy. Many students had never worked with their hands at school; for them, manipulating pipettes, handling slides without breaking them, even touching sensitive equipment took much repetitive practice. Ms. Holland designed the course as a movement from rote and repetitive procedures (using a pipette to move a drop of liquid; pouring from a large flask to a small tube; weighing and reweighing; measuring and remeasuring temperatures of various samples) to more complex problem solving. Students reported that they had done little or no lab work in middle school science classes; those who had some lab experience said that they were graded in those labs on whether they "finished their lab sheets," so they had frequently "rounded up" imprecise answers or borrowed bottom-line results from other lab teams if their experiments did not work. The stakes in such classes had been slight variations in daily or weekly grades. After only a few hours in Ms. Holland's class, the students recognized that they were doing what one boy called "grown-up work." Their clumsy teenage bodies had to be trained to sit on a high stool and handle sensitive equipment, vital samples, and the day's instructions.

Teaching for understanding of the science content came only after students could manipulate the laboratory equipment and only after weeks and weeks of learning to observe and to write observations clearly and accurately. The early lab periods did not require students to explain phenomena, but to follow directions. The students were only beginning to study physical science (which includes very basic chemistry); none had yet studied biology or chemistry. Ms. Holland's task, therefore, was in part to acquaint students indirectly with chemical and biological concepts (oxygen, plasma, pH) while at the same time using the precision laboratory setting to socialize them into one aspect of the culture of medicine.

The other courses in the medical sequence were also geared to have congruence with practical medical settings, rather than with scientific abstractions. The freshman and sophomore years included courses to acquaint students with health care careers, methods of researching medical topics, anatomy and physiology, and CPR (cardiopulmonary resuscitation). The two-hour Med Lab blocks dominated the day and assured a continuity of socialization into an applied stance to medical skills and information.

Credible Academics

Regular subjects like English and History could easily have been eclipsed by the dissection of cow eyes and practice with dental tools, by guest lectures by the inventor of an artificial heart or the discoverer of a new treatment for Parkinson's. The medical courses set the context for serious study with real-world applications, but it was the core academic subjects that transformed these young people into serious students who would be able to take advantage of the openings the school afforded for college and professional studies.

A refrain running through all the magnet schools was the teachers' disbelief at how little the students had read and how little they had written prior to high school. Even at SET and Pathfinder (see chapters 3 and 4), whose students had to clear higher admissions standards, the freshmen entering magnet schools seldom brought rigorous academic learning with them. At MedIC it was the task of their teachers in English, history, math, and the sciences to leverage their interest in medicine into academic studies that would enable them to act on their very abstract dreams of becoming a doctor. The students reported that "you can forget the math department," and in fact the principal did not give permission to observe math classes. The science classes varied in quality, but by senior year linked with the advanced medical classes to provide solid experiences with both conceptual and applied sciences.

The English and history courses, then, bore a special responsibility for students' academic learning. The teachers of these subjects developed their own curricula, sometimes coordinating within departments and occasionally creating cross-disciplinary student research projects. Primarily they worked independently, enjoying a faculty culture that honored excellence in teaching and learning but that rarely fostered collaboration. When asked if there was much interchange between the medical teachers and the regular courses, the history teacher explained that such initiatives were rare and almost always came from the academic teachers: "In the ninth grade World History course and the ninth grade Introduction to Medicine course, they tried to create some lessons about Egyptian and Greek medicine, but that rarely comes off. We are much more interested in what they are doing than they are in us. I get curious and I walk in there when they lay out the dental tools and when they start cutting on the cats. But they never come in to see what we are doing. It is a matter of curiosity."

If the medical teachers had been curious, then they would have seen teachers creating lessons that began in the ninth grade with very basic reading interpretation skills, teaching purposeful reading in both literature and history, and that proceeded through the grades to introduce the students to serious literature and complex interpretations of history and economics. The school's library, shared with the medical/tech campus of the community college, had proportionately few reference books and journals related to social studies; nevertheless, students discussed with great pride their research projects on such varied topics as the economics of rural medicine, early Danish and German settlements in Texas, the history of space exploration, and various wars and elections. The students with friends in honors or Advanced Placement classes in college-prep high schools in the suburbs said that these projects matched those of their friends; students who had transferred to this school from traditionally Black high schools said that their friends in their neighborhood schools reported never having this much homework, never having assignments that took them to the library.

An assignment that demonstrated how much the academic program of this school had advanced the intellectual skills of the students was Ms. Barnes's senior literature assignment. The students had moved from very basic reading of essays and short stories in their freshman year, to analyzing novels and working on writing in their sophomore and junior year, learning to discuss their reading and to venture personal interpretations of text. For this class, Ms. Barnes put out a challenge equal to their rotations in the Medical Center. Each group of five students was to read a difficult novel and interpret that novel through a dramatization of a pivotal scene. The dramatization had to include the text of the scene, the significance of that scene in the novel, and the significance of that scene in the author's life and work. Over several weeks, the students read, talked, passed ideas by the teacher, researched the life and times of the authors and debated the selection of the scenes to be portrayed on stage.

One of the most dramatic renderings, and one that linked "school knowledge" to life experience, was the decision by the readers of *Crime and Punishment* to enact Raskolnikov's crime as a modern-day theft. The theft was the actual stealing of a test by a group of MedIC students; one of the teachers had become somewhat of a hero by breaking up this little theft ring, helping restore confidence in the camaraderie that had traditionally protected this school from the destructive competitions for class rank typical in the honors tracks of other schools. Identifying the culprits did not "solve" the crime, however, because it unleashed an emotional parental defense of one student, fractured the sense of trust students had shared, pitted the nurturing side of teaching against perceived needs to police student behaviors, and revealed cracks in the otherwise amiable relations with school administrators, who found themselves caught between protecting the integrity of the program and appeasing vocal parents. The question of cheating and the nature of consequences, to wrong-doers and those around them, had dominated conversations for days. Through Dostoevsky, the seniors crystallized the issues and elevated them to a level of discourse that was both more personal and more universal.

The players in this Russian work were Black, Latino, White, and Middle Eastern. The diversity of the acting ensemble gave greater weight to the discussion that followed the dramatization, pushing the questions of ethics and choices into cultural as well as personal domains. The young Muslim woman on stage, herself striving to balance family, culture, and educational opportunity without losing the core values of either, unconsciously symbolized the struggles many of these students faced in finding, leaving, and holding values. *Portrait of the Artist as a Young Man, Grapes of Wrath, Pride and Prejudice,* and *The Color Purple* all became in the hands of these players vehicles for examining the cultural and personal values that for these students were not academic but were working themselves out through experiences that were both highly academic and imminently practical.

On Call

The academic and the practical came together most pointedly as the junior and senior students donned their white coats and boarded the bus for the Medical Center. In their junior year they observed and assisted in labs and clinical settings. Students who admitted hating chores at home spoke with pride about changing patients' bed linens, emptying bed pans, organizing supply closets, and "just sitting around trying to figure out what all these different people were doing—they all seemed to know where to go and what to do, though there was no one really telling anyone what needed to be done—it just happens so magically—all those people." The junior rotations give glimpses of the many tasks that need to be done and that can be done in medical settings when people are prepared to do them. These rotations stimulate students' determination to learn chemistry and physiology, biology and lab skills far more than the pressure for grades or class rank. They can see that without more education they will be pushing the wheelchairs rather than setting the bones. An eleventh-grade girl had chosen this school because of her mother's insistence she apply. She valued the small size of the school but missed the chance to participate in sports. Her junior rotation in the public health section of a large public hospital included taking patients to radiology, taking notes on the activities in this public health department for a paper for one of her classes, and assisting with physical therapy patients. She had hoped also to work in an animal research lab but discovered that she was allergic to the animals; that disappointment sparked her curiosity about allergies, prompting a research topic for senior year.

A student who drove more than thirty miles from a suburb to attend the school managed even in her junior year to connect with patient care. She helped the nurses in a pulmonary clinic assist asthma and emphysema patients with blood tests and chest catheters. By her senior year, she earned a placement in a cell biology lab in the medical college and assisted on a research project.

She, too, had an interest in the animal research laboratory and learned to care for and handle the animals, do simple surgical techniques and blood work on them, and in a training center at the Catholic hospital assisted in intestinal surgery on a dog. The medical school library became her favorite haunt during free time, permitting her to search for references for her school paper without the limitations of the school library. This girl said she had always been a fairly good student, but "even at my high school I never would have known I could do these things; I would probably be hating chemistry right now along with my friends. They make good grades, but they don't really see the point to the course. I say, 'are you *kidding*? . . . They may not even believe I operated on a dog, but I did. I could do it." This girl managed to carry gymnastics, History Fair, and Science Fair, and still turn one of her hospital rotations into a paying job after school.

The small size of the school (approximately 750 students) offered close connections between students and faculty and among students across racial and neighborhood lines. The school culture was predominantly Black; the principal was a noted Black educator with long experience in the district, and the school was situated between two Black neighborhoods and the Medical Center. The student body was almost 90 percent Black in the early years, and later 60 percent Black, with 30 to 35 percent White and small numbers of Hispanics. Many of the Hispanics said that their parents or previous teachers had been leery of their chances for success in a mostly Black school, but they had for the most part thrived and did not regret this entree into the medical world. For girl students the chief weakness in the school population was the dearth of boys; in some years the class was 60 to 75 percent girls. The lack of competitive athletics was often cited as a reason fewer boys attended the school. (This was the only school in the entire state given a waiver for physical education credits for graduation; the physical education program was led by a strong, popular teacher, and the cafeteria/auditorium doubled as a basketball gym for most hours of the day, but as one teacher said, "We are supposed to be the school about *health*, and we have the most sedentary students. We don't even have a track.")

A Vietnamese girl from a family of twelve children talked of brothers and sisters who never had homework at their neighborhood high school. One brother had attended this school, and although he went on to study architecture, he strongly urged this sister to apply to MedIC. Her junior rotations at the Veterans Administration Hospital inspired great interest in endocrinology ("Isn't it amazing they know how these things work?") but discouraged her from considering nursing as a career after she watched too few harried nurses carrying out too many tasks. Her senior rotation at the medical school helped set her sights on research; she assisted a graduate student on a study of cervical herpes viruses, learning to don gloves, freeze tissue samples, and identify viral strains. She eagerly added viral texts to her regular senior science homework, a voluntary gesture that mystified her siblings whose few take-home assignments were worksheets or excerpts to read in anthologies.

Students learned of the school through all kinds of information channels. One student who had been admitted to both MedIC and SET had accepted SET but had "overslept and missed the bus to that school." So he agreed to look into the school that had been his dad's first choice for him and three days into the semester enrolled in MedIC. A Latina had moved from Kentucky and had been told that there might be "too many Blacks" for her to succeed. But, having always wanted to be a doctor, she commuted one hour each way every day, defying the grandfather who was very upset about the racial mix at the school. She made friends easily among all groups and thrived in her studies. She could scarcely describe her junior rotation, interrupting herself to say, "Can't you see?" and "You *do* understand, it was just so amazing . . ." Her senior rotations were enriched by her bilingual skills; she was able to assist in a family planning clinic in a community hospital. She spent time in a medical co-op and observed the ob/gyn practice at the teaching hospital. She worked with cancer patients in an outpatient clinic. She also learned lessons about the economics of medicine: at one clinic after she had proved her skills the doctors started asking for her assistance. She was flattered until she realized it was because she, a volunteer, was cheaper help than the nurses. Seeing how easily quality could be sacrificed for a small savings strengthened her commitment to go into public health. This is a student who said, "I have never been a scholar," yet she continued to take upper-level science courses and to make plans for premed studies because she saw them as necessary avenues to work for which she was recognized as skillful in a variety of settings.

From formula derivations to technical vocabulary and careful handling of equipment and people, the MedIC students saw purpose in their studies as they, and the older students ahead of them, brought their stories of illnesses and treatments, drudge work and miracle discoveries back into classrooms.

One teacher confessed that for her the student rotations were somewhat academic, "a nice addition to the program," until she herself was hospitalized. She was aghast to realize that some of the MedIC students were assigned to her hospital; she prayed none would come on her floor. To her dismay, a senior boy walked into her room with the attending physician and the medical students on rounds. The boy did not acknowledge knowing her. He retained the same serious "preprofessional" demeanor throughout the consultation. "And after I returned to school, he never let on that I had been in that hospital. I mean, he was *so professional*. I think they really are learning something here. He is serious about what he is doing."

The MedIC school was not perfect. There was little coordination between the medical and academic faculties; students were left to make the connections. The collaboration with the medical college provided the arrangement for the rotations and clinical placements for the students but left the MedIC faculty in an unclear role within the school organization, even though within their classrooms they exercised wide latitude in course planning, materials acquisitions, and grading policies. Authority in the school was at times ambiguous, with the teachers expressing confidence in and a strong preference for working directly with the principal but having to negotiate around a midlevel administrator who was partly on the payroll of the medical college and not always closely involved with the faculty's goals for the school. The medical college was represented in this institutional partnership by an advisory board for the high school that included physicians and on-site by staff for whom the relationship with the school was one of several "outreach" projects. The MedIC faculty discussed the medical college personnel as "they" and puzzled over their authority and their role. Particularly the Black faculty members expressed concern that because most of the students were Black, some of the medical school outreach personnel tended to treat MedIC like a local charity or at other times a showcase for the medical school, rather than an educational enterprise in its own right. The MedIC faculty recognized that even though relations with the medical college were at times uneasy (because decisions or policies made in conjunction with the medical school tended to be made without broad teacher input), the association with the medical school provided strong legitimacy not only for the high school's distinctive programs and mission but also for the school's relative independence from the central office and from state regulations. Invoking the partnership with the medical school carried symbolic weight in dealing with central administration. In addition, the collaboration was invaluable in recruiting students.

There are many narratives that converge in a school like MedIC. It has opened the doors to medical careers and medical studies to hundreds of Black and Hispanic students, especially girls. It has provided a place for medical professionals from laboratories and public health facilities to work alongside teachers, bringing applied sciences and academic subjects together. And it has served as a door through which teenagers of color, who are often overlooked as future employees in highly skilled settings, are welcomed into labs and clinics, research centers and hospitals, teaching the professionals in those settings as much about the potential of urban children as the students were learning about medicine. Those who originally envisioned that magnet schools would desegregate the schools could not have fully anticipated the ways that they would indirectly help desegregate the workplaces of the city.

MedIC stands out as a school that succeeded with educating its diverse students inside the school because the knowledge of the classroom had to be credible in the halls of the hospitals and health centers, not only in senior rotation but also in their lives beyond school. The independence of the school from generic bureaucratic regulation enabled both the medical specialist faculty and the teachers of academic subjects to shape a curriculum that could encompass not only their own knowledge but also the evolving knowledge base emerging in the Medical Center. The students' development could parallel and build on that ever-growing body of knowledge and expertise without the need for them to bracket what they had learned in school.

Chapter 3

Breaking the Cycle:
The Pathfinder School

Pathfinder people are supposed to have different ways of thinking about things. In physics you sometimes have to think in a straight line. You sometimes have to leap across, and people are good sometimes at one and not the other. But it's good for them to see that sometimes you can solve a problem by breaking it into parts and doing the parts; sometimes you cannot. But in physics a lot of times that's the way you do it. A lot of them need to see that.
    —Ms. Watts, a teacher at the Pathfinder High School

In this one statement, Ms. Watts, the physics and physical science teacher at the gifted-and-talented magnet school captured both the deeply philosophical and the practical daily bases for the difference between an education at her school and the cycle of lowering expectations typical of the schools described in *Contradictions of Control.* In those schools, with the predominance of administrative control over teaching and learning, de-skilled teachers were rewarded for routinized teaching and a uniformity of curriculum, which caused them to use the control of knowledge to control their students. The students, bored by the content and silenced by the teacher-dispensed curriculum, reduced their efforts and settled for a course credit, regardless of their interest or disinterest in the lessons. Their lethargy convinced the teachers that the students were incapable of learning unless the course content was simplified and supplied by the teachers. Ms. Watts and her colleagues and the students at the Pathfinder magnet demonstrated almost the exact inverse of that pattern. The Pathfinder teachers were involved in learning; their students were involved in helping shape what was taught. Together they reinforced in each other an enthusiasm for learning and a shared sense that there was much to be learned and many ways to go about it. The curriculum at the Pathfinder school was one that did not place barriers between personal knowledge and school knowledge. As a result, Pathfinder demonstrated the potential for learning when the curriculum is not artificially packaged to satisfy institutional requirements of credentialing and classroom control.

"Pathfinder people are supposed to have different ways of thinking about things." Ms. Watts was saying, in a sense, this program is here because of people, because of teachers and students. It is here because not everyone learns in the same ways and not everyone thinks alike. Schools need to be built around the many ways people really learn.

"In physics . . ." says that Ms. Watts as a teacher knows her subject and bases her teaching on what she knows to be true about her subject, this may or may not coincide with the standard text or the official curriculum guide. She teaches from her own intellectual engagement with physics and does not leave her best knowledge of her subject outside her classroom. She does not separate "school physics" and her own best understandings as she explains them to the students. She does not see physics as a static field, full of established information she is to pass on to her students. Instead, it is an active way of looking at things, not just a set of formulas: "Sometimes you can solve a problem by breaking it into parts, and sometimes you cannot."

"It's good for them to see . . ." and "you sometimes have to think in a straight line . . . sometimes you have to leap across." She wants to bring her students into this domain of thought where she herself feels at home. She knows her subject, she has thought critically and analytically about its content and its "ways of knowing," and she has definite ideas about how teaching should look if students are to really understand that content and begin to move in those ways of knowing. To Ms. Watts, this is just commonsense teaching; to the school district it is "Pathfinder."

Unlike the city's other magnet schools, the Pathfinder schools are built around an educational philosophy, not a topic or career focus. And Pathfinder was the only magnet program to have not only a high school but also elementary and middle school magnets. In fact, the first elementary Pathfinder program was established in 1972, well ahead of the desegregation court order, in the hopes that a distinctive program of academic excellence could help stem the tide of middle-class families to the suburbs and wealthier families to private schools. The early strong reputation and drawing power of the elementary Pathfinder program made it an important model as the magnet desegregation plan was drawn up. As the citywide magnet program developed in response to the desegregation order, the elementary Pathfinder magnet created demand for Pathfinder elementary programs in other neighborhoods. And, as the children faced going into traditional middle schools after graduating from elementary Pathfinder, a push was created for Pathfinder programs at the secondary level.

The Pathfinder philosophy as established by the school district was child-centered, with recruiting, admissions, curriculum, and pedagogy based in theories of "gifted-and-talented" education. The learning environment was to be nurturing, with possibilities for individual initiative and exploration, and "the having of wonderful ideas" (Duckworth 1987). The curriculum was to be created in the interaction between knowledgeable teachers and curious, independent-thinking students. The brochure of the original Pathfinder elementary magnet signals the district's official commitment to this nonprescriptive education:

> The gifted and talented child—society's most valuable resource—is
> the focus of the Pathfinder program at [this] School. Designed for
> children in grades K–5 who excel in the natural ability to think, rea-
> son, make judgments, create and invent, students are allowed the
> freedom to achieve as rapidly as their special abilities allow. Under
> the careful guidance of teachers especially trained in individualized
> instructional techniques, student creativity and development of
> ability are emphasized. Pathfinder acts as a catalyst to instill an
> interest in learning throughout the child's formative years.[1]

In hindsight, the language of giftedness sounds outdated. Theories of child development (Barnet and Barnet 1998) and multiple intelligences (Gardner 1993) confirm that all children have gifts, a wide range of inherent abilities, and the goal of having all children become independent learners is now articulated in the curriculum frameworks of all the subject fields. (Henry Levin, through the Accelerated Schools Movement, has shown that the children who most benefit from the "gifted-and-talented" pedagogies are those children traditionally labeled at risk, failing to thrive under traditional teaching.[2])

So in one sense the mission of the Pathfinder schools is neither exceptional nor educationally radical in its philosophy and in its instructional programs. However, it is telling that in the Texas context of top-down school policies, with state regulations regarding which books to adopt and how many minutes per day to spend on each subject, and with district rules about content, teaching, and testing, *the creation of a school centered on children's development is so exceptional that it merits a special magnet school status.* Even many of the teachers who had taken courses in gifted-and-talented pedagogy said they did not necessarily identify with those theories; they explained that they had been looking for a school program that would allow, and even *support them, to teach the way they thought all teaching should be.* The "gifted-and-talented" rubric legitimated their ability to act on their own teaching philosophy in an otherwise controlling educational system: to base their teaching on their own deep familiarity with and excitement for their subject and on their belief that teaching should foster development in children. The magnets' role in desegregation further reinforced their commitment to teach diverse groups of students in ways they thought all children should be taught. They invoked the district's stated purpose for the school to further undergird their rationale for their teaching: "An added objective is the fostering of understanding and acceptance among children from different cultural, ethnic, and economic backgrounds." The map on the wall of the Pathfinder high school magnet coordinator's office showed pins stuck in every part of the city and even beyond the city's boundaries—marking homes of children whose very diversity justified these teachers' determination to bring their own best knowledge into the classroom and to invite students to do the same.

What was the "draw" of the Pathfinder magnet? This program was distinctive because the teachers made their own knowledge and especially their own continued learning outside the classroom visible to their students. As a result, although many students entered with weak skills and an uneven background (despite qualifying for admission), in time the students began to take major responsibility for their own learning within classes and in an extended independent project outside of class. By the time students graduated, they could face college applications knowing they had mastered a rigorous college-prep curriculum and in addition had created independent areas of study both within and beyond their coursework.

The exciting learning goals may call to mind a brightly lit, well-equipped school, full of reference works, enrichment materials, and laboratory equipment. The ambitious student-centered curriculum would seem to call for student study carrels or workrooms or common areas, perhaps seminar class-rooms for lively discussion. The gifted-and-talented admissions criteria would seem to imply an elite learning environment for an elite group of students.

In fact, the Pathfinder magnet high school was a small program of 250 to 300 students housed as a school-within-a-school in a very poor neighborhood in the southern part of the city. The "neighborhood" had on some sides been encroached on by freeways, warehousing, and semi-industrial buildings. The area had seen increasing poverty. Some of the houses around the school were painted and marked by carefully tended gardens, but many were run-down; only two blocks away were shuttered and battered strip shopping centers that looked like a war zone and had reputations as drug havens. The plain, even dreary, brick school and its grounds were surrounded by a cyclone fence. The gate clanged shut behind the cars entering the parking lot, where a security guard moved between the school's automotive repair shop and the gates to the street. Allen High was named for a famous city father, and in the 1960s was highly regarded as a middle-class high school. The population then was mostly White. Within a few years, Whites left the area and Blacks moved in. The "neighborhood" portion of the school, whose students come from the sur-rounding attendance zone, had a predominantly Black student population at the time of these classroom observations. The declining population among all groups of students made this segregated school vulnerable to closing just about the time the district drew up its desegregation plans to submit to the court.

Early plans for a Pathfinder high school magnet were to place it at the high school nearest the Pathfinder elementary. That high school, in an old established wealthy part of the city, was often in those days called the "country club" high school because it anchored the south end of an avenue whose oppo-site end led into the gates of an exclusive country club.

But as the Allen High principal and others have related to me, some of the parents at the "country club" high school were afraid that putting a magnet school program there, for the purpose of including the school in the city's desegregation plan, might draw the "wrong kind of kids" (read, "poor, Black, and Hispanic") to the neighborhood.[3] Despite the fact that the Pathfinder magnet would draw students who were by definition academically able and highly motivated and that it would also be open to qualifying students from the surrounding neighborhood, a group of parents strenuously objected to having the Pathfinder program at their school. Seizing an opportunity to keep his school open by increasing its numbers and to raise its educational standards, the Allen High principal stepped forward to claim Pathfinder for his school.[4] His mostly Black high school would gain up to three hundred new students, keeping it off the school-closings list; he would be able to desegregate his faculty; the added students would help raise the educational reputation of his school. In addition, he truly believed in the philosophy of the program. He believed that not all children develop in the same ways and that teaching should reflect attention to those differences. He also believed in desegregation and expressed in an interview that if children are going to survive outside school, they should meet and work with all races of students inside the school.[5]

For those who challenged the elitism of magnet programs, he quietly invited them to visit. No one entering these halls could claim to be in an elitist school. The halls were dark and cheerless. In fact even before entering, a visitor on a rainy day would notice that the drainpipes from the flat roofs drained directly onto the sidewalks, not the grass. Walking through four or five inches of water just to enter this building was not uncommon in this subtropical climate. Like many schools in neighborhoods without rich parents with time to organize school fund-raisers and parent "workdays," the school had no landscaping except for thin grass and a few trees. There was little color outside, little color inside. The school was a series of long, bare intersecting halls with little beyond a trophy case or banner that expressed the personality, interests, or academic pursuits of the students. Like any big-city school in a poor neighborhood, it had occasional acts of violence, including a shooting or two and car thefts and fights. In the halls of the neighborhood section of the school visitors were impressed with how cheerful and friendly the students seemed. Their smiles, banter, and genuine pleasure in seeing each other between classes always seemed out of sync with the dull physical setting and with the sense of quiet with which they entered classrooms. The school seemed a safe, if plain, refuge from the desolate and sometimes dangerous area around it.

During the period of this study, the "neighborhood" part of the school tended to follow the district and state curriculum, with traditional subjects and single-teacher classrooms. There was a nursery school that provided child care for the children of students. The neighborhood school had a football team and other interscholastic sports teams, cheerleaders, choir and a band, a yearbook. It was a regular school, with the regular mix of motivated and dispirited students, inspiring and dull teachers, "good" and "bad" courses. The principal was caring of the students, the parents, and the school. He has never been heard by anyone to describe it as less important to him than the Pathfinder magnet program, the kids on the north hall.

Pathfinder Students

Who were the kids on the north hall? Officially, they had been chosen because of their mix of good standardized test scores, their performance in an essay or a creativity test, their profiles on a developmental test, and recommendations from their middle school teachers. According to an undated report entitled "[Pathfinder], In-Depth Study," from the early 1980s, criteria for admissions included "intellectual ability, the process of creative thinking and leadership potential."[6] Intellectual ability was generally measured by nationally normed achievement test scores, with the 85th percentile as the desired cutoff. Strict use of the numerical standards for admission was mitigated by consideration of a student's race, the quality of the student's previous school, the student's home language, and such abstract qualities as creativity and leadership. These latter qualifications permitted consideration of the student's overall strengths and weaknesses, not just a set of indicators. Motivation to enter such a program weighed heavily, especially at the high school level. Equally important was the match between a student's learning style and the philosophy behind the program.

Constructing the Pathfinder Philosophy

The teachers' co-construction of a Pathfinder philosophy and shared identity came in part from the conceptions of giftedness and honors programs. It is interesting to note that the ways their theories of pedagogy, including the models they distanced themselves from, were built around their understandings of students' learning, especially their own students' learning. As they differentiated themselves and their students from other academic programs in the city, they were using the freedom afforded by the Pathfinder structure to build simultaneously a program and a theory of teaching that honored their own best knowledge.

One Pathfinder teacher found the identity in his teaching by distinguishing it from the district's previous honors program, Master Works. He characterized Master Works as "the same curriculum, but you go faster and in more depth, . . . doing not only the 'basic' assignments but the 'desirable' [optional, advanced] ones as well." Pathfinder teachers who had taught Master Works courses at other schools recalled them as varying in difficulty and pacing from "regular" teaching, but not necessarily engaging of students'—or teachers'—minds.

They regarded the district's two current honors programs, Advanced Placement and International Baccalaureate, as also centered on curricula rather than on students. Through Advanced Placement students could earn advanced college credit; the courses offered high-quality academics, "but it is not a matter of sophisticated connecting of ideas and teaching theme and concept the way we do in Pathfinder classes because the AP has its own rules. You are teaching to a test." The Pathfinder teachers saw both AP and IB, with their external tests, as rigorous and demanding for both teachers and students and as their main competition for recruiting students, but as intellectually limiting because their prescriptive formats and external tests did not invite sufficient student contributions to learning.

They also saw Pathfinder as different from an honors track, which typically reinforces a student's particular strengths but which lacks the spark of a class where "you've got a computer whiz next to an English whiz." One saw traditional tracking as narrowing the definition of a student's strengths. Pathfinder students were characterized more by a curiosity to learn than by a specific academic strength.

One Pathfinder teacher added another dimension to the identification of a "Pathfinder" student: "We'll tolerate weaknesses more, I think than the other programs." She described Pathfinder students as "less nose to the grindstone" than Master Works students: "They [Master Works] do all their homework. They have wonderful attendance and their lack of creativity just helps you keep . . . more efficient." She continued, "But where are you going to send a kid who is flaky and is creative but is an underachiever, but yet has an IQ of some phenomenal thing. . . . We are willing to put up with some of the idiosyncrasies, with some slowness in some courses so that person can be a star in a Pathfinder project or whatever." She saw these students as having great strengths but also great needs. One of their needs was to be in an environment that did not require conformity to a set place of a single learning style. The district's identification of the school as "gifted and talented" rather than "honors" gave the teachers, by virtue of the ways students were recruited, the authority to create an academic program centered on students' different ways of learning—an additional, critical layer of organizational support for bringing their professional knowledge to bear on their teaching.

Significant Differences

The lack of social conformity among the Pathfinder students further helped shape teachers' pedagogy. Because they came from all over the city and represented all kinds of neighborhoods and family backgrounds, they came with different ideas about clothing, music, and ways of talking. A part of the culture of the school was to accept, to tolerate, even to celebrate these differences. Both students and teachers took pride not only in the diversity among students who came to the school but also in the diversity that was preserved and even broadened as students pursued special interests or grew into being more their own person. This acceptedness both shaped and was reinforced by its extension into acceptance of student contributions to course content.

"The biggest strength of this program is the tolerance for other people. And the admiration for other people." That sophomore girls' words were echoed by a teacher, "It's like a microcosm, and that sounds really trite and I hate to use it . . . and of course the thing the kids like best about this program is little things like no cliques, no racial prejudice, none. In fact, probably the best thing I've ever seen, I mean the best feeling is we're all in here to see what minds we have and what character, and color? [Racism] just doesn't exist here."

Race was a dominant factor in admissions because the school was part of the desegregation plan. Although the goal was to have the magnet schools balanced among the three races, Hispanics applied to this school in smaller numbers than did White and Black students, though those who came did exceedingly well. Until recently, according to one magnet coordinator, the pressure on Hispanic girls to attend a neighborhood school, even if its program was inferior, was extremely strong, especially from their fathers. One Hispanic girl said in an interview that her parents had been afraid she would become "a druggie, like the White kids, or pregnant, like the Black girls" if she left her home neighborhood for high school. Once at the school, Pathfinder students found themselves confronting and overcoming these prejudicial expectations because of the ways the courses were inclusive of all students' experiences and knowledge.[7]

The appreciation of diversity helped blur the social class lines. Some critics have wondered if the magnet schools serve only middle-class and upper-middle-class students of all three races, those whose parents value education enough to be entrepreneurs in exploring and selecting schools for their children. In fact, among the Pathfinder students were students who lived with relatives other than parents, who had only one parent and lived in the federal housing projects, whose single mother was holding down two or three jobs while the younger children stayed with a grandparent. The range of income spanned wealth, high family income from two working parents, struggling middle-class and working-class families, and absolute poverty. After the observations were completed at this school, the story was shared of a later

Pathfinder student who very quietly but joyfully told her teacher that she and her family had just moved into a house. The house had no running water, but it was a paradise for this family. For months they had been living in their car. The girl had washed at the bus station each morning and managed to appear at school indistinguishable from her peers; very few of them knew that she did not live in a house.

A teacher spoke about the Pathfinder students' apparent disregard for appearance and fashion trends this way: "And dress codes. The, not codes, but dress, well, *pressures* to be fashionable, whatever, the kids [here] think that is ridiculous. Here the poorest kids, with families that are dirt poor, since everybody. . . dresses so individually, honestly, you can't tell rich from poor. And that's not a planned thing; that's just what happens because the emphasis is not on that here at all. . . . Here you can just be yourself."

This English teacher went on to relate the variety of student cultures and dress to the educational philosophy of the school: "Here we help you to develop yourself, really. *And to see you through all the changes as you try out different ones.*"

The Pathfinder students, then, could be defined by race, as they were in reports to the federal courts, or by academic and creativity standards, as they were in the application and admissions process. Or they could be defined as motivated students who took the initiative to leave their home neighborhood to ride a school bus perhaps as much as an hour each way, into a very poor neighborhood to try to get a college-preparatory education at a place they felt at home.

Feeling at home in a school, feeling valued and welcomed, was no small part of what brought students to Pathfinder. One social studies teacher told me that one reason there was no single stereotype, or prototype, of a Pathfinder student is that different students came for different reasons. The Black students, he said, tended to come because their neighborhood school was not challenging to them and had little connections to colleges. A big part of the recruiting was in broadcasting the college admissions rate: virtually every year every student would be accepted into at least one college, and most students into more than one good college. Most are awarded substantial financial aid. The senior class typically won a total of around $2 million in scholarships for college, among a class of 50 to 60 students. The news that Pathfinder was highly regarded by colleges helped draw many students to this school, particular those bright African American students whose home schools have not traditionally been a part of the college admissions pipeline.

Another group of students drawn to Pathfinder were students who by their own self-description were "misfits." Some of these were extremely bright students who were tired of being thought of as nerds because they preferred to be reading a book than kicking a football or, more typically, just hanging out. They were the math whiz or just the divergent thinker, perhaps more academically inclined than was typical for their schools or their peer groups.

African American students who had chosen this magnet because of a weak home neighborhood school (rather than for desegregation or the learning style here) reported the pressure in their home neighborhoods to emphasize athletics and social activities more than school, or—even greater—the pressure to hang out, to do nothing. Serious studying was hard to do in their home schools because courses were unchallenging or because to do so would be to stay on the margin of the friendship group (Suskind 1998; Fordham and Ogbu 1986). Several students at this school said in interviews that they could have made better grades in their home school, "but I never would have known what was in me—what I could do." Several Hispanic students, boys in particular, said that guys in their neighborhood were openly hostile to other guys seen carrying books or taking hard classes, both of which were seen as "sissy."

Other "misfits," according to one teacher, were the students, mostly Anglo, whose lives were troubled. These students, mostly middle- or upper-middle-class, might have suffered depression or had an unhappy home life; they might have had an eating disorder or have contemplated suicide; they could have withdrawn from friends or school activities or from really trying at school. Their behavior, their moods, or their problems might set them apart at a more conventional school. Or they could have been so emotionally needy that their teachers in bigger, more bureaucratic schools, already overburdened with paperwork and the rush to "cover the objectives," had no time or energy to offer more than sympathy and a few good wishes. A Pathfinder teacher said such students were willing to undertake the academic demands of Pathfinder because they, and their parents, saw that Pathfinder included not only great tolerance for a variety of kids but also a sensitivity to the fact that life is not static, not linear, for any one kid. For them, Pathfinder combined an appreciation for their intellect with the support—rather than pressure—they needed to develop it. Some found emotional support to rebuild their fragile teenage lives.

The teacher who described these students, naming one or two, said that the public perception that Pathfinder was for bright kids who "already had it made" was wrong. He said that these students did bring a great deal with them. But the schools' laurels should not rest on the inherent abilities of the students.

He said, "We see this as value-added education. The first thing we give them is to let them know it is okay to be smart." Many had been misfits simply because they were smart and openly willing to work hard in school. Others were misfits because of serious personal and family problems. Others may have been misfits because they did not fit the dominant culture of their home school but never had the chance to find out who they were and where they might fit.

Many, many other Pathfinder students were happy, well-rounded, eager students who enjoyed life, enjoyed school, and looked forward to whatever would come next.

Pathfinder Teaching

Pathfinder might be called "the program of the unexpected." The gifted-and-talented label calls to mind high-achieving kids in a school full of good resources. The school's location in a poor neighborhood creates expectations of dangers or low educational quality. The "misfits" label might make one think of dysfunctional teenagers who are a constant problem for their teachers. In fact, this magnet school was probably the most complex of the schools studied. It labeled kids and at the same time threw away all labels; it challenged them, yet made caring a programmatic priority. Hearing the philosophy and the labels raised serious questions about what kind of learning could take place in this environment. Teaching in the Pathfinder program must have been something like *Baghdad Without a Map* (Horwitz 1991). In his account of traveling alone throughout the Middle East, journalist Tony Horwitz met Bedouins betting on camel races in the sand dunes, then saw them get into their BMWs, parked just behind the dunes, to return to work when the lunch hour ended. When he arrived in Baghdad, he repeatedly inquired about buying a map. Finally someone told him that Saddam Hussein did not want any maps made of Baghdad; knowledge of the city would give foreigners more information than he wanted them to have. Horwitz's journey became his map.

With a philosophy that placed students at the center of learning but with the textbooks of a traditional school, and not much else, the Pathfinder teachers were left to create their own instructional maps. They chose the school for the opportunities to do so. It is this creating and re-creating the program that makes Pathfinder distinctive in a state where the curriculum has been centralized through state-adopted textbooks for more than one hundred years. The federal court order and the district's implementation documents called for magnet programs that would desegregate predominantly single-race schools. But these programs were merely names.[8] It was up to the teachers to create the courses, the overall academic program, the student activities, the culture of the school. The overall course sequence and requirements had to be approved, but these were approvals based on course titles and outlines, not detailed information about how courses would be taught or what students would do.

What was taught in the Pathfinder program, what was required of students, how the overall program was built was the work of the teachers. This magnet program evolved over time because these teachers shared the assumption that the curriculum grows out of the interaction of the teacher, the student, and the subject. This program was shaped by the fact that these teachers felt most comfortable when they were making their own maps. Many of them had chosen to teach in this school because, as more than one of them told me, "I hate to do the same thing over and over." The lack of a fixed curriculum, which might frustrate other teachers, was for them a tacit permission to teach from their best knowledge and to teach to involve the students. Most important, they placed no walls between their personal knowledge and what they brought into the classroom. They did not water down the curriculum in order to make it easy to learn or efficient to test. The tendency to create efficiencies by fragmenting knowledge, the desire to suppress controversy by omitting potentially volatile topics, the temptation to mystify complicated subjects in order to hide what a teacher does not know or does not believe students could understand without great student (or teacher) effort—these defensive teaching strategies find their diametric opposites in most of the teaching at the Pathfinder school. And there were virtually no passive roles for students in this program.

The course listings did not capture the culture of learning that they created. The core, required courses carried traditional names; they were taught in single-teacher classrooms, divided by the same subject and grade-level divisions that were found in traditional high schools. English IV followed English I, II, and III. Mathematics proceeded through the algebras, geometry, analysis, and calculus. Social studies combined history, government, economics, and sociology. The sciences were separated into biology, chemistry, and physics. Foreign languages offered were Spanish, French, and sometimes German. Physical education was taken with the neighborhood students, as were art, music, or competitive athletics. What the teachers did with these subject frameworks is what made the school a place of authentic learning.

Words. Words. Words.

Ms. Williams taught with passion. To enter her room was to be captured by her visible love of language. On the front blackboard everyday was a new word from a daily vocabulary calendar and a sentence using the word. A solid row of *New Yorker* magazine covers filled the space between the blackboard and the ceiling. Stacks of paperbacks filled bookshelves, the corner of her desk, and random other horizontal surfaces. Samples of student writings were stapled to the bulletin board. Student-made posters and three-dimensional representations of literary works were taped to walls, stapled to bulletin boards, or set in a corner on the floor. Red dictionaries were kept at hand because in Ms. Williams's class you never knew when you might need a word.

There were talking words, as well. Ms. Williams loved to talk about literature. She hated to come into class and find that students had not read the assigned short story; any class time devoted to silent reading meant less time to try out ideas on each other, to probe for meanings, to hear students' papers read aloud. Her own presence conveyed much emotion and she wanted students to feel as involved in the literature as she did. Her ninth graders sometimes looked stunned to hear her exclaim, "I am so excited! Did you *read* the story? How do you think he felt when he found out his grandfather was dying? Has someone that you love died? How did you feel? Doesn't this author just make it all seem so real? Didn't you feel less *alone* after reading this story?" Her questions came in torrents, but because they were so honest, so completely personal, the students found themselves quite unexpectedly talking about their own grandmother's death, or the time their little sister got lost, or the way death was different in these stories from the death they had seen in television violence. More than in any class observed, the students related current readings to literature they had read in previous years in school and to the books they passed around to each other.

Ms. Williams assumed that if students read enough and wrote enough, then they would "learn to write something honest." They would learn how books can extend experience. In a semester of visiting her class, the technicalities of grammar and composition were never divorced from her central passion for helping students discover the power of words. Ms. Williams brought literature to life because she basically did not know any other way to teach it. Many of her students came into the Pathfinder program with weak writing skills: many who had not been in honors programs before had done most of their "writing" lessons on worksheets.

Some said they had never read a whole book before. Their school reading had been mostly from anthologies—brief selections that one reads in order to be able to "find the main idea" or explain key vocabulary words, not whole works that require thinking along with the author. She patiently but relentlessly pushed them to read, to write, to write about their reading, to keep a journal of free writings and to read each other's papers.

Her main goal was to help students find their own connection with language and literature, in a manner both organized and highly chaotic. The class period would be broken up into the introduction of the day's vocabulary word, time for journal writing, a discussion of the previous day's short story, plans for the student's long-term responses to the readings (creating a visual, performing a dramatization, putting music to a reading, making a notebook of character sketches for future story writing). All student talk was welcome and all ideas were valued. Many of these "gifted" students had developed the habit of "reading" by skimming just before class; they assumed they could do the same in her class. Her generous acceptance of any student idea was counterbalanced by her queries that led them back into the text so that they and the author were working together on an idea.

That "school words" and the words of their lives came together in this class was made vivid by a Black student. She had a wonderful African name, a very musical name that sounded almost made up, composed. When the class discussed naming—the names authors give their characters, the use of biblical names to give symbolic weight to a short story character, the renaming among Native Americans after a person accomplishes a great deed, this girl offered the story her own name. It was a legacy of the civil rights era, the gift of Stokeley Carmichael. She told that when Carmichael had come to the city for a civil rights rally, he noted two young pregnant women in his audience. They were her mother and her mother's best friend. After his speech, Carmichael approached them and told them that they should give their babies African names. He told them several names and the meaning of each one. Her mother's baby was born first, and so she chose this beautiful name, which meant "well loved," for her daughter.

Ms. Williams's favorite ways to help her students connect with words were a special set of lessons she had developed on music and poetry and her work with the creation of the Pathfinder literary magazine. Both exemplified the ongoing creation of curricular knowledge at this school and the ways that creation depended on both teachers and students.

The Music of Poetry. The highlight of Ms. Williams's literature studies was a poetry unit she had developed when she was a curriculum resource supervisor for schools clustered in an area of poverty and eligible for federal enhancement funds. In this role, she supported other teachers by visiting their classrooms, identifying and collecting for them curricular resources in the new federally funded humanities resource center. She spent hours gathering, purchasing, and "duplicating, with that purple fluid duplicator" for these teachers. She found that most of these schools in poor neighborhoods lacked paper and lacked any means for supplying the teachers with their most basic classroom needs. She became a creator, resourceful scrounger, mentor, and disseminator of curriculum materials, a one-woman antidote to the rigid state-adopted textbook list.

To her dismay, she found that as she grew as a creator of curriculum, the teachers were becoming dependent on her to supply the same thing year after year. If something "worked," then they wanted to reuse it, to cover known material with efficient results. They were not curious about adapting their teaching to the major changes occurring in student demographics and in teen culture. Rather than reinforce teacher-centered teaching, Ms. Williams decided to return to the classroom to make use of these curricula she had designed to bring students into active learning. Among these was the teaching of poetry through music. In her Pathfinder class, she taught this unit from a dog-eared set of paperbacks long out of print, old photocopied sheets of poems, poems the students would bring in, poems from the officially adopted literary anthology, and poems the students wrote. Along with all of this poetry would be music.

The music could be heard down the hall, giving students a clue to the day's lesson before they entered. "I knew we'd be doing something very serious today," said an athlete, who wasn't sure he wanted a day of serious poetry. "I could hear that symphony music when I was just coming out of my math class." A girl confided, "I didn't think Ms. Williams would know the kind of music we listen to, so I brought my favorite Prince tape. She surprised me! She had her own copy of that tape and wanted us to read this poem by Langston Hughes. I don't really think that's the best poem to read with Prince. I mean, Prince and Michael Jackson are talking about *my* world, well, not really my world, but not Langston Hughes's, either. I wish I knew what jazz is about. I think that's probably what I would listen to with Langston Hughes." The students liked the way the musical selections helped bring the poems to life, and the ways many poems also helped them connect to pieces of music, for example a ballad or a classical guitar selection, that they otherwise never would have listened to. Abstract "elements" of poetry, like mood and tone, became clearer as they were listened for in the music.

Ms. Williams taught poems about love and loss with a break in her voice, or an occasional tear; she also chose strong poems, full of beat and lift and spirit. The whole unit of study was more a framework than a set curriculum, and in later years future visits to her class would reveal the same tattered set of paperbacks along with a whole new set of photocopied poems she had brought in or had gathered from students over the years. From students she accepted everything from doggerel to rock lyrics, from sentimental greeting card verse, to poems they discovered in parents' old college texts. The climate of acceptance created even among the skeptical a poetry workshop atmosphere that virtually all the students joined. Reliance in part on poems students collected meant her classes never fell into the static patterns of those teachers she had worked with whose own desires for efficiency made them reach for the same readings every year.

What stayed constant in Ms. Williams's class was the plan she established for their assignments, giving them plenty of time to develop their writing. There was never the pressure to "write a poem by the end of the period." The "elements" of poetry such as imagery, rhyme, rhythm, and alliteration were taught as they arose in sample poems.

The students received their poetry unit as a packet of poems to read and assignments to be written over several weeks. The assignment to write was carefully sequenced to counter students' stereotypes that poetry is soft, mushy, private. Many of the assignments were topical, moving from distant to near, from impersonal to personal. The first was observational: write a descriptive poem of a place or object. Students wrote about what they saw: roaches or dirty feet, butterflies or dancing shoes, a single stone or chicken little ("if the sky fell, would we get wet?") The assignments then moved from the concrete to the more personal, on "poetic" topics like emotions or friendship. The poetry journal was to culminate in two major poetic writings: a poem about a compelling issue and a personal poem. The compelling issue could be political or philosophical or humanitarian, but it must extend beyond their own personal experience to capture something universal. A great human tragedy, such as starvation and floods in Bangladesh or Ethiopia, the Challenger space shuttle explosion, homelessness in their own neighborhood, or the future of the planet—all took form in very dramatic, forceful poems. Ms. Williams was sure that this was because she did not let them write about "big issues" until they had played with words and poetic forms enough in writing about the more concrete, the close at hand. The final assignment would be to write a personal poem. The personal poems, not unexpectedly, centered on love and loneliness and death. Thomas French, in *South of Heaven*, writes that the students in the at-risk "pod" at Largo High were consumed with thoughts and stories of death—their own, death in movies, apocalyptic visions of the end of the world, and images of death, like skull earrings and skeleton sketches in their notebooks (French 1993). Death in the poems in Ms. Williams's classes seemed to be more close to home, thoughts of suicide or fear of illness, the death of a neighbor child or a grandparent—the deaths that are near and that people think teenagers get over quickly. They found music for these poems in rap themes of violent death, in hymns with resurrection themes, in rock dirges and in sweet sentimental "muzak" tunes, a variety that matched the cultural and peer preferences of the students and their understandings of the poems.

Students bringing and writing poems, students editing each other's poems; the teacher and students choosing music to listen to for parallel patterns or messages or images that make poetry not only conducive to academic analysis but also accessible as a new form of language now at their command. The purposes were fixed, the standards were high, but the curriculum and the students' role in it was dynamic, flexible, changing.

The Pomegranate. This same pattern of creation and interpretation extended into Ms. Williams's other favorite venue for language teaching, her sponsorship of *The Pomegranate,* the literary magazine. In a school where most students rode the tightly scheduled school bus, extracurricular activities were sandwiched into tutorial and homeroom periods and lunch hours. The staff of the literary magazine brought their sandwiches into Ms. Williams's room one or two days each week, where stacks of student writings awaited their editorial judgment. As Ms. Williams described in an interview, "some of the other honors programs in town, they think because we're not strictly geared to the AP test, that we just have fun, we just play around." She invited me to see the editorial staff of the literary magazine, to see them *work.* A group of students, mostly girls, sat quietly reading handwritten poems, examining and passing around ink drawings and photographs, shuffling the pages of a short story, attempting in one lunch hour to review three or four pieces that had been submitted to the literary magazine. All reviews were done blind.

Ms. Williams saw the journal as filling a need for "opportunities either within the classroom or within the activities—to get kids into leadership roles and train them to do things they might not otherwise know they had the ability to do." The student editor guided the discussion. "These editors, even the weaker ones, have grown into the positions." The juniors and seniors would become so invested in the process that they on occasion wanted to keep freshmen and sophomores from voting because "they don't know the technicalities of poetry." One student on the staff said she had always been shy about showing anyone her poetry. She had not realized how difficult it would be to sit as a silent editorial staff member listening to her fellow staffers discuss a poem they did not know to be hers—its merits, its weaknesses, whether it lived up to their expectations as a "poem." "I was just trying to write what I felt. I did want to hear their opinions, but I didn't want to have to make my poem just be what someone else wanted it to be. It felt very strange. I'm glad they liked my poem. But what I really got out of it was now I'm more careful when I talk about someone else's writing. They wrote it that way for a reason. I should respect that." Another girl said, "When I signed up for this, I thought we would be choosing good or bad stories, you know, good poems or bad ones. But when we talk about them, I hear something else. Lucy might really like a story that I think is booor-ing. Maybe it's closer to her life. Anyway, now I know why Ms. Williams keeps talking about *audience* when we write. There's not like, just one audience, you know. There are lots of people out there and one story won't affect them all alike."

To sharpen their ability to make decisions and to work together (and to make sure they did finally make a printing deadline), Ms. Williams encouraged one selection rule: "Once it's in, it's in. So they have to make the right choice the first time." If some of the kids "really blow it," they may come back and say, "We hate this and now we want it out." They wanted high quality so that its being published would be an honor; nevertheless, the first decision would be the final one. They learned not to make frivolous choices; they learned about consequences. "Maybe then they have to work extra hard to find a photograph or a drawing that can be on that same page and add something that the weak piece of writing lacks. They learn to work with things."

Pomegranate fostered a writing culture. Some students who did not write well in class took their writing "baby steps" in submissions to the magazine. Others submitted volumes; they seemed to write all the time. The other Pathfinder English teachers also emphasized writing in their classrooms, personal writing, analytical writing, writing based on the literature—they pushed writing. That push, together with the enthusiasm generated by the literary magazine, created a writing community that came to include many Pathfinder students. Each year several began a piece of writing for the magazine and later developed it into their independent Pathfinder project. This poem called "reflections" makes the connection between being a person and being a student and writing poems to be read and judged.

I look down at my shoes;
"me."
white and new,
 "me," too.
Accepted because I am "me,"
I write my poems so they will be accepted;
doesn't matter if my art is not me,
long as it's "me.". . .

People think they know me,
when really they know
"me."
Chances are, I don't know you.
But I bet "I" know "you."
                                    —C. R., *Pomegranate*, 19xx

Election Central

Two doors down from Ms. Williams's room was another busy classroom where students were finding their voice and learning to work with a variety of "audiences." Mr. Drew also used the curricular authority of Pathfinder to teach in ways that mixed in-class learning with out-of-class learning. He taught government, economics, and, sometimes, sociology through matter of fact, ordinary lectures: here is how a bill gets through Congress. Take notes on role, status, class, primary association, secondary association, interest group. Read the chapter on supply and demand. Write a brief essay explaining the difference between monetary policy and fiscal policy. These are the three branches of government. The government has three branches so there will be a balance of powers, so no one branch has all the power. On certain days, Mr. Drew's class looked like a thorough, traditional lecture course on government or economics. The students were at their desks; maybe they were supposed to read a handout or a chapter before class. The teacher at his lectern, some printed handouts to read, the blackboard, the student questions, the test. Traditional subject matter boundaries, traditional materials, traditional use of class time. This was not defensive teaching, because there was no attempt to avoid inefficient discussions or controversial topics, but it was not distinctively "Pathfinder" either.

Mr. Drew's model for his lectures came from his college teaching. He also taught at a community college and at a local university. He had good lecture

notes and high standards for the information students should learn before getting out of high school. But in his Pathfinder classes, his lectures were only the
beginning. They were introductions or elaborations; they were not the whole
study of the topic. He wanted students to experience the topics, and more
importantly, he wanted them to add new information. Like Ms. Williams, he
involved students in creating the courses. The lectures were just one component, the stage-setting exercise before the real drama began.

De-Mystifying the Way Things Work. Mr. Drew taught politics and government, and indirectly a good deal of economics and sociology, through elections. He explained that every year there is an election, national elections,
elections for state and local offices, school board elections. He made each
year's election the subject of his teaching. The offices themselves and the
authority they carry, the election process, issues of franchise and representation, issues of districting (always an issue in this state), interest-group politics,
the role of the media—all were studied first through succinct lectures and
readings from the text and then explored in the community.

For Mr. Drew, there were no walls between "school knowledge" and what
went on in the real world. He had worked in a corporation before becoming a
teacher; he had taught in various parts of town in the community college system; he had many contacts in the community. It probably never would have
occurred to him to try to make electoral politics, or any other aspect of
democracy, simple, neat, or noncontroversial. He especially would not have
tried to sanitize or oversimplify those aspects of community life on which he
knew his students were likely to disagree with him or with each other. Their
varied backgrounds required making differences of opinion explicit. Students'
diversity required bringing the processes of give and take in a democracy out
into the open to be talked about, worked on, lived out. In Mr. Drew's government classes, this was accomplished through in-depth study of the candidates
and issues through role-play. Beyond the classroom, this was the mission of
Election Central.

Presidential Debates. Election time in Mr. Drew's government class meant
strong opinions, hours in the library, and a lot of laughter. This teacher whose
lectures were so organized and who even used Scantron (computer-graded)
answer sheets for the tests on the lectures, tolerated great uncertainty in turning the curriculum over to the students during an election. He could count on
the regularity of election cycles and an ever-changing set of candidates and

issues. For the class to learn government, economics, sociology, and history through an election, every candidate had to be studied, every issue had to be investigated, every interest group and voting pattern explored. Class time had to be flexible enough to allow discussion of issues that arose that were not originally in the candidates' platforms. "Precinct" was not a vocabulary word to be matched with a definition on a test; it was a place to visit. And "issues" were contested inside the classroom, not just memorized on a list as the "issues of the election of 19—."

The candidates were the subject of much study, all of it organized by the students. It was they who were responsible for teaching the rest of the class about the qualifications, weaknesses, views, and proposed policies of the candidates and parties. They did their teaching through debates, in which they would speak as the candidate. In each group of four students, one took the role of a presidential or vice-presidential candidate, one the role of issues adviser, one the campaign manager, and one a media expert. As a group they studied the issues from this candidate's perspective. If an issue required additional background, such as a foreign-policy or tax issue, someone in the group had to research it. They read news accounts of likely sources of support or opposition and studied the candidates' campaign literature and media coverage. Together they put together what was essentially a set of briefing notes for the candidate to study and use in debating the opposition.

When the day came for the debates, the room was filled with excitement. Sometimes friends from other classes would peek in to see the candidate, whose usual uniform was t-shirt and baggy pants, now dressed in Sunday best for the debate. There was a problem in one particular election year, because several students wanted to play the part of Geraldine Ferraro. No one wanted to be Ronald Reagan. "No way! You think I'm gonna stand up there and say we don't have any problems with the environment? Oh, sure." An Anglo student, who one girl said had to play the part because he had Ronald Reagan's hair color, escaped the role. No Black student wanted the part: "That man is evil. He doesn't even like us. Forget it." A Black girl answered, "I don't think he's evil. Sometimes he's funny. I just don't like anything he does."

Finally, a Black girl took the part. She out-Reaganed Reagan, having carefully studied and imitated his manner of speaking. Her Ronald Reagan was mostly in his own words, carefully researched by her team. Even if she had the least desired role, that of an actor playing an "actor playing a politician" as she put it, she had the benefit of the best briefings. She did not try to ad lib a role so far from her own ideas, but rather fully immersed herself into the part. She smiled a huge, beaming smile as she sat down to strong applause, winning no votes for Reagan in this class but much respect for herself.

Through the debates, students became very invested in their candidates. They weighed issues as though they themselves were standing for election. They moved beyond simple slogans about abortion or immigration to more complicated lines of thought. Just when they felt confident in their positions, Mr. Drew confused things further. He made them switch. The Reagan team now had to be Mondale. The feisty Ferraro team had to transition into George Bush. They had to "live" in the opposition camp for the next round of debates, this time challenging the information they themselves had provided just a few days before.

Everyone in the class depended on everyone else for their information. The room filled up with newsmagazines and photocopied articles from a foreign-policy or health journal. Each team made an original contribution, and on each team every individual was a specialist. Mr. Drew had to be the kind of teacher who could tolerate ambiguity, since his curriculum was truly constructed by the students for several weeks each semester. He had to convey to them a sense of trust, and he had to provide them with the skills to gather and weigh information. He arranged for them to be able to use the nearby university library, sometimes taking them as a school field trip. Their own school library, just down the hall from his classroom, had almost no reference material; anything beyond a very few news magazines had to be found off-campus. Given their long daily bus rides and the fact that most of these students did not have many books or subscriptions in their homes, it would have been easy for the teacher to justify teaching government as a straight lecture course. Because of the potentially wide range of political and cultural values represented in the class, it would have been very convenient for him to teach defensively by "omission," avoiding all controversies by giving an official interpretation for them to memorize or to use their intellectual talents merely to accept and elaborate (McNeil 1986). A large part of the success of his teaching was that early in the semester, the students learned that their ideas were valued. By the time they undertook their election research, they knew there were no library exercises just for the point of doing a library search, no group work just for the sake of "small-group activities." This was real information building, with the students functioning as gatherers and interpreters of information.

Polling Places. Election Central was also work. Mr. Drew had found that teaching voting patterns, socioeconomic status, interest-group politics, and demographics in lecture meant very little to the students beyond being able to match the term with the definition. From his university teaching, he became acquainted with a political science professor whose expertise was public opinion polling. Talking with him, Mr. Drew decided that his students could understand politics better if they went into the community to find out what makes people vote the way they do. To motivate them, he posed a challenge. They would do exit polling and try to project the election winners before the local television stations made their projections. Theirs would not be a wild guess. They would spread out across the city to poll people on how they voted. Since the numbers were limited to those students in the government, history, and economics classes, they could not hope to canvas the entire city. They would need to learn to sample. The university professor explained sampling and polling, his own data on the city's demographics and the concept of representative sampling.

As the students learned more about economic and cultural differences in neighborhoods, they looked into past voting patterns. They wondered if all rich neighborhoods were likely to vote Republican. Did middle-class Blacks vote like middle-class Hispanics? Did they vote the way poor Blacks vote? Did people vote because of habit, or party loyalty, or the candidate, or persuasive ads, or an issue they really cared about? They worked and reworked their questions. How could they ask strangers how they had voted? Was this not an invasion of privacy? How would they know where to go to do the sampling? What if some people voted in ways unlike others in their neighborhood or ethnic group or age or income bracket? What would that do to their sampling?

The classroom became a laboratory of confusion, with students draped over or slouched in desks, or seated on the floor surrounded by stacks of papers describing neighborhoods and precincts. In contrast to the orderly classrooms of *Contradictions of Control,* where the content of the curriculum was subordinated to the goals of maintaining efficiency and a single informational authority, this room clearly exhibited the priority of students' delving into a complex topic and getting physically and vocally involved with the materials. The deadline for mastering the ideas and designing the plan of action was not an arbitrary test date, but rather the upcoming election, a very real-world, nonschool constraint. Working through the details of sampling and the questions about voting patterns took a great deal of work on the part of students. In this highly mobile city, the teacher could not have supplied "the answer."

Election Day was "the test." One group of students stayed at school with the teacher to operate the computer program the professor had helped the "computer whiz" students develop for collecting and analyzing their polling data. If the program worked, and they had selected their precincts carefully, then they would be able to enter their exit polling statistics and project the winners at least at the city level. The rest of the students went out in pairs to neighborhoods they had identified as representative of certain voter characteristics.

This would have been an interesting way to learn about electoral politics if nothing more than interviewing, data collecting, and data analysis had occurred. But the lesson took an unexpected turn as students actually arrived at the polling places. The numbered precincts from the maps became the reality of neighborhoods and shops and streets and campaign signs and people, many of them people very unlike the students. Two encounters in particular made the day, and the activity, unforgettable. Two students, a Black boy and a White girl, had been assigned (as the students worked out the placements) to a very wealthy White neighborhood. Residents of the area emerged from the polling place—a school—to be met by these two students with their clipboards and questions. The students saw many voters visibly shudder, or step aside, or begin to walk faster. They knew they were not welcome. They were dressed slightly better than they would have dressed at school, but not "dressed up." Was it their clothing? The fact that they looked like an "interracial couple"? The fact that they were teenagers ("aren't you supposed to be in school?")? As these well-liked students later explained to their classmates, they had expected to learn about voter opinions. But the immediate and lasting lesson was to know what it is like to be rejected, to be "different," to be in the "wrong" place. They had worked at making eye contact and greeting voters and over time had broken down some of the barriers that had perhaps made the voters avoid them.

Their experience was uncomfortable but less dramatic than what two Black girls faced when they arrived at their assigned polling place in a very conservative working-class area known for White racism and for a history of John Birch Society and Ku Klux Klan activity. This was not what they had expected from their precinct number. Their reception ranged from icy stares to hostile threats. The students were very frightened. The driver had dropped them off to take other students to other precincts; so now they could not leave. And besides, the students at Election Central, the computer in the corner of Mr. Drew's room, needed their data. After all, they reasoned, these people were city voters, representative of one sector of the voting public; without their answers, the whole equation would be thrown off.

The girls stayed, interviewed voters, and eventually returned to school safely. The next day's class was devoted to comparing the newspaper accounts of each precinct's vote counts with the numbers from the student exit polls. The classroom buzzed with stories of funny answers, nosy questions, and quirky behaviors they had observed. The race with the television station was recounted, complete with tales of computer glitches and searches for pay phones to call in the data and the pride of missing by only a few minutes and only a few percentages. But overwhelming all of this was the story of the two Black girls who had ended up alone in Klan territory. They were still shaking. Quietly, then sometimes excitedly, they recounted the comments and looks and threats. They talked through how they had felt so trapped and how they had made their decision to try to stay and finish the job.

No textbook lesson on racism could have had such a powerful impact. These were not girls who wore "race" as a badge in class or school activities. For these two to bring back this story of terror brought the class to a halt. Their experience had to be dealt with. The White students in the class could not put themselves in the place of the violent and racist comments any more than could the Black students. Together, they and their teacher tried to understand: "Why do White people feel superior?" "She's smarter and harder working than those guys—how could they think they're better?" "Do you think this is ever going to change?" "Of course it will—we don't have slavery any more!" "But this is our town. How could you think people are better or worse than you because they are another color?" "Well, if you're White in this school, sometimes you feel funny walking through the rest of the building. Or going into the cafeteria. I don't feel very wanted there." "Yeah, but that's different from being afraid." The questions sound simple, almost scripted for a teen conversation on racism. But there was great emotion in the questions, and great pain. This was not an academic discussion. Their friends had had their lives threatened, for a school project.

Living History

The day after Election Central Ms. McDonnell's U.S. History class was in session. She typically organized her lessons around a series of introductory lectures, followed by student research into primary sources and student presentations or activities that gave them an opportunity to learn from each other. On this day, she was lecturing on the Progressive movement when, in the middle of a sentence, she interrupted herself to say "I'm so *glad* you're all right!" She was speaking to one of the two Black girls who had gone to exit poll in the Klan neighborhood. She had tears in her eyes, and she couldn't keep from looking at the girl now and then as she proceeded to go over the relation of the labor movement to the Progressives.

Normally, Ms. McDonnell was much cooler, much less emotional than Ms. Williams. A young woman, she taught with a dry wit and straightforward style that brooked little silliness. She conveyed absolute confidence that her students could learn and conducted class accordingly. She began each new topic with a lecture and the handing out of a learning packet that included key names, dates, and ideas; reading assignments (references to them, or photocopied articles); questions for analysis; and dates for tests. Students learned from her lectures, from discussion, and from examining primary and secondary sources representing varied historical interpretations. Perhaps more than any other teacher in the program, she felt hampered by the lack of a functioning library in the school. She wanted her students to be to able read actual historical materials, to investigate issues for themselves. Her solution was to bring her own books from home and make them available to the students. She had to keep them locked up because the community college used the school at night; she said that anything left out would be taken, mislaid, or in the case of magazines, missing articles that had been ripped out. Of the school texts the district supplied to all U.S. history teachers, she was provided with only ten copies (to be used by all five of her classes). (There were no additional "Pathfinder level" texts or district-supplied resources.) Although she maintained a calm presence all year long, she faced a constant struggle to have adequate materials for her students. She had chosen Pathfinder because she thought that creating materials and involving students was what teaching is all about. But clearly she would have preferred to have more materials accessible so that her students could have much richer experiences in reading, in discovering new perspectives, in encountering the many forms of historical information.

Her special concern was that the students came with so little background. Although they had qualified for admission to a "gifted-and-talented" school, many could not write well and few had read or remembered much from earlier social studies classes. She explained that her teaching had to assume that social studies students came in with no background (they had taken the courses; her concern was not for courses they had taken but for *what, if anything, they had learned*). Her lectures, then, were central to laying out basic information, but they were not monologues. Every lecture was interrupted by many student questions and ideas. When she lectured on the Progressives, students interrupted to ask how current nativist groups might differ from progressivism as a social movement. When she described labor disputes and the violence of late-nineteenth-century labor-management relations, students asked why the United States had used violence in Nicaragua and El Salvador and whether a woman president would be less violent. She sparked their curiosity and let them know that if they would read their history and keep up with current issues, she would create time for them to explore the connections.

When her students who had participated in Election Central debriefed the exit polling, they more than the government students went into great detail about what people wore, what students had asked them, what they were asked in return. The Black girl who went to the working-class neighborhood described the "guy who had KKK on his sleeve." Another girl told about a very poor woman in a Black neighborhood who was sure that the "elderly would all be on welfare if [the Republican] were elected." A White, middle-class girl talked of going to a precinct where "I thought I would know someone." But the people there, who looked just like her, evaded her and tried to avoid her questions. One woman had told a student pollster that she voted the way her husband wanted her to because he had "gotten into some trouble" and couldn't vote. From this the class launched into a discussion of how the idea of one vote per household (because a husband "represents the wife's thinking") had been used to keep women disenfranchised. They got into a very animated discussion about when a Black or a woman or a Hispanic would be elected president, and whether the Hispanic boy in the class who aspired to politics might not be the first to be elected vice president. In contrast, a history teacher in the "neighborhood" part of the school saw Ms. McDonnell's students' debate preparation and said with a sigh, "One of my students this morning talked to the class about why he thinks 'Mondale Ferraro' will be elected president; he thinks *he* has a great chance.")

Ms. McDonnell took her students' impressionistic and wishful discussions and pushed the students to probe further. She pushed them to learn as much as they could about the issues that shaped the election and what its consequences might be over four years. She reminded them that by the next election they would be voters. The pattern of exchange in her class was always an acceptance of a student contribution, a chance for other students to elaborate, then a new question that pushed the thinking. These bright students had been accustomed in the lower grades to talking (charming) their way through subjects like history, with a little knowledge and very little work. In her class, the atmosphere was accepting and supportive, but the method was to push.

Positive Identification. This combination of pushing the thinking and accepting the attempts to think became crucial as the class discussed a pending bill that would limit immigration and require immigrants to carry identification cards. The Black and Anglo students debated for about twenty minutes whether under this bill an employer would ask for an I.D., whether asking for one would be the same as checking to verify its authenticity. The discussion ranged back to the turn-of-the-century immigration they had been studying and this new legislation that tried to cap the very kind of immigration they had seen resistance to during the days of early industrialism. The same problems of city services, housing, jobs, and poverty were arising now, with the same mix of welcome and intolerance for immigrants. Ms. McDonnell arranged a debate on the current legislation. Articulate students took their classmates through the issues: Did illegal immigrants take jobs away from U.S. citizens? Did they increase the costs of welfare and education and medical care? Could the U.S. limit the influx of family members drawn to this country by relatives already here? The Black girl taking the opening position made the case against illegal immigrants, giving statistics from several states. Her Anglo challenger focused on a provision of the bill that would give amnesty to immigrants who could prove that they entered the country before 1981; "legal" immigrants would have to carry an I.D. card. He refuted the statistics about immigrants' drain on resources, saying that a major report, which he had found and cited, had concluded that the majority of immigrants pay social security, sales taxes, and property tax and are afraid to collect even those benefits due them for fear of being deported. He thought the bill would be punitive to citizen and legal immigrant Hispanics, that employers would be afraid to hire any Hispanics lest they have forged papers. The debate covered racism, economic statistics, the issue of border guards and migrant workers. The debaters had searched widely for information (beyond the most recent issue of a newsmagazine) and had prepared well. After the formal debate, the class talked about whether such a bill would actually limit the flow of illegal immigrants, as was its intent. It was a good lesson, a good class discussion, demystifying and demythologizing the issues surrounding immigration.

Roberto made it less academic. He stood up by his seat, not the custom in this class, and said, "but my parents are immigrants and they do not have papers. And if this becomes a law, what will they do? What will *I* do?" The class fell silent. Another Hispanic boy spoke up, "Put yourself in my place. I am a citizen here. So are my parents. But with a card—I'd be afraid of being harassed by my friends. My Black friends would not have to carry a card." A Hispanic girl spoke up, "If you can prove you have been here, you probably came legally. If you have had to keep quiet about how you came, you have not been doing the kind of things [jobs, applications for social services, credit purchases] that have a lot of paperwork with them. You mow lawns or work as a maid. You have been careful *not* to have records so you can stay unnoticed."

Students who had only a vague interest in the bill, taking just enough notes on the debate to be able to answer a test question comparing current and past immigration policies, suddenly cared what the pending bill proposed. Someone offered to get a copy, to call a congressman. This discussion would come up again after Congress voted. The students' feeling that they could bring into class the personal ramifications of the law stand in stark contrast to the "wall" that the teachers in *Contradictions of Control* classrooms often erected between students' experiential knowledge and course content. A student in one of those classrooms had been almost in tears in an interview when she explained her opposition to the tax dollars spent on the space program when there is so great a need to find ways to overcome hunger and poverty. But just after the interview, as she walked into her Forest Hills High history class and listened to the teacher's brisk list of facts for the Kennedy presidency, the student showed no sign of interest or emotion as the teacher listed as one of John Kennedy's three main "accomplishments," the space program (McNeil 1986). The girl knew that any comment from her would be seen as an unnecessary digression or interruption of the teacher's carefully paced coverage of "the material," all of which resided with the teacher and the text. Students were not sources of course "material." In contrast, the current, the historical, the personal, and the political all came together in Ms. McDonnell's class because what students brought to class in the form of experience and questions was just as important as the scrounged materials and borrowed books that she herself brought in. As students made connections, there was more than once a moment of unplanned drama.

On Trial. Planned drama was also a part of her repertoire. To make the robber baron period come alive, the barons themselves were put on trial. Ms. McDonnell served as judge and provided advance materials in the form of questions, resource articles, and her reference books. She explained courtroom procedures and how they would be adapted for this mock trial. The rest was up to the students. Each had to assume a role, such as injured miner or widowed mother, railroad tycoon or Teddy Roosevelt. Someone served as bailiff. They spent days researching their characters and the kind of experience each would have that would make him or her a witness for the prosecution or defense of a railroad tycoon or banker. A wealthy senator might take the stand on behalf of the patriotism of the railroad baron and in gratitude for all his railroads had done to link the country together and create jobs. Because there was no script, the prosecutor would need to be informed enough to know that the senator might be beholden to the robber baron and to use that to raise questions about his testimony. Each had to know his or her own character and the issues that linked them to the others.

The class learned the material as it was presented at trial; this was not a replay of a lecture. The lectures had covered corporate organizational forms, the rise of industrialism, economic theories that supported or challenged the creation of trusts and monopolies. The lectures and readings explored Marxism, social Darwinism, and the notion of the self-made man. The trial put faces on workers and owners and gave voice to their relative power in emerging industrialism. The railroad porter tried to make a case for minimum wage; the widow of a miner, her arms full of pickaninny-style baby dolls, charged the robber baron with being unconcerned about worker safety and providing no benefits when workers were injured or killed. The arrogant captain of industry shot back that workers only got hurt when they were careless. The senator argued that any legislation to prohibit child labor or protect workers would be unconstitutional—it would interfere with the *industrialists'* pursuit of happiness.

Teachers who teach defensively do so in order to create efficiencies for themselves. They simplify content, reduce the number of information sources, and severely limit student interaction. Ms. McDonnell of all the teachers observed would have had the most convincing justifications for teaching defensively. Her school provided the authority but virtually none of the resources she needed and essentially created no efficiencies for her. She would have taught a respectable course if she had done nothing but provide students with her knowledgeable lectures. But her commitment was to the students and their need to learn. She wove skillfully between history and their present lives, between the historical knowledge in books and the historical understandings they came to by working through that knowledge—in debates, in costumed theater, in soul-searching discussions. She seemed unaffected by any theory of gifted education or other pedagogy. She said that the way she taught "is just what people do who have been born to teach; it probably cannot be taught or learned." She knew it could be done without a lot of materials but not without enormous effort and, in the case of this school, the legitimacy the magnet program afforded her "natural" gift of teaching. And, as we will see, her sense of the innateness of teaching would be threatened when standard tests were brought in to prescribe the means and content of teaching.

Teaching as Experiment

The physics and biology teachers agreed in philosophy but differed in style. Ms. Watts and Ms. Bartlett had as their primary goals bringing students into scientific ways of thinking. Ms. Watts began her physics course with the reading of *The Physicist,* a play about the ethics of science. As one girl remarked, "I thought you always started science courses with converting from regular measure into the metric system. I couldn't figure out what she was doing. Was this English class?"

Getting away from teacher demonstrations and into hands-on labs for students was not easy in the physics classroom where the ancient lab benches were tall and few in number. Desks moved in for the overflow students were sandwiched in between the tall lab benches or pushed against the back wall. Students in the desks could not have seen a teacher demonstration, and they certainly had no lab equipment. Students at the fixed lab benches had little more.

Ms. Watts had come to this school after much persuading by a colleague, from a mostly Hispanic school where she had helped equip the labs. She had loved the setup and the students there and so left only reluctantly. Now she was beginning the task again, with few funds from the district but with the promise of modest annual support from a corporate donor to help the science teachers acquire equipment and simple lab tools for their classrooms.

She preferred to teach by posing a problem and then having students work through it from varying perspectives. She wanted them to have to be able to reason out when something should be considered a measurement problem, when it was an investigation of the effects of a variable, or when it was a search for an unknown variable. As will become clear in chapter 6, she felt caught between what she as an engineer and scientist knew about thinking in science and the simple problems, mostly mathematical, that the district curriculum defined as school physics and physical science.

Ms. Bartlett also wanted to bring her students into thinking in science. In fact, she modeled scientific thinking for them in a number of ways. She was always bringing into class new articles she had read or new things she had learned in summer courses. She introduced herself to a group of magnet teachers from other schools, saying, "I'm in biology and I like to write curriculum. . . . It's my way of experimenting with kids. My scientific activity for the year is to write curriculum and test it out and then find out how well it tests." She went to say that she hated to do the same thing twice, so she was always looking for new ways to teach. She felt hindered by the lack of lab equipment and facilities, students' weak background in science coming into Pathfinder, and the ever-growing wonderful field of biology, from which she had to choose those ideas and skills which she had some hope of teaching meaningfully in the brief time she had her students.

Ms. Bartlett organized her laboratory classroom as a series of learning centers, partly because there was not enough equipment for everyone to do the same thing at the same time and partly because students came into her class with such different levels of science background. Like most of the other teachers at this school, she created a learning packet for each set of lessons, with background materials, basic information, and a list of requirements. Common to all the learning packets was that students would read the required sections of the biology text (a college-level text), listen to lectures and films, and be tested when they were ready. The other requirements involved exploring a number of choices—three or four lab stations were set up for examining specimens or working through experiments, or the chance to construct models or collect specimens or write a paper. There could be as many as a dozen choices of required and elective activities. The core concepts of the unit would be explored through several operations, the mathematical, the experimental, the explanatory language of the text, the diagrams in the text and those drawn by the students, visual observation, and manipulation. By the time a student worked his or her way through the required and elected activities, the lesson's terminology and concepts would have been worked with and applied in a variety of ways.

The study of cell nutrition began with a beautiful film about the cell, actual footage of living cells as well as animations; she followed with an overview lecture. A second, elaborating lecture would follow in a few days, after students had had a chance to investigate cell processes on their own. Assigned readings were the next step for most students, although those who wanted to proceed to set up an experiment could come back to the readings later or do them at home. The first time through this difficult reading material was begun at school by many of the students, for whom the reading needed frequent checks with the teacher or peers. Suspended from the ceiling, and made of everything from styrofoam to wire to found objects, were models of cells made by former students. This group would add their renderings as the unit progressed. Lab stations were set up for investigations of plant and animal cells, examination of protozoa cultures, and for later in the unit experiments with nutritional processes of cells. A cell nutrition board game[9] was set up for two to four students to play, a game based on enzymes and "foods," with little cardboard pieces notched like enzymes and amino acids color-coded to help students understand the sequences and relative quantities in enzyme reactions in cell processes. The manipulatives allowed students to give physical arrangement to the ratios and processes that in the text were presented as formulas and complex vocabulary. For the entire unit, a guide sheet of descriptive and synthesis questions provided students a means of tracking their understanding of the concepts and helped link lab stations to text. Very popular with the students was a computer simulation of cell processes designed by a former student.

The biology course relied less on student-supplied knowledge of content than did Mr. Drew's government class or Ms. Williams's poetry students. The students' contribution was more one of making decisions about their own learning. Their chief role was to learn to make good choices about ways to learn and to voice to the teacher what they did not understand and what they needed to help them learn. She said, and interviews with students confirmed, that many Hispanic students resisted the structure of her class. They tended to come from more traditional schools where they had been taught there is a right answer. Learning how to get those right answers helped them get into Pathfinder and set them apart from their peers back in their home neighborhoods who were disengaging from school. They were confused as to why she did not "do her job" and tell them the answer, or at least the way to get the right answer. Better yet, since she knew the material, why did she not just tell them by lecturing? Each year the search for a balance between choice and structure was a chore for her because she aimed for real, rigorous coverage of as much of the increasing field of biology as possible, yet she felt success only when students really understood and could work in-depth with a concept. She tried to listen to her students, and their parents, in making these decisions, but the struggle for a balance was ongoing and shifted with each new group of students.

When pressed, Ms. Bartlett cited two important influences on her teaching: the new learning she was doing outside the classroom and the requests from her students. Each year she tried to leave one class period undesignated in order to teach a course "on demand." In response to student requests, she had created a marine biology course, a microbiology course, a biochemistry course, and an environmental biology course whose topics varied from year to year. Her flexibility to teach in these areas came from the school's Pathfinder designation and the learning she was doing outside of school.

Teacher Learning. From a marine biology institute offered by a major state university at a facility on the Gulf of Mexico, Ms. Bartlett learned about estuaries, plant and animal life in and near the Gulf, and about the applications of biological laboratory concepts (cell processes, for example) to particular life forms. Marine biology held a special fascination for her and her students. With virtually no lab equipment or money for supplies or field trips to the Gulf, she seemed to have little likelihood of translating her new expertise into curriculum. She decided that she and the students would have to create the materials themselves. With modest funding from the biology share of a corporate grant to the science department, she bought supplies. She and her students would build aquaria. The building and stocking of the aquaria would be a part of the study. Before standardizing reforms were put in place (see chapter 6), she was able to work marine biology into her regular biology classes. Her enthusiastic stories about the Gulf and about marine biology were contagious; this became a popular choice for students who wanted to stay with her for another semester of study. The university marine course and her personal study of environmental issues gave her the background to offer similar electives in various environmental biology courses. She also created an environmental unit for her regular biology course, which gave students a chance to see practical applications of their lab-based learning.

In addition, Ms. Bartlett had been selected to have a mentor from the research faculty of a local medical school. The federally funded program linked a pair of teachers with a medical school researcher of common interest, who was to meet with them occasionally and help them establish a program of independent study to update their science knowledge or lab skills. During the two years of the program, she studied problems in microbiology and was able to meet a number of medical researchers as well as the other teachers in the program. She also became much more alert to science and medical news. Her students came to expect that if an exciting new development in genetics or pollution research or infectious diseases made the news, then they would hear about it from Ms. Bartlett. Her real love for the new discoveries and applications in biological sciences lifted her course out of the "memorize the taxonomies" mode of much high school biology. She came to see biology as a problems-based subject, not separable from chemistry and physics. That she made her own learning, and delight in learning, so visible drew a number of students into biology-related topics when it came time to design an independent Pathfinder project.

Of particular importance to the understanding of the role of students at this school is their role in teaching. The history debates and mock trial and election central, the arduous process of editing the literary journal, the creating of biology electives in concert with student interests all demonstrate ways teachers at this school created conditions in which students could teach each other. Ms. Bartlett saw an even broader impact of students' teaching: the questions students came to her with and asked to do independent study on, the topics they developed for their Pathfinder projects, the questions they raised in class were as influential in her continued learning as the formal courses she took in the summers. Her "experiment" in teaching extended to testing her ideas to see if they pushed her students into territory she herself had not yet explored.

This continued learning also enhanced her sense of herself as a professional and enabled her to take advantage of the school's supportive environment. Following Ms. Bartlett's teaching career beyond the year of data collection in her school showed her becoming increasingly assertive in trying to shape district goals for biology courses, for creating methods of assessment that would incorporate problem solving and applications and essays (extremely rare among public school science courses in this city). She worked closely with the chemistry and physics teachers to explore lab equipment and materials that would fit their student-centered teaching so that as their corporate donor continued the annual gift ($5,000 to $10,000 per year), they could make wise purchases. The district estimate for equipping a science laboratory classroom ranged from $25,000 to $50,000 [early 1990s dollars], assuming basic furnishings and utilities were in place (at least $100,000 if they were not). None of those assumptions could be made for any of the labs at this school. And what little equipment did exist included, as she said, "dinosaurs" like unlighted microscopes. The facilities problem would have made it easy to simply lecture, to have students memorize, to keep students in a passive role. The prior background in engineering and physics that Ms. Watts brought into teaching and the continued learning that bolstered Ms. Bartlett's teaching kept them directed toward more authentic science learning for their students despite the lack of provisions in place for it.

Affirming Personal Knowledge. These Pathfinder classes were not performances arranged for the benefit of an observer. Continued informal visits to the school over several years showed that they were the courses Pathfinder students encountered every year, courses which were evolving as specific topics or activities came and went. The organization and philosophy of the school helped to sustain teaching that brought teachers' personal and professional knowledge and invited their students' personal knowledge into the classroom.

The world history course was always in flux. It was taught by a former band director, who literally acknowledged no discipline boundaries. He taught world history as the history of culture and the arts, as the history of peoples and ideas, as well as the history of nations, wars, and governments. To explain the baroque, he played a flute and recorder duet with a university teacher education student who was in his class for her pre service observation hours. For years he had struggled with the lack of books, photographs, and other resources beyond the standard survey text, but he was finally liberated by the invention of the video cassette recorder and the proliferation of video-taped cultural performances and documentaries. "I can show three versions of *Carmen*. My students don't have to take my word for anything any more. They can compare. They can see for themselves. We can go everywhere now." When they were freshmen, the students did not speak of "seeing for themselves." They could only groan over his insufferably long and detailed, "outrageous or insane" in their words, tests. By their senior year students were proud of all they learned from him as freshmen or sophomores, and they remembered and used more from his classes than they had ever imagined they would.

Throughout Pathfinder the curriculum changed as the teachers learned, as they found new needs in their students, as their students' curiosities sent them into unknown territory, but the basic format of creating and re-creating the curriculum together remained the key to Pathfinder in the years I have stayed in touch with this school. In retrospect, one of the more interesting features of the co-creation of the curriculum was the fact that more of these teachers designed and developed curricula with their students than with each other. There was strong rapport among the faculty. There was a collective sense of being part of an important school with a distinctive philosophy that they shared and guarded against outside claims of elitism, administrative threats to close magnets, and competition from other magnets and especially other honors programs. Much of their curriculum and their teaching strategies derived less from collaborations with other teachers than from the needs and creative contributions and curiosities of their students. That so many of these same students had come initially to the school having never read a whole book, having written so little of substance, having so little to remember from middle school science and social studies classes gives evidence to the value-added nature of the teacher-student collaborations central to a Pathfinder education where both could bring their personal knowledge into the classroom.

Pathfinder Projects

The Pathfinder program was designed long before Theodore Sizer wrote *Horace's Compromise* and advocated assessing student's learning through "exhibitions" of what they know. When they planned their school program, these teachers did not know Sizer or Newmann (Sizer 1984; Newmann, Secada, and Wehlage 1995) or the now-extensive literature on alternative or authentic assessment. They had not read Howard Gardner's theory of multiple intelligences (Gardner 1991, 1993). Their commitment to individualized learning and to child-centered pedagogy extended beyond fostering active student involvement in classrooms. To explore beyond the assigned, to integrate across the boundaries between school subjects, and to develop their own abilities to be a part of creating learning experiences, the program from its inception included an independent study project. The Pathfinder projects, according to the magnet coordinator's guidelines from 1984–1985, offered "an exciting and challenging opportunity" to "develop your intellectual talents." Interestingly, the projects were seen as a way of evaluating how well the Pathfinder program was helping the students develop as independent learners, not just measures of what students could do.

The Pathfinder project was not just another research paper, science fair project, or math competition. Each student was to pose a problem or a line of inquiry and write a proposal about how to investigate, or solve, or create a solution to the question or problem. The student would design the mode of inquiry or creative enterprise, would develop the project in conjunction with a teacher advisor and, if possible, a community mentor, and, in the doing of the project, would create something new to be shared with an audience. The topic could grow out of something learned in class or an out-of-school interest. It had to involve research but also had to go beyond the information-gathering typical of high school research papers to synthesize the information and act on it in some way. The research process and "findings" did need to be presented in a documented, written form but should also include visual displays, performance, construction of models, experiments, or other public format so that others could learn from the work. The student had entire responsibility for the project but was urged to seek the guidance of knowledgeable people outside the school. From elementary to high school, Pathfinder independent projects had an explicit goal of sending students outside the walls of school for information and for models of learning and doing. As such, they challenged teachers' domains of expertise and opened up "school knowledge" to comparison with nonschool knowledge.

The project had several incarnations, depending on grade level and school culture. At the elementary level, the projects were not overseen by teachers or connected to a particular class. After their topics were approved, students worked on them at home, sometimes under the guidance of a parent and if possible with the help of a mentor. For elementary students to work on a single project for several weeks or months is unusual, particularly in schools were there are state rules that govern how the school day should be broken down minute by minute for each subject. Yet the students managed, by trial and error, to find projects that were manageable given their skill levels (and lack of a driver's license). A third-grade girl studied species that are endangered because of human destruction of their habitat. She checked out library books and called environmental groups to get their literature. She interviewed a zoo scientist responsible for the zoo's breeding program for endangered animals. Her written report told what she had learned from these resources. To make the lessons vivid for her peers, she held a foot race with a one-dollar entry fee to raise money for a nature group concerned about endangered species. Participation was voluntary, and the field was muddy, but many children brought dollars and ran. The race, along with other children's posters and handmade puppets and specimen collections, showed third graders' ingenuity in overcoming such obstacles as needing an hour to write out even one neat page of a report.

At the middle school level, students felt the pressure to do projects that would impress their peers. They also were more aware of competition, parental and peer, and the difference financial resources could make in their presentations. A particularly memorable middle school Pathfinder project was called "26 Flags Over My School." The boy had become aware of the increasing number and variety of immigrant children at his school, but no one in the school had collected any organized information about this diversity. His curiosity led him to notice this information gap. His mother taught him how to do a survey questionnaire. He interviewed students in his grade (in a very large middle school) and learned that they represented twenty-six different countries. His questionnaire asked the students from where they had immigrated, how long they had been in the United States, what they missed most about their home country, what they liked best in the United States, and what they liked to eat. He presented his data in the form of a written report with simple percentage statistics and in a scale model of the school, around whose roof flew flags he had made representing the twenty-six countries.

At the Pathfinder high school, the projects were in some years independent graduation requirements and in other years tied to a particular course
and counted as a portion of the grade for that course. Each student drafted a
proposal to submit to a faculty review committee; the proposal included a
request for a particular mentor. Teachers like Ms. Bartlett who had created
elective courses around student interest in science topics were in great demand
as advisors. Students had several months to work on the project, almost all of
that work completed outside of school except for the conferences with the
advisor or perhaps use of lab space (rare because labs were so underequipped).
The Pathfinder projects shared many of the characteristics, and fulfill many of
the goals, of the "exhibitions" recommended by the Coalition of Essential
Schools and "authentic" assessments advocated by those who see a need in
schools for students to demonstrate what they know (rather than to have student learning represented only on tests common to all students in the class or
by what they "miss" on tests). Like exhibitions and other forms of authentic
assessment, the Pathfinder projects have been a means by which students
could demonstrate how they know, and how they were developing as thinkers
and learners.

The Pathfinder project assignment included a dimension of assessment that
was rare at that time and is still rare in the district, the requirement to include a
reflective component, reflecting on how the work on the project, particularly the
ideas, developed. One racially mixed group of students made a joint project of
performing a play on teenage pregnancy. The author was a community center
director. The students created the production and along with it did research on
teenage pregnancy. They performed this play for a group of teenagers at the
community center but thought the language was too strong for adult groups.
When they were invited to perform for younger teens and adults (United Way
agencies, PTAs, church groups), they had to weigh their self-consciousness
against the need to get the message out. They had each kept a journal about how
it felt to play their characters—the pregnant girl, the teen father, the parents and
friends of the couple. Their journals reflected their thoughts on playing these
characters before different audiences. Their research was about teen pregnancy,
their own moral and social development, and about the potential for community education on this issue. It was an unconventional but educational project,
one that invited students to "complexify" a topic and continue to work through
the complexity with a variety of people in and out of school.

A second project on teenage pregnancy was done by a boy who was troubled to learn many girls at the middle school and high school in his home

neighborhood, in a poor Black area, were pregnant or new mothers. He devised a questionnaire to ask them their plans and how they were managing to stay in school. The sociology teacher, his advisor for the project, helped him structure the questionnaire; the boy did research on the subject through the library and social service agencies. He had been influenced by a public television program in which a noted journalist had explored the same issue and found that the girls who were mothers wanted to stay in school and prepare for careers. The journalist discovered that the fathers had little interest in the babies, school, or planning for future jobs that would help support their children. In addition to his written report, the Pathfinder student had conducted a class discussion based on his findings. That discussion and his presentation were videotaped for future sociology classes. Both of these projects demonstrate students' taking very seriously the strong dialectic between learning and teaching, between learning and reflecting on learning. They crossed the "school knowledge" boundary and exhibited students' capacity for understanding their communities better as a result of serious study in school and for bringing that new understanding back into the school to hold school knowledge up to the reality of experience.

Teachers and a committee of parents and others spent hours carefully examining each project and listening to the students' explanations, then writing thoughtful notes to them. The projects in a given year ranged from a computer program to help students prepare for various citywide math contests to a systematic cataloguing of sources of natural dyes.

A Hispanic boy who later attended an ivy league university and became an environmental engineer had wanted to know more about aspirin. He thought he might want to make aspirin and had attempted one sample. He asked Ms. Bartlett how he could learn more about aspirin and its effects. She put him in touch with a medical researcher she had met during her work with the medical college mentor, who was very excited to know that a high school student shared his interest in aspirin ("I haven't found anybody here at the medical school who is interested in working on this right now") and who suggested that they work together on the effects of aspirin on blood clotting. To do an experiment, the student had to learn about human subjects review approvals, informed consent and experimental design as well as about blood and aspirin. His design included three groups of students, those to whom he gave aspirin every day, those to whom he gave a placebo every day, and those who took nothing. At three-day intervals, he made a cut on their finger and used an absorbent paper to collect the blood. By weighing the paper he could chart the rate of blood flow and blood clotting. His charts showed a clear relationship between the use of aspirin and blood-clotting rate; even more impressive was the representation in his charts that aspirin could not account for all the difference. To know what other factors were involved would have to be the subject of future study.[10]

A ninth grader, whose advisor was Mr. Goodman, the world history teacher, did a study of the Holocaust, collecting photographs and maps of concentration camps. He wrote a diary from the point of view of a Jewish survivor of the camps. He also wrote a diary from the point of view of a collaborator. Two boys who said they had not finished the introductory-level physical science course or ever worked with technology tried to puzzle out how future transportation could work if solar energy could power magnetized tracks. Their idea was that a car could move along a magnetized track if it the car's magnetization repelled that of the track. They had produced schematics and a simple model.

A boy who Ms. Bartlett described as a genius pursued his interest in astronomy by testing the effects of Mars's conditions on certain bacteria. He subjected the bacteria to minerals and to heat conditions known or thought to exist on Mars in order to chart the changes in properties or conditions in the bacteria. Searching the community for people and materials that could be helpful to his experiment was a major learning component of the project. He said he expected to "stay curious" about this topic as he went on to college.

Reflections on the Absence of Walls

Reading about the inventiveness and passion in Pathfinder teaching makes it easy to forget the scarce resources in the school, the extreme poverty in some of these students' lives, the weak background many of them brought into the school despite its admissions criteria that might suggest otherwise. It is easy to forget that these students had a school day one hour longer than other students' and a one- to two-hour bus ride on top of that. It is easy to forget that the district supplied the school with (some) adopted texts not necessarily relevant to program goals, and only $25 per student per year (per year, not per subject per year) for additional instructional materials. Although it was officially defined a magnet school by the district and has district administrative help on arranging the students' admissions and bus schedules, it was created as a magnet philosophy and sustained as a magnet program by the teachers and students. They, at the "bottom" of the bureaucracy, created and re-created the curriculum. As a result, there was little sense of "school knowledge" here as separate from "real knowledge." The authenticity of what was taught, its connection to their personal situation as well as to cutting-edge knowledge (for example, in biology) and quality (as evidenced in the study of literature, not anthologies of cuttings of literature) came from what the teachers construed as the curriculum. They came to their various instructional choices from various perspectives, but their shared focus was on helping the students learn and develop.

When teachers mystify a subject, they convey to students that it is important but unknowable, or that they, the students, should not worry about learning it. Mystification may be used to obscure the teachers' lack of knowledge on a topic, to avoid having to create a complex teaching strategy for a difficult subject, or to avoid making explicit the potential complexity or controversy that may arise if the topic is explored thoroughly (*Contradictions of Control,* ch. 7). The Pathfinder social studies faculty worked with their students to *demystify* political processes, the effects of social class and race in this urban community and this school, economics (both theoretical and applied, both historical and current), and the "way things work" in the media and government. Most important, they demonstrated for their students how they themselves investigated a previously unknown or little-understood topic, and they made explicit for their students the processes by which they as a class were getting behind surface definitions and slogans to understand complex processes. Mr. Drew did not pretend that on his own he fully understood statistical sampling of voting populations; he called in an expert and worked closely with him. And he encouraged his students, particularly the ones developing the Election Central computer program for the class, to meet with the consulting professor on their own. Mr. Drew did not fear that they would learn something he did not know. He went outside school, to the university and community, for ways to make his social studies courses valid in content and involving for students. He wanted his courses to provide them with realistic knowledge of social and political factors, knowledge they would need as they took their place as participating adults in the community.

Contact with working scientists and opportunities for continued learning were keys to Ms. Bartlett's contagious enthusiasm for science. She talked directly with her students about what she was learning, about things she had thought she understood until she worked with the medical professor or got her hands wet studying marine biology specimens.

Beyond avoiding fragmentation to create immediate efficiencies and working not to mystify but to demystify complex topics and complex ways of learning, these teachers were more remarkable because even with very few teaching materials, they did not simplify topics to elicit student compliance. Yes, they had some students who wanted to just get by; they had some students whose weaker academic skills or middle school background made the teacher have to rethink the sequencing of assignments or topics. But they did not yield to a simplification of the curriculum to avoid student complaints, student resistance to assignments, or low student effort. Taken as a group, they constantly pushed the students to try things, to extend their thinking, to move beyond the quick, facile responses "gifted" students so ably give to teacher queries. This spirit of confidence in what students can learn should not be remarkable. But in class after class, school after school, in this urban area, university researchers and teacher education students conducting preservice field observations have found that the prevailing teacher comment across thousands of pages of field notes, noted by dozens of different observers, is "I knew you wouldn't do it," or variations such as "I knew you couldn't do it," "Since I know you won't really do this, . . ." or "I can't believe you actually completed/wrote/read the assignment."[11] For the Pathfinder teachers to exhibit genuine excitement about learning and to make even the missteps and uncertainties of their own learning visible to students is not typical teacher behavior in this district. For them to further push their students to "complexify," rather than simplify, their thinking is one of the hallmarks of Pathfinder.

A teacher like Ms. McDonnell will justify this kind of teaching as what naturally born teachers do. Others will attribute it to discussions the Pathfinder faculty had in its early retreats and planning meetings to arrive at a working definition of "Pathfinder." Some teachers invoked the school's founding theories of gifted education to shape their curriculum. Whether they invoked theory, philosophy, or personality, all of these teachers ultimately justified their teaching style by what they personally knew and were learning of their subject and what they saw as the capabilities and needs of the students. Their ability to articulate their justification for their teaching, for the centrality of students and a strong teacher knowledge base, was at no time more needed than in the years immediately following the Perot reform legislation. As chapter 6 will show, not even the Pathfinder school was exempt from attempts to align all school practice in order to "fix" the schools.

The Pathfinder program was established at the central district level, in compliance with a federal court order and located at this school by the initiative of the principal. It developed into a program of credible, authentic curriculum by virtue of the focus on the students, the individual teachers' personal knowledge, and the school culture that supported the building of an instructional program on that knowledge. The program was threatened from time to time when teachers were assigned to it who did not understand or espouse its philosophy and who as a result taught the required text in standard sequence in teacher-centered classrooms. The program was buffeted by the many reorganizations of the district and regular political pressure to do away with Pathfinder or with magnets. It was always fragile because of the extreme energy required to create courses, sustain active student involvement, and provide emotional support for students. It was vulnerable because the teachers had to create and scrounge materials in a district that was known for start-ups based on initial grand ideas but which many times left teachers to fend for themselves after the administrators first involved had moved on to the next [flashy] start-up. The teachers and students managed to keep Pathfinder "Pathfinder" until the state decided to reform the schools of Texas. As chapter 5 explains, the reformers did not visit this or other strong programs to learn about teaching and classrooms before they wrote their reforms. Chapter 6 shows the damage that occurred to this program and others as a result of the reformers' lack of acquaintance with what teachers and children can contribute to learning.

Chapter 4

════════════

The School for Science, Engineering, and Technology: A Different Kind of Bargain

The thin, meager light that managed to filter through the grimy windows exposed the gouges and scratches on the faded old blackboard. The room was entirely bare, with no hint of the name of the class, the work of the students or the personality of the teacher. Broken desks sat empty under the windows, still aligned in straight rows. Twenty students sat in the four rows closer to the door, slightly to the right of the teacher's lectern. They looked to be typical teenagers: boys slouched down, with long legs extended into the aisles, girls sitting slightly straighter. A mixture of races and sizes—alert but not animated, they waited for their teacher. On their desks were a few pages of notebook paper, but no books. Visually, the scene could be a third-world school, a photo from a Peace Corps brochure, a request for donations for school supplies and equipment. Sam Beshara, huge and huffing, burst into the classroom, a heavy engineering text tucked under his left arm, chalk in his right hand, and a stack of papers clutched between the two. "Moment!" The students registered surprise and amusement: what next? "We have to be able to work with 'moment.' What is it? You can't build, you can't understand materials, you can't make anything work until you understand 'moment.'" He set down the book and the papers, picked up the chalk, and jabbed the blackboard with numbers. The numbers grew into equations. The teacher boomed, "Of course, we have no books, so you

*are just going to have to pay attention up here." He chalked in geometric
diagrams, sketches of structures. "Now, if we had a book or any materials here, you could test this out. Instead, we are going to just have to get
this through the formulas. Now, who can tell me what we have here?
And you, the university visitor, you had better get this, too." Another day
in "Applied Engineering Lab II" had begun.*

The School for Science, Engineering, and Technology (SET) is the school that
shows what teachers and students can do when they make a contract, even an
unofficial one, to make their school work. Their contract is a "different kind of
bargain," because it is almost the inverse of the cynical bargain of lowered
expectations that students and teachers struck in the high schools described in
Contradictions of Control. In those schools, teachers controlled the content in
order to control the students. The teachers masked their personal knowledge of
the subjects in order to convey a simpler curriculum that would meet the minimum institutional requirements. They deliberately placed few demands on the
students to prevent students from resisting assignments or completing only the
minimum course requirements (McNeil 1986, ch. 7). The students did not
know that the course knowledge being presented was less than the teachers
knew or felt to be important about the subject. But they did learn early in the
year that if they did not speak up, did not challenge the teacher's lecture, did
not fail to do at least a minimum level of work, then they could make a good
grade and pass the course. Students learned not to ask for elaborations or further explanation; they did not question the information or otherwise disrupt
the clean efficiencies of teachers' covering the minimum material.

Together the teachers and students participated in a cycle of lowering
expectations: the less "real" the lessons seemed, the less effort the students put
into mastering them. The more students disengaged, the more the teachers felt
justified in keeping tight control over content and classroom interaction. The
result was a strangely perverse incentive system: each rewarded the other for
doing little and for demanding little. The institutional requirements did not
call for more. Neither the students nor the teachers found out over the course
of a semester what the other really knew or cared about; neither students nor
teachers discovered what the other could do. By mutual agreement, they made
school painless but also unproductive.

This cycle of lowered expectations had origins in the particular histories of
the four high schools documented in *Contradictions of Control.* The teacher-

student agreement and the way it played out in the classrooms took on a different character depending on the contextual factors within the school organization: the pervasiveness of administrative preoccupation with control and neglect of academics, the lack of teacher influence over decisions of tracking or de-tracking, the career paths of teachers who once exerted extra effort to engage students but now reduced that effort in the face of administrative disdain for exceptional effort, their memories of the resistance to teacher-supplied knowledge among their students during the Vietnam War era. The particular circumstances might vary, but in those schools where over time the structural and administrative purposes emphasized efficiencies over learning, teachers translated their powerlessness in the school as a whole into an assertion of counterproductive control over students, students who responded by merely going through the motions of schooling. They taught "defensively," requiring little of their students in order to avoid student resistance to the substance or the difficulty of course content. Their defensive teaching strategies did not enable them to see the silent resistance of disbelief even among those students who seemed to be achieving (McNeil 1986, ch. 7). Even those students who acquiesced to the forms of schooling in order to meet minimum course requirements held such oversimplified school knowledge as suspect.

These particular, situational bargains are confirmed in the discussions of Sizer and others as a cycle of lowered expectations around mutual agreements endemic to the typical American high school (Powell, Farrar, and Cohen 1985; Sedlak et al. 1986; Sizer 1984). Horace Smith's famous "compromise" was not just a compromise of effort, easily labeled as teacher burnout, but also a fundamental compromise between what he as a teacher knew his students needed to learn and what he was willing to put forth. Neither the course content nor the skills and ways of thinking that he knew to be essential to learning matched the superficial lessons he provided for his students. He knew that in his large bureaucratic and impersonal high school, no administrator would notice the weak quality of intellectual engagement in his classes. And, most significantly, no demand for more was forthcoming from his students. Sedlak and his colleagues, in *Selling Our Students Short,* document the pervasiveness of the cynical bargain students and teachers often strike to assure that each meets the minimal institutional requirements with the least personal effort. In a very distressing analysis, they indicate that many students feel that to be untouched by school is not to be deprived, but to be unscathed (Sedlak et al. 1986, ch. 1). More recently, emerging research on the relation between children's cultural identity and learning has pointed to the intentional withdrawal, physical and mental, from schooling by students of color who feel that doing so is their only self-protection from the cycle of low expectations they and their teachers are caught up in. When they physically remain in school, but emotionally and mentally distance themselves from the lessons, they are acknowledging that the school may emphasize their continued enrollment as more important than whether they learn (Irvine 1990; Valenzuela 1999).

The School for Science, Engineering, and Technology stands out for turning this model of defensive teaching and silent resistance on its head. It is a school where teachers and students entered into a constructive bargain to make the school all that its name implied, when little ongoing support from inside the building administration or the district could be counted on to do so. How they came to strike this bargain, what it meant for teachers' work, the student role and the curriculum, and how it was sustained against great odds demonstrate ways authentic schooling can be co-constructed by teachers and students.

SET is a school that began as a compelling idea for a magnet program. Like many good ideas in big-city school systems, it was given much more attention as an idea than as a working school program with continuing needs. To be fully realized, and sustained over time, such an innovative program would require qualified teachers, special equipment, time for continued planning by the faculty, rich curricular materials and abundant references in rapidly changing fields, and resource people available to students and faculty. That the school has served so many students so well without many of these components is a tribute to the sometimes explicit, sometimes hidden, bargain the teachers and students made with each other to make this program come close to what is implied in its name, the city's School for Science, Engineering, and Technology.

Like the MedIC magnet, SET was one of several magnet programs based on key economic sectors in the region. The school district could count on the business leadership to endorse the economic rationale of generating "human capital" locally through these specialized magnet schools. The desegregation pressure to broaden minority students' access to specialized careers in science and science-related industries linked the federal court requirements to a vital local economic issue. The expectation that corporations in these sectors (many of them with national or regional headquarters in the city) would be contributors to industry-related specialty schools gave the district confidence to open schools for which they had inadequate internal funding. All these factors helped shape a constellation of magnet programs identified with career objectives. SET would be the school that helped attract minority students, and particularly girls, into sectors of the economy from which they had been traditionally excluded by both the cultures of the technology-based corporations and the cultures of schooling, which tracked them away from science-related fields.

The name of the school and the frequent public announcements of corporate gifts of money and equipment to the school gave the impression that this school, unlike the impoverished setting of the Pathfinder magnet, would provide an education congruent with the cutting edge of ideas and technology typical of the local economy. This magnet program at the high school level would parallel the inventive research fields that give the region its reputation as a major producer not just of chemicals, petroleum, computers, and space ventures but also of the innovative ideas that drive these fields. The gap between school knowledge and the knowledge "out there" in the working world of the sciences would be bridged by this school.

This ambition is not far from the original dream of the school. But this was a city with a history of underfunded schools and of wide disparities in the allocation of resources to schools according to neighborhood, race and family income patterns. It was a city that tried to open enough magnet schools with sufficient speed to satisfy a federal court order to desegregate.[1] The economic, political, bureaucratic, and racial issues embroiling all the city's schools did not fail to make their mark on even this potential showcase for education in the sciences and engineering.

The placement of the SET magnet at Carver High mirrors the location of the gifted-and-talented magnet at Allen High: A predominantly African American high school in a mostly African American neighborhood was losing enrollment as shopping areas, warehousing, freeways, and changing family demographics eroded its student population. But there was a crucial difference: Allen High, named for a longtime civic leader who was White, had had a mostly White student population until the late 1960s and early 1970s, when the surrounding neighborhood rapidly shifted from White to Black. Placing the Pathfinder magnet at Allen High had helped not only to counter the trend of declining enrollment but also to bring White students and their families back into a school now designated as segregated and "Black." By contrast, Carver High had one-hundred-year history as an important anchor in the African American community. It was the alma mater of generations of African American leaders. The social contact, job referrals, and community cohesion provided to Blacks by this school over many years would all be endangered if the school were to close. As a single-race school, its hope of staying open hinged on desegregating, but its history as an "all-Black" school made volun-

tary transfers from Anglo and Hispanic neighborhoods an unlikely desegregation solution. These students would need a special program to draw them.
(One Carver graduate recalls that in her senior year, one of the first "crossover"
years for voluntary integration transfers, only six Anglo students joined her
class; most of these had lived on the border between this school's attendance
zone and that of a predominantly White high school.[2])

A regional administrator in the school district, an African American, had
made the idea of an engineering and science magnet his pet project. He had
long-standing ties, personal as well as administrative, to the school. He became
a strong advocate for situating the SET program at Carver. Such a visible,
important magnet would widen the base of support for the school, and the
program, if it succeeded, would bring the scientific and engineering enterprises of the community close to students traditionally excluded from careers
in those fields. The building had the space, the principal was eager, and the
pressure to provide the school with a "draw" sufficient to make it an agent for
voluntary student desegregation made the decision seem in later years to have
been inevitable.

The planning of this magnet program, like the others that were rushed
into place, combined a great deal of enthusiasm and goodwill with little clear
idea of how to go about creating a first-rate science high school. Even more
serious was the early message that these magnets would not be receiving the
kinds of funding needed to provision them at anything approaching the quality implied in their names. Among the reasons for the lack of special funding
were strong community resistance to integration, on the one hand, and, on the
other, criticisms of magnet schools as elitist. The desegregation dollars had to
cover central office administration of magnet student transfers and program
oversight and expanded research and evaluation staffs to track desegregation
ratios for the courts. In addition, those dollars were allocated to the busing of
thousands of students, the advertising of magnet choices, and many other
non-instructional expenses. The funds given to start-up programs included
the usual per pupil instructional funds plus a modest increment.

Basically, a faculty was assembled, a magnet coordinator hired, and the
planning begun a few weeks before school was to open. To establish this magnet school, there was little special funding for equipment, for hiring professional scientists or engineers as faculty or as long-term consultants, for field
trips into scientific workplaces, for specialized library materials, or for non-
standard textbooks. A community advisory team was created to participate in
the design of the school program, a committee which did include corporate and

university-based engineers and scientists. This advisory group took a great interest in the goals for the school and expected to be an important continuing resource for the faculty. Once the magnet school opened, and the Carver High principal took charge, however, the advisory committee found its voice diminished and, in fact, not always welcomed. It soon disbanded, and teachers and students in later years were rarely aware that this potentially vital group of advisors and advocates had once been a part of the vision for the school.[3] After the school opened and its first students enrolled from across the city, the magnet program was left to survive or fail without substantial district or organized community support. It had been created with an impressive name, a strong billing, and large claims for creating futures for students in fields that had been traditionally closed to them. It was a school with few material resources, severely inadequate facilities, and no administrative support for a systematic plan to rectify these deficiencies. That it became a school that in time held its good teachers and served students well is almost entirely due to the bargain its students and teachers struck to make the school live up to its advertised promise.

Why Did Students Apply to SET?

Students came to the SET magnet from across the city. From its inception, the program attracted African American and Anglo students, and, in smaller numbers, Latino students. For admission, students had to apply during the districtwide magnet transfer application period, submit middle school grades and teacher reference letters, and qualify on an admissions test. Grades and test scores in mathematics and sciences were weighted heavily in the admission process. Each qualifying applicant had an interview with the magnet coordinator. Student and parental commitment to the program were essential because attendance at this school required willingness to attend school for an extra hour of classes each day. The expected academic rigor of the course work, the assurance of homework and the newness of much of the subject matter were only a part of the load students would be undertaking if they enrolled. In addition, many would have a daily bus ride of from forty-five minutes to an hour and a half each way. After-school jobs, home chores, sports, and many other personal activities would have to be dropped or rearranged to accommodate to this schedule.

Finding students meant a combination of active recruiting as well as reviewing applications. Even this first contact brought together the cultures of the communities with the cultures of the schools. The students discovered very early that the magnet schools offered personalized learning environments: the coordinators from the magnet high schools spent much of January and February presenting their programs to eighth-grade assemblies in middle schools, trying to impress them with the distinctiveness of their programs. They hoped to make "high school" less abstract to help students picture their future in a specialized program. Of particular importance was attracting sufficiently balanced numbers of Hispanic, African American, and Anglo students to satisfy desegregation goals. A number of SET students credited these assemblies and the chance for conversations with magnet school representatives with helping them think of high school as a step toward college, and not merely as their next level of schooling. The presence of the magnet coordinators on the middle school campuses helped prompt middle school teachers and counselors to regard their students with more of a sense of their futures: several minority students in particular recall being surprised when a middle school teacher, especially in math or science, called them aside to encourage them to apply to SET.

Especially interesting is the way the application process meshed with the changing perceptions among families of many minority youth. Many of the Latino and African American students said it was their mother who urged them to apply to SET. A mother would have heard about the school from a co-worker in the offices of one of the oil companies, from a neighbor whose child had gone there, or from younger co-workers who were graduates of magnets. When the mother was the source of the information, or the pressure to apply, typically she did not have a college education herself but was working in order to provide a better future for her children. These women were on the lookout for opportunities for their children; they wanted high schools that would recognize their children as "college material."

Parents for whom higher education had seemed an unreachable goal were learning that SET and other magnets were helping students become acquainted with college admissions and financial aid processes and, even more important, had counselors or faculty who were helping the colleges learn about the potential of minority youth as future college students. Although there is the widespread perception even today that many minority families do not value advanced schooling for their children, the fact is that the access remains mystified for many. Sadly, students report a pervasive lack of information given to "regular" students in "regular" schools regarding courses to take to be on a pre-college path, procedures for monitoring one's own progress toward college, the early steps in the college admissions processes, and the ways of finding out basic information regarding universities and their requirements.[4] From some of the city's high schools of 2,000–3,000 students, it is not untypical for only 300 to 400 to graduate and fewer than 50 students to be enrolled in college the year following high school graduation. In fact, in a year subsequent to these observations, school records noted that only 5 percent of the students in the regular, non-magnet Carver High senior class went on to college.[5] These numbers do not reflect the range of student potential, nor are they solely an issue of poverty; poverty of information is as critical as financial poverty, because the former helps perpetuate the latter for many urban students.[6] The school's commitment to open opportunities for Latino and African American youth in the sciences and engineering converged with the growing understanding among their parents that it was not their children's ability that had prevented their attaining higher levels of education. SET students reported that their parents wanted them to be at a school that would take their abilities seriously; their parents, especially mothers, prompted many of these students to at least try this school.

The students' own expectations were more immediate, and those expectations became half of the key to the school's success. In interviews they shared their reasons for choosing the school. Overwhelmingly, they had thought SET meant "computers." They had imagined computers in classrooms and special computer labs; they had imagined learning to work through complex computer applications. In addition, they had envisioned cracking the mysteries of highly technical engineering equipment. Since most of the applicants had toured the school or had their admissions interview there, it was difficult to understand why they had not noticed the lack of facilities and equipment. One explanation offered was that the one piece of showcase equipment in an engineering lab classroom implied the presence of other equipment available but not on display at that moment. Several students also explained that anything had seemed more complex than what their middle school had to offer. One teacher suggested that the lack of congruence between the setting and students' expectations had made them trust their expectations because they could not believe a science and engineering specialty school could have so little equipment.

A senior African American boy said plaintively, "I had heard so much about the wind tunnel. I thought it would be big." (The wind tunnel was an expensive piece of lab equipment, purchased by the school and used, according to two of the teachers, in only one or two sets of lessons each year. The teachers felt that for the price of the wind tunnel, many supplies and pieces of equipment needed on a regular basis could have been purchased. Some of the teachers speculated that having those very basic supplies and instruments available on shelves and lab tables would not have signaled to visitors the technological image conveyed by situating a 12-foot-long wind tunnel in the middle of the lab. Others welcomed the purchase, thinking it would be the first of many that would give their students new opportunities for hands-on learning.) From an Anglo student who for a hobby collected and reviewed computer magazines and who attended a major engineering university after graduating from SET, "I expected hands-on science and better scientific equipment, more up-to-date computers and harder—harder *everything* [his emphasis]."

Others had heard that the school had a pedagogy particularly suited to scientific inquiry and technological experimentation. This included the perception that the magnet program would be structured to allow students to work at their own rate: "They said they'd assign all the work at the beginning of the semester and you could work at your own pace." Such a plan appealed to these bright students who were accustomed finishing class assignments well ahead of other students and then having to wait with nothing to do. An African American sophomore girl expressed an expectation that any teacher or magnet coordinator would love to hear: "I thought it would be *so challenging* that it would be like fun and games [emphasis hers]."[7]

Whether they came from middle school magnet programs in science and math, from "gifted-and-talented" middle schools, from regular neighborhood middle schools, or from Catholic schools, they came because they wanted a school to point them toward college. From what they could see when they arrived, the school did not live up to its advertising. To leave would mean being perceived back at their home school as having "failed," as having "not made it." To leave, after going to the trouble of transferring, would mean having to re-enter changed social groupings and peer relations at the beginning of high school in their neighborhoods. It could mean returning after places on sports teams and class activities had been claimed. The students described poignantly the *loss of face* they could expect if they gave up on SET; leaving would signal that they, and not the school, were deficient. Staying meant many unknowns; during that first semester, students could not quite decide whether they had made the right choice. Yet most of them stayed, and most of them succeeded. The story of their staying is a part of the different kind of bargain they struck with their teachers in the course of their first year or two in the school.

Realities

With so much promise and so much anticipation from the community and the district, what were the weaknesses the students encountered? First, there was a dramatic disparity between the quality implied in the list of required courses and the facilities in which those courses were taught. The students knew they would be taking a course load that included both more courses and more difficult courses than the district's regular graduation requirements. They would study four years of English, three years of history and social sciences, four years or more of both sciences and five of mathematics (far exceeding the one or two years of each required for regular students). Their studies would include a year of technical drawing (called engineering graphics in some years), a semester of technical writing, courses in engineering and technology (including computer programming). They would also study computer math, freshman-level introduction to engineering sciences, and a senior-level synthesis course in applied engineering and technology, which incorporated at the least a precalculus knowledge of mathematics. Additional electives in computer applications, independent projects in technology, and problems in engineering were available in most years, and students had to take two years of a foreign language. Most of the courses in the magnet program carried honors credit, on a parallel with the Advanced Placement and honors courses of the city's other high schools. Physical education, fine arts, and foreign-language study were provided through the regular, "neighborhood" part of the school, and SET students took those courses with the Carver High nonmagnet students.

Taking on this heady list of courses fresh out of middle school was a challenge the SET students eagerly awaited, even if they felt a bit overwhelmed once they arrived. It was not the difficulty of the academics that first daunted them. It was the contrast between the course titles and their setting. The school was housed in a building that had long been scheduled for renovation, but which kept being bumped in the renovation schedule by the district's other priorities. (It was not lost on the students nor the teachers that those "other priorities" were frequently school buildings in richer neighborhoods, not buildings even more dilapidated than this one.) The building was old and dimly lit; the classrooms were ill-equipped. The library had scant materials, journals, or reference volumes, particularly in the specialized fields the magnet courses represented. The science labs for the magnet courses, shared with classes from the neighborhood part of the school, had outdated equipment, with no lighted microscopes, for example. The labs were severely understocked, even for lessons and experiments required by the state or district for all students, not just those in magnet specialty courses. Rulers, simple weights and balances, scissors, tubing, glassware, and other basic nonconsumables were missing or in short supply. In addition, the SET classrooms were "upstairs," and the labs downstairs. Several SET science teachers, on days they were not scheduled into labs, taught in regular classrooms furnished with single-student desks, with no tables, sinks, or equipment for demonstrations. Computers were scarce, with the earliest ones received from corporate donors going first to the school's central (nonmagnet) administrative offices and to various teachers throughout the building. Later computers went to a single computer lab classroom assigned to the magnet program for programming courses, not for computer applications related to science or other classes. Computers available for instruction and daily student use in a variety of scientific courses were many years in coming and not evident when these observations were begun, although by then the magnet program had been in operation for more than ten years.

The equipment and technical shortages were not limited to the magnet specialty courses. Some classrooms had few electrical outlets; one had none. Teachers in English, social studies, and the natural sciences did not always have a copy of the basic textbook for each student (although by the state's textbook adoption law, every school must supply every student with "the book" for each subject). This problem was compounded in those advanced classes, in English and social studies in particular, that were not using state-adopted texts but that were furnished no other books nor a budget for creating course materials. Moreover, for those classes that were taken a year ahead by SET students (for example, with freshmen taking sophomore-level English), the district might issue the standard grade-level book rather than the books actually needed for the subject being taught. None of these teachers taught primarily from textbooks, but the books assumed importance as the only district-supplied instructional materials in those courses, beyond a few basic maps for history classes or dictionaries for English classes.

For materials appropriate to their class topics, levels of difficulty, and varied instructional approaches central to the magnet mission, teachers were on their own to try to acquire or produce what they needed, although they received no more than $50.00 per teacher per year (not per course, but per teacher) for instructional purchases. The teachers at this school were less able than their Pathfinder colleagues to sit down with donors and plan over time how corporate contributions would be coming into the school and how such enhancements could support a long-term plan for program design and acquisitions. At this school, donations came in through the principal, who felt pressure to allocate them throughout the building to the people who over many years had been "his faculty." Given the seventy-year history of inequitable distributions of resources in this city, by race and by neighborhood income, it is understandable that this principal would see any resource as critically needed to bolster his whole school, not just the magnet program. Contributions to this magnet program frequently came in the form of equipment; its dispersal beyond the magnet into "regular classes" could have been a significant help to the neighborhood program but often had little impact because it was allocated to faculty who had not requested it nor been trained to build their teaching around it. SET students frequently reported to the magnet faculty sightings of computers or other equipment sitting idle in other parts of the building.

What students found, then, behind the exciting name of the magnet program, was a very heavy list of courses, yet an underequipped building, regular single-teacher classes, insufficient books, and a scarcity of basic materials. They found a rather cheerless atmosphere and fellow students who were wondering to each other, "Why doesn't this look like a science and engineering high school?" And, "Why am I here?"

Building a Faculty

Their questions mirrored those of the researcher. The school was chosen for this study as an exemplar of a school whose organizational structure was designed to support authentic teaching and learning, to be more than a school that processed students through a canned sequence of graduation requirements. Initial appearances conveyed the sense that the organizational and administrative support was limited to the establishment of an advertisable magnet specialty and to assistance in attracting racially balanced groups of students. Such support, while essential, was not extended to the development and sustaining of an engaging, high-quality academic program. That initial assessment proved to be correct in its general outline. If it had proved to be definitive throughout the content and processes of the students' educational experiences, then I, like the students, might have been in "the wrong place." The bare facts about the administrative context of this school pointed to the likelihood that the teachers would feel caught between the pressure to comply with administrative definitions of the magnet specialty, which were quite limited, and the pressure to keep students in the program until they finished. Such a caughtness could easily lead to defensive teaching and a precarious balance between educational substance and appearance, between raising expectations just enough to attract students but not so high that their disappointment over the realities of the program led to early exit.

This potential for defensive teaching did not materialize because of the teachers themselves, the circumstances under which they came to the school, and the bargain they struck, over time, with their students to make this school a place for authentic learning. SET teachers were experienced teachers. Most had taught in more than one previous school, several for many years. Those who had taught in schools where administrators valued covering the curriculum in the standard textbook felt that that was not "real teaching." They had sought out a magnet school as a place where they could be involved in the ongoing constructing of a curriculum. Several had taught in schools that, while having no "special" programs, nonetheless had principals or faculties that valued creative teaching, teacher involvement in instructional program development, and attention to the children's learning rather than to finishing all the chapters in the book. Two had taught in other states, without centralized state curricula, and so had begun their careers in schools where teachers were presumed to be curriculum makers. Now that they were in Texas, with its centralized curriculum and textbook selections, they wanted to teach in a school that permitted teachers' expertise to help shape the curriculum. Prior to coming to this school, the SET teachers had for the most part worked as inventive, involved teachers. They came to a magnet school because they felt the need to be in a program where that model of teaching was the accepted professional norm, not the exception (Carlson and Apple 1998; Cochran-Smith 1991; Craig 1998). They were hungry for collegial interaction with other teachers also committed to creative teaching and to the ongoing creating and refining of curriculum. Individually they knew themselves to be "good teachers." They wanted to be a part of a school whose philosophy they shared. And they wanted to be in a school where teachers helped shape what was taught as they, as educators, continued to learn more about their subject and their craft.

From interviews it was clear that several of these teachers had left teaching situations in which they had felt de-skilled (McNeil 1986, ch. 7). They did not think that covering lockstep curriculum was real teaching; they did not think it fostered real learning. Even where they personally had managed to avoid the de-skilling pressure to cover the state-adopted texts and to keep all their classes on the same page, they had observed smart and dedicated colleagues who, once they had complied with this common practice, began to burn out and leave teaching or, worse, remain in the classroom but lose credibility with the students (McNeil 1986). The core faculty of SET, particularly the teachers in the academic, nontechnical subjects, had chosen this program because they thought it would give them permission to be the kind of teacher they felt real teachers to be. As Cheryl Craig discusses in her studies of teachers' professional identity (Craig 1998, 1999), teaching is not merely individual and technical work but is also situated in, shaped by, and determinative of the context of a particular culture of teaching.

The SET teachers sought out and at the same time worked to create a shared culture of teaching that supported their individual philosophies. The philosophy they shared centered on a desire to *open up knowledge and ways of knowing to their students.* They wanted their students, regardless of home situation or race or other factors, to leave high school able to think about complex issues, able to find information, and more important to contribute to the knowledge of their communities and their chosen field.

Bringing together a faculty with a shared definition of teaching was not the result of happenstance, nor was it the product of a single visionary administrator's staffing plan. Just as they helped create the curriculum of the school, the teachers had a role in constructing the faculty, recruiting colleagues who shared their philosophy. Once at SET these initial teachers had seen that the school could be even better if they could convince other teachers like themselves to join them. Having consciously left employment at a school that was de-skilling, or having taught in another state or in a local school where professional teaching was valued, these teachers were at little risk of falling into patterns of teaching artificial content for the sake of efficiency. They were even less likely to oversimplify course materials to maintain their own authority over class discussion. They became enthusiastic recruiters for like-minded faculty. They had come to this school precisely to reduce the conflict between "doing school" and living out their definition of what it takes to make school meaningful to students and to themselves. As one teacher said on more than one occasion, "if you can't teach at this school, you can't teach."

A personal goal of the teachers of the core academic subjects, and an official goal for the SET magnet subjects, was for teachers to engage students with new knowledge and with many ways of knowing. These teachers took great responsibility for enabling students to learn much more, and in much more depth, than they would have been taught at their neighborhood school. They also worked to initiate them into ways of knowing that would enable them to be creators of knowledge, not just passive recipients. They envisioned an ideal in which the students gained knowledge in their core courses and applied or extended it in new, inventive ways in their technology and engineering courses. The loose linkage between the core academic subjects and the magnet specialty courses made this cohesiveness problematic at times. But SET students did feel that they were expected to learn in ways that engaged them in both discovering and applying new knowledge. The ways the teachers managed to open new knowledge domains and new ways of knowing became critical given the many limitations of the school.

The congruent philosophy and definitions of teaching that created a shared professional culture among the teachers of core academic subjects (English, sciences, social studies, and, to a lesser degree, mathematics) framed for many of the students the fundamental nature of their educational experience at SET. But this congruence did not in every case extend to the teachers of the magnet specialty courses, many of whom came to the school with less experience with teaching and with children and so tended to center their courses on a specific technical domain. They were more visible in the public display of the school and yet less involved in shaping its dominant culture of teaching and learning. Some had come to teaching from industry or private practice; one had previously taught in parochial schools. Their courses, although required for the students and central to the magnet specialty, were not always integrated into the fabric of the school culture. A few of the technical courses were seen by academic teachers as of lesser intellectual quality, despite intimidating course names such as Applied Engineering Lab or Engineering Drafting or Advanced Computer Programming. Like many other named programs in the district, the technical parts of this magnet school carried labels that were not always matched in substance. Administrative support was limited to creating or approving the titles and appointing people to teach the courses; it rarely extended to working with the faculty to integrate the traditional core subjects and the magnet specialty courses into a unified school program.

The dissonance between the two groups of teachers was an ongoing source of confusion for the students and a source of frustration for the core subject teachers. It challenged the quality of the magnet specialty but did not override the overwhelming sense in this school that the teachers of core subjects were not likely to be de-skilled, were not likely to see the lack of direct administrative involvement as a reason to bring less than their best knowledge into the classrooms. They confronted the school's inadequacies, its fragmentation, and the lack of resources from the district with the determination to make the school the place they as professionals needed it to be if they were to be able to stay in teaching. Their efforts to forge an authentic learning experience for their students did not rely on sophisticated pedagogies, nor on abundant materials. Their efforts relied on their ability to engage their students and build enough credibility with them that the students helped them make the school work.

"The Blood of the Faculty. . ."

Working day after day in a setting renders commonplace the particulars of the material environment. Stepping out of the setting, for interscholastic science contests, for sports events with other schools, for district meetings held in other school buildings, reminded the SET teachers of what they lacked. A science teacher who frequently consulted to other public and private schools on designing and equipping school labs and who taught summer school at another school saw the utter inadequacy of his own lab space in light of these other schools, schools where his expertise was solicited in ways that it was rarely invited and only rarely heeded by those who controlled the budgets at his own school. He remarked on his classroom's lack of a gas supply, water, electricity, basic microscope slides, or even lighted microscopes (bemoaning that his "available light" microscopes were not old, but in fact too new to discard). He spoke about going into schools within the same district where halls were carpeted, the library "worked," and the "teachers have a decent chair to sit in." He spoke for all these teachers who knew that they were working under primitive conditions, yet responsible for creating a first-rate academic program in sciences and technology. He saw the school's importance to the district as symbolic; the district role in the school was, in his view, often limited to promoting and exploiting that symbolism. After sharing many reflections on his teaching, he concluded, "This is a good school because it runs on the blood of the faculty and the brains of the kids."

Mr. Walton was not engaging in hyperbole. He saw the teacher role at this school as vital, as life-sustaining, and, it is not too strong to say, sacrificial. The "blood" of the faculty meant more than long hours and hard effort; it also conveyed the way the faculty poured themselves out for the school. The faculty's part of the bargain to make SET a good school included extraordinary and sacrificial efforts by individual faculty and collective endeavors within and across subject departments. The individual efforts included creating an authentic curriculum from a mere skeleton of course titles and taking personal responsibility to overcome resource scarcities. The collective efforts extended from recruiting other faculty, to sharing scarce resources, to intentionally working to create a culture of academic quality and of caring for their students.

The Faculty's Part of the Bargain

Most of the teachers who came to the school in the early years were as seduced as the children were by its promise as a cutting-edge science school. They brought high expectations for their own practice and for the potential of the school to create wonderful futures for children of all races. They came committed to working together to create new courses and new programs. All knew they would be volunteering to do much more than a "regular" teacher taking over a regular teaching assignment; for most, that chance to create and to do so with like-minded colleagues was a large part of the attraction of the school. Yet none anticipated the rawness of the assignment, the abject scarcity of resources, or the continuing absence of any plan for the district itself to put additional financial and programmatic support behind their task. Like the students, the teachers had given up familiar school settings to take on this work. They were motivated to make the school a good place because they saw the need to be shapers of their own workplace, not passive employees, if they were to have a place to teach as they thought teaching ought to be. And, after meeting and working with the students, they expressed a determination to make the school worth the students' four years.

This is a state where individual teachers work on the basis of individual contracts; there is no collective bargaining. The subject-matter professional organizations are not a strong presence among teachers and districts. The SET teachers' responses to the inadequacies of the district's provisions for this school reflect both their histories as individual professionals and their desire for a collective response, for a professional community. They took on extraordinary individual burdens to create good courses, equip their classrooms, and create a climate of academic excellence for their students. In addition, they found creative ways to support each other and to create a shared culture that would engage the faculty and the students in a collective effort to make SET what the students needed it to be.

School Scarcities and Faculty Generosity. Any bureaucratic school system runs in part on rules and regulations: there is the presumption that a requirement implies resources. For example, if the science courses must have a certain number of days per week in the laboratory, then there should be laboratories. It is not uncommon, however, for urban schools to lack the resources to do those things they are *required* to do by their central office or state department of education. SET was no exception. The school lacked the basics to support a regular school program (the Carver High neighborhood curriculum), much less the enhancement materials to make the magnet a credible school for sciences and technology. As the teachers entered into the tacit bargain to make the school function, a typical first step was to make personal sacrifices in order to compensate for resource deficiencies.

The Library. The librarian embodied the determination of the faculty to make the program academically creditable. Ms. Hamner's goal was to make the library a "safe place" for students. "It may sound silly. What I have worked on is that the children feel free to come here and ask questions, whether they feel their questions are stupid or not. And they like to come. It's a friendly place." Making the library a safe place for personal questions and a place to discuss problems was not difficult; the librarian herself was caring and accessible. "I have to be; we have quite a few misfits who come in regularly." The library could be a welcoming space because of her presence.

Making it a safe place for inquiry, for research, and for finding help with their studies was far more difficult. The obstacles she faced were many: scarce materials, unreliable acquisition procedures, and virtually no relation between the contents of the library and the special focus of the magnet. Because her own vision for the school called for a "real library," the librarian took as her personal mission making this thin collection into something of value for the students. Telling of her efforts may only give fuel to those school critics who believe that schools do not need any more money, that the people in schools just need to work harder. But her efforts do need to be recorded because they exemplify the lengths to which the faculty went to compensate for the weaknesses of the school.

For the magnet specialty collection, Ms. Hamner pulled aside every visiting engineer or scientific corporate representative who entered the school to ask whether their company had any used or extra copies of engineering manuals, technical specification guides, scientific references or journals they could donate to the library. Many were eager to do so, enabling her over time to acquire a small but decent collection of texts, problems books, and references related to computers, engineering, sciences, and technology. While some references in fields like mechanical and electrical engineering remain standard over several years, others, particularly in fields such as space exploration, computers, and the natural sciences become rapidly obsolete. Being alert to new developments, and working with a faculty committee or professional engineers and scientists to keep her collection both current and sufficiently broad and deep, was not structured into the plan for the school. The cost of new books in these fields meant that the purchase of even a few titles would rapidly deplete her annual acquisitions budget for the entire school. Moreover, the district's central, generic purchasing for school libraries compounded her problems by her lack of authority over expenditures appropriate to this unique school program. She did not want the deficiencies of the library to be a hindrance to children's active learning or to the teachers' ability to make this a real science and technology school. An immigrant from Europe, she came to U.S. public schools with the high expectations she had been taught in her home country. Although dismayed by public resistance to adequate tax support for schools, she was not embarrassed to beg on behalf of the students to assure the addition of materials they needed.[8]

This librarian did not limit her energies to the needs of the magnet students and their teachers. She was eager for the students in the "neighborhood" part of Carver High to become readers and researchers. The library needed to have materials, and she wanted it to be a place where the use of those materials was eagerly modeled and shared. But her friendliness and interest were the only reliably abundant resources in the library. Fiction and the traditional nonfiction topics in high school libraries, particularly biography and history, had been in very short supply when she became the school's librarian. Few of her students had many books in their homes and no public branch library was nearby. She felt hampered by her inability to pull a book off a shelf when a student was searching for help with an assignment or just cruising the library bored but perhaps open to an enthusiastic librarian's extemporaneous review of a book. She wanted to be a teaching librarian, not the protector of a skimpy collection.

Ms. Hamner refused to be limited by what was missing. She set out in search of books. This tireless professional spent her weekends searching garage sales for used books. She became expert in timing her calls to schools that were closing or libraries that were weeding out their collections. She obtained the principal's permission to use library fine money to buy used paperbacks. She added her own money. And she unashamedly begged for the rejects from fellow librarians' shelves. Her library came to have abundantly stocked wire racks of paperback novels, perhaps more attractive to casual or reluctant teen readers than clothbound hardbacks in neat rows on the stacks. Her heroic sacrifices of weekend after weekend to stock the library from secondhand sales do not excuse the school district's failure to provide a basic library collection for every high school, nor did they come close to rectifying the district's long history of discriminatory resource allocations to a historically Black high school. Her efforts do, however, demonstrate in a poignant and visible way the faculty determination to make this school worthy of the students' investment of time and long bus rides.

A 40-Percent Solution. The state and district required that all secondary school courses in the natural and physical sciences be based in a laboratory for a minimum of 40 percent of class time—two days of each week. All of the science classes and the applied engineering classes fell within this requirement. The primary space assigned to lab science teachers, however, was traditional classroom space. "Lab" time meant moving to a laboratory classroom in another part of the building, shared by the teachers in the neighborhood part of the school. The distance from each teacher's classroom, the scarcity of supplies, the lack of control over budgets, the randomness of acquisitions, all mitigated against fulfilling even the minimum state requirement for laboratory-based instruction. It was not atypical for many science teachers in this district to substitute a teacher demonstration for student lab work or, more commonly, to stipulate that a worksheet (typically an exercise in labeling a diagram or working through calculations) was a "lab."

It was the SET teachers' ingenuity, dedication, and generosity that enabled the students to engage in laboratory experiments, to view lab demonstrations, and to get their hands into scientific operations. Perhaps the most impoverished setting was that for a course required of all ninth graders in the district, not just these magnet students: a course called Physical Science. The content for this course, as outlined by the district, was to include an introduction to chemistry and introductory physics concepts. (As will be discussed in the next chapter, it was more typically centered on algebraic functions for solving for one unknown, even though Algebra I is neither a prerequisite nor a corequisite for this course.) The district curriculum was straightforward: simple machines, basic molecular structure—a set of formulas, principles, operations, and terms that extracted from the processes of chemistry and physics those concepts that on the surface seemed "simple." One of these was a required unit on the basics of electricity.

The required curriculum called for students to learn the basics of circuitry and currents, including alternating and direct current, parallel circuitry, resistance, and other simple concepts in electricity well known since the 1800s. To do the required labs called for circuit boards, batteries, wiring, switches, light bulbs and sockets, and a base on which to secure various circuit configurations. None of these supplies was available in the school, nor were there budget accounts teachers could access to order them.

Ms. Bachrach had left a middle school where she had designed and equipped science labs for sixth grade through eighth grade (also an underresourced school in a high-poverty area). She was accustomed to being enterprising, and she was determined not to turn the electricity lesson into a worksheet activity, where students labeled lines and points of contact on a circuit diagram but never "turned on a light." She went to her neighborhood hardware store and purchased from her own cash all that she needed to make the circuit boards. She spread out the supplies on her driveway and spent a Saturday sawing boards for the bases, drilling holes for screws and switches, and cutting lengths of wire. She knew that if her students could not work with fundamental electrical principles, they could never engage intellectually in the more advanced electronics applications ahead in their applied engineering courses. A great irony of these lessons is that during her sequence of activities involving nineteenth-century electricity, a professor at a university in the city announced to the world his breakthrough discoveries in superconductivity. Only 5 miles from her campus, common understandings of the nature of electricity were being shattered. In this city of Nobel-worthy scientists, her students—students in a science and technology magnet school—would have been left in a Third-World science learning environment without her constant personal intervention.

The circuit boards were visible evidence of the less visible but constant vigilance with which she approached course requirements and materials. She also spent weeks rewriting the district's lab manual into a guide that was rich in ideas and that connected the processes and terminology of course topics into lab-based phenomena to be subjected to students' hands and problem solving. The "teaching for understanding" language would seem redundant to Ms. Bachrach; she would not recognize any other kind . Her rewrite of the lab manual provided students with opportunities to experiment, to elaborate on their findings, to make application of their growing knowledge of physical principles to unfamiliar phenomena. Consistent with the later theories of Harcombe, Perrone, and others, teaching for understanding of physical science in Ms. Bachrach's class was predicated on students' having opportunities to think through discrepant findings. She encouraged them to question lab results and to explain and compare their findings with those of fellow students (Cohen et al. 1993; Harcombe 2000; Perrone 1998). Because the district's own lab manual offered strict recipes for lab practice and presumed a convergence of answers aiming for accuracy, Ms. Bachrach had to create her own materials for student inquiry in order to bring students into what Sass calls "Thinking in Science" (Sass 1993). The creation of those materials was not something new, but was for her the heart of teaching.

What was different in this situation was that in the other states where she had taught, the paradigm of teacher-as-curriculum-maker had included time and budgets and a teaching schedule structured to support that work. In this magnet school, the need to create curriculum was accompanied by no com-

mensurate resources. Without Ms. Bachrach's creativity and energy, the centrally supplied lab manual would have been the curriculum for these students,
in complete contradiction of the mission of this school to prepare students for
college studies in the sciences, technology, and engineering. Like many of the
SET teachers, she seemed to have infinite patience with the students; she had
much less tolerance for oversimplified curricula, empty lab rooms, and a sys
tem that made it so personally difficult to be a good science teacher. That she
sustained a sense of caring, a contagious sense of humor, and a great enthusiasm for teaching science to these students is evidence of the wisdom of the collegial pattern of teacher recruitment to the school and of her own vision of
teaching and learning. The school's structure permitted, almost by default, her
methods of teaching but did not support and make provision for them.

Lab without Walls. Mr. Erickson wanted his biology students to move beyond
the simple taxonomies in the textbook; he wanted them to experience being a
field biologist. He wanted them to develop a keen capacity for observation and
for the diligence needed to learn from those observations. In the context of a
school highly focused on computers and machines, he wanted them to see the
life sciences as alive, as vital, as full of intellectual problems worthy of their
engagement. The program budget offered him few live specimens and no
growing space. Skimpy grass and asphalt surrounded the school building, an
urbanscape seemingly barren and totally inadequate for teaching the life sciences. Mr. Erickson would not be limited by those resources inside or around
the school. He made the students into the curriculum gatherers. They were
each to collect, draw, label, identify, and research one hundred different kinds
of leaves. The assignment seemed impossible, and student response ranged
from incredulous to resistant to fatalistic—this would be one assignment
where a bad grade would be inevitable. Many students left home before dark
and arrived back in their home neighborhoods long after dusk. The school
buses would not stop for leaf collecting. Few of these students had visited the
city's arboretum, and their childhood visits to parks had focused on play-
ground equipment, not foliage. For the first few days, students came in with
two or three leaves each, beginning with unnamed leaves from nondescript
"bushes" or leaves from the city's magnificent and ubiquitous live oaks.
Someone, in an attempt to be clever, would bring in a blade of grass or a leaf
from a house plant. Someone fortunate enough to visit a relative in the country would earn the envy of the class by dumping out a paper bag full of leaves,
only to find that researching leaves away from the whole plant posed unex-

pected difficulties and challenged the adequacy of the available botany reference guides.

Then one day a student would bring in leaves from a dozen vegetables from the grocery, or another would suddenly realize that his mother's garden was "botanical." Heated challenges to these as "not tree leaves" pushed the definitions of tree, leaf, and plant. These marginal specimens literally awakened the other students to the trees and plants around them—plants they passed everyday but never noticed. Suburban kids, who usually had the advantage on books at home, suddenly found that the mono-planting of suburban landscapes yielded less variety than one trip to an urban public park or abandoned lot. The inherent competitive nature of the assignment gave way at some point to a sharing of clues about large "finds" of trees: perhaps a student who had grown up visiting the city's major parks would organize a "leaf day" for several who had never spent much time outside their own neighborhoods. In a conspiracy against the teacher and his unreasonable assignment, they plotted to help everyone find and analyze one-hundred leaves.

The resulting co-constructing of the botany curriculum expanded the teacher's repertoire, giving him each year a larger and more complex map of the city's trees and made the students absolutely invaluable as curricular resources: they brought in the lab material. In the beginning, the teacher's personal library of botanical references and the information derived by a few students with access to a public library were the chief sources of research material for the students. Over time, the teacher worked with the librarian to acquire books in the biological sciences, including good references on leaf-bearing plants. The most impressive books, though, were the ones made by the students, with leaves, layout and lettering giving evidence of becoming alert observers, careful researchers, and articulate explainers of their specimens. "Forty-percent lab time" for this teacher meant reaching beyond the building for lab materials and being willing to stretch his own knowledge to encompass the wide variety of plant life his students discovered in this subtropical city once he taught them how to see it.

Teacher on Call. One teacher's classroom was exceptional for its abundance of books—novels, biographies, histories, political analyses. The room was always filled with books and with students. They came there, in their few "free" moments during the day, to read or talk or eat lunch. The room served almost as the de facto commons area for the magnet students. One day two boys came in joking and laughing, jostling each other and clowning. As they neared the teacher, one became very solemn and pulled a crumpled dollar bill from his jeans pocket. He handed it to the teacher, and said quietly, "This is a good one, Mr. Moore—I gotta keep this one," gesturing with the paperback he held in his other hand.

Mr. Moore lived on a teacher's salary. But he taught on a department store salary. He carried a second job in sales, which, although part-time, paid more than his teacher's salary. He used that second income, in part, to support his teaching. He bought books for his classroom. Students could check them out; if they wanted to keep the book, they had to bring in a dollar. "Even our poorest kids can give up a couple of sodas if they want a book badly enough. And paying for the book, even just paying a dollar, makes them feel it's really theirs. They own a book." He also used the extra money to buy gas for his car. He was notorious for announcing a trip to the university library with the caveat that "you have to get your own way home." One morning he came into class quite sleepy and admitted that he had had to drive students home from the university library, and "home" for this magnet school meant making the circuit of every quadrant of the city. When he was reminded that he had promised to get students to the library only if they could get their own way home, he replied, "Oh, I just say that so if anyone does have a parent or older brother with a car, they'll come get them. Then I won't have to take so many. But you can't leave a kid sitting in the dark on the steps of the university library." The lack of good public transportation linking all sectors of the city was a barrier external to the school, but one Mr. Moore was determined to conquer so that his students could learn to write real research papers, even at his own expense.

His generosity extended to subsidizing field trips (although students rarely knew he was the source of the funds), to summer trips to cultural sites outside the city, and to bail money for a student in trouble. One day, a police officer had called to tell Mr. Moore that his son had been arrested; Mr. Moore, who had no son, listened for the rest of the officer's explanation. "Sam Moore" needed to be picked up at the police station; he had been so terrified that his parents would find out that he had been arrested for shoplifting that he had given Mr. Moore's last name as his own. Mr. Moore paid the bail, then found this student the help he needed with the authorities and with his family. According to one girl, Mr. Moore gave her a "loan" to secure her dorm room so that she could accept admission to a prestigious college. This girl's mother had given up her own dreams of college when she found herself abandoned by the father of her three young children. She worked menial jobs and lived a spartan life in public housing so that her daughters could avoid her fate. Her

daughter's scholarship did not cover the housing deposit; Mr. Moore understood that like a ride home from a library, a modest loan at a strategic time
could make the difference between taking advantage of an extraordinary
opportunity or giving up.

Mr. Moore was also generous with time, available to be called about
homework questions at almost any hour. He knew many of these students
were in courses far beyond their parents' level of education, and they needed
to know there was someone they could call. He remained available to students
away at college, again because he knew that negotiating dorm life, registration,
an unfamiliar schedule, or even more unfamiliar culture was difficult for any
freshman. It was even more daunting when no one in the family had ever
attended college and there was no "cultural capital" in the family network for
surviving the university or for making the university years productive. Mr.
Moore served as a counselor, academic adviser, tutor, and referral service, linking current and former students to each other in order to foster the formation
of "cultural capacity" across informal networks of SET graduates (Anyon
1997a; Ladson-Billings 1998b; Valenzuela 1999).

His own class sessions were typified by lectures. There was no discernible
"pedagogy" other than well-researched and organized lectures, delivered in a
kind and conversational manner, from detailed notes drafted and redrafted over
years of reading, lecturing, and listening to his students' questions. He stayed
attuned to current political and economic issues and always connected past
events with the history his students were now living. As a teacher of both literature and history, he made thematic connections between the two. "Discussion"
emerged naturally out of the reading or in response to points in the lecture.

There was no wall between Mr. Moore's personal knowledge, the content
of his courses, and the invitation he posed to students to engage with him in
thinking about things. He was determined that students see the world as complex and understand that they were capable of the kinds of complex thinking
needed to understand it. His lectures and discussions with students are
marked by questions: "What else might explain Truman's decision to bomb
Japan?" "Why do you think it's so difficult to know the truth about the
Rosenbergs? Some people were terrified of Communism and the Russians.
Some people say the judge could have been anti-Semitic. The idea of the bomb
as a threat to us, not just a tool in our own arsenal, was very scary. How *can*
you best study these things? What else would you want to know?" Nothing was
presented unreflectively as a fact to write down and memorize. Nothing
appeared as a fragment out of context. There were no lists to mask the dynam-

ics of history as a consensus set of facts (McNeil 1986, ch. 7). "History" was our understanding of the past. He pushed his students in class discussion and in their research papers to look for more than one interpretation, to consider the source of the information, to ask many questions and to consider opposing interpretations. In describing Mr. Moore's teaching, one student blurted out, "He let us see his mind at work." His was compelling pedagogy.

In this diverse class, the students' families had not all experienced "American history" the same way. By presenting to the students the debates among professional historians, he modeled a willingness to consider all ideas within the class as well. As a result, his students developed both a greater acceptance for others' ideas and the skills to investigate and weigh various sources of information before accepting simple interpretations. The research papers his students wrote reflected an earnest curiosity about significant historical events, particularly those presenting a question of justice. One boy investigated historians' assessment of factors shaping President Jimmy Carter's presidency. A boy usually thought of as the class technology wizard wrote on what he called the "three P's of Nuremberg: people, power and psychology"; his analysis showed a strong grasp of Nazism, based on a wide range of sources (all of which he had to find outside the school itself). A Latino boy who had never before conducted historical research wanted to know more about Nixon's role in détente. He consulted U.S. State Department materials, newsmagazines, several British writers, and the journal *Foreign Affairs*—in his first-ever attempt at research. Along with several other students, this boy marveled at his own thoroughness and his insistence on reading more and more sources before he ventured his own interpretation. Mr. Moore's pattern of asking students questions just when they thought they had an acceptable interpretation, and his continuing to push and pose alternative ways of thinking, became the implicit model for his students when they began to make their way as beginning researchers. His combination of generous transportation, patient questioning, and insistence on rigor created the conditions necessary for these students, by their own accounts, to far exceed anything they had previously done for a history class. Such novice renderings as "the Warsaw Pack" in a student's paper gave evidence of their newness to the process and made even more impressive their willingness to tackle difficult and unfamiliar topics.

Mr. Moore's classroom was famous for having no electrical outlet; he surely must have violated some section of the fire code by stretching an extension cord across the hall to another classroom on those rare occasions when he wanted students to see a film or hear a tape recording. Only something as strong his passion for Franklin D. Roosevelt and the country's creative energy under this president's leadership during the Great Depression and World War II could make him bother to rig up the electrical cord. He wanted his students to hear Roosevelt's voice and imagine themselves, without a job or in the midst of a war, listening to the weight of Roosevelt's speeches and, reminiscent of Mr. Moore's own style, the fireside chats.

His teaching of the Roosevelt era provides a powerful contrast to the teaching of that same time period in the classroom of a teacher called Ms. Langer in one of the schools documented in *Contradictions of Control* (McNeil 1986, ch. 3). Ms. Langer kept control of the content of the curriculum by presenting history as lists of facts that "historians all agree on," permitting no discussion, stifling students' questions with witty one-liners, and asserting her authority and that of "the historians" by tolerating no ambiguity. As she lectured on the Great Depression of the 1930s, she taught the New Deal social legislation (social security, workers' compensation, federal deposit insurance, and other federal protections for workers) as institutions created "for you to appreciate." She saw student questions as challenges to her authority (and the authority of the consensus history she was providing them) and to the efficiencies needed for all her classes to cover all the chronology of American history by the end of the course. Her tight control over course content inadvertently led her students to question the veracity of her assertions, of this "school knowledge" she was dispensing (McNeil 1986, ch. 3). By contrast, Mr. Moore taught the New Deal laws and agencies as evidence that courageous and imaginative people could work together to solve social problems. He invited the class to discuss those issues that they saw as the persistent social problems of their day. One class entered into a passionate discussion about homelessness and the issues of who bore the responsibility for providing adequate housing for the poor. Another class identified the most critical social problems as the lack of ways for regular citizens to be effective in helping bring about and sustain peace. This discussion branched into lively comparisons between international "hot spots" and both the latent and visible violence in cities.

Mr. Moore's "Roosevelt" was not a dead icon, but rather a model for creative action. In his class, these students could discuss how they could expect to be shapers of policy, their dreams of inventing, a central idea in their technology labs, extending into their anticipated futures as citizens. This attention to the fostering of democratic ideas and active civic participation was significant because these classes included all the races and cultures represented in the city; all the students, not just one group, were hearing that they would be shapers of their communities and their country. This spirit of a collective citizenry mindful of particular histories echoes the discussion of citizenship identification cards in Ms. McDonnell's history class at the Pathfinder school. In both classes, the history course content was important not just to bring these students into analyses by leading historians but also to create a context in which their own contemporary histories could be examined. Both teachers brought in their own books, their intellectual depth, their spirit of inquiry. Both encouraged students to speak from their cultural and personal experiences, not just from what had been read in a standard text. It probably does not need to be said that for his memorable study of Franklin Roosevelt, Mr. Moore personally supplied both the Roosevelt tapes and the extension cord.

In interview after interview, students and teachers credited Mr. Moore's accessibility, his dedication to the students and his generosity to the overall sense of shared mission within this school. His capacity to underwrite school expenses was in many ways unique, but his willingness to make personal sacrifices on behalf of his students and in support of the vision of the school that had first attracted them did not differ significantly in kind from the efforts of many of his colleagues who were determined to make SET worth their own and their students' four years there.

Time to Read a Book. Ms. Foster matched Mr. Moore's energy and passion for teaching and did not stint on personally providing classroom resources. She had taught in other high schools and at one time left this school to teach in a more traditional high school, but she returned to SET because of the students and their determination to learn. (She had reported to her SET colleagues that the parents at the other school refused to believe their children could fail, and so did not support her high academic standards for all students—even those with prominent parents; she saw at SET a chance to set those high academic expectations for children too often excluded from them.) She too dipped into her wallet to buy books for her class. She spent hours creating literary studies and writing assignments for her students. These students came to the school having passed the admission standards but admitted—in large numbers—that they had never read a whole book. Their middle school English classes had been taught from large anthologies (the state textbook) comprised of brief selections or passages abridged from longer works. Ms. Foster knew that SET students would not be served well if they were admitted to colleges, but arrived at college utterly unprepared to enter into class discussions of literature, philosophy, and the arts. Her course curricula were in a constant state of development. After her seniors studied a novel, she analyzed their learning and, on the basis of their weaknesses, revised her freshman or sophomore course to assure that future seniors would be stronger in their writing or in their capacity to analyze text or write critically about literary themes.

Ms. Foster was praised by the students for pushing them to find out what they could do. They had come to this school expecting to put all their energies into technical and scientific courses; English, history, and math were areas they thought they had already mastered. Ms. Foster's wide-ranging knowledge of literary selections, her persistent focus on what students could do when they engaged with that literature, and her determination that all SET students would leave the school as fluent writers and thinkers gave reluctant teen readers and writers no place to hide in her class. Interviews with students reflecting upon their SET experience reveal a sense of surprise and gratitude that this teacher met each student with compelling and personalized reading suggestions, with a stubborn insistence that they actually read, and with patient attention to their individual development.

Ms. Foster, like Ms. Bachrach, built her course from her own professional sense of her subject. She had a strong grounding in what constitutes good reading and writing. She had an exceptional talent for linking her curricular knowledge with an understanding of each student. She built and rebuilt her courses to assure that each student left the school fully prepared, not only to succeed in English classes but also to be able to hold their own as thinkers.

Like Ms. Bachrach, she created this level of excellence with little in terms of material resources from the school or district. In fact, hers were the academic courses least likely to have even the standard textbook, since her courses were among the English courses that SET students took a year ahead of the district's course sequence in English. At the beginning of a new school year she often received the books appropriate for her students' grade level ("ninth grade"), rather than for the content of the course. For her senior course she used a book not used by any other teacher in the district, an anthology of literary selections organized by historical periods across an international, mostly European, literature. She was proud that for her diverse students this book challenged them with literature by German, Polish, and Chinese writers. "Chekhov is in it—it's not an easy book." She saw her seniors as avid readers, "the seniors read just incredible amounts in the last two years." But her juniors were "basically nonreaders. You have to force them to read outside the class." She struggled over their resistance to reading, avoiding simple diagnoses but raising questions about the skimpiness of their reading assignments in the first eight grades, the likelihood that their parents were nonreaders, and the powerful draw of computers. She declined to ascribe nonreading to socioeconomic factors alone, suggesting that except for a lack of English language in some of the homes, she suspected that economic status was not a primary factor in whether these students had developed an identity as readers. She was very concerned that in addition to the pull of computers, videos, and television, there was the stark fact that so many of them told her that prior to coming to this school they had never read a whole book or been taught to write about even a short story.[9] She had seen reading and a strong background in literature vary from class to class; the trend was toward nonreaders, but she was unwilling to concede that this was a trend that was irreversible. In the meantime, she took personal responsibility for connecting these students to print, to great literature, and to their own growing fluency as writers.

When asked what they learned in her classes, Ms. Foster's students always began with her determination to help them learn to *ask* questions. She nurtured in them a stance of inquiry into literature but also into institutions, including this high school, and into the political and social aspects of the literature being read and the policies that governed their lives. She was an advocate for their general education and saw literature as a means to engage their minds with significant ideas. She said more than once that these students' lives were heavily shaped by their socioeconomic circumstances. She saw the "economic" part of that as remediable. More problematic were the social issues, including race, prejudice, and powerlessness. She used literature as a means to examine "voice" as not only a literary device but more importantly as personal and collective expression. If she discovered that a student felt no connection between that student's own voice and the assigned literature, then Ms. Foster would seek out, and photocopy at her own expense, a selection more appropriate for that student, not as an "alternate" assignment but as a door into the shared studies of the class. She broadened her own reading lists and her selections for whole classes as she sought out titles that could connect individual students' lives with literature.

These sacrifices of time, money, and energy are indicative of the contributions of many of SET's teachers as they tried individually and collectively to overcome the particular deficiencies or barriers they saw to the school's capacity to deliver on its advertised purpose. For many of these teachers, the financial and time commitment were the silent renewables in each year's contract, year after year. It is somewhat ironic that the teachers who made the greatest personal sacrifices to make SET live up to its name were typically these and other teachers in the core, nonmagnet, nontechnical subjects.

Engineering a Curriculum

The magnet courses in technology, engineering, and applied sciences provided the official "draw" of the school. The SET program had no parallel in the city or in the state. The advantages of teaching wholly unique courses were enormous: there was no state-adopted textbook, no limits on format or content, no prior weaknesses to overcome. Many of the teachers who joined the faculty in the early years were excited to be creating a program, a school-within-a-school. They had expected to work together across the traditional and the specialized disciplines to create a unified precollege program around the sciences and technology. The lack of time to plan the school and the continuing lack of resources and facilities long after it opened were among the factors mitigating against such a collective creation of a unified, integrated curriculum. Yet they managed to have enough strength in these courses that many students found within them the skills and opportunity to explore significant concepts and topics in the sciences, in several engineering areas, and in computer-based applications. While most of the graduates of this school did not pursue engineering majors in college, all graduated with extensive exposure to technical fields and to ways of applying scientific and mathematical knowledge to problem solving.

Despite initial program-building meetings and an occasional faculty retreat in the earliest years of the school, the curriculum in the magnet specialty courses tended to develop as a collection of individual courses, rather than as parts of a highly integrated program. One reason for this was the tendency to teach the technical and applied sciences courses on the basis of available personnel. Individuals brought in from industry or from technical professions might be able to teach a variation or specialty within a particular domain; they were not necessarily expert in how that specialty fit within a larger technological education. And they were frequently even less knowledgeable about how their technical specialty related to the traditional academic courses. There was also a higher turnover among these people, including the built-in turnover in the upper-level applied science and engineering course whose teachers were on a rotation from a major technology corporation. Reliance upon a highly contingent pool of personnel resulted in most years in a loosely federated group of technical courses and academic subject courses, rather than a coherent "school." The teachers of the technical courses had the task of creating something of quality out of little more than a course title.

Technically Writing. The magnet program called for a course on technical writing, but the district had no materials on this subject beyond one or two courses at vocational high schools. The instructional paradigm in those courses, according to one teacher, centered on writing about technical specifications or technical drawings, the kinds of writing that might be expected from a technician rather than a scientist or engineer. Writing to explain or analyze processes, writing to convey highly complex information, writing to persuade a technical audience were goals the technical writing teacher at SET had developed that went beyond the initial outlines for the course. As an English teacher with a strong interest in the history of science, Mr. Roberts had eagerly taken on the course, but he found over time that because it sat between the traditional English courses and the new courses in engineering and technology, it risked being viewed as the lowest course in either field. His goal, by contrast, was that it be the bridge between the core subjects and the magnet courses. When first invited to teach the course, he had taken time to examine curricula and texts from technical drawing courses from the community college, from vocational high schools, and from university engineering departments. Like his colleagues, he devoted his personal time to designing the course in its initial year and to upgrading and adapting it over the years. He was philosophical about the time he had invested in this course. He had neither expected nor received financial support or paid time from the school to create the materials, to visit other school sites, or to consult with colleagues about the link between this course and others. He did take pleasure in having been able to take his knowledge of the history of science and apply it to his English teaching. He tried to develop writing assignments that incorporated the processes of design, observation, and problem solving inherent in the work of engineers.

Most of his students had come to the school having written only formulaic pieces in answer to a strict writing prompt ("What is the main idea of this story? Give three supporting examples for your statement of the main idea") or "creative" writing that encouraged children to write a poem or a piece of descriptive prose or stream of consciousness reflection. According to the students, they had virtually no experience writing in science classes or writing informational pieces whose content *mattered* to an audience. Mr. Roberts organized the semester so that students moved from writing based on careful observation of objects, to writing to explain a process, to researching a technical process and creating both written and visual explanations of the purposes and mechanics at work. He required an oral presentation from each student after he saw that even those who were developing as writers stumbled over their words when they were asked to talk about their projects. Over several years, he acquired sufficient computers and enough knowledge about computer drawing and editing that he increasingly based much of the course on computer-drafted writings and computer-generated images to accompany them. He was proud that this course reflected his personal effort and credited his students over the years with helping teach him about computer applications at the same time he was helping them become good problem-solvers through writing.

Introducing Engineering. The freshman applied engineering lab was a hybrid course, introducing students to simple mechanics, to calibrations and gauges, to weights and measures, and to engineering concepts typically limited to mechanical engineering. The content of the course depended entirely on who taught it in any given year. The original outline of the course had been derived by the planners of the school, but it presumed equipment that never materialized and a common level of preparation among the incoming students. The freshmen coming into this course were highly motivated to learn complex operations, to conduct experiments, to becoming expert on high-tech equipment—generally, to become immersed in the advertised specialties of this magnet. Some of their expectations were met through this course. Depending on the teacher, many of them designed and carried out their first experiments in mechanics in this course. Others learned precision of weights and measures and observation. If the teacher was inventive, the course included hands-on activities and open-ended projects calling for student ingenuity. Unfortunately, students came to the school with widely varied backgrounds in mathematics and in sciences. Some of the concepts they needed for this course were just being taught to them in the concurrent physical science course or in their ninth-grade math course, generally geometry. Because the math and science teachers did not plan their courses in concert with each other or with the teacher of this introductory engineering lab, the issue of students' prerequisite information led some teachers of this course to rely heavily on lectures and teacher demonstrations.

This class did have the luxury of lab space, but there was little usable equipment. A few highly visible and expensive pieces of equipment, including the 12-foot-long wind tunnel, dominated the budgets and the space. The teachers had to improvise to do even teacher demonstrations of some concepts. Over time, corporate donations of equipment became more available, but there persisted gaps between what was needed for developing the concepts of the course and what various donors had to give.

Advancing in Engineering. The senior-level applied engineering course had the advantage of building on the students' previous years of math, computers, and science courses, as well as technical drawing and computer graphics. Students brought a great deal of knowledge to this course and, by this point, had disciplined study skills for tackling complex topics. As we have seen from the introduction to Mr. Beshara, this class did not, as its name would imply, take place in a technology laboratory. The lack of supplies, equipment, and texts caused this teacher, on loan for two years from a major computer company in the Northeast, to build his course around math and physics problems central to mechanical engineering.

An engineer who studied the curriculum of the school, herself a former structural engineer for a naval subcontractor, noted that mechanical engineering dominated the applied science and technology courses. She was surprised to see the lack of environmental engineering or biotechnology, given the industries and needs in the community, or the basics of electrical engineering, which have application across a wide range of technologies. She speculated that "the teachers are unaware of what is really going on in the field of engineering today," or "the teachers assume that the mechanics is easier for the students to understand than most fields of engineering," or that "mechanical engineering and its fundamentals are the easiest for the teachers to teach, test and grade" (Wallace 1994).

The students would question the latter interpretation. Mr. Beshara's tests consisted of a small number of well-chosen pencil-and-paper problems, each of which required a student to figure out what concept was being represented, what practical problems needed to be solved, what formulas might apply, and only then how to solve the particular mathematical operations. For example, during class Mr. Beshara might present the students with six different ways to calculate the points of downward thrust on a trestle, or the upward pressure points on a structure designed to remain stable while bearing varied amounts of weight along its length. Only rarely would the students have had physical objects with which to create and test models, to try out alternative configurations, or to hypothesize about the effects of using varied materials. With their teacher or a classmate at the board, they would have worked through a number of examples of formulas and chalk (or pencil-and-paper sketches) over several days. Key concepts required careful application and precision of measure. But generally Mr. Beshara tried to foster thinking. He invited students with variant procedures for solving the problems to write them on the board and explain them step by step. Comparing varied approaches was, in his mind, the only way to introduce students to the kind of intellectual teamwork central to engineering; working with others to solve problems was more of a goal for him than traditional measures of accuracy. He taught them to represent their final calculations as a relationship (the multiplication of several factors, a ratio, and so on), rather than a precise mathematical answer down to the *nth* decimal point. He felt that grading for that kind of accuracy tended to over-shadow attention to the means by which students reached their solutions.

By the time students made it to his class in their senior year, they brought a level of assurance and confidence, albeit a skeptical confidence, because even reaching this level in the program represented a milestone. By senior year, many of their friends at their home schools had dropped out of school or elected to take a light senior load. They knew their opportunity to study with "Mr. B." was exceptional. These students hovered over calculators and dia-grams rendered in sharp pencil lines. They designed structures that met the specifications Mr. Beshara presented in the problems, or they analyzed struc-tures as that were being subjected to various pressures, weights, and material strengths. They wrestled more than once with "moment": the product of a quantity and its perpendicular distance from a reference point (from the *American Heritage Dictionary*), the rotation produced in a body when force is applied (from a student's notes), and torque ("and you'd better know what that is, because otherwise you won't get these rotation problems, and Jeanie, I know you know this so would you please make sure your friends there get it and don't just do a bunch of math calculations without really knowing what we're doing here. I'm not looking for the exact right answer. I want to know if you can draw that structure and figure out what the torque is when all you know is these other dimensions. And I know you can do it because you drew it up here just yesterday. And if we had a place to set these up as working mod-els, you know that would be the right thing here. But instead I have just copied these problems out of my old college mechanical engineering text. So, you don't get to build the models, but hey, look, you're doing college level stuff here. You should be very proud. So let's make sure everybody gets this by tomorrow. I'll be in my office if you need some help, all right?")

Mr. Beshara had come to the school on loan from his company; with their children grown, he and his wife had made the temporary move across the country, intrigued with the idea of teaching engineering concepts to inner-city students. He was delighted by the diversity of the students, by seeing minority girls frequently make the highest grades in this highly technical class, and by the camaraderie of the students as they helped each other through this totally unfamiliar territory of struts and balances, trestles and beams. But he never accepted the discrepancy between the name of the school and the lack of resources in the very fields it named. Upon arriving and finding he would have no lab and the students no books, he carefully drew up a list of essential books and supplies and took it to the principal. Unlike the veteran teachers, he fully expected the principal to place an order and have the missing supplies delivered promptly. He repeated the principal's response to everyone he met: "What's this? We can't order these. This would be expensive. We don't have money for books on engineering. That's why we're glad to have *you* here. You'll just have to do the best you can." Mr. Beshara never gave up on the students and, in fact, sent for his old college texts and castoffs from his friends' engineering lab manuals and proceeded to walk these students through complex structural problems. The naval engineer who observed that the school emphasized mechanical engineering to the exclusion of most other forms of engineering might have traced some of that narrowness of focus to the failure to build over time a cumulative collection of books, manuals, lab equipment, and manipulatives in the engineering and technology courses. Without an assembly (even a random collection) of such materials, the engineering courses, particularly at the advanced level, were highly dependent on concepts that could be operationalized with pencil and paper. And they were equally dependent on the expertise of those who rotated in to teach them.

Computers and Special Problems. After the school had been open for several years, the computer teachers seemed to be the only applied sciences and technology teachers with adequate equipment, although closer inspection showed limitations even there, in software, printers, and capacity. The computer laboratory accommodated both the introductory and applied or advanced courses, with a computer for every two students at first, and later even more computers were added. The problem with this course was that unlike computer math courses that existed at the time in several suburban high schools, this course was designed as a computer-programming class, sometimes called by that name and in other semesters labeled "computer science." The materials were aimed at teaching students to learn to program in a certain format: BASIC in the early years, and a series of other programming languages after that. The goal of learning to program a computer superseded learning how and why to use computers. The computer teachers, like their colleagues in the other subjects, spent an inordinate amount of time outside of school, including taking courses at their own expense or returning to their former schools to be updated by colleagues, in order to create a computer-programming course appropriate for SET students. Programming that required higher math could not be taught until senior year, yet for students to use computers in their courses they needed these courses earlier.

So long as "computers" was a freestanding set of skills, these teachers carried the solitary burden of creating the programming activities that would mesh with their students' current skills and laying the groundwork for the facility they would need with computers in their upper-level science and engineering courses. The teachers developed instructional packets that enabled students to pace themselves as they worked through the programming activities and then to self-schedule examinations. The most elementary computer course covered balancing equations, learning to code data, and learning to "decode." By the third computer course, if they had reached this level in their math classes, they were using the computer to work with functions.

Over time, programming for the sake of learning to program would recede in importance and give way to a wide range of computer uses, from graphics and data presentation to the kinds of operations in mechanics taught by Mr. Beshara through formulas written on a blackboard. The computer lab hummed with purposeful activity in the second- and third-semester computer classes. The introductory course seemed to lack a coherent focus for either the students or the teachers, with kids who were computer whizzes thoroughly bored with BASIC and kids new to computers utterly baffled by both BASIC and the need to learn it. When compared with the advanced computer applications courses observed in suburban high schools, these courses seemed disjointed and aimed more at sitting in front of a computer than learning how and under what circumstances a computer might be a helpful tool in applied sciences and engineering. On the other hand, when compared with these same students' likelihood of learning computer applications at their home school, these classes, created by teachers who had little to work with except programming manuals and simple freestanding computers, captured students' attention and gave them a new set of skills. The creaky line-printers, long out-of-date, hampered producing print representations of students' work, but such a limitation paled before the chance to sit at a computer. Concerns that computers and a technological mind-set would overwhelm all other forms of learning and discourse (Bromley 1998, 18) may have been unfounded at this school precisely because for so many years, the available computer-based technologies were inadequate.

Other courses in applied sciences, technology, and engineering were taken by upper-level students depending on available faculty. The advanced graphics, special problems, and applied engineering courses were generally of one-semester length. Virtually all were taught by people new to the classroom; some were experienced in industry and others were fresh from related graduate-level studies. Again, these courses were idiosyncratic to the teacher and sometimes to student demand. Students who came expecting a great deal of hands-on science and applied mechanics became obsessed with robotics. If they could build a robot, then they themselves could create a piece of the school's missing technology. The special problems course developed for a time into a robotics course; scientists and engineers were brought in to talk about or demonstrate robotics. The principal worked with the students, the teacher, and magnet coordinator to secure some of the materials and funding needed for students to build and operate a simple robot. Sometimes a highly technical focus such as robots produced in students a real understanding of complex concepts and sometimes it devolved into random activities that did not add up to much student learning. The highly situational nature of these courses was characterized year after year by high potential, occasional brilliance, and at the minimum a chance to engage with fellow students in a hands-on activity.

Such a focus was not consistent. Many semesters, students complained that these courses seemed random in content, poorly planned, and under-resourced. Some students used them to pursue their own passion for a particular scientific or technology application, while others drifted in parallel to the drift of the course. Their Special Problems teacher might have expressed a frustration similar to the students', having been hired to teach in a first-rate magnet school for technology and sciences and having been left to create a course with little budget or time to take students off-site to see actual engineers and computer experts tackling the "special problems" of their average workday. Somewhat marginal to the faculty culture shared by the teachers of the core academic subjects, the Special Problems teacher was less likely to be as involved with the students' total educational experience at the school, but he, like those teachers, did have to be involved in inventing the curriculum if there was to be one.

Happy Hour. SET was more than the sum of "the blood" of individual teachers. A strong collegial faculty culture was forged in the connecting of the individual efforts into collaborative strengths that in many ways helped compensate for the scarcities. This collaborative strength, as will be seen in chapter 6, became a vital source of resistance to the coming standardization policies. The magnet school faculty culture, as an entity in its own right, became clear when after many weeks of patiently answering the questions of a daily observer, two of the teachers said almost in chorus: "If you really want to get to know what we do here, meet us for Happy Hour." This was a puzzling invitation; these did not seem to be teachers with time to stop at a bar on their way home. "We don't mean after work. We mean 7:00 A.M. That's when we meet at Kinko's [a twenty-four-hour photocopying store]. You'd be surprised how many of us meet there every morning before school. We have to have some place to copy the things we'll need for our class." And before the question could be posed, Ms. Foster supplied the answer, "Yes, we pay for our copies out of our own pockets. But believe me, it's what you have to do if you want your students to have anything good to read."

The Happy Hour symbolized the collective effort that went beyond the individual contributions these teachers made to the school. Quite accidentally, one day Mr. Moore and Ms. Foster had stopped by the same copy shop on their way to school. For her classes, Ms. Foster produced collections of poems, extended the range of diversity and interest levels in the short stories she taught, and developed new exams based on what each class had learned about the literature. More important, she made special trips to the copy shop to photocopy a particular story for a student having trouble with the class assignment or perhaps already beyond the class's discussion and ready for a related reading. Mr. Moore copied materials for his classes and also often brought in things for students, for other teachers, and for the program as a whole. The English, history, and science teachers formed the nucleus of the Happy Hour group, but on any given morning, any SET teacher might be found there juggling a styrofoam cup of coffee, a stack of papers, and a stapler.

It is scandalous that in a rich city, classroom materials would be paid for by underpaid teachers working an extra hour before school. The SET teachers were not martyrs, nor were they seeking praise for their efforts. They were acting on a shared commitment to bring academic quality to their students. The Kinko's Happy Hour created a rare moment for sharing stories of their students, ideas for the courses, and strategies for overcoming continuing scarcities. The photocopier donated to SET by a local corporation sat in another part of the school. They had permission to use it, but rarely had the time and often did not have sufficient paper.[10] Hurried trips to the copy machine at school did not build the shared culture found in that 7:00 A.M. Happy Hour.

When the standardization reforms would, in a short period of time, deskill these teachers, it is the added benefits of their generous contributions—not any weaknesses in their practice—that would be "reformed" away.

The collective efforts of the teachers to make the school work went far beyond such informal meetings, but they were co-created by the teachers within the school's structure, not initiated by the structure or administrative leader-ship of the school. The teachers had anticipated that as a specialized faculty, they would meet regularly to review and adjust the program and to discuss its relation to the students. The observed teachers recalled various styles of faculty meetings during their tenure at the school. Early collaborative ventures had been eclipsed by the pace of the work and by the working relations established by the succession of magnet coordinators. One coordinator had been highly collaborative, establishing the expectation that the faculty would work as a group to design and maintain the magnet program (not just their individual courses). One coordinator was described as "starting each meeting with the appearance of being collaborative but actually just doing everything himself."

The magnet coordinator during the period of these observations pro-posed to a local corporate donor that this company fund a two-day retreat during the summer in order to bring the faculty together to reassess the cur-riculum, to discuss how and whether the program was meeting students' needs, and to consider very carefully the culture of the school as the students were experiencing it. The corporate donor was enthusiastic: he proposed funding the retreat and supplying the management expert on organizational efficiency to conduct it. The potential donor declined to make a contribution that did not come with the efficiency expert. The request was withdrawn. The coordinator would later recall the parallel between the donor's ties of funding to efficiency and the rationales behind the states' imposition of standardized reforms.

But the lack of a retreat did not diminish the collective efforts already typ-ical of this faculty working to make the school an educational one for their students. The teachers were very generous in sharing students and time. The small number of students and the hopes for coherence across the subjects made most of the teachers very willing to be mutually supportive of the need to be flexible, especially when students were highly engaged in a project. The scarcity of materials also prompted the sharing of items personally purchased, of items carefully stowed to prevent losses but willingly shared with someone equally respectful of the need to avoid breakage and loss. The forced sharing with the neighborhood part of the school in the labs made those spaces "no man's lands," with no one responsible for storage and inventory. Sharing among colleagues who purchased and stashed pipettes or tubing, measuring gauges or circuit boards assured that emergencies were covered.

Teachers also gave each other support in dealing with the school's admin-istrative context. Some teachers found the principal and operational procedures direct barriers to their work. Requests for supplies and equipment would be routinely ignored, only to be followed by new requirements to fill out requisitions that would also be ignored. Other teachers appreciated the principals' public backing of the magnet program and his general hands-off management style. Still others found his management intrusive and arbitrary. The role of the principal became a critical component once "reforms" were underway (see chapter 6), but prior to that time, those teachers who were able to elicit the principal's support leveraged it on behalf of those who could not.

Shared Values and High Visibility. The core faculty worked to create a shared ethic. A part of this was creating an ethic of mutual support and caring for students, and a part of it was fostering a climate in which ethical concerns could be raised regarding practices within the school. This became critical to the survival of their program during the "reforms" described in chapter 6, but it surfaced long before in the use of resources and the public promotion of the School for Science, Engineering, and Technology. In a context of scarce resources, every expenditure is eyed with interest; those expenditures that take dollars away from basic needs are especially closely watched. For the science and technology teachers struggling to buy or borrow basic lab instruments, an especially frustrating expense was the wind tunnel, which they saw, rightly or wrongly, as having been purchased for its visual impact on visitors to the school. (When questioned about whether there might have been other, more educational motives behind the purchase, they would not even entertain the question because of the symbolic importance this purchase had assumed in their feelings about the material context of teaching at SET.) The wind tunnel could be used for student experiments, but only rarely. More troublesome was the purchase of an expensive rooftop weather station that students and faculty could *not* use. (The initial rumor was that this equipment had been purchased with donor funds, but other personnel said it was purchased with the school's funds from the district. The silences regarding the sources of funds and purposes of use, even if both were completely legitimate, added to the sense of unease among faculty working so hard to compensate for institutional scarcities.) Having no voice in the larger expenditures and having no way to leverage very basic supplies was dispiriting to the teachers, and several said that only the close cohesion among the faculty helped mitigate their frustrations both with the procedures and with what they viewed as the disregard for their expertise and students' needs.

Another contextual dilemma involved students directly. For the Special Problems in Engineering and Technology course, students had been encouraged to design and build an experiment to be launched in space on a NASA shuttle. Numerous problems emerged, including disjuncture between the school calendar and space launch schedules. The project took much longer than expected to design and early designs were not operational. The project included both a biological experiment (testing the effects of space travel on certain organisms) and the mechanical/structural component: the design and functions of the casing and other components to house the experiment. The specifications for design quality and safety had to conform to the safety protocols space vehicles. Any leak or other weakness could jeopardize not only this experiment but also adjacent experiments and even the space craft itself. Unlike many experiments in which school children participate in analyzing plant seeds or other specimens that were a part of a larger experimental project designed and overseen by adult scientists and engineers, this experiment would be freestanding and thus dependent on design and construction capacities of this group of students. The school employed a consulting engineer to assist the teacher and the class. The students reported later that the consultant had actually built much of the unit and set up the experiment. A group of students who had been in the class were invited to Florida for the shuttle launch; the launch was scrubbed and they returned to school.

Several classes of SET students did work on various initial phases of this project prior to the hiring of the outside engineer. They had learned many new things about not only the experiment but also the potential problems that arise in collaborative ventures and in enterprises in which both expertise and materials are in short supply. They and others saw close-up the conflict inherent in making the school look good at the cost of candor about what part students (and paid consultants) played in the project. Many of the teachers were distressed that such activities undermined their attempts to create a shared set of values in the school. Others felt it trivialized the work that students had actually done by turning the project into a public relations piece done by adults, rather than an opportunity for students to work on problem solving in the real world of engineering. Still others were grateful their students had had a firsthand experience in this cutting-edge venture. Having a group of teachers with which to discuss the ramifications of such events gave members of the faculty greater strength when they were later faced with curricular reforms they saw as highly questionable.

The collective faculty culture extended to many activities beyond individual faculty duties. For a few years, SET, although a science and engineering magnet, had no Junior Engineering and Technology Society chapter. JETS sponsors competitions and engages students in engineering games and opportunities for independent and group projects. When no science or technology teacher stepped forward to serve as the faculty advisor, an English teacher took on the job. JETS, with its regional and statewide activities, came to supplement students' creative learning by providing a continuity for experimental activities even in those years when the applied engineering and technology special problems courses were not strong. The teachers, already teaching an extra hour per day, took on Model United Nations, debate, and other activities so that these students could build the skills and precollege resumes they would need upon graduation. In a regular high school, these duties would be compensated and spread across a larger faculty. At SET the core teachers took on all these activities so that their students would not feel they had missed too much by being bused into SET.

Faculty and Race

The faculty dealt not only with resource scarcities and a diverse and unevenly prepared group of students but also with the persistent underlying issue of race, given the role of the school in the desegregation plan. A part of the faculty strength was the collective commitment to desegregation and to providing a high-quality education for students of all racial and cultural groups. Students could see that faculty viewed racial and cultural diversity as a strength and as a motivator behind their work, a component essential to academic excellence. Students were asked directly whether they felt any one group was privileged at this school, whether the teachers or students held higher expectations for one group over another, and whether students of any one group received more help or attention than any other. The students, boys and girls, Blacks and Hispanics, Anglos and Asians, expressed surprise at the question. Their immediate answers, and their responses after some reflection, were unanimously "no." They saw the faculty working together to assure that regardless of the quality of a student's previous schooling and regardless of gender or race, all of these students would graduate and would be fully prepared for success in college and the professions. Many of the teachers had chosen this school for its dual mission of desegregation and quality academics; others were hired in to teach the technical courses on the basis of their expertise, quite apart from any political or educational philosophy. Some of the technical teachers, according to faculty members, came with few prior predispositions; others had taught primarily boys or Anglos and so had to learn what the other students could do. The dominant faculty culture of commitment to all the children eventually embraced virtually all of these teachers as well.

Issues of students and race seemed almost simple and matter-of-fact when compared to the role race played in faculty appointments. There were strategic times in the history of the school when hires had to comply with racial quotas. Interestingly, these quotas could be used both ways: when the emphasis was on increasing the number of non-Blacks in this previously all-Black school building, White teachers would have to be hired, even if they were not the most qualified (very few of the teachers here were Hispanic). Any arbitrary hire of a White person who seemed to be chosen for racial or political reasons rather than educational philosophy or competence was a source of great embarrassment to the Whites on the faculty.

The result of using the SET faculty to change the ratio of Whites to Blacks in the building was that the SET faculty was less diverse than its student body. When the emphasis was on adding more diversity within the predominantly White SET magnet faculty, a Black or Hispanic might have to be hired. Sometimes these hires seemed arbitrary as well and not always linked to philosophy. Both arbitrary "White" or "minority" hires pushed against the faculty culture of the school because they cut into the faculty voice in hiring and into the tradition of recruiting like-minded colleagues. The distrust and lack of confidence in a perceived "racial hire" or "political hire" was the same whether the new person was Black or White. They felt that any hire not based on educational philosophy and expertise trivialized the very identity of the school as one committed to both equity and academic excellence. In one case, the teachers felt that the person hired was less qualified than other candidates, less qualified than they themselves, underprepared for the job, yet paid more than other teachers because of having come in from industry. The teachers knew the city well enough to know that there was no need to sacrifice academic quality to satisfy racial quotas; there were many strong teachers of all races in the city. For that reason, they disrespected the concessions to expedience which sometimes resorted to arbitrariness.

When race meant "not necessarily the best choice" instead of "diversity among colleagues," the strong faculty culture around academic equity and excellence was threatened. When "political" meant "privileged by connections" rather than "a person who will be able to make things happen for the school," the faculty felt that the school (especially the students) was not being taken seriously. Mr. Beshara told a story that reinforced teachers' sense that political and racial hires, or hires based on nonschool experience in industry, were threats to academic quality. Mr. Beshara was covering the chalkboard in his empty classroom with formulas when a new teacher stepped into the doorway

and watched admiringly as the symbols and equations filled the board. The
new teacher held an advanced degree and had some experience in the technology fields he would be teaching, but the other teachers were wary of him
because he was regarded as a political hire. He knew Mr. Beshara to be a sea-
soned engineer and the teacher of the advanced engineering lab. He spoke, "I
would like to learn what you are doing here. Do you think you could teach
me?" Mr. Beshara said he would be only to glad to help this new teacher learn
these formulas and equations. They agreed on a time to meet and the new
teacher came in for two or three sessions. One day he asked, "This is hard—
what is this we are doing?" Mr. Beshara replied, "Algebra I." The new teacher
never came back for another tutorial with Mr. Beshara. Mr. Beshara waited a
discreet period before he shared that story. It was a story that would confirm
in the teachers' minds the importance of maintaining a strong faculty culture
and collective voice that included continued influence over teacher recruitment around a philosophy that linked equity and academic excellence. They
were working too hard to have issues of manufactured diversity trivialize, or
issues of politics make a mockery of, their ideals.

A Culture of Caring

The collaborations on curriculum and hiring, while important in a specialized school, held less direct significance for the students than the faculty's
collective creation of a culture of caring. Certainly individual teachers cared
about and cared for the students. But what students discussed in interviews,
and what the graduates interviewed validated, was the collective sense of caring the students came to depend on in this school. Gloria Ladson-Billings
describes a difference between "caring for" and "caring about." She describes
the successful teachers of African American children as those who "care for"
the children (Ladson-Billings 1994, 1998a). Angela Valenzuela, in analyzing
the ways U.S. schools subtract from Latino children's capacities to learn by
subtracting from their cultural identities, also makes the distinction between
"caring about" and "caring for." She notes that American teachers, particularly Anglos, express dismay that Latino children (both American and immigrant) do not "care about" school. Those teachers predicate their willingness
to teach on whether the children care about school. But the Latino children
know very well if the teacher does not "care for" them; they know if the
Anglo teacher does not exhibit or seek a caring relationship. In those children's culture, one does not "care about" until one is "cared for." The teachers and children have such oppositional views of caring that each feels the

other withdraw from the potential for productive teaching and learning (Valenzuela 1999).

SET students, across all variations in grade level, achievement, neighborhood origin, and race, expressed the presence of caring as a strong basis for remaining at the school: "These teachers care about me." "They take care of you here; they want you to do well. They want you to go to college." "If I have a problem—and sometimes I was in over my head here—I had never had courses like these—but you can talk to the teachers here. They will help you figure out what you need." The seniors especially feel that teachers' caring had been the key to their being able to survive, even thrive, despite their freshman fears that they may have been "in the wrong place."

This caring took the form of accessibility, of openness to questions, of fairness in assignments and in assessments, and of an acceptance of all the students. It came across in teachers' willingness to share their personal knowledge with the students and to consider student contributions as seamless with the curriculum. Even more, it took the form of high expectations for all the students. Almost every student interviewed volunteered the information that at this school, the teachers believed that every student can succeed. Many of these students transferred in from schools where they would have had higher grades and lighter senior course loads. But over and over they said that the fact that the teachers believed they can learn and then worked together to insure that they learn was the most important benefit they have derived from the school. The students were particularly awed by the fact that the teachers expressed this belief in the students' capacity long before the students felt they had demonstrated any evidence that they merited that confidence. They described this confident caring as a characteristic of the magnet program as a whole, not merely the kindness of any one teacher. It invited their mental engagement; it invited them to risk staying.

The state's standardized reforms would soon impose a "teacher appraisal instrument" to measure teacher's work. That "instrument" would try to enforce generic teaching behaviors, splitting teachers' knowledge of their children from their teaching. Teachers like these whose pedagogy was inseparable from caring would find their capacity to engage children threatened by the need to comply.

". . . and the Brains of the Kids"

The SET students contributed to the success of the school in ways that might not seem remarkable if they had been the students in a traditional honors program in a regular school. The honors program would have predated them and would continue after they left. At SET, however, the students' very presence was vital to the sustaining of the magnet program; too few admissions or too much attrition over the four years would mean closing the school.

Students and Race

Their presence was tied to their racial diversity. They were valued as individuals but admitted as a class for representing the city's Black, Hispanic, and Anglo populations. Many of these students would have been valedictorian, class president, athletic hero, or social leader at their home high schools. Some left those schools because they feared losing their friends if they succeeded too well in academics, and others left because they feared they would lose their academic focus amid pressures to "hang out" with their friends. Even the self-described nerdy kids, who had not anticipated popularity and class office, said that they had left both the possibilities for higher grades and the possibilities of dropping out from boredom. "If I had not come here, I would never have known what I could do."

In some schools in this city, the resegregation in a multiracial school follows social groupings, friendships forged in home neighborhoods and reinforced on the bus rides to and from those neighborhoods, or reactions to perceived rejection by students of the "other" groups (Suskind 1998; Tatum 1997). At SET, the students quickly made friends across racial and neighborhood lines and across such differences as family income and parent occupation, in part because many had already attended integrated lower schools and in part as a survival strategy in the face of the strenuous academics all ninth graders had to confront. They simply needed each other too much to divide into cliques. Thus, one contribution the students made to the school was wholehearted buy-in to the school's desegregation mission. If the teachers had had to deal with divisiveness, student prejudice, and claims of privilege by one group or another, then they could not have directed so much of their energies into the creation of the academic program. Because the students created friendships across racial lines, and generally settled into a good rapport with each other, the teachers were free to forge ahead, building positively on the cultural diversity rather than having to overcome fractious feelings or just the separateness seen at many other schools. Although the students had had to leave their neighborhood school and there was no Spanish spoken in the school (and most of the Blacks were quite separate from the student organizations in the neighborhood school which built on long-standing traditions of culture and school spirit in this famous old Black high school), the students said in interviews that they saw this education as adding to what they would be able to do *for* their communities, not ultimately taking them away from their communities. Not entering into someone else's school (as crosstown busing requires) made them all potential co-creators of the culture of this school. This is a complex issue and not mentioned lightly here; but it is remarkable in that the students' perceptions while they were in the school was that the school was respectful of them, and more respectful of their capacities to learn than some of their single-race home schools might have been.

Two moments most captured the issue of race at this school. One showed the utter ease with which these students dealt with their diversity of culture, home language, and race, and one revealed the tensions imbedded in the use of race as a category for stratifying educational opportunities. The first was the reenactment of a drama entitled *The Night Thoreau Spent in Jail*. In Mr. Moore's class the roles of Thoreau and his New England neighbors were played by an international cast of students: Thoreau was Hispanic (appropriate since he was protesting the payment of taxes to support the U.S. war against Mexico, although that connection was not mentioned in class). The roles of the associate justice, Henry David Thoreau's mother, and the bailiff were played by Black girls. An Asian girl served a co-defense counsel. Anglo boys played Thoreau's defense attorney, the court reporter, and the Chief Justice of the court. One Black boy took the role of chief prosecutor and another, the assistant prosecutor. The defense at one point called Thomas Jefferson to the stand, an Asian Thomas Jefferson. Testimony about Thoreau's refusal to pay war taxes and his "draft dodging" came through a witness played by a Vietnamese boy. Some of the lessons of the play remained muddled after a few of the characters ad libbed and emphasized the issue of taxes more than the underlying principle of a citizen's conscience in time of war. But the lesson of this school as a productive meeting place for the widely diverse children in this city was writ large. Without this school, few of these students would have been seen in their home school as having a future in the sciences or engineering or as able to discuss the intricacies of Thoreau's night in jail.

The other moment of clarity about race as lived by these students came in the interview of an African American boy in his second year in the SET program. Approximately 60 percent of the SET students were African American. Of those, most were bussed in from other neighborhoods. This boy, however, lived in the Carver High School zone and had attended middle school with some of the students in the downstairs, "regular" part of the school. While some of the Anglo or Hispanic SET students had said that they felt uncomfortable downstairs, mostly because the teachers in the classes they took there (physical education, foreign language) expected them to make straight As, their unease was temporary, not a challenge to their identity. For this boy, his sense of identity as a Black and as a student were confounded by his treatment in the regular part of the school. He said that the students in that all-Black school would shun him; even those who did not know him would treat him coldly. If they spoke, then they accused him of trying to be "White" or of acting superior to the Black students of Carver (Fordham and Ogbu 1986; Suskind 1998). For old friends to feel that he had left them behind was understandable; what was less clear was the treatment by students who did not know him. "If they don't know you, how do they know you are a SET student?" The boy faced the interviewer with complete incredulity: How could any outsider, even a White one, be so clueless? He answered politely but firmly: "I carry books."

A graduate student observer watching students from both groups arrive in the morning and leave at the end of the school day, noted that Carver students bolted from the doors, carrying no books, backpacks, or notebooks (Wallace 1994). The SET students left slowly, in small conversational groups, laden with books, lunch bags, and other gear. These unobtrusive indicators speak volumes about the structural inequalities in this district, inequalities perpetuated when no one tried to extend the teaching methods or curricula of the successful magnet programs over into the "regular" schools that housed them, and no one tried to learn from the teachers in neighborhood schools what their students might have needed to be able to see an academic future for themselves. The structural message is the relevant one for policy. It is, however, the personal message from this student that tells how race and racial identity forced choices for those students who had to cross a peer culture boundary that included race in order to have access to a college-bound education. This student carried not only books to school but also a conflicted sense of place. For many of these students, similar conflicts over gender and education, neighborhood and family and education, careers and family, and adolescence and education all lay just under the surface of their struggles to succeed at SET.

Knowing and Being Known

The students also helped make this into a "learning" school by their willingness to be known. Nel Noddings writes that caring involves both the caregiver and the one cared for (Noddings 1992). The SET students, perhaps because many were more than an hour away from home and academic light years away from their home school, were for the most part willing to enter into a personalized learning relationship with their teachers (Meier 1995). Even those who had thought of themselves as brainy outsiders at their home school found a place—perhaps in a computer lab, perhaps in a JETS activity, where they felt enough at home to get to know a teacher, to contribute ideas to how things should work, and to make that place welcoming for other students. The rigor of the program prompted older students to tutor the younger ones, especially during the long bus rides, and they passed on a school culture of student involvement.

These students also contributed to the success of SET by studying. While this seems to be an obvious role for students, there is much evidence that students do not take school seriously, that many do just enough to get by, that the content of schooling is not of great importance to teenagers. Page writes that a science teacher in a privileged high school, one expected to have a rigorous science curriculum, finds it difficult to engage his students' minds because their lives are filled with so many of the activities, consumer goods, social relations, and entitlements of the wealthy that they do not see the value in having to study and learn (Page 1999). Valenzuela has documented that Latino youth disengage from the content of schooling when they do not see in it respect for their cultures or for themselves (Valenzuela 1999). Suskind records the same phenomenon in the poorest high school in Washington, D. C. (1998); and French paints an equally bleak portrait of the student-school disconnect among lower-income White students in a Florida high school (1993). There are numerous other studies indicating that for a variety of reasons, ranging from the lack of credibility of school knowledge (McNeil 1986) to the pressures of peers and consumerism (Steinberg 1996), students often disengage from schooling even when they are physically present.

The SET teachers had claimed a role that rejected de-skilling, in order to teach what they hoped to be authentic knowledge, embodying significant social values and coinciding with their own best understandings of their subjects. The SET students met this kind of teaching, most evident in the core subjects, with diligent study and a willingness to work through very difficult assignments. Their earlier schools did not necessarily prepare them for this tough work. Ms. Foster noted that many (in some classes, most) had never read a whole book. Before SET, these students had made good grades by doing what was assigned, and in some cases not much was assigned. They went from reading brief excerpts of stories in middle school to novels, plays, and short story collections

in English classes and primary sources and writings by historians and econo-
mists in their social studies classes. The math they had mastered for admission
to SET consisted mostly of accuracy in calculations; now they were asked to use
math to note relationships and processes. All of this was new and daunting. The
very difficulty caused many of them to create study groups and to spend hours
on the phone at night comparing answers, in essence re-creating a student version of teachers' Happy Hour by phone and bus ride.

Significant Differences

The casual dress of these students masked family income and parents' occupation and neighborhood, the kinds of variables expected to influence the students' school success. Appearances were often deceiving, a mark of the capacity
of the school to be fully inclusive and to treat all as having bright futures. One
student might be the child of a university president, the next the child of a day
laborer and the next the son or daughter of an engineer or a teacher, a secretary
or a beautician. One Latino was especially memorable. More than many of his
more isolate "techy" friends, Pedro was poised and articulate, comfortable in a
class discussion or serving as master of ceremonies of the annual awards dinner. He seemed to be that middle-class Latino student destined for a lead role
in the community; SET was just a stop on his way to starting his own company
or running for Congress. Watching Pedro in action raised the question of
whether this school served primarily middle-class children of all three racial
groups, or whether it provided a "pipeline" for poor students of color, students
whose families would not have otherwise been able to send them to college.
Was this school opening up opportunities for students who, unlike Pedro, did
not already have the social and cultural capital to succeed?

Mr. Moore accepted the question politely, then began to describe Pedro's
life. Behind this popular class officer's seemingly carefree spirit lay extraordinary family problems. The newspapers had been carrying stories of a small
child struck by tragedy. The mother, described as very poor, was attempting to
address this emergency, care for her other young children, and at the same
time bring in a small amount of income. There were many legal and family
complications surrounding this child's story. Mr. Moore said in a quiet voice,
"That is Pedro's mother. That child in the papers is her baby." Pedro was able
to give his classwork and school activities his full concentration at school,
while immediately upon leaving school assuming the financial, emotional, and
pragmatic support for his mother and her younger children. In the past few
weeks he had spent every nonschool moment helping his mother resolve this

crisis involving one of her younger children (his half-sibling). The few teachers who knew the situation offered to be flexible with deadlines so Pedro would not have to choose between school and family. Even with the newspapers and television news stories filled with this child's plight, Pedro's friends did not recognize it as including their successful classmate. This was the most dramatic story of a student's need, but atypical only in degree. The teachers came to know the students well and knew that for many of them, this school offered an exceptional chance for them to move beyond poverty, beyond family conflict, beyond gender barriers, beyond the disillusionment and lack of direction of many of their friends.

Because many of their parents did not have college degrees or advanced educations in math and science, the students relied heavily upon each other for homework support. They created study groups. Older ones tutored younger ones. Students with computers at home helped teach the ones seeing computers for the first time (short-circuiting the labored lessons in the official "computer" classes), by going directly into applied graphics (record jackets, architectural renderings, fantastic space modules) and operations, then working backwards into programming. Students found ways to make the school into a teen social scene, stealing corners for conversations, giggles, friendships. They found boyfriends and girlfriends, planned parties, and decorated the walls with posters to celebrate a JETS victory or winning essay. All of this along a single hall of a large school. They created a student culture apart from the rest of Carver High because their schedules rarely permitted participation in the larger school's assemblies, sports, newspaper and yearbook staffs. The students in the "regular" school had social clubs, Black social societies of long-standing with loose affiliation to the school; the Latino, Anglo, and Asian students of SET would not have found a place in those. But neither did they treat SET like a somber academic setting—it was their home for at least eight hours every day. They brought food to class. Their teachers looked at the growing kids, the long bus rides, the quality of cafeteria food (a student almost jumped between me and a dish being served in the school cafeteria to persuade me not to take it) and agreed that snacking in class was probably a healthy thing to do. Some teachers even kept food in their rooms for students famished midmorning after rising at 5:30 A.M. to catch a 6:30 bus.

Co-creating the Curriculum

Just as they contributed to the making of a life in a school where no sustained extracurricular activities did that for them, the students added to the curriculum materials of the school. Learning from their teachers' scrounging and collecting, the students became alert to news from the medical center and the National Aeronautics and Space Administration (NASA, located in the state), the university scientists and local computer companies. The computer jocks among them brought in their knowledge of new software and computer magazines. They advised teachers on printers to buy, on models to avoid. They learned to beg science reference books from parents and literature books from friends in college. They compared notes with friends at other high schools and let their teachers know what other schools were buying for science labs or computer applications. The students began to see scarcities as a call for their own resourcefulness. African American girls, for example, in reading a book by Alice Walker or Toni Morrison, would "sell" their fellow students on reading these important authors and make sure the English teacher added their new titles to the class book lists. Books of all kinds would pass among these previous nonreaders, supplied in part by Mr. Moore's paperback collection, in part by the librarian's scrounged titles, but also by the enthusiasm of students using cross-city bus rides to educate their peers about "really great" books. As a result, students became (although unaware of the term) co-creators of the curriculum in a very real sense. Not only did they not resist the teaching and learning at this school (McNeil 1986, ch. 7 and 8; Page 1999) but they also became invaluable to the teachers for what they added.

Giving Back

Visible during the observations at this school were many ways students brought in ideas for JETS activities (three more ways to make a carton to protect an egg dropped from the seventh floor of a parking garage), for readings, for software. Less visible but vital to the health of the school were the contributions made by SET *graduates*. Several times when questioned about how they came to teach a particular lesson or use a particular software or lab activity, the teachers would say, "We learned this from one of our former students." Just as the graduates would call teachers like Mr. Moore for advice on professors, choices of majors, and other challenges of college life, they would also phone to let the teachers know what they should continue teaching or what they should change. "I'm sorry I complained about having to read so many books. Now that I am here, I find that everyone else has read much more Black literature than I have. Please add more Black authors to your reading list—in every grade, not just junior lit." "We only had to do one formal research paper. I still feel like I need help. Maybe you need to think of a way to have a couple of short research papers, just so people really learn how to do it before it counts so much at college." "The computer course is way out of date. You had us programming BASIC. Nobody needs that any more. I am sending you the syllabus for my freshman computer course. See if you can't get newer software. I am really behind. I was good at what we did, but now I find out it wasn't what I should have been doing."

Because they credit SET with opening the college doors for them, many SET graduates feel an enormous obligation to make the school even better for those who are coming along behind them. Former students' calls about the computer courses caused the faculty to redesign those courses. They took student suggestions very seriously, because these students now at college were offering suggestions in the spirit of the school's mission. This school was established to be the best chance for minority students and girls to get into scientific and technological fields in college and to prepare them to succeed once they gained admission. But it was not provisioned at the level of the private or suburban high schools against which their students were competing. The students, once out of school, took every opportunity to help the faculty bring the school up to the level it should have been for them. The practices of other schools were rarely accessible to these teachers; their students filled the gap.

The role of students as co-creators of the meanings of the curriculum and of the curriculum itself is rarely visible or understood at the policy level. That SET became a place of authentic learning *because of its students* is a concept far removed from those who attempt to improve education through policy mandates. The impending standardization of curriculum and teaching would not only not recognize but also would actively devalue the role of students in creating learning.

"We learn from our students. We learn from them while they are here, and if we are lucky, we keep learning from them after they leave. We do not want to send them off unprepared. If they don't let us know, we have no way of knowing that what we are doing is not right." The magnet coordinator went on to say, "Our students are our best curriculum advisers. I mean that."

Coming Together

If SET is the product of the blood of the teachers and the brains of the kids, two events crystallize the coming together of the teachers, the students and the goals of the school. The first of these greeted all visitors during April and May of each year. On a huge butcher paper banner on Ms. Foster's door was a list of all the seniors. Beside each name, once chosen, was the college that senior would attend and the student's usable scholarship money. A college could not be listed until the student had sent in the acceptance and turned down all others. By May there was a college or university beside every name. Students were admitted to regional state universities, historically Black colleges, church-related colleges, small liberal arts colleges, and undergraduate programs in top-tier research universities; the diversity of college size and specialty mirrored the students' own range of interests and family backgrounds. One year four students were admitted to one of the nation's top scientific universities, three by early admission. The usable scholarship total for a class of eighty-five came to more than $2 million (this amount held fairly steady between the late 1980s and the early 1990s). In one year during this time period, only *five* students from the regular Carver High senior class of more than three-hundred went to college. That figure was not listed on this poster, but these students were aware of the uniqueness of their opportunity; all credited this school (and the teachers credited the kids' efforts) with this promise of a future.[11]

The technical and humanistic goals for this school were made poignant during a night at the theater. The city's renowned theater company was presenting the Arthur Miller play *All My Sons*. Mr. Moore and Ms. Foster arranged for a group ticket rate; 150 of the 300 SET students attended. Engineering, ethics, family, economics, and citizenship all came together in this play. Mr. Keller, the manufacturer of airplane engines, had a partner who went to jail when it was revealed that their plant had let 120 cracked engines be shipped for installation in planes during World War II. Mr. Keller was ill the day the engines were shipped out. The pilots of twenty-one of the planes lost their lives. Now Mr. Keller awaits word on his own son, a pilot who has been missing in action. As the story unfolds, it comes to light that Mr. Keller was not sick, but that he stayed home to avoid responsibility for sending out what he knew to be defective engines. He justifies his decision saying he did it for his family; a factory that acknowledged producing that many defective parts would not be awarded future war production contracts. Without the contracts, he could not support his family. He kept thinking maybe someone else would catch the defect before the engines were installed or that he would produce replacements before any damage was done. While his younger son is reeling from his father's use of the family to justify this business decision, the older brother's fiancée discloses that he is dead. Just before he died, he wrote to tell her that his plane would crash. He could not live with the knowledge that his fellow pilots had lost their lives because of his father's negligence. The father is sure that he did it all for his family; but to this son, "family" has a new definition. He is connected to every one of those pilots. He ended his life rather than face the shame of his family's role in their deaths. And after finally reading the letter his son wrote just before crashing his plane, the father comes to see that to his pilot son, these young pilots were *all* "his sons." He too takes his own life.

The play brought together the technical and pragmatic aspects of engineering, the business and profit side of engineering, the issues of ethics, quality control, and responsibility. The students were rapt. The actors came on stage after the performance to field questions from the students. There were no questions about memorizing lines or selecting costumes. All the questions went to the heart of these students' futures in engineering and technology. An African American student stood up and asked in a clear and authoritative voice: "How did you feel playing the part of a man who did something so terrible? How did you learn to act like nothing was wrong when you already knew what he would soon find out?" A second African American student stood up and challenged the first student as well as the actor: "How do you know you wouldn't do something like that yourself? He did say he had to feed his family. I'm going to have to feed my family someday too. It's not easy when you are Black. And I will still be paying for going to school and all of that. How can you be so sure you wouldn't do the same thing?" One of the girls asked, "How would this have been different if he had not known in advance? What if you produce something that you think is good quality, but it still ends up hurting someone? Would you be more like Mrs. Keller who all this time thought her husband was innocent?" The students pressed the actors to delve into the ethical dilemmas of their characters. They knew little of war except for World War II movies and more recent stories of the American involvement in Vietnam. But they could identify with being put at risk, and several questions followed about choosing to be at risk or being put at risk by someone else, perpetual issues in engineering design and technology. They pushed the actors just as their teachers had pushed them in class discussions and in their papers not to stop with simple explanations. The discussion carried over into class the next day. More than any experience since they had come to SET, the students found themselves connecting the formulas and diagrams from Mr. Beshara's class in advanced engineering lab, the themes of family and personal responsibility from literature in Ms. Foster's literature class, the World War II battles and the "homefront" stories from Mr. Moore's history class, and the side conversations they had had with teachers and with each other as they tried to figure out what their studies at SET might mean for their future careers. They were not quick to condemn Mr. Keller, because they were beginning to envision themselves as people who would one day have knowledge and responsibility for that knowledge.

All My Sons and the senior college scholarship banner give evidence that the bargain the teachers and students struck to help each other make SET a place of authentic learning paid off in unexpected ways for these students. They did not learn on the latest equipment, but they had an education based on reciprocal relationships with teachers who were committed to their futures and who opened up their ways of knowing to them. In a later year, after the new lab wing was completed and the equipment, needed for twenty years, installed, one of the science teachers wanted to make sure the real benefits of the school were understood: "Some of these newer teachers think they can teach because we now have these labs. But this is just the icing on the cake. It's nice to have these labs, but they aren't the school. The real key to this school is what the teachers and the kids do. It's always been this way. It's nicer now, but it's not a better school."

The power of the students and teachers' bargain to make SET an educational school is power invisible to policymakers who locate authority over teaching and curriculum at the top levels of central bureaucracies. It is an educational resource unseen by those who equate educational success with measurable outcomes. If this school *had* been noticed by those who wanted to "reform the system," then they would have seen it as idiosyncratic and "not replicable" rather than what it was: the evidence of what teachers and students are willing and capable of doing—and growing into—when a school is structured to be educational rather than controlling and credentialing.

Part III

The "Perverse Effects" of Legislated Learning

Chapter 5

"We've Got to Nuke This Educational System"

"We've got to drop a bomb on them, we've got to nuke them—that's the way you change these organizations."[1] When Texas got serious about school reform, no one sat down with Ms. Watts to ask what she needed for her physics lab. No one called in a group of Hispanic students from inner-city Houston to ask how the engineering magnet program was changing their understanding of mathematics or their plans for their future. No one from the legislature spent a week at the gifted-and-talented magnet trying to understand how teachers and students can create a whole school culture that makes learning something everyone works hard on with excitement and diligence. No policy-maker expected teachers or students to provide expertise into what schools needed. No one was looking into schools for answers. After all, schools were the problem. Instead, a businessman was brought in to "fix" things. And to fix it, Ross Perot decided to "nuke" the system.

The state reforms did not start out as a bombing raid, but they did proceed completely independently of anything going on in schools. They were driven from the top, defined as management problems waiting for an expert manager to solve. They were formulated on the assumption that schools are at the bottom of the bureaucracy. If schools are to be improved, then the bureaucratic machinery needs to be running more smoothly. And bureaucratic machinery runs best when strict management controls are in place. If this sounds like a deliberate plan to create schools full of defensive teachers and bored, disengaged students, who merely go through the motions of schooling in order to produce credits and credentials, that in fact became one of the dangers good teachers had to try to overcome once the reform controls were all in place. The distrust and cycle of lowered expectations found in the schools portrayed in *Contradictions of Control* were in fact inadvertently implemented by official policy when Texas tried to "reform" its schools. They provide a powerful lesson for a nation increasingly preoccupied with calls for "standards" and for narrow measurement indicators as keys to holding its public schools "accountable" to those who would control them. They provide a powerful warning about effects on teaching and learning when all the authority over all the significant decisions about teaching and learning is centralized and all the means are standardized.

The impetus for reform came from a simple fact of Texas school life: the teachers were seriously underpaid. The governor valued teachers' votes but did not trust the legislature to raise teacher salaries. The legislators did not trust teachers and refused to fund raises without "quality controls" on teachers' work. H. Ross Perot did not trust the state school board, the state education agency, local school boards, superintendents, administrators, school principals, or coaches (he had figured out that many coaches grew up to be superintendents and principals). In this climate of distrust, it is remarkable that there was any initiative for school reform. That the distrust led to top-down policies aimed at controlling teachers, rather than at learning from the best of them, should not be unexpected. The nature of those policies, the assumptions about schools that shaped them, and the politics behind them provide a graphic case study in the seductiveness of top-down reforms. The Texas case shows a painful intersecting of good intentions, scarce resources, and the push for a one-size-fits-all quick fix.

For decades, Texas public schools have been almost self-caricatures in their reputation for low per-pupil expenditures, state-adopted texts and the forum the textbook adoption hearings provide to right-wing objectors to literature and science curricula, generous outlays for football teams and marching bands, and low teacher pay (McNeil 1986, 3). When statewide reforms attempted to shift priorities away from these legendary weaknesses, it is somehow not surprising that even the reforms should play to stereotype: the choice of a billionaire to chair the blue-ribbon advisory commission, ungrammatical public pronouncements by legislators bent on testing teachers for basic literacy skills, and galvanized resistance by football coaches faced with enforcing No Pass/No Play rules on their players. The Texas role in the national educational reform movement seems on the surface to be too unique a parody on educational reform to be instructive to the national debates. But school reform in Texas, despite its theatrics, is not an aberrant case.

Within the policies, which taken together comprise educational "reform" in Texas, converge political pressures that are playing themselves out across the country. Some of the legislated reforms in Texas are very close to policies of centralized testing and centralized curricula currently being advocated for national implementation. There has been no clear "end" to the Texas school reform policies of the 1980s, so their final "result" cannot be measured. Those policies have been contested, revised, and amended. (The succeeding governor, not party to the legislation, advocated shifting earnings from teacher retirement funds to prison construction.) Their most far-reaching impact has not been the success or failure of any of the specific provisions of the reform but the precedent set for centralized controls based on accountability to a corporate elite, not to a citizen public nor to educators. These policies established a structure of centralized controls and they operationalized the assumptions that only those aspects of teaching and learning that are externally prescribable and measurable are worthy of state support. Even though some of the specific policies are no longer in place, the bureaucratic structures that grew out of the 1980s top-down reforms have legitimated centralized student testing and have so strengthened the state's already top-down education structure that attempts in the 1990s to decentralize have been undertaken only at great cost and are given little chance of success against an established culture of rigid, short-term accountabilities. (As will be discussed in concluding chapters, 1995 legislation provided options for more local decision making, but only when in accordance with state standards as measured on centralized tests over centralized curricula and skills; the commissioner of education has said that under "decentralization," the only thing that cannot be waived is the state test.) The system of testing legitimated by this legislation directly harms instruction by its narrowing of the curriculum and externalizing of the criteria for teachers' practice and children's learning. The Perot reforms also legitimated the direct intervention of business interests, long influential behind the scenes, as the appropriate locus for decision making over the structures and practices of schooling. Chapter 7 will elaborate on the controls now deeply imbedded in the system that have their origins in the mid-1980s when the Perot reforms became state law and state educational policy.

The ongoing Texas story serves as a prototype of two central features of this kind of school reform movement. The first is the direction reforms take when schools are defined in terms of the rhetoric of economic restructuring, rather than in terms of children's learning or democratic (and other noneconomic) ideals. The Texas economy was still thriving when a reform-minded governor took office; as the price of oil dropped, so did the resources for school improvement. Yet the unstable economy inspired reconsideration of the role of public schooling in the economy. One Texas school reform policy that has national import is the idea that public education should be responsible for economic recovery. In this particular state, economic chaos gave rise to the thought that schools should create certainties, should test and be held accountable to standardized measures. Yet, the same educational commissions and legislative packages calling for standardization demanded that public schools somehow provide the imaginative, intellectual "capital" needed for a high-technology future. Behind the economic improvement rhetoric were models of accountability anachronistic to the economic future the reformers articulated. Examining the relationship between the language of economic structuring and educational restructuring in Texas may provide an analytical focus for questioning links in other states between perceived economic ills and recommended educational remedies. The success of educational reform in enhancing the economy may well depend on the model of education employed. In Texas, the economic justification for increased state support for public education led to the implementation of a nineteenth-century industrial management model of "reform," anachronistic to the rhetoric of highly technological and inventive economic futures and ultimately counterproductive to educational improvement.

The second central feature the Texas case brings out in the open is the critical need to look beyond the "lightning rod" issues of educational reform to examine the ways centralized, top-down reforms reshape, and in this case constrain, possibilities for substantive teaching and learning. In Texas, No Pass/No Play and teacher testing became the public battlegrounds upon which competing educational interests fought for their claims of educational quality. While teachers complained that literacy tests for them were demeaning, reformers assured the public that minimum standards were being raised to rid the classroom of illiterate teachers. Athletic coaches descended on the state capital in grief and anger to protest linking eligibility for participation in competitive sports to students' passing grades, while the governor and billionaire Ross Perot basked in the knowledge that only a reform that really made a difference would have generated so much heated opposition.

While the debates were filling the evening newscasts and becoming in the public mind synonymous with "school reform," the significant policy changes were occurring out of sight: authority over curriculum, teacher assessment, student assessment, funding, attendance, athletic participation, and teacher discretion in a host of instructional areas were all shifting from the local school boards, district offices, and classrooms to the Texas Education Agency (TEA) in Austin. Both these shifts in the locus of control and the linking of educational reform to economic restructuring place Texas in the mainstream of *philosophies* of school reforms that are shaping national and state legislated policies in the United States in the last decades of the twentieth century. Because the Texas reforms have anticipated some national reforms and have been so publicly debated, they offer a unique opportunity for policymakers to see in action the conflicts behind the reforms, the historical and economic contexts of reform policies, and the unanticipated consequences of some of these reforms. Because Texans little bother to disguise or moderate the political and economic rationales behind their public policies, what may remain hidden at the federal level or in other states in linking educational policy to the economic and political power structures nationally is more fully visible in Texas. To see the contested policies in Texas, and the overt and hidden shifts in control accompanying them, is to have a window on the kinds of power relations becoming imbedded or contested in other states or at the national level, where they may be less visible. And while these reforms and the power plays behind their design and implementation seem far removed from classrooms, the magnet school classroom data will demonstrate how centralized reforms can have devastating effects on teaching and learning when they define teaching as the problem and administrative controls as the solution.

While several pieces of legislation and numerous efforts by local school boards and building-level staff have addressed the need for public school reform, the key to Texas's role in the national educational reform movement is state legislation that still goes by its House number, "House Bill 72." House Bill (HB) 72 is a complex piece of education legislation passed in 1984. Many of its components became effective soon after passage; others were referred to state agencies and local school boards for implementation. Others were never adequately funded. Resistance to the bill came from many quarters. The story of this "reform" legislation is a continuing one. There is a public perception, and even a perception among legislators and school board members that this legislation is no longer in force, that it has been superceded by decentralizing legislation.[2] While school-based decision making is now required by the state, the primary control generated by House Bill 72, the state-level testing of children, cannot be waived at the local level regardless of the locally derived educational plan. Thus, the appearance of obsolescence of the Perot reforms is misleading; they are lived every day in classrooms by teachers who have to juggle teaching children or teaching to the state tests, tests aimed at generating standard measurable indicators to assure the powerful people outside schools that the people inside schools are following the scripted curriculum.

House Bill 72 itself, the intentions behind it, and the assumptions guiding it offer an opportunity to frame an analytical perspective on top-down school reform movements, using Texas and its contested legislation as a case study in reform policies. The combination of unique historical factors and economic conditions that produced HB 72 (and much of its opposition) exemplify the dependence of educational policy on the broader historical circumstances. Yet the uniqueness of these external factors in Texas has contributed a model of centralized control over schools advocated in Washington, in business leadership circles, and in many state legislatures where such centralized schooling has not been historically prevalent.

Something for Everyone

Ernest Boyer (1983) and John Goodlad (1983), in their contributions to reform debates, have said that in American high schools "we want it all." That could have been the motto of the drafters of the Texas HB 72, in the 1984 legislative session called to pass school reform legislation. Gubernatorial candidate Mark White, a Democrat who expressed deep concern for education and the working conditions of teachers, had seen the uneven quality of education in the state where he had been serving as attorney general. He faced a close race with incumbent governor Bill Clements, an extremely conservative Republican millionaire oilman. One of White's campaign promises was to raise teacher salaries more than 20 percent; his promise paid off in teacher votes and in the votes of supporters of improved schools. Once in office, however, he was unable to persuade the legislature to pass such a pay increase. Many legislators believed teachers were generally not qualified for the higher pay increase. Education analyst Thomas Toch reports that the chair of the Texas House Ways and Means Committee and the Speaker of the House both thought many teachers "didn't deserve the increase" (Toch 1991, 73). They thought that an across-the-board increase would benefit "bad" teachers as well as good ones. To get the pay increase, White had to promise that there would be quality control, that the taxpayers would be receiving benefits from their expenditures. White's strategy was to put together a comprehensive education reform bill that would provide benefits for as many constituents of education as possible. The teacher pay increase would be one of many features of a broad-sweeping legislative reform for Texas education. The result of White's concern was HB 72; meant to upgrade education and directly help teachers, it drew more heated opposition from teachers than any legislation in recent memory. The distance between its intent and its reception is only one of its many ironies.

Ross Perot, a billionaire who made his fortune in computers rather than in ranches and oil, also cared about education, but knew very little about it except for having graduated from a public high school in Texarkana many years before. To mitigate against the business community's resistance to the anticipated tax increases that the reforms would require, White appointed Perot to chair a task force charged with "studying" the teacher pay issue (Toch 1991, 74). The task force was named the Select Committee on Public Education (SCOPE). Although no other state is known to have had such a wealthy and illustrious planner of reforms, Texas was different only in degree, not in kind, from its use of the rhetoric of economic competition typical of the alarms sounded in *A Nation at Risk* (National Commission on Excellence in Education 1983). This economic rationale for improving schools has been given at least acknowledgment, if not central status, in most of the other major reform reports and current state and federal "standards" initiatives. To bring Texas schools, and the Texas economy, to a competitive level, Perot's commission, as officially established by the legislature and as reconceptualized by Perot himself, did not limit its work to its original instructions to conduct an investigation and documentation of the "salary needs of teachers." Instead, under Perot's leadership and with the blessing of the legislature, the Select Committee on Public Education broadened its jurisdiction to consider "the issues and continuing concerns related to public education in Texas." (Toch 1991, 74, quoting Texas House Resolution 275, May 30, 1993.) With this expanded mandate, the committee set out to consider aspects of schooling they (especially Perot) considered to be problems. These ranged from funding formulas to attendance, from athletics to teacher pay, from class size and length of school year to mandatory kindergarten (Select Committee on Public Education 1984).

SCOPE's first stated responsibility was to the teachers. White had promised teachers a significant pay raise. The most obvious benefit of any new bill would have to be higher pay for teachers. The Perot commission agreed and the final bill reflected this priority. Second, ostensibly also for teachers, was a system of documenting and assigning merit so that only those who performed to higher standards would be appropriately rewarded.

While such a proposal was likely to gain teachers' support, it would not necessarily be popular with voters once they had calculated the expense of using state funds to raise the guaranteed minimums of teacher pay across the state (from $11,000 to $15,000 per year). In addition, local school taxes (property taxes) would have to be increased to pay for merit raises in the future and to provide for those raises expected by teachers in districts where pay already exceeded state minimums but remained low. Going against greater expenditures for this and other components of school reform was the long-standing marginality of education to public policy in Texas. Unlike many midwestern and East Coast states, where education has been long valued and made accessible to wide sectors of the population (and where higher education has been seen as key to generating correspondingly greater economic and political power), Texas has traditionally viewed education beyond the primary level as something of a luxury. In fact the Texas Constitution guarantees that the children of Texas be provided with a "basic" education, not an excellent one.[3] Unlike those states whose economies were driven in part by highly skilled labor, complex mastery of international economies by management, or the production of "knowledge capital," Texas had predicated economic success largely on the presence of fairly easily exploited natural resources. From agriculture, and then oil, had arisen an economy, so the myth goes, based on hard work, luck, and land (or what lies beneath it). Many of the state's most powerful corporate owners, oilmen, and politicians have traditionally been proud of their relative lack of formal education. A sociology of Texas knowledge would have to study the relations between *savvy and power,* rather than *knowledge and power* in their formal senses (Apple 1992, 22). Neither intellectual nor credentialed knowledge has been seen as crucial to personal or collective economic development in this entrepreneurial state.

In addition, the state has a very poor history of supporting public goods of any kind. It has consistently ranked in the bottom tier of states on almost all measures of payment for public goods, including those which include the channeling of federal funds to residents and communities.[4] It is critical for understanding educational reform movements in this state to note that even in times of great wealth, individual prosperity, and a bulging state treasury, Texas has not spent on public goods (mass transit, parks, health care, pollution control, schools) in amounts proportionate to its wealth. The entrepreneurial presumption is that you take care of yourself and your own; if you are not successful right away, then either your luck may turn any day, or you are not working hard enough.

Teacher pay, within such a culture, is generally regarded as public employee pay, rather than as an investment in a public good. And in a state where public employees are barred from collective bargaining, high pay for public employees has had few advocates. One way to defuse the reluctance to pay for higher teachers' salaries was to have business leaders represented on the Select Committee. They could forcefully argue that business and industry in this state, whose agriculture faced strong international competition and whose oil reserves had been severely depleted, would be becoming more and more dependent on "human capital" and "knowledge capital." As the state's economy shifted to a high-technology focus, higher educational standards would become an imperative from a private enterprise, not from a public goods, perspective. The business community needed better schools in order to have a more skilled and knowledgeable labor pool and in order to attract new industries to the state. That the message would have to come from the business sector was underscored by the lack of any teachers, and very few representatives of higher education, on the Select Committee.

The second way to elicit support for teacher pay was to promise more benefits for the costs. The parallels to the social efficiency movements of the 1910s and 1920s here are startling: in that era (Callahan 1962), increased immigration, burgeoning secondary school populations, and a history of corruption and patronage in the running of many big-city school systems made business leaders decide to take control of public education. They ran for school boards, promising to increase productivity and efficiency in schools. They bypassed the teaching profession, inviting efficiency experts like Frederick W. Taylor to come in as industrial consultants to redesign secondary schools to resemble the factory and to emulate factory productivity. From this era come such commonplace school features as ability group tracking (cost-effective allocation of "raw material"—students—on the assembly lines), standardized tests (testing the factory's "raw material"), the superintendent as businessman, and teacher as hired worker in the credential machine (Kliebard 1986, 26–27). Schoolmen (and they were men) reasoned that the public would be willing to pay if the public could see tightly managed organizations and measurable results. The short-term accounting practices of industrial production came into widespread use in schools, and the structures designed by those factory experts persist in most American high schools to the present.

In Texas in the 1980s, the promises of productivity to taxpayers came in the form of trade-offs within the reform legislation. Teachers were promised an increase in base pay, with the state making up the difference between poor districts' salary scales for teachers and the state-specified minimums (McNeil 1987b).

In return, the tax-paying public was promised a guarantee on their investment: teachers would be worth the extra pay, first as entering teachers and later as practicing professionals. Quality control for current teachers was to be in the form of a test to be taken by all teachers requesting certification and by all currently practicing teachers wishing to retain their teaching certificates. As will be discussed below, this test, the TECAT, became a lightning rod issue that alienated teachers far more than the promise of greater pay pleased them. A system of tests in the subject fields and "professional knowledge" would be the screening device for people entering the profession after the one-time administering of the TECAT.

Second, for the benefit of both taxpayers and teachers, the law would institute a career ladder program by which teachers could be evaluated and rewarded according to criteria other than years of seniority. For the taxpayer and legislators the promise would be that no teacher would get merit pay raises who did not earn them; teachers, in turn, would see that high quality effort does not go unacknowledged. A central component of this career ladder merit system was to be a systematic, regular assessment of the classroom performance of all teachers. Previously, only probationary teachers were typically evaluated more than once each year. In some districts, career teachers were observed and assessed only in alternating years in a two- or three-year cycle or in no regular pattern at all. For teachers the benefits of being observed and assessed were to be that they would experience less isolation and have more potential to have their work seen and rewarded. For administrators and taxpayers, there would be the move from intuitive (and political) assessments to "fair," "objective," "rational" ones. Teachers would receive at the beginning of the school year a copy of the state-mandated teacher assessment criteria and behaviors for which they would be judged. Both they and their administrators would have greater certainty about what their evaluation was supposed to accomplish. The system of assessment and rewards would be aligned in the form of a Career Ladder. Each step up the ladder was expected to result in a merit pay increase.

Other benefits for teachers in the omnibus reform bill, and for education in general, were to be new attendance laws. The most famous, or infamous, was the No Pass/No Play provision. To counter teachers' frustrations that their students were missing class for pep rallies and athletic games, especially in rural areas on Thursdays and Fridays, athletes would be held to strict grade requirements before being allowed to play in sports during each six-week grading period. The provision gave teachers more leverage over class attendance and student activities, especially in varsity athletics (traditionally seen as the domain of coaches and alumnae, not teachers). In addition, it sent the message to parents and students that the educative purposes of schooling are to be taken seriously: teachers are to be supported.

In addition, the school year was to be lengthened and strict attendance rules set by the state were to establish the exact number of unexcused absences that would merit a failing grade in a course.

The attraction of these portions of the law for the business community were both stated and implied: education was to be valued, but it was also to be accountable. Even if it cost more, there would be quality control checks to make sure productivity matched investment. There would be testing and assessing of teachers and state testing of students in specified subjects in specified years. Teachers entering the profession would be tested on "professional knowledge" (e.g., "Which of the following are characteristics of a standardized test?") and on basic literacy. Stricter attendance policies and enforcement would accrue to local districts in the short term in per-pupil dollars from the state based on the basis of actual pupil attendance and in the long run in increased graduation rates. In each provision, the locus of authority was the state. These important educational issues were not to be left to local communities, schools, or districts.

Other provisions of HB 72 dealt with issues of school finance and the role of the state education agency. The state agency, for example, was empowered to design (or contract the design of) the "instruments" for testing teachers and it was authorized to codify the new attendance policies. "Guidelines" of implementation were to be developed by various offices within the Texas Education Agency. A previous bill two years earlier had put in place a statewide curriculum, identifying by legislative requirement and state agency enactment a detailed set of "essential elements" for curriculum in all major subjects at all grade levels. The new legislation would ensure that teacher performance and student performance and attendance made compliance with the agency's "essential elements" a responsibility of teachers and students as well as of local districts administrators.

One of the most popular provisions of the law for those who worry about the quality of education in such a huge and diverse state was the clause moving toward greater equalization of funding. Texas had not had a history of universally bad schools; instead, the state had generally assumed that the reputation for educational quality would reside with a few select high schools in wealthy neighborhoods or oil-rich towns. If Bellaire High School in Houston, or the high schools of the oil town of Midland, for example, turned out Merit Scholars and "good students," there would emerge leaders for business and the universities and the professions. Many other, poorer neighborhoods were written off as just not having "good schools." Litigation in the 1970s had attempted more than once to redress the maldistribution of tax dollars across school districts on the grounds that local property taxes should not be the primary sources of school funding in a state with such enormous gaps between rich and poor (*Rodriguez v. San Antonio I.S.D.* and *Edgewood v. Kirby,* among others; Toch 1991, 87). These lawsuits largely failed or made incremental changes, and over time the vast inequities widened. HB 72 took a step in the right direction by mandating a new formula for the distribution of state education funds to local districts. The provision was helpful enough to please legislators representing extremely poor, often minority districts, but not so radical as to alienate those representatives of the affluent districts which would lose funds once the formula went into effect.

HB 72 looked like a popular law, a genuine attempt to build a coalition in favor of greater spending on public education. It appeared to be an attempt to provide something for all the constituents of public education: teachers, parents, business people (a direct voice in state-level educational policy, as evidenced in SCOPE), legislators, the state agency (greatly increasing its power), school boards (giving them the role of assessing teachers at the local level, while being able to blame state agency for designing the assessment instruments), and children (mandatory kindergarten, longer school days and school years).

Lightning Rods and Loss of Faith

The lightning rod issues, those which drew the greatest and most public opposition, were the teacher tests and No Pass/No Play. Both pitted school personnel against each other and against the state agency. Both figured strongly in Mark White's eventual loss in his second very close gubernatorial context with Bill Clements.

The No Pass/No Play rule is not very radical: students must be passing all their subjects at any six weeks grading period in order to play in a sport or participate in other major activities (band, cheerleading, class officer, editorships) during the following six weeks. No Pass/No Play is seen as a reform aimed at supporting teachers of academic subjects whose leverage over their students during a sports season is often overwhelmed by that of the coach. Small towns especially construct a sense of community and special identity around the successes of the football teams. In larger cities, poor and minority students often envision sports as their ticket to college scholarships and perhaps even professional teams. Interscholastic sports so dominate some small-town schools (and some suburban ones) that for all practical purposes classes have been dismissed at noon on Friday so that students (spectators as well as athletes) can travel to out-of-town games and pep rallies. Also, even when school continues to be in session on game days, booster activities may cut into classroom time. While coaches were less vocal publicly in their opposition to the tighter attendance rules in HB 72 (six unexcused absences equal a failure in the course for the term, regardless of the student's grades), they were furious about the grade requirements for athletes.

Of all the opposition to provisions of HB 72, it was the coaches' that was best organized, best disseminated around the state, and most frequently heard in formal hearings. Coaches managed to have extensive media coverage of star players, band members, drill team members, and cheerleaders whose tears were flowing over exclusion from participation based on failing grades. Some high schools had to cancel games because of insufficient players; others canceled marching band performances at games. In their small towns coaches became political leaders on state education reform overnight; their professional association sent spokespersons to legislative and agency hearings to protest this rule. Most argued within the spirit of "school reform," asserting that rather than hurt academic performance, sports participation increased motivation for students who might otherwise see no reason to attend school. The coaches were able, thereby, to appear to buy into the school improvement rhetoric without giving up their intense opposition to No Pass/No Play. While this has generally been viewed as a conflict between athletic and academic interests, No Pass/No Play is critical also as one more manifestation *within this legislation that discretion and authority were passing from the local to the state level.* The locus of power over this issue was at the last as important as the rule itself. Coaches exerted far more clout than many political observers imagined possible and are credited with helping, at least in a small way, stir up enough opposition to Mark White that Bill Clements, who promised to amend the rule, was elected governor in the next election. (The rule still stands today.)

The other lightning rod issue became the testing of teachers. Although most Texas teachers held "permanent," "lifetime" certificates (according to

the language printed on the certificate), HB 72 required that to remain certified, all previously certified teachers would have to take the Texas
Examination of Current Administrators and Teachers (TECAT), a pencil-
and-paper test of basic grammar, professional knowledge, and a writing
sample. Because the commission, the legislature, and governor had used the
promise of competence to legitimate higher expenditures for teacher pay, the
legislation had to provide for a way of assuring teacher competence. They
searched for a way to measure it. The idea of competence, translated into
terms that could be both statewide and measurable, quickly shifted from
professional expertise and classroom effectiveness to an issue of basic literacy,
something much more measurable. According to one analyst, the cost to
develop a series of subject-matter tests for teachers, especially to create high-
quality tests for teachers in all subjects at various grade levels, would have
cost tens of millions of dollars.

The cost issue shifted the discussion of *teacher quality* into *quality control*. As one of the first overt trade-offs between quality and the appearance
of quality control, the reform plan settled on a test of the basic knowledge
teachers would need for teaching and legislators would need to show that
teachers were *not illiterate*. Disproving the worst case, then, became the
rationale for the teacher certification test: Did Texas teachers know the basic
skills they were supposed to be teaching to children? Could they read and
write? An objective test of basic literacy and simple information about classroom practice would satisfy two objectives: it would not be so threatening to
teachers that they would balk at taking it (as would, say, the equivalent of the
College Board's Advanced Placement examinations or college-level exams in
the subject fields), nor so expensive that the costs would be prohibitive. At
the same time it would provide some assurance that no illiterate teacher
could "hide" within the system. A standardized test seemed the quickest,
most expedient, and least expensive way to approach a problem that many in
the public and in the legislature saw as the cause behind low educational
quality: the teachers.

Teachers immediately grasped that the trade-off between pay raises and
quality control could work against them. The *quality of their teaching* was not
to be considered as a basis for recertification: certification would rest solely on
performance on a single, generic standardized test. Because so much of the
rhetoric of the reform movement was couched in the language of blaming
teachers, teachers were not irrational to fear the test and its consequences.
Older teachers, minority teachers, and many teachers who had studied at

underfunded, small colleges most feared that they were to be judged against a test designed for people whose education mirrored greater privilege. While most teachers agreed that illiterate and incompetent teachers have no place in schools, they did not agree that the test would capture this incompetence, nor that all who failed would in fact be incompetent. The abstract fears and ambiguities that arose during the months the test was being prepared turned the teachers against the very governor, Mark White, who had initiated these reforms to increase teacher pay. Lawsuits challenging the requirement to be tested were filed by individuals, unions, and teacher groups. A small number of teachers retired early rather than face failing the test; many schools offered cram courses for teachers who needed to review their writing and professional literature (or to hone their test-taking skills).

Those in government and business supporting the test saw it as a marker of basic literacy, of absolute minimum standards for teachers. Common sense had it, they said, that the teachers' fear of the test must itself be an indicator of teacher incompetence; if teachers were competent, they would have nothing to fear. For teachers, those arguments held little weight. It was the presumption that teachers were the ones in schools that needed reforming that most galled them. They knew that where there were weak teachers, principals knew who they were, just as teachers knew which principals were not competent. And they knew that principals and other administrators did not want to have to deal with instructional quality or personnel evaluations that called for their own professional judgment. Also, they knew that many of their schools were weak because of decades of underfunding and of stark inequities across schools and districts. Teachers resented this plan that placed the blame for weak schools on all teachers. And they were equally offended because with their careers, their livelihoods, at stake, the quality of their day-to-day *teaching* was held to be of less importance in recertification than a test score from a commercial testing firm from out-of-state.

More than 97 percent of the teachers taking the TECAT passed on the first try; their fears of losing jobs because of the test were unfounded. But their fears of losing a *voice* in their teaching were right on target. Consoling words from the governor ("I knew our teachers could do it.") were not enough to compensate for months of uncertainty, for the lack of input into policies that were increasingly de-skilling their teaching, for the lack of public credibility that built as easy sample questions appeared in newspapers alongside interviews with worried teachers. Classroom teachers never became as articulate and unified in their reasons for opposing the test as the coaches were over No

Pass/No Play. Teachers' public voicing of fears, rather than of positive alternatives, planted in the public mind (and certainly in rhetoric of the governor and the state education agency) that teachers do need "improving," that they need tighter controls from management, that they need more supervision over their teaching. (It is interesting that with so much of the school reform rhetoric aimed at helping economic recovery, no teacher groups noted the cash drain out-of-state in the creation of this test. Dr. James Popham of IOX Assessment Associates of California held the contract to develop the test [McNeil 1987b, n. 4].) In a time of great debate over money for teacher pay raises, the contract cost was almost $5 million to develop, administer, and score the test. In addition, the Texas Education Agency subsidized the appropriation with more than $200,000 of its own staff time. An independent economic analysis of the test production, preparation courses (many of which aimed at test-taking skills, rather than the substance of reading or grammar or pedagogy), personal time, and outlay costs by administrators and teachers yielded a conservative estimate of more than $78 million. The TEA noted these direct and indirect cost estimates to be credible (Shepard and Kreitzer 1987). For a test that changed few staffing patterns, had little lasting impact on teachers' reading and writing skills, and no discernible impact on their teaching except to cut into lesson-planning time, the financial costs are staggering. The costs of status and confidence and public esteem for teachers have had even longer lasting negative effects. The strategy to build consensus through an apparently rational objective process only exacerbated divisiveness. And the shift to centralized controls over teaching and over "educational quality" were not dislodged once the test figures were in and teachers were seen as overwhelmingly "literate" by the standards of the test (an irony that has had no public discussion).

There is much more to be said about teacher tests as instruments for certification and recertification. What is significant in this case is that the symbolic politics that merged quality control with increased costs backfired dramatically. Teachers contributed to their own alienation from their public by failing to explain their opposition. In addition, by failing to articulate that these tests lowered standards rather than raised them (by reducing the complex craft of teaching to a simple computer-scored test), they failed to gain credibility as a voice in educational policy. Because the vocal resistance to state-level reforms tended to come from coaches, who favored lenient attendance and grading policies at the expense of academics, the governor and others in policy positions felt they had truly set in motion policies that would create public confidence that they had upgraded education. On the other hand, because the governor failed to listen to those teacher groups that did try to speak out, because he saw teacher responses as irrational fears, rather than pedagogical concerns, he miscounted his votes. Although no one will know just how individual teachers voted, they did not support him as a group and he lost his reelection bid in 1986 by a small margin.

Lasting Ironies and Hidden Controls

The lightning rod issues of No Pass/No Play and teacher testing were responses to the sense that Texas public education was out of control. Both of these policies attracted vehement opposition because they attempted to bring under "control" conditions of schooling (athletics dominating academics, allegedly illiterate teachers) that traditionally local administrative practices had failed over many years to correct. Texas school reforms generally have been characterized by a controlling reaction to anything perceived as a problem and by a shift of the controls to a level removed from the classroom. For example, there was no sustained debate over the possible value that could emerge from student assessments of teachers or teachers' personal assessments of their work as relevant to teachers' recertification. And there was clearly no consideration of increasing provision for classroom resources and for holding communities and districts (and the legislature) responsible for providing teachers and classrooms with the instructional materials and professional enrichment opportunities that could have immediately raised the quality of children's learning. There was no attention to engaging communities and interest groups in a plan to rectify persistent inequalities. The mentality of reform was that "we need to do something about (or to) those teachers."

Such controls over teacher practice can be contested because they are so public, so overt. As one high-level curriculum supervisor stated, "Every time they try to improve schools, they end up just adding more controls." So long as such controls are new and in the press, they remain problematic and debatable. Over time, however, overt controls tend to become imbedded in the structure and taken for granted once they are in place. These Texas school reforms demonstrate how the imbedding of controls can occur while the various constituents of public schools are focusing on momentary distractors tangential to the larger issues. These "reforms" also point to the complicated relationships between the economic goals of school reform and the tendency to solve educational problems by adding management controls and undermining teacher authority. In the case of Texas, the model of school reform embodies the controls reminiscent of a time, and an economic circumstance, long past, ironically helping to lock Texas into a position far short of the high-technology economy that reformers said they were hoping would develop alongside "reformed" schools. (A clearer picture of their ultimate goals is the subject of chapter 7.)

If one purpose of bureaucratic rules is to gain control over uncertain environments (K. McNeil 1978), the bureaucrats in the teacher assessment division of the state agency followed the textbook on bureaucratic controls. The uncertain environment they faced included great geographic, economic, and cultural diversity across school districts; the politics and personalities and favoritisms in local areas; and the varying levels of professionalism among both teachers to be assessed and administrators charged with carrying out assessments. The TECAT would not address those issues and their impact on children's educational experiences. But it would create a large enough financial and bureaucratic response to those issues to appear to deal with them, or at the least to prevent them from being dealt with seriously. This last point was important because to deal with the issues substantively would take time, money, complicated ideas, and a large number of participants, with no certain, measurable outcome. Certainty and continued control, rather than educational quality, was the political goal; a bureaucratic fix became the means.

The swelling opposition and alienation in the ranks of teachers did not subside after the initial administering of the TECAT. The test's trivial questions and the classroom management slant to the test's pedagogical topics surfaced again, this time in the state's new "instrument" for teacher assessment. A part of the quality control promised in exchange for higher school taxes for teacher pay was a way of monitoring teacher performance. The means of monitoring was not left to building principals nor to the teaching profession. It was created as a uniform statewide checklist for administrative oversight of teacher quality (Texas State Board of Education 1987). The bureaucratic tool for certainty about teacher performance was the Texas Teacher Assessment System, the TTAS. The political and personal uncertainties of teacher evaluations were to be made "rational" and "objective" by placing in the hands of administrators and teachers a list of behaviors thought to be typical of productive, effective teachers. Teachers' ratings on these classroom behaviors would provide the basis for their eligibility for mobility up the career ladder and thereby for merit pay increases. The state would micromanage teacher performance. Early versions of state-required assessment tools had such sections as "uses praise words" and "varies verbal responses," followed by a list of approximately one-hundred acceptable "praise words" for teacher to use with children in their classes. This and other trivializations created such resistance by teachers, and such unwieldy paperwork for administrators, that the agency was compelled to begin anew.

The new instrument was aimed at bureaucratic precision. Modeled, perhaps unwittingly, after the activity analysis model of factory assembly line pacing (Callahan 1967), the checklist reduced the tasks of the teacher to fifty-five generic behaviors. They were generic in that the same list of behaviors was intended to pertain to all teaching situations, all courses and subjects, all grade levels, all students. Derived from the language of classroom management, the list enumerated such teacher behaviors as having a clear objective, making sure all students' attention is on the teacher, varying activities, and waiting the appropriate time for student responses to teacher-asked questions. The checklist was an inventory, a list of behaviors to look for and rate; it was not a description of what is taught, or how the lesson progresses, or students' skills and conceptions, or their developing levels of understandings. The checklist included little about the students except in terms of their compliance with teacher directives (all eyes on the teacher; all students listening). The "instrument" held no provision for a description of or an evaluation of the curriculum content of the lesson, or of the ways the students were encountering it. The "objective" measures included just three choices of rating by the observer: "satisfactory," "unsatisfactory" (stated on the form like the "needs improvement" boxes on children's report cards), and the elusive "EQ," which indicated "exceptional quality."

Leaving little to chance, those in charge of implementation (as so charged by the very general enabling language of the legislation) developed detailed instructions about the frequency of these assessments, the level of personnel who may conduct assessments, and the necessary training workshop hours the evaluators must have before doing the classroom visits. Two administrators (or an administrator and an experienced teacher) were to visit each teacher. The primary administrator's assessment was to count 60 percent; the other observer's portion of the ratings counts 40 percent.

The number of visits to a teacher each year was later contested, as was the appropriateness of evaluations by administrators who were not knowledgeable about the subjects being taught in classrooms they would be evaluating. Teachers saw the assessment as ignoring their personal style and knowledge of their subject. They particularly objected that nowhere in the assessment was there a space for a teacher to explain why she or he chose a particular approach to the lesson or how the observation day's lesson followed on what had come before it, what was to come after, and ways the students in that class best learned. There was no attention to the "ways of knowing" and none to the relationship between the lesson and the cultures and experiences of the children.

In press conferences, the state commissioner of education defused teachers' criticisms of this assessment device as typical of any system that "needs to have the bugs worked out of it." He anticipated fine-tuning the "instrument" and continuing the training of the assessors so that the procedure would work smoothly once all were familiar with it. Such deflection carried with it the strong message that to be against a generic evaluation is to be against improved teaching. (As with the TECAT, the public spin put on dissent, from the governor, Ross Perot, and the Texas Education Agency, was that the dissenters were the incompetent teachers, afraid that at last their incompetence would be made public.)

If the assessments went into the personnel file for only rare future reference, or if they were to become the basis for constructive peer discussions about improving classroom teaching, most of the teachers interviewed in the magnet study, and in other schools, said they would not have objected to being rated by a knowledgeable observer. In fact, the generic assessments of standardized teacher behaviors were to be the central feature of a teacher's advancement on the career ladder. A teacher had not only to attain a certain level of ratings but also to maintain those over, say, three consecutive years, before career ladder salary increments would result (TTAS instruction booklet 1985). In a nonunion state, such a merit system makes the teacher entirely vulnerable to the politics, and to the professional knowledge (or lack of it) and personalities of those administering the checklist. Although the teacher assessment instrument was supposedly standardized and objective, the instruction book (which all teachers received at the beginning of the school year) had only very brief instructions guiding assessors (and teachers to be assessed) in designating EQ status to their work. Some administrators used Exceptional Quality to mean exceptional as compared to other teachers; others used it to indicate a teacher who went beyond his or her own usual norm. Some administrators used this designation liberally, eager to present a positive image of their faculty; others reserved its use for truly extraordinary teaching. Still others, considering budget implications of teacher eligibility for the salary increases attached to career ladder mobility, allocated EQs sparingly. No teacher could know in advance whether an administrator would reward (or even recognize) a particularly insightful question or explanation to a student in a given subject, or understand the characteristics of a well-taught lesson in their subject.

Although the detailed effects of such an assessment model on the magnet teachers follows in chapter 6, and are the subject of a separate paper (McNeil 1987a), it must be noted here that most teachers felt that to perform well on the fifty-five-item checklist in a forty-minute class period came closer to a song-and-dance routine than to teaching. If only a few items on the checklist were applicable to a given day's lesson, then the teacher was forced to forfeit a high rating or to alter the teaching style for that day of observation, even if to do so divorced the lesson from its content and the students. *The instrument thus de-skilled the teacher, artificially separating a teachers' knowledge of pedagogy from overt behaviors.*

For an assessment to be fair, according to the reformers, it would need to be uniformly managed and administered. The rationale for the checklist is to maintain objectivity in an area that can easily become political and irrational. Of course, the checklist itself is highly subjective in its creation and has been variably applied. For example, one teacher with twenty years of experience stated that her biggest objection to the assessment checklist was that nowhere did it ask for her explanation, for her *why.* The checklist included no way of checking off attending to a particular student's need because this assessment instrument was built on a classroom management model that assumed the teacher addresses an *aggregate class with the teacher at its center.* The assessment instrument, ostensibly neutral, also omitted variations in teaching style that accompany subject matter considerations, including whether the teacher had developed the curriculum or taught from prepackaged materials. Students, their cultures, and their development as learners were notably missing as well.

The assessment mechanism is one more area where Texas teachers participated in a trade-off, gaining a system of merit pay in exchange for an assessment system to be generic to all subjects, grades, and students. These trade-offs at first seemed fair and reasonable (or at least not dangerous), especially if they resulted in new revenues, because they were supported by the economic establishment without whose support, in this non-public-goods state, increased financial support for schools would be unlikely. That forced trade-off of professional judgment for the support of the corporate elite was veiled or backgrounded during the implementation of these policies, yet it remains the most important part of the continued legacy of these policies and will be discussed in the concluding chapter.

Of great distress to teachers in impoverished schools was the considerable expense the state would incur to produce the assessment instrument (again, an expensive contract to a vendor) and create training materials on compliance for teachers and on observation-and-assessment procedures for administrators. It would lead to the creation and maintaining of new divisions of the bureaucracy, both in the Texas Education Agency and in local districts, to administer this assessment system. The costs of the contracts, materials, training, and new bureaucrats would show up as "educational expenses," making taxpayers think they were paying for school improvements, when in fact none of the funds were in support of children and instruction.

The Faustian component of the agreement is that within a linkage between controls and benefits, *the controls can remain in place even after the resources for the benefits disappear.* This is essential to understand in the current calls for a national test for teachers and a national set of tests for students. One widely discussed vision is that such tests will not revert to the lowest common denominator because they will include multidimensional "performances" and multidimensional criteria. Such non-computer-graded assessments are very expensive. Once the tests and their criteria have been legitimated as the province of government (in this case, the state) or of a national board to be somehow ratified by or complied with by the states, the locus of control for these matters will be out of the hands of local people, particularly local teachers. And if the resources to support their highest level of educational expertise should disappear, or shrink in competition with other necessary public expenditures, then the controls themselves, the tests, and the "instrument" will persist. Evaluation of children and of teachers will have been nationalized at great cost to professional teachers and to local communities.

This ratcheting effect raises controls each time resources are needed (for example, higher teacher pay). Yet, it is very difficult to lower the degree or level of control if the resources are taken away. Texas has already demonstrated this ratcheting effect. Governor Mark White and the Perot committee (SCOPE) laid the plans for a complicated package of new expenditures and controls at a time when the state had a surplus of almost $5 billion. The checklists for teacher performance were tolerated because they were thought to be the only politically expedient route to capture some of those state resources for higher teacher pay.

The Texas economy soon weakened, with no clear end of the decline in sight. The price of oil fell to an extreme low; agriculture suffered; and the wealth built on those two came near collapse, especially in real estate, banking, and savings and loan sectors. The next governor, Bill Clements, no friend to education, suggested that the Career Ladder pay increments due for the years immediately following implementation of the Career Ladder be postponed. (This represented a huge disappointment for those teachers already above the state minimum, who had followed the legislation with great anticipation of a pay increase; steps two and three of the Career Ladder would have been their first real benefit from House Bill 72.) The standardized assessments were, of course, to remain in place. Governor Clements made several public statements about the Career Ladder. At first, he indicated that the state treasury could not possibly honor the commitments to higher teacher pay. There was not enough money budgeted to cover all the salary increases for all who might upgrade their Career Ladder status. The governor explained that since there was not enough money for the *teachers,* the surplus should be invested back into the *further production and refinement of the assessment instruments.* In other words, assessments were to continue even though additional Career Ladder steps in pay could not be taken. The testing and consulting firms, the administrators who traveled to workshops on teacher assessment—all these would reap the benefits of the "not enough for teacher pay raises" fund. Even more cynical was the governor's later suggestion that education money remaining in the Career Ladder fund be switched to prison construction.

Because it is more complicated and because teachers were not all gathered on assessment days ready to be photographed by the news media as they were on TECAT test days, the teacher assessments did not become the volatile public issue that accompanied the one-time teacher testing. Rather, as the management-based assessment continued in place, it became taken for granted. Its controls have become imbedded in the structure of administrator-teacher relations. The emphasis on observable behaviors, the absence of substantive content and pedagogy, and allowance for teacher style and student differences have become as routine as student report cards. In such an instance, the hollowness of the assessment categories becomes a secondary problem; the first is the necessity of linking resources to controls, in which the controls come to serve only controlling purposes rather than educative ones. In the tension between the educational goals and the controlling goals of schooling, the teacher assessment system built into HB 72 represents a serious tilt toward the controlling goals. This is evidenced, in this instance, by the continuation of the assessment instrument as a management tool for several more years after the Career Ladder model as a system for merit pay was abolished in 1992.

A Problem for Management

An enormous leap of imagination is needed to connect the provisions of HB 72, the state's first comprehensive school legislation since the Gilmer-Aiken Act of the 1940s, to the problems of schools identified by the magnet teachers and other good teachers. The checklist of teacher behaviors for Career Ladder advancement gave no hint how a teacher should be evaluated who used worksheets to count for the required 40 percent lab time in her science course because there are only two or three lighted microscopes for a class of thirty students. It provided no suggestion whether a teacher who did not send students to the library for history class should be seen as lazy, as frustrated because the school has no library, or as generous and enterprising because she brought her own books from home for her students to use. As state testing of children became incorporated into the teacher assessment system, there was no provision for an asterisk by test scores of those students whose schools run out of photocopy paper in March and textbooks in September. The conditions of teaching that the magnet teachers had to overcome could not be solved by teacher checklists, nor by statewide testing of children, longer school years, or praise words. Far less would the legislation solve the problems of the neighborhood schools many of their magnet students had left behind, where student test scores hovered in the 40 to 60 percentile range (scores that represented the students still in school after 25 to 30 percent had dropped out before ever getting to the final years of high school). Students reported in interviews that they managed to get all the way to high school, even a magnet school, without reading a whole book. Their teachers would be asked to prepare them for multiple-choice statewide tests and to do so by carrying out two- or three-dozen operations in a single class period if those teachers were to receive high marks on the Career Ladder assessment. HB 72 added five days to the school year, then took away more than that many with added standardized testing days.

By what logic did SCOPE, the governor, or the legislature think that the separate or collective components of House Bill 72 could take Texas schools into the high-tech future of the twenty-first century? In order to understand the full impact of this law on teaching and learning, particularly the unintended consequences of the law and its implementation, it is essential to understand how the "issues and continuing concerns related to public education in Texas" were identified, what the source of the solution was expected to be, what knowledge was brought to bear on the legislation. It is critical to know what assumptions about the organization of schooling guided the selection of reform items and the authority for implementation and accountability.

Who's in Charge Here?

By selecting Ross Perot to head up SCOPE, Mark White signaled to educators and to the larger public that he thought the expertise for improving schools lay outside the education community, in the corporate elite. Ross Perot let it be known, by organizing the Select Committee and personally underwriting its financial costs, that he thought the education problem was a management problem. Perot had looked at the schools and asked, "Who's in charge here?" (Toch 1991, 79). His role in the Select Committee proceeded to answer that question.

Perot identified the problem of Texas public schools as a management problem. He articulated three great needs. First, he believed that schools are about being able to compete in society. He saw success in society as the survival of the fittest. He expected, even advocated, the same kind of competition in schools. But he said over and over, according to Michael Kirst who was his adviser on school finance, that everyone needs to be "equal at the starting line." Kirst reported that Perot would say, "It's get them to the starting line *even* and whoever wins, wins." Perot would add, "We've got to get them pretty much even, otherwise the race is rigged." His interest in equalizing funding and in making prekindergarten and kindergarten mandatory was genuine according to Kirst, two ways of leveling the playing field for children.[5]

Second, he thought (according to Kirst, who read the notes Perot had written up after making visits to schools) that teachers "were working hard and they needed help." He saw his role as doing something "positive for the teachers," whose work was made harder by the "terrible" administrators. He thought the teachers were held back by local administrators.

Third, Perot also looked at the dollars and focused on the bottom line. He noted that state funding for public education in Texas had increased from $1.75 billion in 1973 to $8.3 billion in 1984 with little evidence of improved achievement (Toch 1991, 79). An analysis of costs might have revealed increases in numerous noninstructional areas such as energy, transportation, and construction. In addition, international immigrants and an influx of families moving in from out of state as well as new federal guidelines for special education and bilingual education all put pressures on school budgets. A number of noninstructional factors could be isolated from the cost increases. In addition, the increasing challenges children were facing, including divorce, poverty, geographic mobility, limited English proficiency, deteriorating school facilities, deferred construction, and other factors that affect student achievement could have been examined. Finally, the means of calculating costs and the measures of achievement themselves could have been questioned. Instead, Perot saw the two sets of numbers and concluded that the benefits were not commensurate with the costs: competent management was needed.

Few teachers observed for this study would believe that Ross Perot started out sharing their concerns—for young children, for equalization of resources across the state, for teachers and the conditions of their work, for better use of tax dollars. Very few, as SCOPE began to report out its findings, would believe that Perot thought he was acting on their behalf.

Top-Down Management

H. Ross Perot had earned his millions by leaving IBM and starting up his own company when IBM rejected his idea of selling computing services, rather than just computers. The record of his spectacular fortune includes his successful maneuvering to acquire government contracts for processing medical claims, among other ventures. However, the aura surrounding the success of Electronic Data Systems (EDS) rarely includes references to its reliance on government contracts but spotlights the leadership of Perot himself. In the way he ran the Select Committee and in his prescriptions for Texas schools, Perot's model for effective management was himself and his own corporate leadership record. He knew very little about schools, and frequently said so, but just two weeks after opening the SCOPE hearings around the state and making a few visits into schools, he was "ready to tell Texas that its schools were failing" (Toch 1991, 78). He lay the blame on all levels of administration (again, an idea he and many teachers shared, although as the reforms played out, teachers would be surprised to remember Perot's original disdain of school administrators).

He thought the elected state school board was a group of political hacks, influenced by old-boy politics and the cabal of coaches. The first step he advocated for effective management was to have a state board appointed by the governor, to align top management into a single command structure. In his view, the old, twenty-seven-member elected board was too indebted to constituents and too tied to old, ineffective ways of thinking (too much a part of the problem) to be trusted to implement the legislated reforms. A nine-member *appointed* board was a feature of the SCOPE recommendations; the legislature, more inclined to a board accountable to the public, added the compromise that after the initial term of the appointed board— just long enough to implement HB 72—the members would have to stand for election.

Once the top command was in place, the task was to sharpen the chain of command, clarify the content of the commands, then set up strict accountability systems to make sure the command signal reached the troops in the trenches. Perhaps Perot's old Navy training superseded even his strong corporate model as a metaphor for bringing Texas schools under control.

The top command had to have strong authority because Perot completely distrusted the middle-level managers, the bureaucrats, the local school boards, the superintendents, and building principals. He especially hated that so many of them were former coaches, saying, "Half of them still have whistles around their necks" (Toch 1991, 80). According to Kirst, Perot thought teachers were "held down by local administrators" and he thought these administrators were "terrible." To his advisers, Perot would say that the local leadership was "essentially bankrupt, and irreformable, irreformable." He completely distrusted local control. This was not only his corporate management style and his strict Navy training but also his assessment of the capacity of the particular kinds of people currently holding administrative positions in local school districts. He thought that because local school boards and superintendents and principals "could not be trusted," the state had to go around them to influence classrooms. He did not start out with the idea that "teachers are lousy and you have to micromanage them" (Kirst 1994b). It was that their administrators were incompetent. It is interesting that SCOPE's provisions for No Pass/No Play to govern athlete's participation and for the UIL (state interscholastic league) to report directly to the state board of education, rather than the state education agency, were informed by Perot's distrust of bureaucrats' and local administrators' ability to withstand the pressures of coaches to subordinate academics to competitive athletics. The appointed board, to include corporate leaders, would in his model be presumed to be immune to "local politics." In these and other areas of schooling, he concluded that the top commands cannot reach the bottom employees (teachers) unless the objectives and sanctions are made public and the command structure tightened. Perot was explicit that only tight management could solve the problems of the schools:

> In any basic management course [you learn that] there are certain things you need to do to run a business. All these things are missing the Texas public schools. . . . There are no management goals; there is no management philosophy; there is no management training. . . . There is no accountability. Now think about that in your business. (Perot, cited in Koppich 1987, 9)

Managing a "business" from the top-down, for Perot, was a matter of identifying individual problems and "solving" them. Timar writes that this is a central feature of hierarchical policy implementation (Timar 1988). Since there is no single definition for "educational excellence," the tendency is to see "issues and continuing concerns" as isolated technical problems in need of a fix. This is particularly true when those charged with the reform know very little about education. They have to borrow metaphors and technical solutions from what is familiar to them. For Perot, the issues were competence, efficiency, and accountability. Most of all, the issue was control. He addressed the issue of competence not by proposing an alternative governance structure (although in corporate management as well as in education, there were, at that time, a number of organizational alternatives to the Texas educational hierarchy), but by jerry-rigging around the "broken" links in the present structure to affect classroom practice.

The Experts. For issues of efficiency, Perot did what he would do as CEO of his corporation: he called in experts. SCOPE was made up of business and legislative leaders nominated by the governor, the speaker of the Texas House, and the lieutenant governor (Toch 1991, 74). It had subcommittees on teacher pay and finance and other matters before it. What appeared to be a deliberative body, however, soon came to be a parallel universe to Perot's own "deliberations" about how to fix Texas schools. At his own expense Perot engaged experts to advise him about school finance and equalization, about teacher pay and a possible merit system, about public polling on attitudes toward education. He ran the work out of his corporate offices at EDS and his secretary made arrangements for all the meetings of SCOPE. Some estimates place his personal financial contribution at $2,000,000; the state supported the committee with something closer to $200,000. He kept his own personal experts separate from each other and from the Select Committee. Each problem he or the committee identified was dealt with in isolation from the others.

This fragmentation may make it easier to control the process of producing a reform report, but it has serious consequences when it isolates elements that can work only in tandem. The school finance plan and the proposed teacher career ladder provide a case in point. Michael Kirst of PACE was hired by Perot to advise him on school finance. Texas had two problems to be addressed: an antiquated unit of allocation (by instructional unit rather than per pupil), and gross inequities because of unequal property tax bases across districts. Kirst, along with a Dallas businessman and another school finance expert, were to come up with recommendations that would solve these two problems. Kirst said that he was told to work within a "conventional" school finance model. He was given the tax base figures and asked to create a model that would equalize resources across districts. Perot was fascinated by California and so planned to rely heavily on this California-based finance expert. Kirst came up with a plan that provided near equalization for the 95 percent of school children "in the middle." The high and low per-pupil expenditure extremes were left out of the equation, but within the main distribution the plan went a long way toward equalizing dollars across districts. He also recommended allocations per pupil, rather than by the "unit of instruction" allocation calculation from forty years before. The third major finance recommendation, one which Kirst had tried unsuccessfully to sell California on, was to have state dollars weighted according to their buying power in regions of the state. Both Texas and California are huge and include high-cost cities and remote rural areas and lower-cost small towns. A dollar spent in Houston does not go as far as a dollar in Plainview. This potentially common-sense, cost-saving economic factor was not incorporated into the SCOPE finance recommendations.

Kirst had expected to meet the members of the SCOPE finance subcommittee, but Tom Luce, Perot's attorney and assistant during the SCOPE proceedings, informed him that that would not be necessary because Kirst was working for Luce and Perot. As a result, the formulas applied by Kirst and his associates did not include any changes in educational program policies. Neither the proposed mandatory kindergarten, the prekindergarten, nor the Career Ladder was factored into what amounted to the financial "hypotheticals." "We worked on what one would call a conventional-concepts-at-that-time form of school finance. Career ladders and teacher merit were unconventional, and we were not intending to do anything with that whatsoever.... Our concern was around property tax equalization and equal yield for equal effort and rationalizing the system so that it was converted from a classroom unit to a per pupil expenditure." Their data were current property tax/pupil ratios and differentials across the state, not projected costs of new programs.

By having all the experts report to him directly, Perot could keep to a minimum any alternative ideas or criticisms of particular proposals on which he wanted to prevail. His distrust of school administrators seemed to extend to any kind of deliberation he did not control. Because of his distrust of educators, he did not turn to teachers or other educators in the design of the system of merit pay for teachers. He brought in (and paid) a management consulting firm from the Turtle Creek area of Dallas, a firm that had advised him on internal management issues within EDS. The "Turtle Creek Gang," as one person called them, had no experience with schools but had designed a rationalized system of merit pay for a corporation. That model, slightly modified, became the Career Ladder. Interestingly, in a strictly top-down management model, labor carries out tasks assigned and defined and measured by management. The assembly line worker does not have the choice of the placement of door handles or side mirrors; the sewing machine operator cannot move the pocket or add a belt unless directed to do so. The use of this model to direct and measure teacher behavior does not omit the intellectual capacity of the worker by accident. It does so because worker discretion will create inefficiencies. As the magnet teachers and others have reported, they often pull out a standard, de-skilled lesson (a grammar exercise, a set of math problems that require routine operations, a prescripted recitation) on the days they will be observed, so their teaching will fit the assessment instrument (see chapter 6). The Career Ladder plan, according to those close to the reform process, was constructed in isolation from any expertise on children's development, teacher practice, or the curriculum in any subject or grade level. In addition, it was planned in isolation from those financial advisers who might have been most likely to be able to generate a plan for adequate funding of Career Ladder increments.

The Organization. Perot was right about the quality of many of the bureaucratic layers of Texas public schools. He was wrong about how they worked. Like his helicopter rescue of his employees held hostage in Iran (Follett 1986; Toch 1991, 75), his "rescue" of the schools was predicated on an end-run, a dramatic circumvention of the villains holding teachers and children captive in administrative mediocrity. As a result of attempting an end-run, he left the basic structure intact. And as a result of little curiosity about teaching and learning, he strengthened the bureaucracy as a controlling mechanism, rather than strengthen it as a support for teachers and students or weaken it altogether. His assumptions about how the system worked, and how it would work after HB 72, were flawed.

First, Perot believed that if the top command sent clear directives, they would be followed. This presumes top management would know what should be taught and learned, and it presumes the same command will have the same effect across a widely diverse number of school subjects in widely differing communities for students who differ in every dimension of culture, learning style, ability to learn, and stage of development. It assumes that teachers function as de-skilled laborers dependent on and observant of instructions from management. It assumes there is a correlation between teachers' overt, measurable behaviors and the quality of their teaching. It assumes that local or personal variation is something to be remedied, brought into line, rather than understood and valued.

And a strict top-down management that would permit a recommendation from Ross Perot or the legislature to go straight down to a classroom teacher assumes there is no Texas Education Agency. What Ross Perot did not understand was that even with an appointed school board, not all the signals from the top would go directly to local districts for implementation. What the state board of education proposes, the Texas Education Agency disposes. The SCOPE plan did call for having the commissioner of education report to the school board rather than to the governor, but it did not fully deal with the role of TEA in drafting guidelines, creating implementation procedures, generally bureaucratizing legislative and board-initiated policies. After the SCOPE report was adopted, with minor adjustments as House Bill 72, it was TEA that arranged for the contracts to create the teacher assessment instrument to be used for the Career Ladder, TEA that contracted with vendors to create student tests, TEA that took the language of raising standards and turned it into quality control checklists for minimum teacher performance and minimum student learning.

In *Legislated Learning*, Arthur Wise writes that assuring educational equity is best done by central governments. But he goes on to say that improving the quality of education is not (Wise 1979, vii). He describes the search for a tight mechanism of goals and controls in a domain where such a tight mechanism can undercut the fundamental purpose of the enterprise as "hyperrationalization." (Wise 1979, 65, 69). As the Career Ladder and student testing systems required by HB 72 were implemented by TEA, the state agency's budget and its authority increased at the expense of local districts, dollars were diverted from instruction, and local administrators, as receivers and interpreters of TEA directives, increased in power relative to teachers. By treating public education as a single corporation, Perot changed out the board and CEO and put in a few quality controls. But he, his committee, and the legislature did little to enhance the working conditions of teachers. They tinkered at the margins, looking for a single fix. If the TECAT was a cheap alternative to substantive subject matter tests for teachers, then either was inexpensive com-

pared to the cost of seriously remedying the deplorable and inequitable conditions in the state's poorest schools, enabling all teachers to continue to learn
(as a number of the magnet teachers were doing at their own expense), and
seriously addressing the strengths and weaknesses of particular schools and
districts. *Absent a complex understanding of schools, Perot's efforts strengthened
the very bureaucrats he had hoped to undercut.*

Because Perot and his experts functioned so separately from the Select
Committee, and because he set the terms of so many of its meetings and its
recommendations, it is easy to forget that the larger committee, made up of
prominent political and business and educational leaders, was supposed to be
a part of the process. If Perot had run the committee as a truly deliberative
body, then it is likely that some of the mistakes of bureaucratization and
pseudoaccountability could have been avoided or at least partially mitigated.
Some on the committee knew a great deal about schools. Perot's control over
experts and the committee's processes prevented SCOPE's consideration of the
package as a whole until the very end. According to one member of SCOPE,
the committee did not see the recommendations for an appointed board or for
the TECAT until the very last minute, when Perot and Luce were drafting the
amendment for the appointed school board. The governor, anticipating organized teacher opposition, strenuously objected to the teacher test. Several
members of the committee met the night before the SCOPE's final meeting to
come up with a plan for opposing the proposed TECAT. One of the committee members told me that the group went into the meeting thoroughly prepared, knowing they would have a difficult time making their case. They never
had a chance. Perot walked in and announced that unless the report included
the appointed board and the TECAT, his name was going to be taken off the
report. One noted "statesman of public education," according to his colleague,
stood up and said, "There is a saying that when the eagles fly, the sparrows
should go to roost, but this little sparrow's not going to go roost." (This report
came from another member of the Select Committee, one who had anticipated a lively debate, hard pushing and resisting, and then a decision resulting
from tough bargaining.) This statesman made a strong and reasoned case
advocating an elected board and elimination of the more controlling portions
of the committee's recommendations. But Perot prevailed.

SCOPE's report and the ensuing legislation are a patchwork quilt of recommendations: a state-established passing rate to qualify athletes to play a
sport and to set minimum passing rates for students in their courses; the
requirement that districts offer free tutorials for all students who fail, without

a requirement that students attend them. The legislation included the requirement that all districts offer full- or half-day kindergarten, but added the qualifier that the state funds will be calculated on the basis of only half-day
programs. The state was to establish a forgivable loan fund for people going to
college to become teachers (but never authorized funding for such a loan program). The law required that the state formula would equalize funding, yet the
planners all had the understanding in advance that the state share would be
small compared to what local districts would eventually have to raise in additional property taxes to fund the Career Ladder and to comply with other provisions of this law. The limitation on elementary class size (recommended by
SCOPE to be fifteen, but enacted into law as twenty-two) was one of the few
provisions that would directly benefit children; yet, the financing of this law
carried no provisions for capital expenditures for adding onto schools or
building new ones. The TECAT, which all teachers had to pass to keep their
certification, and the Texas Teacher Assessment System, the checklist of classroom behaviors on which Career Ladder promotions depended, were situated
in the context of these other piecemeal provisions.

The teachers I observed saw this "omnibus bill" in terms of what it omitted. It seemed scattered, fragmented and, except for the equalizing and class
size provisions, unrelated to the needs they and their children faced every day.
This did not seem like a comprehensive education bill to them. It certainly did
not seem like major reform.

Michael Kirst offers some insight into how this collection of policies
looked to Perot. He said that when the various experts made their presentations to Perot, Tom Luce invited Kirst to stay and listen to the others. The
meetings took place in Perot's EDS office, away from the Select Committee.
"This was where I saw the Career Ladder people come in from Turtle Creek.
We had the whole thing [all the experts' proposals] in review." Everything from
kindergarten to No Pass/No Play? "Right. And people came in to give their
reports. I did the finance part. . . . And people were ushered in and ushered
out. . . . So in came a public polling group that had done some polling about
Texas attitudes. . . . That was a group he had used for EDS. . . . He of course
paid; all of this, as it was documented, was paid from [his] personal accounts."
As the day went on, Kirst was shocked by what he was hearing.

"So they [the Turtle Creek consulting firm] came in and I had never seen
a Career Ladder before. I had heard of career ladders, but I had never seen a
design for a Career Ladder. . . . I made no comment about that. I was just listening. I thought, gee, this is really bold. You have guys that have never done

anything in education before designing a system the likes of which I have never seen in education before."

Finally, Perot asked for comments on the overall nature of the recommendations. Kirst, basing his thinking on "general organizational theory" said, "I think you have too many things going on here at once." He pointed out that with something like sixty or more changes hitting the organization at once, the organization would not be able to implement them. "I was arguing classic implementation theory. That you overload the organization and you'll end up with partial implementation and they [the state educational system and local school districts] won't be able to handle it."

Perot lashed out and said to the rest of the group, pointing at Kirst, "That's the kind of thinking we don't need around here." Perot was sure that if reforms were designed to be incremental, the "good ol' boys at the local level" would just "incrementalize them to death." They would fake compliance and kill the reforms. He said, "We've got to drop a bomb on them, we got to nuke them— that's the way to make changes in these organizations." The quote made the papers and Perot made his case. The implementation would proceed military style; he would give the orders.

When the legislature received the SCOPE report, there was much political debate, much lobbying. Teacher unions opposed the TECAT and coaches opposed No Pass/No Play. The legislation was opposed by the sitting commissioner of education, the state board of education, the association of school boards and many other educator groups. Perot and White believed that so much opposition signified that they were successfully challenging the entrenched incompetence in public education. There were reports that Perot hired Luce and other "$100,000 boys" to lobby for the bill, that Luce hired beautiful women from Dallas to lobby for the bill, and the Perot even outbid the opposition by paying a lobbyist or two working the other side to go home (Toch 1991, 89–90).

A key part of the lobbying was the pressure from Perot *not* to pass the finance authorization bill until the "quality control" provisions of HB 72 had been passed. He and Gib Lewis, Speaker of the House, were determined that teachers would receive no additional pay, that not one additional tax dollar would be raised for education, until the controls were in place. If the reforms had originally been initiated to support teachers with a pay increase, then they came down to the wire demeaning teachers in the public eye as needing state control. The National Education Association affiliate broke with Governor White over the TECAT, desperately trying to remove it from the bill. White had to stay committed to the total package, Perot's "nukes." The union lost its chance to have a voice in the final passage of the bill, and White lost a key base of support in his attempt for reelection. The voices of teachers were not welcome in this top-down reform effort. As a result, the reforms remained silent on the content of schooling, on the lives of children in schools, on the potential to learn from good practice across the state if improving education were the goal. Teachers were right in their skepticism that the legislation would impose regulations without adequate funding. Texas is a state that can legislate requirements without legislating funding to meet the requirements. The mechanisms of control—the teacher checklist and teacher and student testing contracts and the bureaucratic expenditures necessary to implement them—received funding, as did the initial step toward equalization. (The equalization plan remained inadequate and was challenged later in the courts.) The Career Ladder created a series of measures of classroom behaviors that trivialized the craft of teaching and placed the teacher, not students, at the center of the classroom. The requirement for standardized tests for students set in motion a series of state tests, all of them aimed at minimum skills and managerial controls. (As will be seen in chapter 7, these tests are, in this period, increasingly divorced from pedagogical theories or learning theory and increasingly tied to the privatization of public education because the narrow set of accountability measures can be easily adapted to for-profit school settings.)

Ross Perot and the Select Committee, along with the legislature, by structuring tight controls but offering too few resources, created a top-down structure with the stated purpose of trying to bring up the bottom, the lowest level of educational performance. They tried to do an end run around the worst administrators; instead, they gave those very administrators more power over teacher assessment and discretion over the increased state aid (Stahl et al. 1984, 6). They tried to teacher-proof the curriculum with the checklist for teacher behaviors and the student minimum skills tests. By doing so, they have made schools exceedingly comfortable for mediocre teachers who like to teach routine lessons according to a standard sequence and format, who like working as de-skilled laborers not having to think about their work. They made being a Texas public school teacher extremely uncomfortable for those who know their subjects well, who teach in ways that engage their students, who want their teaching to reflect their own continued learning.

Wise suggests that educational policy is on firm ground when it addresses issues of equity. He states that when it ventures into areas of educational quality, it usually only makes things worse (Wise 1979). That was true of many provisions of House Bill 72, the nuclear attack on Texas public schools. The next chapter examines the civilian casualties caused by the "nukes" as they fell on classrooms. And the concluding chapter traces the longer-term effects of these reforms, the imbedded controls which de-skill teachers and subject curriculum, classroom practice, and the very definitions of what it means to learn from externally derived artificial measurements. Together the stories from classrooms and the extension of these findings into the current context will provide a picture of the immediate and lasting collateral damage we can expect when the locus of external control over what is valued in school becomes institutionalized in standardization.

Chapter 6

―――――――――――

Collateral Damage

I am tired of having to lie to do my work.

―a magnet teacher

Everything they make us do takes me farther and farther from my students.

―an English teacher at a Latino high school

When the state school system was "nuked," the bombs did not fall on the targeted state education agency or middle-level managers in the state bureaucracy. They did not fall on the central office administrators in the local school districts, or others ("ex-coaches and bureaucrats") whom Perot had publicly blamed for the poor quality of education in the state. The legislated reforms, and the mechanisms put into place at the state and local level to assure compliance with them, fell instead on classrooms, on the teachers and their students. Teachers and students suffered the "collateral damage" from Perot's reform "nukes."[1] These reforms included systems for testing teachers and for evaluating their classroom performance. They included reinforcement of systems for prescribing curriculum and for testing students. Together, they had the effects of de-skilling teachers' work, trivializing and reducing the quality of the content of the curriculum, and distancing children from the substance of schooling. More important, the "nukes" assured that this pattern of de-skilling and reduced quality would be institutionalized: the legislated reforms emerging from House Bill 72 shifted the locus of control over instruction away from those closest to the children. By trying to do an end run around the state bureaucracy, Perot, knowing little about education, ironically strengthened the very bureaucracy he and his committee had identified as the source of the ills in public education. His attempted helicopter rescue of the teachers landed them right into the domain of bureaucratic controls.[2] Once these policies were in place, teachers would have difficulty remembering that when Perot began, his charge from the governor and his own expressed passion was to raise the salaries of overworked, underpaid teachers and to nuke the bureaucratic system.

The data from the magnet schools demonstrate very compellingly that these "reforms," ostensibly meant to improve education, reduced what was taught, constrained teachers in the ways they could teach and, as a result, set in motion dynamics in which teachers would have to choose between course content they felt to be valid and content that was required by the state. They would have to choose between creating lessons that were meaningful and engaging for all their students, students of varying ability and cultures and learning styles, or lessons that would earn them, the teachers, high ratings on their own annual performance evaluations. As they shifted their teaching to accommodate to the mandated curricula and teaching techniques, they saw their trust relationships with their students eroded, their relationships with administrators become increasingly adversarial, and their carefully constructed school programs jeopardized.[3]

The research that underpins this book was designed to document and analyze students' access to knowledge in schools structured in support of authentic teaching and learning. It had the purpose of analyzing schools where the administrative controls, long a source of tension in the traditional public high school, did not drive decisions about teaching and learning. These controls include excessive concern with discipline, mass processing of students for credentialing, overemphasis on efficiencies to the detriment of quality instruction (McNeil 1986). The magnet schools proved to be appropriate choices for this research. Their distinctive missions set them apart from the state controls over curriculum, particularly as exercised through the state textbook adoption system. Within their local district they were unique, and their uniqueness gave them a latitude for interpretations of and compliance with a variety of central office directives meant to apply to all schools. The reputation of these schools, as supported by the federal courts and the local district, to be specialized was validated in this latitude and in such central services as bus transportation for their students and the assistance of the central office for magnet admissions and student transfers. For their academic programs, this "structural support" more frequently took the form of a lack of direct control rather than adequate provisioning of the program. Nevertheless, taken together the schools provide a powerful record of the ways a non-controlling administrative and organizational structure enabled teachers, even in extremely under-resourced schools, to work together with their students to create successful academic experiences for highly diverse populations of urban students. The data emerging from these magnet schools would have made an important contribution to our understanding of the positive dynamics that can shape educational experiences under less controlling organizational environments if, in fact, the story had stopped with their precarious place in the structure of an urban district: supported by permission to be distinctive but not provisioned so as to act on that permission. As events developed, they became even more important as examples of the losses that can occur when curriculum and teaching are standardized.

The research took an unexpected turn during the middle part of the field observations, when teachers at SET began to murmur, "We hear we are about to be reformed." An observer may be forgiven for hearing the teachers' dread with a naive sense of optimism: surely "reform" would mean library books, lighted microscopes, budgets for instructional materials, funds for updating equipment, new procedures for acquisitions, and new opportunities for planning. The teachers with considerable seniority in this state and in this district were far more prescient; they had endured "reforms" before. And they were correct in their apprehension: when the legislated reforms were enacted, no member of the state Senate legislative committee called a teacher from SET to inquire about adequate laboratory facilities. No member of the House committee called Pathfinder teachers in to discuss how the successes of the Pathfinder program might be extended to the students in the "neighborhood" wing of Allen High, so that they too could have a chance at a productive future. Nor did Perot, in his personal hiring of experts, invite a MedIC teacher in to advise SCOPE on how teachers' work should be evaluated in light of their responsibilities for preparing students for critical fields such as medicine and scientific research. The governor, the legislators, members of SCOPE, and Perot himself relied on technical experts from outside education and on their own limited knowledge. They acted precipitously and at the same time proceeded timidly and reactively (afraid of those who did not want to pay more for public education). As a result, they set in motion "reforms" that changed the nature and content and relational contexts of these teachers' work and that of teachers who would follow them.

The Myth of Standardized Reform

Being present as these reforms were rumored, piloted, implemented, revised, and institutionalized provided a rare opportunity to see the reality behind the myths of centralized reforms. The myth promulgated by the state commissioner of education, Perot, and others involved in selling these reforms to the public is that policies that centralize and standardize teaching and learning generate "improvements" by setting minimum standards, by "bringing up the bottom." The myth further says that of course "good teachers" will not be hampered by these minimum standards, but in fact will go far beyond them. The "good teachers" are not the target, or so the logic goes; it is the "illiterate" and "bad" teachers whom the reforms are supposed to improve or drive out of the system. Classroom observations, extensive interviews with teachers, conferences with teacher groups brought together from across these schools, and examination of course content after House Bill 72 reforms were put in place paint a very different story. The clear picture that emerges is that the standardized reforms drastically hurt the best teachers, forcing them to teach watered-down content required because it was computer-gradable. The standardization brought about by the state policies forced them to teach artificially simplified curricula that had been designed by bureaucrats seeking expedient (easily implemented, noncontroversial) curricular formats. The quality of their teaching, their course content and their students' learning all suffered. In addition, those relations within the school essential to fostering a culture of both equity and authentic academics were undermined.

The teachers found themselves having to shift their teaching away from a focus on children's learning in favor of a format that held the teacher at the center. At one point they were required to translate all assessments of their students' work into matrices of meaningless symbols, proxies for substantive responses to their students' work. The resulting teaching and curriculum took on two dimensions: either teaching and curriculum suffered in quality as a result of compliance with standardization requirements, or the teachers' workload took on the dual tasks of compliance (or working to create the appearance of compliance), on the one hand, and attempting to hold on to authentic, substantive teaching, on the other. The reforms required that they choose between their personal survival in the system or their students' education.

Classroom examples that follow, and the teachers' voices as they reflected on these new constraints on their work, show teachers having to exclude their richest knowledge from their lessons. They capture teachers' voices as they describe having to shift their teaching away from their particular students into a generic mode of presentation, generic not only within their own school but also across the district or state. The data show teachers presenting "double-entry" lessons with the "real content" explained as distinct from what student would need "for the [official] test." In interviews teachers reflect on making these conscious decisions to teach a split curriculum. Classroom observations will show teachers, already working many extra hours to create their school programs and producing materials not provided, now having to spend time—previously devoted to their own and their students' learning—on strategies to get around the undermining effects of the controls. The pattern is pervasive across these schools. The examples cited are not exceptions, but rather representative practices as the state reforms, and their local manifestations, began to be implemented. The particular strategies vary by subject or by the teachers' relation to colleagues and the school-level administration, but the overall pattern is one of curricular losses. It is, further, a pattern of pedagogical gamesmanship as the policies to control curriculum and monitor the "quality control" of teaching were imposed on these schools.

When the centralized curricula and testing remained as loosely enforced directives, the faculty cultures established in these schools sustained the teachers and their efforts to maintain authentic teaching. When the controls became "aligned" with the teacher assessment system (especially Career Ladder pay increments) and student testing, teachers faced an imposed de-skilling to which they did not want to acquiesce, but which became much more difficult to avoid. Some threatened to leave; some left. (Perot and the governor mistakenly saw teacher exit as proof their reforms were driving out the bad teachers, the ones who "couldn't make it.") Others stayed and tried to minimize the effects of the collateral damage on their students.

What Was at Stake

No single pedagogy or recipe made the magnet schools academically successful for their students. The approaches to teaching varied widely, depending on the subject, the teachers' personalities and philosophies, the teachers' perceptions of their students' interests and capabilities, the role of a particular course in the overall school program, and many other factors. The curriculum in the magnet schools was in a constant state of flux, as teachers updated and reworked their courses from year to year and from class to class within a given year. The curriculum itself, then, was not an "independent variable" that could account for the schools' accomplishments. The curricula grew as teachers' knowledge and students' experiences grew and shaped the possibilities of topics and activities.

Nor were the students themselves, although perceived as an elite group, carrying the school reputations by their very demographics. In fact, the students varied along every dimension: academic preparedness, measurements on intelligence and achievement tests, family economic circumstance, parental employment and education level, neighborhood, and level of motivation and engagement. They included boys and girls, Hispanics, Blacks, Anglos, and Asians. Many of them, as the teachers kept reiterating, had not been well prepared in the sciences and social studies, had not developed rigorous study skills, and had not even read a book at school, despite qualifying for admission to a magnet school. The only common trait among these students was that someone in their family had heard about the school and that they had applied. That initiative made them somewhat different from the average student who did not seek a magnet transfer, but since the person most motivated to have them at this school may have been a parent, someone other than the student, even the fact of applying does not account significantly for the fact that in each of these three schools, even with all the weaknesses they brought with them to the schools, more than 95 percent (closer to 99 percent in most years) of these students went to college and most graduated.

To understand their successes, it is important to review the strengths of the magnet schools as schools that made authentic knowledge and varied ways of knowing accessible, even commonplace, for their students prior to the reforms:

- **MedIC** was the school that exemplified teaching and school course content that has *credibility in the world outside schools,* in this case the hospitals and research labs of the city's famed Medical Center. Laboratory equipment, lab skills, scientific concepts, and the ability to communicate and understand complex concepts were essential inside the school because the students would have responsibilities for carrying out "real-world" tasks during their junior and senior rotations through labs and clinics. The teachers could not water down, oversimplify, or omit information just because it might be complex or inefficient to teach.

- **The Pathfinder School** was notable for the lack of barriers between teachers' knowledge and the knowledge they invited their students to study and explore in class. The *congruence between classroom knowledge and personal knowledge,* the teachers' and the students', enabled teachers and students to work as co-creators of the curriculum. They built the curriculum out of their individual and shared experiences, enabling the teachers' formal learning, the children's cultures and family histories such as work or immigration, their curiosities about new subjects, and their diverse perspectives to be brought to bear on traditional subjects such as the branches of the U.S. government and elections as well as on emerging topics such as changes in immigration laws and the political and naturalistic ecologies of the coast of the Gulf of Mexico.

- SET also exemplifies a school whose course content and educational activities provided students with intellectually engaging content and skills that would serve them well beyond the walls of the school, beyond the credentialing requirements of a traditional high school. The teachers were able to provide such an education and prepare their students for college studies in the sciences, technology, and engineering as well as liberal arts, because *they and their students struck a bargain to make the school work.* The district had provided this magnet program with a name, entrance requirements, bus transportation, and an initial group of highly dedicated faculty but very little else that would have been needed to create a first-rate science high school. The faculty created a culture of academic excellence and mutual support in the face of severe shortages, but they ultimately credited their successes to the willingness of the majority of their students to help make the school live up to its name.

It is against these models of authentic teaching and learning, and the dynamic relational organizational factors at work within them, that the standardizations of teaching and curriculum need to be weighed. Those standardizations made it increasingly difficult for teachers to incorporate complex "real-world" information into their courses, to draw on their own personal knowledge and their student's experiences, and to affirm the students' role in the co-construction of the learning experience.

As "school reforms" began to take shape at the state and district levels, no distinction was made between strong teachers and weak ones, between productive school programs and faltering ones, between successful programs within schools and those programs within schools that neglected or underserved certain groups of children. These teachers, in their more optimistic moments, listened to the politicians' reform rhetoric with hopes for policies and funds that would help overcome barriers to good teaching; these hopes turned to cynicism as the reforms began to be implemented. Both the reforms originating at the state level, prompted by the Perot commission and subsequent legislation, and related district-level policies aimed to bring up the low-est levels of educational quality aimed to accomplish these goals by standard-izing teaching. The district reforms removed the design of the curriculum and of student assessment from the teachers' control. The state-level reforms dic-tated the teachers' role in the classroom and redefined teaching as "teacher behaviors." Both shifted the authority for decisions about teaching away from educators and families. And when they came together, they worked to the detriment of the students in these strong schools.

Anticipatory Standardization

Standardization in education tends to originate at the top of bureaucratic structures. In the case of the first reform policy felt by the magnet teachers, the standardization of the curriculum came first from the district level, not the state. The planning of the state-level reforms, and uncertainty about the form they would ultimately take, caused the local superintendent to set in motion an anticipatory strike in this war on school mediocrity. The first curriculum controls (in this 1980s round)[4] were originated within the district in the antic-ipation that such controls by the state were inevitable and would probably be "pilot-tested on some podunk town that isn't at all like us."[5] The superinten-dent wanted to create a test-driven curriculum system within his own district and, according to several of his co-workers, ultimately hoped to be able to market the local system statewide and eventually nationally. Having a stan-dardized curriculum and testing system that would be handed down from the state agency was not consistent with his view of the district as needing to stay "ahead of the state."[6] He did not challenge the idea of centralized controls, only on their locus of authority; he wanted the local plan to shape the state controls that would soon align curriculum content and student testing with the more visible state teacher assessment systems being implemented.

The district innovation in curriculum control was a proficiency-based system. Like the Perot reforms being planned at the same time, the district's plan was announced as being directed at the weakest classrooms and schools. The steps in the district's creation and implementation of this plan follow the same general outline as Perot's work at the state level: first, exclude teachers and others who know curriculum, learning, children's development, instruc-tional practice. Second, decide, as Perot would say, "who's in charge," in this case the central administration and its evaluation office. Third, decide what will be measured and by what instruments. Then shape the content by the capacity of the measurement instruments. That step involved calling in the curriculum and instruction staff to tell them that whatever is to be taught has to conform to the evaluation (read, measurement) instruments. From that point, the curriculum (or at the state level, the teacher assessment "instrument") is rewritten not from the basis of any expressed learning theory or theory of schooling or child development and definitely not from an understanding of the epistemologies of the subject disciplines. Also omitted are any considerations of the contested nature of the curriculum (Apple 1992, 1993; Kliebard 1986), the relation of classroom learning to external authenticity (such as the congruence, for MedIC, with the science as practiced in the Medical Center) or to the lived experiences and learning of the teachers and students. The idea that curriculum could be co-constructed by teachers and students, or situated in communities and cultures, was entirely missing from this model. *The curriculum,* under the proficiencies model, was a management response to unevenness within and across schools. The curriculum would be what the district could test; it would be centrally provided, supervised, measured, and scored. The teachers were merely to make sure all the proficiencies were covered before the test (Callahan 1962; Wrigley 1982).

Proficiency-Based Curricula

With Ms. Williams and others having to help students overcome their lack of previous reading in schools, and Ms. McConnell having to make the assumption that her ninth graders, although having taken history classes, were coming to her with little or no knowledge of history, a case could be made for the provision of a centralized curriculum and curriculum resources. Certainly these teachers would have welcomed having more books, more instructional materials, more activities for their students (and for those students' elementary school years). Teaching in a district where children's poverty prevented teachers from being able to require students to buy copies of books, paperback novels for example, was a serious constraint not faced by faculties in wealthier districts. A central curriculum that assured each teacher an adequate stock of books and other course materials could have been an asset. The district curriculum, however, was not an investment in resources for teachers and classrooms, not a provision for selecting more varied materials than the single textbook, not a call for professional educators to discuss what they needed to teach their subjects with depth and breadth and appropriateness to their students.

The district's response to both the weaknesses already apparent in some local schools and to the state's movement toward central controls was to implement a curriculum based on a computer-graded evaluation system. The model chosen was called "the proficiency curriculum" because all subjects were to be rewritten not as narratives (history, literature) or systems (earth sciences, biology, languages) or conceptual domains (chemistry, physics, mathematics), but as discreet microcomponents of the subjects. These microcomponents were labeled "proficiencies," with subcategories called "objectives." These components were to be parsed out, sequenced in a linear format, numbered and given to all teachers and students. Teachers were to teach the proficiencies, the reorganized version of their subject that conformed to a central office computer-graded test. Each semester's proficiencies would then be the subject of computer-graded multiple-choice tests, with tests and the scoring of the tests to be done by central office.

The rationale behind the proficiency-based curriculum mirrored much of the thinking in the Perot reforms that would reshape the parallel assessment of teacher practice. When the two converged, as they would do very soon, they would share several notable underlying assumptions. The first assumption is that poor quality resides with the teachers. Teachers are "the problem" and have to be managed differently for purposes of quality control. By extension, the quality of education can be managed; bureaucrats should hire experts to tell them what needs to be done and then those same bureaucrats would issue the mandate and begin to monitor compliance. The second, as mentioned, is that quality is static; something is "good" or "bad." The idea that "bad" schools could be mandated to be "good" (provided the people in them followed directions from their superiors) was the justification for enforced uniformity. If the curriculum were the same for everyone, as one evaluation office staff person explained, then Algebra I at the city's weakest high school would be "the same" as Algebra I at the high school with the most National Merit Scholars. (This rationale carried no acknowledgment that the latter school had a history of strong principals, who were able to leverage funding from the district for labs, libraries, drama and music halls, sports equipment, and supplemental materials for classrooms; and who were able to select faculty from waiting lists of teachers wanting to teach there. The neighborhood demographics had begun as middle-class, suburban; became increasingly Jewish middle and upper-middle class; and now, quite diverse, still had a strong base of middle-class, university-educated parents. Unlighted microscopes would not have been sent to this school, nor tolerated by teachers or parents if they had been. Fifty years of discriminatory allocations and many other factors stood between "Algebra I" at that high school and "Algebra I" at the weaker school that had piloted the minimum skills testing on its most at-risk students.) *Sameness* was a symbolic proxy for equity, but not an investment in equity.

This idea of *sameness* is also one that differentiates *standardization* from *standards*. The staff involved with creating the proficiencies for each subject did not consider the research literature or literature on professional practice to inform them on what the curriculum "standards," or benchmarks or possibilities, would be in that subject. Even though many organizations were working at that time (post–*A Nation at Risk*) to rethink the substance of knowledge and ways of knowing in the sciences, in the teaching of writing, in the teaching of mathematics, none of that work was consulted. Nor were exemplary teachers whose courses might be seen locally as "setting the standard" for academic quality and intellectual engagement. The goal behind the proficiencies was to create a curriculum management system that could fit any subject into a multiple-choice, computer-graded test.

There was a second goal behind this system that kept the planners from consulting curriculum theory and child development research as they planned the proficiency curriculum—the system was also to serve as a personnel management system. The "personnel" to be managed were the teachers.

In an extended interview, one of the designers of the proficiency system explained that the superintendent was trying to preempt the state by creating a system that would "allow principals to fire teachers."[7] The superintendent reasoned that principals could avoid messy personnel reviews, subjective classroom observations, consultations with parents, and confrontations with weak teachers (all of which were fraught with fears of lawsuits and accusations of ageism or racism or even just burdensome paperwork over an extended time) if they had an indirect way to measure teacher performance. That indirect way would be the testing of their students. Student testing, to be an accurate personnel performance measure, would have to be based on a curriculum all teachers had to cover. The central office, through a standardized curriculum, would provide all teachers with "the same" course material. Any variations in the quality of student learning then (as measured on the test over the standardized curriculum) according to their logic, would be caused by variations in the quality of teaching. Students with low scores on the proficiency tests would be students whose teachers "should be fired." (All historical, cultural, fiscal, organizational, and other "context" factors were ignored in this model, as though being "held constant" in the causal attributions.)

The standardizing of the curriculum at the local level, then, echoed the distrust of teachers heard in the halls of the state House. The difference was that at the state level, the Career Ladder was being planned (at least ostensibly) as an incentive system to encourage higher levels of performance; the proficiency system was meant to target and punish the lowest levels of teacher weaknesses. The two lines of assault would converge in the magnet classrooms, to the detriment of educational quality.

False Economies

The proficiency system encompassed all the basic subject fields at all grade levels. To create such a system on short notice and, always a consideration, at low cost, the district did not engage the services of curriculum specialists or testing experts. According to personnel involved in the planning, they looked for "a model already in the drawer," something local that could be adapted. (The efforts of the SET teachers, for example, to create the best quality curriculum materials for their students, at great costs of time and their own personal finances, stands in sharp contrast here to the district's reliance on expediency with little regard to quality.)

A member of the proficiency-system planning team identified in an interview the "drawer" from which the district pulled the model it would use to build a comprehensive citywide system of curriculum and testing. This planner recalled that one of the district's poorest and academically weakest Black high schools had attempted to improve its weakest students' achievements through a test-based curriculum. That curriculum was a list of remedial skills, a compilation of the most rudimentary components of reading, writing, mathematics and selected other subjects. The resulting "curriculum content" bore little resemblance to the academic subjects as taught in traditional classrooms. This content was even less substantive than that found in the state-adopted textbooks, already highly abridged and oversimplified to conform to eighteen-week semesters, and neutralized of political, cultural, or intellectual content that might offend extremely conservative organizations regularly monitoring textbooks slated for adoption cycles (Apple 1991; Marshall 1991; *The Texas Observer* June 1999). The test-based curriculum was just that, a curriculum of reductive skill components that could be tested by a multiple-choice test. It was not a curriculum constructed to raise the academic standards in this very poor school, nor to provide a means for the school's weakest students to become prepared to enter mainstream academic classes. It was not a curriculum to be used as a guide to rectify inequalities of staffing and instructional resources at the school. It was a curriculum specifically designed to further stratify an already highly differentiated curriculum into a remedial content at the very lowest level, which if mastered on a multiple-choice test, could appear to reduce student failures by giving "these students" something to pass. And it was a curriculum that could be easily computer-scored. The format of that test-based curriculum, aimed at the barest minimum standards, became unapologetically the model for the district's proficiency tests for all students in all subjects.

The district proficiency tests were, following this model, constructed in a format meant to drive curriculum. The district's evaluation staff, who were charged with creating and implementing this system, called the curriculum supervisors into a meeting to tell them of the new plan to "reform the curriculum." They asked the curriculum supervisors, both the subject matter supervisors and deputy-superintendent-level curriculum directors, to pull their curriculum guides for the evaluation staff to review. Most of the curriculum guides were out of date and seldom used; in most schools the state-adopted textbook provided the de facto curriculum, except where teachers were active curriculum makers as at the magnet schools and in many individual classrooms across the district. The curriculum guides bore none of the creativity and complex substance typical of the magnet school classrooms, nor the rigor of the curriculum being proposed by national science, mathematics, and language arts organizations. However, these considerations did not enter into the evaluation staff's assessment of the curriculum guides. Their complaint with the curriculum guides for each subject was not that they were not current with knowledge in the fields (nor in the field of pedagogy), but that the curriculum in them was not "testable." They meant "testable by multiple-choice, computer-graded, standardized tests." And as one staffer recalled, relative low cost and speed of implementation were key considerations as their planning moved forward.

The research and evaluation staff borrowed, then, from a minimum skills test for at-risk students at a weak high school and made it the model for tests that would drive the curriculum in every subject. Curricula had to be rewritten into "measurable" and "testable" "objectives." The rewrites were done by committees. The official district information on this curriculum reform was that teachers were involved in designing the proficiency curricula. The magnet teachers had heard that this was true but were unable to confirm that any teacher was involved. Ms. Bartlett, the Pathfinder biology teacher, was determined that the biology proficiencies not undercut the Pathfinder and other honors biology curricula. She herself designed a series of curricular categories and test questions that would foster the kind of thinking she was working on with her students. She took her test questions and curricula to the central office and asked for a meeting with the science supervisor or the "biology committee" to discuss her ideas. She was shown into a room where around a table sat several secretaries and office clerks. Open on the table were several high school biology textbooks. From these the "biology committee" was selecting facts, terminology, and formulas to be included in the biology proficiencies. There was no biology teacher or biologist present. The content, outlined as numbered "proficiencies" and "objectives," selected by this group of clerical staff, would then be sent to an out-of-state test production company that would render the content list into computer-scorable multiple-choice question tests.

The format of the proficiency curricula was simple. Every subject was parsed into numbered categories of topics on which students were to demonstrate "proficiency" on a standardized test that would be issued by the central district office near the end of each semester. Under these numbered categories were subcategories and sub-subcategories of the microcomponents of the subject. For history, these subcategories took the form of dates, events, names of historical figures, arranged chronologically; in the sciences, the proficiencies were vocabulary words (names of organisms, processes, chemicals, measurements). For English and language arts, the proficiencies were grammar skills and isolated reading skills; the test over "literature" would not be a test of students' reading during the semester, but rather their ability to find the main idea or main character in a brief reading selection provided on the test. Mathematics proficiencies were largely computational and operational, rather than conceptual.

The fragmentation of knowledge under the proficiency system recalls the fragmentation of content by teachers who were, in *Contradictions of Control*, trying to control their students by controlling the content. They omitted controversial subjects, limited student discussion, oversimplified complex topics—all to maintain their own authority over content and their control over the pacing and dynamics of the classroom (McNeil 1986, ch. 7). Under the proficiency system the control had shifted to the administrative level, but the intent was the same: substitute controllable components for educational activity, then create a control structure for monitoring compliance. In this case, it was the teacher who was to comply.

For each school subject, the proficiency system required following a strict linear, chronological sequence. Teachers could vary from that sequence at their peril: the test covered a specific content each semester; deviating across semesters could result in a low score. The compliance mechanism lay in the processing of the scores. The district would create the test, send it to schools, then collect completed tests and score them. The proficiency test was to stand as 20 percent of the course grade in the first year and gradually increase until it stood as the complete semester grade. (The undocumented accusation that "grade inflation" was widespread, especially overgenerous grading by minority teachers teaching minority children, was used as an additional justification for the need to implement this "objective" system of grading that would minimize the role of teachers in determining their students' grades.)

Costly Calculations

The proficiency system, the first of the "reforms" to hit the classrooms being observed, presented the magnet teachers with a critical ethical dilemma. Following the prescribed proficiency-based curriculum would rob their students of experience with the curricula and the learning activities the teachers had been creating. In developing curricula over several years, these teachers had attempted to include the fundamental concepts of their fields, varied ways of thinking about those concepts (or that cultural heritage, as in literature and history), and many ways of applying and working with the knowledge content of the courses. The history and literature teachers had worked to make their treatment of history and literature more culturally informed and inclusive. The science teachers had made connections between their courses and new breakthroughs in medicine, ecology, space physics, genetics, and biochemistry. They had done so by extending their own learning (through mentorships, summer courses, reading, sharing among themselves), all at their own expense. Ms. Bartlett's exuberance over new medical discoveries was especially contagious: she frequently burst into class with press releases from the local medical schools, world renowned for breakthroughs in heart surgery, space medicine, genetics, and cancer research. Each piece of scientific news might excite another student to think about going on in science; each new breakthrough recharged their thinking about the topics already under study. Hers was one of many classrooms where the stuff of schooling was not so far from the spirit of inquiry in the subject as lived outside the classroom.

The magnet teachers faced serious ethical dilemmas. They could teach to the proficiencies and assure high test scores for their students. Or they could teach the curricula they had been developing (and wanted to continue to develop) and teach not only a richer subject matter but also one that was aimed at students' understanding and their long-term learning, not the short-term goals inherent in the district testing of memorized fragments. This was not an easy choice. Most of the students in these magnet programs were African

American and Hispanic, students historically excluded from the currency of standardized testing (historically scoring lower than Whites on Scholastic Aptitude Tests, ACT precollege tests, and normed achievement tests). Not to teach to the proficiency tests was to risk low scores for these very bright African American and Hispanic students. The linking of the proficiency curricula to students' permanent academic records made noncompliance very serious. The tie of the proficiency tests to course grades put student transcripts at risk.

Yet to teach to the proficiencies was to compromise teachers' knowledge of their subjects and their view of their students as learners. The proficiencies presented a "given curriculum," which for the students would become a "received curriculum." The entire proficiency system put students in a passive role; they were to memorize the proficiencies (facts, formulae, grammar rules, dates) and be able to reproduce them on multiple-choice tests made, not by their teacher, but by a distant testing company. Such a passive role for students completely undermined the kind of teaching that enabled Ms. Williams at Pathfinder to engage even reluctant writers in poetry through the use of music. The poetry brought in and written by students was as much a part of the curriculum as the poetry in her well-worn anthologies. Ms. McConnell's class enactment of the robber baron era might be powerfully instructive for one class, but less effective for another class. She might choose for her other class to study the period through making a mural or writing historical dialogues or formal research papers. The concepts and ideas in the study of that historical period would remain the same, but her means of engaging students would depend on her latest reading of historians as well as her sense of what might prompt a particular class to delve deeply into the subject.

The myth of the proficiencies was that because they were aimed at minimum skills, they would change only the weakest teaching. The "good" teachers would as a matter of course "already be covering" this material and so would not have to make adjustments. In fact, the transformation of the curriculum into received knowledge, to be assessed by students' selection of one answer among four provided on a computer-scored test, undermined both the quality and quantity that "good teachers" could present to their students. The testing format limited the quantity of course content, but more seriously for these teachers, proscribed the nature of the content that could be considered. "Objective" information, such as dates and formulae and rules for comma placement, fit the testing format and so were listed as proficiences to be mastered. These would displace interpretive studies, analytical topics, and the notion of the origins and sources of information. The historiographic bases for historical interpretations, the social context of scientific discoveries, the debates inherent to such fields as economics and literary criticism—the heart of Pathfinder pedagogy and much of the core academics of the School for Science, Engineering, and Technology—were not only devalued but also inadmissible in the proficiency system. The testing format assumed a consensus knowledge base, an "official curriculum" (Apple 1992, 1993). That format transformed "curriculum" into highly reductive and fragmented test items, and by doing so, countered these teachers' attempts to foster in students the ability to make connections and to apply what they were learning to new situations. The teachers found the proficiency curriculum so artificial that they were unable through their preferred pedagogies to assure automatic coverage of the proficiency-based content, even if "coverage" had been their goal. The transformed and limited curriculum was not merely a minimum on which they could base their more complex teaching, but a barrier to substantive teaching.

Knowledge Control and the Sciences

The proficiency system threatened the quality of the curriculum by institutionalizing a consensus curriculum, by divorcing the knowledge of the teacher from the curriculum, by divorcing the knowledge and questions held by students from the required content, and by subjecting all knowledge to a fragmentation filter that artificially altered its substance. These teachers often found their subject to be unrecognizable when processed through the proficiency system.

Ms. Watts, the Pathfinder physics teacher, also taught ninth-grade physical science. She found that students came to her with little understanding of science as a way of thinking. Her entire goal for the ninth-grade physical science course was to engage students in scientific inquiry, in investigation, and in the weighing of possible approaches to a problem. Physical science, her ninth-grade course (and the course taught by Ms. Bachrach at SET), was one of the first to be recast in the proficiency model. Ms. Watts had typically begun her physical science course with surprise phenomena that she would ask students to observe and explain. For example, on one of the first days of classes, she might roll clay into a ball and throw it against the wall. She would ask students to describe what they saw. At first they would be describing what she did and venture guesses about a teacher who throws things. Then she would direct their attention to the clay. Why was it flat on one side? It had changed when it encountered the wall. Had the wall similarly changed? What was at work here?

Throwing clay balls against a brick wall was not on the district's physical science proficiencies, nor was dropping objects of various weights and shapes from different heights to record the speed and direction of their fall, nor was testing out different paper airplane designs for observing motion and speed and resistance. Mass, weight, gravity, molecules, resistance, velocity—most of these concepts she was teaching were included in the proficiencies. But they were presented as vocabulary terms to memorize, and they were often tested for what they were *not*: "Which of the following is not true of gravity?" or "Which of the following is not a chemical reaction?" They were not encountered as phenomena to be observed and explained nor as properties to be subjected to experimentation.

The problem of reducing physical phenomena to disembodied terminology was but one limitation of the proficiency treatment of physical science. The other was its prescription of what constituted a unit of study and how much time should be spent on each unit. Simple mechanics and simple machines are a staple of physical science courses. Ms. Watts, an engineer prior to studying for her graduate degree in education, preferred to teach the concepts of simple machines through a variety of activities that might span four or five units of study, units she had organized around other concepts (studying levers, for example, in comparison with passive resistance and inertia in nonmechanical processes). She saw the strict, formalistic organization of the proficiencies to be a disservice to scientific inquiry. "You have to spend a month on [the physics of] machines," she said. "You get to the end of it, and the students hate it, and you hate it for what it does to them. They may be able to figure out the right answer on the proficiency test, but they don't know anything about machines."

She and Ms. Bachrach at SET also noted that the proficiencies for physical science were much more computational than their own conceptual approaches to the course. Both noted that the proficiencies mandated a set of operations centered on finding one unknown; much of the district's physical science test (and curriculum), therefore, was essentially Algebra I. Students were not required to take Algebra I prior to or concurrently with physical science; in fact, many non-college-bound students took a non-algebra math at this grade level. These teachers estimated that in light of the reliance, in the proficiency version of physical science, on algebraic concepts, at least 25 percent of the district's physical science students, and probably more, were set up to fail the physical science proficiencies. The transforming of the course from scientific principles to computational ones to make physical science operations testable through multiple-choice questions penalized students whose academic programs met one set of bureaucratic requirements at their school (the acceptable course sequence of taking physical science before Algebra I, for example) but were out of compliance on another set of bureaucratic requirements (passing the physical science proficiency test in order to pass the course).

Ms. Watts saw the proficiencies as turning students against science, or against the science as represented in the proficiency curriculum. "The students aren't going to remember those formulas—never. They are only going to remember that it was a pain. And this will add to the general population of people out there who say, 'Science is hard. I don't want to do science.' This [proficiency-based physical science] is not a conceptual course, an introductory course. It's a calculation and manipulation course. I'm not allowed and don't have time to give them a conceptual basis—to say 'You can make a better machine' and still cover the proficiencies." In her junior/senior physics class, Ms. Watts was able to maintain a conceptual course that linked student thinking to scientific principles because there were as yet no physics proficiencies. After struggling to hold onto authentic content in their ninth-grade physical science classes after they came under the proficiency system, both she and her counterpart at SET said independently and equally emphatically, "If the district makes a proficiency test for physics, I will quit. That's it, period. I will quit."

Proficiencies and English

English teachers found compliance with the proficiencies to be somewhat less controlling of their daily lessons, since the English proficiencies were skills-based, rather than based on coverage of content. These teachers at first thought they could teach the literature they had always taught without having to shift to a story or poem that would be on the proficiency test, since these were not known in advance. The emphasis would be on skills, both in interpreting literature and in grammar. Once they saw the tests, however, more than one English teacher described the "skills" being tested as highly questionable. Mr. Moore took out a ninth-grade English proficiency test. It included detailed questions over a printed reading selection. The selection was an esoteric poem, with arcane language, by a poet unfamiliar to any of the students. He guessed that this poem was selected because it was so unlikely to ever be taught to students at this grade level that no group of students in the city would have an advantage over any other from having seen it prior to the proficiency test. The poem was remote and difficult to read and substantive questions about its meaning, structure, and imagery would have been in conflict with the requirement that all the answers be multiple-choice, "objective." Mr. Moore was sure students across the city, including his own, would have difficulty with this poem until he looked at the questions. The first was "The pre-vious example is a) a novel, b) a poem, c) an essay." Students would not even need to read the literary selection to be able to answer the questions; the lan-guage arts "skills" test in fact would positively reinforce those students who had "never read."

The grammar section was no better. Ms. Foster at SET pointed out that there were grammar errors in the first versions of the English proficiency test answer key and worried that her students' scores would be hampered by their growing skills in grammar and punctuation, skills that could put them at odds with the four choices given as possible answers if the "right" answer was "wrong." After a proficiency test, her students insisted on discussing questions that they felt had had more than one "right" answer or no good choices; these debriefings, from questions they had remembered from the test, were good learning sessions, but they pointed to the gap between the level of thinking she wanted in her students and the simplistic and often misleading guesses they were called to provide as answers on the test. She, and other teachers inter-viewed during the early administerings of this test, feared that students would learn that they would not have to study so hard or would not attempt complex writing assignments to earn a course grade once the proficiencies were fully in place and made the basis of a greater percentage of the course grade; they would merely have to learn to play the "proficiency game," and their teachers' efforts to engage them in serious learning would be undermined.

Deletions and Omissions

Teachers could respond to the proficiencies in a number of ways. They could ignore them and maintain their own curricula, risking their students' scores and their own personnel performance records. Some successfully took this course. Other teachers found that they had to respond to the proficiencies by deleting courses or units not covered. This was the solution several biology teachers came to with great regret when they found that their integrated sci-ence units could not be adapted to proficiency testing. For example, Ms. Bartlett had organized a part of her biology course around habitats. She would vary the habitats from year to year to keep the course interesting for herself and to enable her students to take advantage of opportunities to explore urban settings or Gulf Coast estuaries, for example. Her students' motivation for the study of "cells to systems" was greatly increased when these were organized into purposeful study of a natural habitat. But such study brought together concepts and terminology the district had parsed into different semesters, different testing periods. Under the proficiencies, amphibians were to be studied separately from plants; aquatic organisms were in a different section of proficiencies from birds. Single-cell organisms came early in the year; more complex systems midyear, and habitats, if studied at all, near the end of the second semester, in an "ecology" section optional for those classes that had managed to cover the basic proficiencies and the required chapters in the standard book. Studying the interdependence of a variety of organisms within a single habitat did not conform to the proficiency sequence. And studying a local phenomenon, where students had access to live specimens and could experience the habitat as a living system, was definitely prohibited by the generic curriculum devised to be the "same" for all children in the state. To diverge from the district's linear sequence of generic topics, even to teach such high-interest, complex science, was to risk low scores for her students. In the habitat lessons, half of what they needed for the fall test they would not encounter until spring, and half of what they were studying in the fall would not be tested until spring. The habitat studies were not add-ons to Ms. Bartlett's biology course; they were among her core laboratory bases for the study of concepts and skills central to biological knowledge. To eliminate them meant reordering her course, decoupling individual organisms from their interdependence in a living environment, and sequencing topics and biological organisms according to what she saw as an archaic taxonomic system, not scientific inquiry. She saw these deletions and reorderings as serious intellectual losses for her students. One of her school administrators, on the other hand, saw the deletions as a simple, low-hassle way to "implement" the proficiencies.

As time went on and she became more sophisticated in dealing with the proficiencies, Ms. Bartlett acquiesced in part to the reductive transformation of her biology course. But to free her teaching from the artificial simplifications of the proficiencies, she also created an elective course entitled "Environmental Biology" and another called "Creating Coastal Aquatic Environments" for students needing elective credits. The flexibility to "save" a part of her curriculum by *renaming it under a course title not covered by proficiencies* was not an option open to teachers at traditional schools; when those teachers had to delete course content, they reported that that content remained absent from their curriculum. And at Pathfinder, these elective courses, although a creative solution for a small group of students, did not protect what Ms. Bartlett believed to be approaches to biological studies essential for the majority of the students, whose only exposure to biology would be the regular nonelective biology course.

Ms. Watts found that problem-based lessons, essential for student understanding in physical science, almost by definition required ignoring the proficiency sequencing of topics. She refused to give up her problems-based experiments and observational activities, but she frequently interrupted them to point out what would be "on the proficiencies." In addition, she was very clear about those concepts in the lesson that were counter to the proficiency rendering of them. "You won't need this until the proficiency test" became a familiar refrain in the science classes where teachers tried to hold on to scientific ways of inquiry.

Social studies teachers also found themselves having to exclude some of their more productive lessons. Economics had typically been taught as a dry series of terms and theories, failing to engage students beyond simple memorization or even failing to attract them to enroll in the subject, until Mr. Drew at Pathfinder designed the course as an experiment in manufacturing, marketing, and sales. Following the model of Junior Achievement (a national organization through which corporate volunteers help high school students create small companies that manufacture and sell a product), and drawing on Junior Achievement volunteers' expertise, Mr. Drew scheduled a course called "economics." Instead of the traditional economics textbook and lectures, he used a student-run start-up company as the laboratory for studying markets, consumer behavior, marginal costs, supply and demand, investments, and other economic principles. The students researched potential products that would be environmentally safe and marketing strategies that balanced risk against potential profits. Once they had decided on a product to make, they conducted a market survey, invited manufacturing bids, accumulated capital, and began to make decisions regarding the scale of the investment and the ways of sharing the work, the risk, and the rewards. The product was often directly linked to the students, a mug with the Pathfinder logo or a T-shirt designed by a student graphics team; the economics principles being studied were traditional market economics. Except for the ethical and environmental concerns, the activities closely matched the concepts outlined as the Economics course proficiencies put forth by the district.

As with the environmental biology course, the applied economics course integrated various concepts into a dynamic model rather than a linear sequence of vocabulary fragments. It included students' judgments and information generated by student research. While the interactive and applied approach to the topic mirrored much corporate behavior and allowed Mr. Drew, who had worked in industry, to draw on his own experiential knowledge, it did not conform to the proficiency sequencing. Pathfinder graduates reported back from college that participating in the applied class had given them an advantage when they studied formal economics in college. Even so, the applied course could not stand as the economics credit course if students were to pass the economics proficiency. Mr. Drew tried in some years to offer this same course as an elective with a name like Independent Study in Economic Behavior, decoupling the course from official economics proficiencies. Smaller numbers of students had space in their schedules for an elective, so much of the power of working with a team of student researchers was diminished, and in some years the course was not offered at all. He also created a Futures Study course to engage students in study that merged history, sociology, psychology, economics, and literature, again creating a course not on the proficiency list from the "deletions" caused by filtering regular courses through the proficiency. Such electives gave students research skills essential for college and were protected by being too complex and interdisciplinary to be prescripted and measurable. These weaknesses, from the point of view of the central administration, were the very strengths Mr. Drew and his students were committed to, but these side-bar courses were powerless to displace the prescriptive, reductive curriculum that was being imposed on all regular academic subjects.

Double-Entry Notebooks

Teachers did not have to delete all of their substantive lessons in order to comply with the proficiency material. Another strategy was to teach two different lessons. This "double-entry" approach included presenting the official proficiency-based material and then doing lessons around the "real" curriculum. This became the most pervasive strategy across the disciplines, but it shows up most tellingly in another of Ms. Bartlett's biology lessons. One day she went to the board and wrote a formula. After she wrote it, she insisted that everyone in the class write it in the back of their notebooks. Then she said, "Now, I don't want to see anyone in here using that formula again until it is time for the proficiency test at the end of the semester. It is the district's formula and it is wrong. Here is the right formula. Write this down. Do you see the difference? This is the formula for photosynthesis. See the district's formula? It has an equal sign. This is not an equation. It is a process—see the delta sign [in the second formula she had provided]? That can also be shown as an arrow. This is a *process*. Now, the district proficiencies list this as a formula about plants. 'Plants make food.' They think this is an equation for plants making food. But this is much more. They leave out the delta; delta means change. We are going to study the changes. We are going to study enzymes, the catalysts for change."

The three weeks of lessons that proceeded from that introduction included lab stations, computer simulations, board game simulations, model making, chemical experiments, readings, lectures, and films—many ways of knowing and applying the concepts surrounding the role of enzymes in plant cell functions. By the time students completed the required components and the ones that they had elected, they had a thorough knowledge, which they could explain and apply to a number of formats, from hypotheticals and lab station tests to essay tests and oral examinations. None of the "real science" in photosynthesis, nor the skills of experimentation and inquiry that the students mastered, could have been deduced from the district's formula.

The teaching of history was also seriously compromised by reducing the dynamics of history, the divergence of historical interpretations, and the inter-sections of varied peoples' historical narratives into lists and facts. Mr. Moore found the effects of the proficiency approach to measuring students' study of history particularly troubling. He also found himself "double-entry" lecturing. He used his history course to engage students in analyzing varying points of view, divergent interpretations of historical events, and different sources of historical information. He distinguished in his lectures between those aspects of American history about which there has been general agreement and those on which historians disagree. He challenged students through class discussion and their research papers to investigate how various events come to be con-sidered "historical." One reason he went to such lengths to transport his stu-dents to the university library was to make them less dependent on the school's single history text as a source of information so that they would not mistak-enly think of history as a single narrative. Also, he fully recognized that his stu-dents included those whose family histories encompassed legal and illegal immigration from Southeast Asia, Mexico, and Central America; whose par-ents might be an engineer or a small-business owner or a janitorial worker; who studied in anticipation of being the first in the family to graduate from high school; and whose cultural roots extended across the United States. Knowing many of these family stories and circumstances, Mr. Moore wanted his students to see themselves as actors in and interpreters of "history." He wanted them to learn from the collective experiences in the classroom as well as from testing their own first impressions of a historical event against other possible interpretations. Neither he nor the other history teachers in these schools could speak the word "proficiency" without scorn; there was no forty-item, computer-scorable list that could capture what they wanted their students to learn. Separating the "proficiency" content from the "real" lectures and discussions was essential as he guided his students through the decades. Teaching a double set of lecture notes, even with the dominant emphasis on what he viewed as his "real" curriculum, he faced the problem shared by many of these teachers: considerable reduction in the subjects he and the class could study because of time taken away by having to separate out the proficiency curriculum from the "real."

One challenge was to assure that the proficiency content did not supplant the more substantive historical information. Another was not to lose the skills essential to the study of history, skills these students seemed eager to acquire, whether in holding their own when pushed by a Mr. Moore question or in making their understandings public through the role plays in Ms. Hughes's Pathfinder history classes. At times this attention to skills provided another push for conveying two sets of information, as the science teachers were beginning to do. Typically, the complexity of an event or the changing interpretations of that event since it occurred would be the direct subject of the lesson. Within that study as certain dates or names or isolated facts emerged ("Pearl Harbor, 1941," or "Roosevelt's vice president," or "the Cuban Missile Crisis"), Mr. Moore or Ms. Hughes would say, "write that on your proficiency page— that's a district proficiency." The message to the students was to set aside and ignore the sound bite until later; keep the intellectual focus on the complex content, not the proficiency.

In addition to double sets of lecture information, teachers found that they sometimes had to alter chronologies in order to conform to the proficiency sequence. One semester Mr. Moore decided to follow the proficiency outline more closely to see what effect this would have on his teaching and on students' test scores. What he found was that the students were penalized when he followed the strict chronology of proficiency topics. The reason was that if the strict chronology were obeyed, items being taught during the last two weeks of the semester would not have been covered in class by the date of the proficiency exam, which was given prior to the end of the semester. To avoid this unexpected penalty for following the proficiency sequence carefully, both Mr. Moore and a history teacher in another city reported that they had had to teach Lincoln and the Emancipation of slaves prior to the study of the Civil War. Each predicted that his students knew enough from middle school about pre–Civil War slavery and the rough outlines of the war itself to get those questions correct, but they doubted the students would know Emancipation.

In Mr. Moore's case, he had looked ahead to see what time period the proficiencies covered. On seeing that the Emancipation Proclamation and the beginnings of Reconstruction would be on the semester's proficiency test, even though they were scheduled to be taught during the two weeks *after* the test, he fast-forwarded to "cover" that period, before his class studied the Civil War, in the hopes of gaining one or two more right answers for his students on the proficiency test. His students took this in stride, but saw it as a divergence from the "real" study of the Civil War period.

Mr. Moore also pointed out the absolute arbitrariness of the content of the proficiency test questions. One forty-item administering of the U.S. history test included four questions about Birmingham, Alabama—one-tenth of the exam. When asked what besides Birmingham Sunday (the murder of four Black girls in church by anti–civil rights terrorists) and the steel industry would have been asked, he answered, "Oh, those would have been good questions—things we have studied, but those weren't on there. Somebody [who] made up the test must have been from Alabama." A standardized curriculum was not "objective," but instead embodied someone's valued knowledge or questions of convenience.

In addition to giving separate sets of information—"double-entry" teaching—several teachers said that immediately prior to the proficiency test they had to spend time "unteaching" some of what they and their students had been studying. A science teacher explained, "You really have to *unteach some things* when you get to the proficiencies. That's what I have found. 'Forget these expansions into things. Go for the simple things.' And we defeat our purpose in the sense that if we teach creative thinking, if we teach analytical thinking, and it we teach children to look beyond the obvious into the not-quite-so-obvious, then the proficiency test comes and they think analytically, think beyond the obvious, and they will get them [the proficiency test questions] wrong because they know all of the exceptions to the rules and they say 'but what if. . . ?' And so I try to reserve at least a week prior to the proficiencies and throw everything aside and they check in their books and we close down the school and we give them the proficiency drills." Mr. Drew told of having taught his class that economic cycles varied in length and intensity, depending on complex national and international circumstances and events. To his dismay, he saw that the proficiency for economics stated that economic cycles lasted "18 months—I had to unteach everything we had been studying and say, 'They say each cycle lasts 18 months and that they all have the same named components, so just forget what we learned. Think in terms of very simple things,' because the first thing they'll think of when they start taking these tests is, 'Jeez, I know it's not always that way.' And the tests are not designed to handle that—so I start six weeks before the test practicing some of the proficiency questions and trying to figure out why they don't want you to know how it really is."

These assessments of the negative effects of the standardized, test-driven curriculum—assessments cutting across subjects, grade levels, and schools—counter the myth that such curricula set the minimums, "bring up the bottom." In these schools, as well as in many individual classrooms in other schools and districts across the state, it is the higher academic quality that is compromised by the standardization. A history teacher at MedIC confirmed the need to subtract from teaching time to prepare students to take the test; his preparation also was aimed at reducing students' thinking as they went into the test. To prepare them, he frequently included several "proficiency" questions on his own tests. He told students they would be able to tell the difference because "the proficiency questions do not permit discussion. If you see a question that cannot be discussed, that does not invite higher level questioning, then you know that's 'their question,' not mine. And you just have to think, 'What's the least dumb answer here.' Do not try to use your mind on those." He added, "I wish their [the district's and the state's] tests would come up to our standards, so we would not have to lower ours to theirs." Like his colleagues at another magnet school, he kept two grade books, one with the students' marks on the required "dumb" tests and one with his own evaluations of his students' works; the former he could show to administrators, the second he kept for himself, his students and their parents. A Pathfinder history teacher challenged his colleagues who described the proficiency system to be hampering their creativity: "We *are* having to be more and more creative—creative to find ways to make sure these things do not ruin our courses and that they don't keep us from teaching our kids. That is taking more and more creativity."

The proficiency system, designed to help principals identify teachers who "should be fired," de-skilled teachers by forcing them to split their knowledge of their subjects from the knowledge they presented in the classroom. It split their judgments about their students' learning from the grades their students would earn as the proficiency test scores became factored into course grades by a central computer with a set formula. It caused them to have to play games in front of their students, appearing to conform while attempting to teach. It trivialized curriculum by transforming the content of schooling into testable pieces scarcely recognizable as components of academic subjects.

A Culture of Resistance

So long as the proficiency curricula were being piloted, with ambiguous (and ever-changing) connections to teachers' evaluations and students' permanent records, teachers could attempt various strategies for compliance, noncompliance, or some combination such as double-entry lectures. Their strong faculty cultures, centered on desegregation and academic excellence for their students and on their own strong professional identities, individually and collectively, helped mitigate against the worst effects for themselves and for their students. As the linkages tightened, however, many threatened to leave. Most took the initial stance of "this too shall pass," which had served them through many previous reforms. Others spent enormous time and energy appearing to comply while attempting to continue authentic teaching, and they did so in concert with their colleagues who shared their distrust of the reductive requirements of the proficiencies.

One principal took great pride in what he considered to be this innovative new system for marking student progress. He insisted that only proficiency scores, and proficiency-like, teacher-made tests during the semester, could be used for assessing students. A group of teachers at that school collaborated (conspired) to create the appearance of compliance while maintaining their own practice. They posted by their classroom doors the required matrices showing their students' performance on the proficiencies. But the charts they posted, with Ps opposite a student's name under each part of the course mastered (or "passed") and Fs opposite each student's name under those not yet mastered ("failed"), were just for show. The teachers had had students fill in the boxes randomly, distributing arbitrary Ps and Fs, or even arranging them in patterns. The marks had no meaning. The upper margin of the proficiency report was changed each term to reflect the new date, but otherwise was left unchanged. These charts of mastery and competency were to be posted by the door for the passing principal to view. A teacher could create a new chart each grading period or merely cut the top off the existing one, photocopy the matrix onto a chart with a new set of dates and repost it by the door. This small act of collective resistance helped create a shared sense of humor about the imposed proficiency curriculum. In addition, by showing that compliance with the controls, or even the appearance of compliance, was in fact more valued than any teaching and learning that the proficiencies were purported to be "improving," both the students and the teachers could feel justified in ignoring them as much as possible so that they could go on with their real lessons.

At first, while the proficiency controls were being pilot-tested, these teachers managed to continue to give essay tests and require oral presentations and projects that represented student learning. They managed to assign research papers and laboratory experiments and readings that bore no resemblance to the proficiencies. They then had to turn the grades for these assignments into "competencies" and "proficiencies" that conformed to a computer-generated matrix. One principal expressly required his teachers to report only computer-gradable scores—on every assignment. He backed the magnet school program on its surface but—counter to both the spirit and substance of the program—insisted that all student assessments on all assignments in the courses be reduced to computer-scored indicators. His teachers spent hundreds of hours responding to student work with long comments, suggestions for revisions, rationale for evaluations—just as they had always done, then attempted to mask those in the administrative reporting, through computer-scorable renderings. The teachers at that magnet supported each other to maintain substantive learning activities and meaningful assessments of them; their students entered into the culture of subversive response to these bifurcated lectures and grading systems because they knew that their teachers' real evaluative comments were the ones that made a difference in their learning. They had no illusions that, as one student said, "This proficiency stuff isn't about us. It's about the administrators and I'm not sure what else." The principal had told these teachers that the requirement to translate all grades to computer-scoring and to post the results was district policy. Several semesters later (when this researcher found that none of the teachers at the second school being observed for the study were complying with this "requirement"), the teachers discovered that, in fact, this requirement was specific to their principal. They then felt even freer to post fictional scores by the door. The proficiency scores, except for those at the end of each semester processed by central office, were merely for show. The teachers worked together and essentially covered for each other to create the appearance of compliance so that both teachers and students would have the space to do their "real" teaching and learning.

It was at this school, after months of these compliance games and having to face his students with two sets of lecture notes and instructions to learn isolated fragments of fact for the proficiencies but "do not bring them to class before then," that a teacher sighed after relating these increasingly negative impacts of the proficiencies on his teaching: "I am tired of having to lie in order to do my work." He was expected to pretend to his students that the proficiency curriculum was the real knowledge they should learn and that the tests were important; he was expected to comply with the requirements by his principal and central office that he teach to the proficiencies. His hallmark, and that of his colleagues, had always been honesty and openness with his students. He resented being put in a position where phoniness was a part of the new job description. When the Soviet Union collapsed, the schools there suspended the teaching of national history for an entire year while the curriculum was being rewritten. The old national history had celebrated Soviet accomplishments uncritically, not only within the country but also within the world, attributing every major invention to a Soviet scientist or engineer, every war to a capitalist country, every victory to the Soviets. When Russian history was again being taught, many of the same history teachers were employed. They were afraid their students would not believe the new history because the teachers were so identified with the old, even though many of *them* had not believed it. When students were interviewed about the "new" Russian history, they surprised their teachers by saying, "We never believed what you were teaching us, but we thought *you* believed it." They had been meeting to exchange "official" knowledge, "school knowledge," which neither fully found credible. This same pattern has been documented in U.S. schools where teachers taught an oversimplified curriculum in order to maintain order in their classes (McNeil 1986). The teacher who was tired of lying had built a career of authentic teaching; he saw in the centralized, standardized curriculum the beginnings of a system that would pit the assessments of his students' learning (and of his teaching practice) against an official, but highly questionable body of knowledge.

"The Examiner"

Ms. Williams, at Pathfinder, had another response: she made the controls the subject of inquiry for her students. "The Examiner," the poem at the beginning of this book, was a poem she read with her class precisely so that they could discuss what was happening to the Pathfinder curriculum and to the spirit of learning there under the new tests. Her goals of helping her students find their voice in their writing, helping them engage with poets and novelists in dialogic interpretations—all these seemed threatened by the "wave after wave" of reform coming down as mandates. She wanted her students to know that she was not willingly complying and that their education should include examining requirements, not merely conforming to them.

> "Shall we open the whole skylight of thought. . . bring them our frontier worlds And the boundless uplands of art for their field of growth?" Class, this is what I want for you. There are so many worlds to explore and you can do it. You have been doing it in the things we have been read-

ing. But now look at this part—"*Or shall we pass them the chosen poems with the footnotes, Ring the bell on their thoughts. . .*"—this is what [Urban District] is trying to make us do. They want us to teach this way.

"*Print one history book for a whole province, and Let ninety thousand reach page 10 by Tuesday*"—doesn't that sound like these proficiency tests you are having to do? Doesn't this sound like what we have been seeing? How does it feel to you? Here are the pages in the grammar book for Proficiency #1. Don't you feel like someone is "mowing down" what we can do?

A girl asked, "Is this really going to happen to Pathfinder? I saw this at my brother's school—I thought it was just for problem classes or something. They can't do this to Pathfinder—we have too much to do. *Can* they?" The teacher replied, "I hope not, but look at this last line—they aren't cutting the grass so that it won't grow at all, just so that it won't grow *unevenly*. Let's talk about that."

And they did. Many of them had gone to regular middle schools and already knew the drill about memorizing isolated facts from standardized textbooks and reproducing them on short-answer or computer-graded tests. They had struggled at first to meet the intellectual demands of Pathfinder. In discussing this poem, they related the "boundless uplands of art for their field of growth" to the endless connections between literature, music, anthropology, the arts, and social history they had unexpectedly mastered in their world history class. They had seen themselves move beyond "screw-desk rows" into independent study topics. They knew that when they had been in "numbered rooms, blackboarded," they had not read books, they had not written. Now that they were doing well and seeing an academic future for themselves, they were not eager to regress into a curriculum that seemed to be more for keeping all 90,000 on the same page. Their teacher compared the grass cutters in the poem, attempting to cut all the grass to an "inch-high green," to the designers of the proficiencies, saying, "They are putting you in a role—you'll come out the same." The class—a diverse mix of races and personalities—talked about how much easier it might be to teach a "uniform class." If that would be easier, then one girl's comment summed up the impossibility of making all these students alike: "Too bad, Ms. Williams! You have *us!*" Ms. Williams retorted, "You all look alike to me!" The absurdity of that comment, and of the push for sameness—in the poem and in the proficiencies—drew laughter.

The class moved on to lively discussion of the poems of Auden and Dylan Thomas and Nikki Giovanni and Dore Previn and Robert Frost and Roethke, knowing they were studying something special and that their personal responses to the poems were as important as the formal explication skills they were developing. When they came to the "inexorable sadness of pencils" and the "duplicate grey standard faces" of Roethke's "Dolor," a student called out, "there's that *sameness* again."

Ms. Williams was the most direct with her students, but most of these teachers shared her desire to be honest with their students in differentiating the "real curriculum" from the proficiencies. They did not want to lose credibility with the students by having students think the proficiency content matched the teachers' own knowledge of the subject (McNeil 1986, ch. 7 and 8), and they did not want students to carry an artificial knowledge into college or work settings. As they struggled to meet the test score issue while at the same time keeping their course content authentic, they found themselves constantly caught. And several noted that increasingly with the proficiencies and other mandated procedures, their students were cheating more, less likely to be intellectually engaged and more likely to be playing the game to get the test score rather than learn. They saw the trust relations eroding along with the quality of learning.

The specific proficiency system developed locally in anticipation of the coming state controls over curriculum and testing. It anticipated in form and in philosophy the system the teachers across the state were soon to face. That system bore out the teachers' concerns about the negative effects a centralized system of testing can have over teaching and course content. When combined with the Perot reforms, it created the basis for a statewide system of computer-graded testing that persists today and that carries with it the same de-skilling of teachers and the same artificial treatment of curriculum. That system of testing, the TAAS, will be discussed in the last chapter as the legacy of this "reform" of curriculum, teaching, and the control of schooling.

Measuring Teacher Behavior

While the proficiency tests and their successors (the TABS, the TEAMS, and now the TAAS) de-skilled teachers by separating their knowledge from the content of the curriculum, the state's teacher assessment instrument de-skilled them even more by separating their pedagogical craft and their knowledge of their students from their classroom practice. The issue of quality control, specifically the quality of teaching (by teachers) had been the barrier to the full funding of the SCOPE committee's recommendations for teachers' pay raise. Leaders in the state House and Senate refused to give the governor the money for teacher pay raises because they were sure that "bad" teachers would get raises along with "good" teachers. They wanted assurance that the quality of teaching could and would be objectively measured and that raises would be based on the merits as judged by a system of teacher appraisal. The teachers all had to sit for the TECAT in order to maintain state certification (see chapter 5), but the concern was that the TECAT measured only minimal literacy and numeracy, not classroom practice. Even after sitting for recertification by the TECAT, veteran teachers would still need to be monitored and the quality of their teaching assessed on an ongoing basis.

Measurability was paramount. The state mechanism for assessing teacher quality, like the proficiency testing at the local level, had to be cheap, quick, generalizable across all subjects and school settings and capable of being used by school-level administrators independent of their knowledge of the subjects being taught. As described in chapter 5, the absence of a model for assessing teacher practice (or at least Perot's assumption that there was no model; he did not investigate the extensive literature assessing teaching in the subject fields) led Perot to employ a management consultant firm to design a model for advancement on the Career Ladder. The model they outlined, which was then refined and implemented by the bureaucrats at the Texas Education Agency (the organization Perot intended to nuke), was a generic checklist. This checklist was meant to be applicable to all subjects, all grade levels, all children, and all teachers—from kindergarten to calculus. It was modeled (perhaps inadvertently) after the factory-floor activity analysis checklists from the social efficiency era (Callahan 1962), reducing an hour's teaching to fifty-five observable, measurable behaviors. (This list was later reduced to forty-five observable, measurable behaviors.) These behaviors had nothing to do with the subject being taught, nor with the particular students in the class. The required behaviors, for which teachers would earn points, included maintaining eye contact with the students, having a "catchy opener" and definite closure to the lesson, having the objective for the day written on the board for all to see, and "varying verbal responses" to students. To insure that all teachers knew a variety of positive verbal responses, the TEA supplied along with the guidelines for the assessment system a list of one-hundred approved "praise words."

Every teacher was to be observed and assessed every year by two administrators in the school. These administrators did not need to be expert in the subjects they were observing; the assessment focused on behaviors, not course content. The teacher assessment system was touted as "objective," but the marks to be earned on this checklist were anything but objective: "Satisfactory," "Needs Improvement," or "Exceptional Quality." Despite printed instructional manuals and extensive (and as Shepard has noted, expensive) training workshops for the administrators who would be conducting the evaluations, both teachers and administrators remained unclear as to the meaning of these. Their application was highly variable within faculties. "Exceptional Quality" could mean exceptional within a faculty, exceptional among teachers of that subject in the district, or exceptional beyond one's own past history as a teacher. In addition to the ambiguity inherent in the checklist was added the highly subjective nature of the evaluations. Science teachers in magnet programs noted that their less qualified science teacher counterparts in the regular part of the school often received higher marks from the principal, in one case because the teacher emulated the principals' dress (coat and tie) and manner of patrolling the halls. Teachers noted that the checklist system gave administrators a vehicle for putting certain favored teachers (particularly those who bought into these prescriptive systems of testing students and teachers) onto a track for Career Ladder promotions.

Many teachers noted that the principal or other observer did not know their subject, yet there was no place on the checklist to note that lack of knowledge. In addition, there was no provision on the checklist for the teacher to explain how the lesson related to the particular students, to the previous days' lessons or to future lessons. There was no provision on the checklist for teachers to explain why they taught a particular lesson in a particular way; the relation of content to pedagogy was absent from the assessment instrument. There was no way to indicate whether a teacher understood his or her subject, whether the explanations or demonstrations or discussions advanced children's learning. The checklist focused on teacher behaviors, presuming a teacher-centered classroom, with whole-class instruction. (One principal, when asked what he did when he entered a classroom where students were working in groups, answered, "That's easy. It's like when they are seeing a film. I just come back another day when they are really teaching.")

The artificiality of the list of behaviors, like the proficiency system, prompted a wide range of responses from those teachers who found the behaviors to be antithetical to their philosophy of teaching. Even the magnet teachers learned that a complicated lesson, a lesson in which students worked independently or in groups, a lesson with ambiguous open-ended tasks and discussions would be seen as "teaching that Needs Improvement." Ms. Watts would not throw a ball of damp clay against the wall on a teacher assessment day, nor would Ms. Hughes have her students changing costumes in the hall for a trial of the robber barons. The collecting of one hundred leaves or working computer simulations of cell nutrition would not be helpful on the day the teacher was to be observed under the checklist. The magnet teachers learned that to gain high points on the teacher assessment instrument, they needed to pull out a structured lecture-discussion format or a very traditional grammar lesson or set of math problems. Such a lesson would allow them to stand at the front of the room as the center of all the students' attention.

Their students became adept at falling into a listen-and-recite mode when evaluators came into the room, stifling their questions and interpretative comments for a day when an authentic lesson, actively engaging students' minds rather than focusing on teacher behavior, was in the offing. Although their students could be accommodating, these teachers resented that the teacher assessment system so depersonalized their students. At each of these schools, an important draw for the students was the teachers' reputation of accessibility and attentiveness to the students. The programs were designed around particular groups of students, their needs to compensate for gaps in their academic background, their interest in the magnet specialty, their individual talents, and the collective cultures they and their teachers developed. There was almost no "generic" teaching in these schools. Yet the teacher assessment instrument required generic teaching, teaching each class as though it were exactly like the others, in order for a teacher to earn high points. The behaviors did not have to relate to the students except in very impersonal ways, such as gaining eye contact; there was no mention of what benefit could come from that eye contact, except the presumption of classroom order.

The checklist itself, and its use in the hands of administrators not knowledgeable about the subjects being taught, reinforced a view of teaching as deskilled labor, the assigned and prescribed labor of the factory-shop floor. The tasks were designed by others, checked off by others as acceptable or needing improvement, and rewarded by still others. The students were cast in a completely passive role under this model, directly oppositional to the active role the SET students had assumed in helping shape their school's program and its academic quality. The teachers were distanced from their students, evaluated for teaching a generic lesson explicitly not geared to a particular class or subject.

Whereas the proficiencies, and the state tests which built on them over time, had truncated the course content, the teacher assessment system trivialized teacher-student interactions by reducing them on the evaluation "instrument" to observable behaviors. The life of the mind was explicitly structured out of the system of valuing classroom practice. The potential for collective discourse, for co-constructing of the curriculum, for what Duckworth would call "the having of wonderful ideas"—all were devalued or "disappeared" by the checklist of teacher behaviors on which a teacher's career would be judged.

What was left? First, such overt behaviors as writing the day's "objectives" on the board required a deliberate link between the prescribed curriculum (and the format of that curriculum) and teacher practice. Second, as has been noted, the content of the curriculum and the engagement with students' ideas was displaced by observable teacher performances. One of these was the requirement to have a catchy opener to the lesson; another was to have "closure" to each lesson. And a third was that all student eyes were to be on the teacher, as though visual attentiveness correlates with mental participation. Each of these seems benign until weighed against what all these teachers had done to create meaningful learning environments for their students. There was certainly no way on the checklist to reward those teachers who met at the copy shop at 7:00 A.M. to photocopy stacks of poems for their students; no way to indicate teachers' growing knowledge as they participated in mentorships in the Medical Center or internships in environmental centers. The kind and patient attention to students who had moved beyond the formal education levels of their parents, the persistence in getting kids to read whole books for the first time—none of these efforts were captured by the checklist.

One extremely capable biology teacher had a mild manner and was given to understatement. He was not, like Mr. Beshara, effusive. If he told a student, "that's good," in his very quiet and serious tone, the student knew his or her work, or idea, to be exceptionally good and felt motivated to tackle something even more difficult. A quiet "that's good" fostered new student effort, new student thinking. The principal heard his "that's good" as a failure to "vary verbal responses," and gave this teacher a lower rating than he gave biology teachers in the regular wing of the school who taught virtually no labs and whose students were much less engaged in learning biology.

The use of the checklist to reward teachers liked by the administration usually shortchanged magnet teachers who were seen as less a part of the "regular" school than teachers who had been there many years and were a part of the principal's longtime cohort. But occasionally the checklist helped a magnet school teacher. Mr. Moore was smiling broadly when he announced that he had earned the highest rating in "effective use of audio-visual equipment." When asked when he had used such equipment, he replied, "Never. I never use it. You know I don't even have an electrical outlet in this room. I don't know what that [rating] was about." Then he added, "I also kept a list of the praise words on my lectern and managed to use several of them; it's the first time I've ever received a 5 [highest rating] on praise words!" He found great humor in these developments and shared them with his students. His students were fully aware that the real power of his teaching was nowhere to be found on the checklists.

Chapter 5 discussed the danger of linking resources to controls, especially in education. The controls are accepted in order to gain scarce resources (a checklist system of teacher evaluations is traded for the opportunity to advance on the Career Ladder in order to receive the salary enhancements attached to each new level of the "ladder"). All too often the resources can disappear while the controls remain in place. The Career Ladder pay increments disappeared years before the checklist assessment system was discarded. (It persisted for ten additional years.) The legacy of the system is not that all teachers conformed or that the expected pay increments were not forthcoming. It is that the relations between teachers and administrators became less trusting, more adversarial, more given to playing games of compliance or resistance, rather than working together to sustain programs of high academic quality.

The merging of the test-driven prescriptive curriculum and the checklist system of teacher behaviors had the effect of de-skilling teaching, splitting the behaviors of teaching from teachers' knowledge of their subjects and of their children. It had the further effect of rendering artificial what had become authentic learning, forcing students to split much of their new knowledge from what they brought into the standardized tests.

There is no evidence in these schools that the teacher assessment instrument improved the teaching of the weakest teachers. Anecdotal evidence, from these schools and from across the state, point to ways the emphasis on observable behaviors actually brought rewards to the weakest teachers. The teachers widely known to be weak could not create year after year the kinds of rich and complex lessons that found their way into these literature discussions, biology labs, and history lectures. If they had been evaluated for their ability to design learning activities that engaged students' minds, then those teachers would have been shown to be severely in "need of improvement." Under a prescriptive system of curriculum, student testing, and teacher assessment, however, the weakest teachers were given a system to which they could readily conform. Many would practice a lesson with their students, then repeat that lesson, with identical recitation questions, the following day when they were being assessed. One African American elementary teacher who left teaching said she did so because she had been hopeful the new assessment system would help the principal see how undereducated and unprepared the teacher next door to her was. Instead, that weak teacher achieved high ratings through prepracticed lessons. When the strong teacher heard word for word the identical lesson from the previous day being performed for the principal, and then heard of the high rating given the teacher, she tendered her resignation. The assessment system could not engineer good teaching by conformity to its required behaviors, but it could easily mask weak teaching.

In a like manner, complying with the proficiency curriculum (and as will be discussed, its successor tests from the state) did not engender better teaching and learning. The traditional indicators of student achievement, from students' failure to complete their schooling, to performance on national standardized tests, failed to show marked increase as a result of the proficiencies.[8] Problems in children's learning and in their staying in school to graduate persisted. The prescribed curriculum was test-driven; it was finally discarded because there was such a gap between students' scores on the proficiency test and teachers' grades. A new superintendent ended the local experiment in test-driven curricula, but by that time the state had built upon this model a system of statewide standardized tests for which there can be no waivers.

Hired to Specialize, Evaluated to Standardize

The magnet teachers had been hired to specialize, to bring special expertise into the creation of specialty schools whose strong programs would draw students from racially segregated neighborhoods into integrated, highly academic schools. The teachers accepted the challenge to develop curricula, design school programs, create new school cultures, and teach students whose promise often exceeded their prior academic preparation. They further took on the work of helping create course materials and lab equipment in severely underresourced schools. They helped sustain schools used by the district to satisfy a federal court order and to showcase local public education to businesses thinking of locating in the city. And they brought schools not supported by the district to the level required to live up to their magnet specialty names. Many of these teachers had sought out these schools because they wanted to stay in teaching, and they wanted to teach urban children. But they did not want to be de-skilled by requirements to follow a state-adopted textbook or prescribed curriculum. Like their students, they had sought out a school environment where it was safe to be smart. The imposition of the teacher assessment instrument and the increasing requirements to comply with test-driven curricula threatened to de-skill their role and to de-skill them personally. They who had been hired to specialize now found themselves evaluated in ways that required that they standardize. They worked alone and collectively to fend off the de-skilling. The intellectual and philosophical bases for their programs were threatened. The dilemma of remaining in teaching, while being required to bracket one's own best knowledge and one's commitment to children's development as thinkers and learners, confronted some of these teachers on almost a daily basis.

These teachers had created schools in which the knowledge of the classroom held credibility outside the classroom; of this MedIC was the best example, but this credibility and congruence was a goal achieved in many ways at all these schools. They had worked to enhance their own knowledge of their subjects and of the cultures and capabilities of their students and had attempted to create courses and classroom environments where there were no walls between their personal knowledge (and their students') and the curriculum of the classrooms. While this lack of walls is most evident across the academic disciplines at Pathfinder, most of the observed teachers had chosen these schools because an authentic curriculum, and a school environment that did not require them to bracket off their own knowledge in order to cover an artificial curriculum, was for them not a "magnet" pedagogy, but merely the way teaching should be. Finally, these schools demonstrated, prior to the imposition of the teacher assessment instrument and the test-driven curriculum, the ways that students, as active agents in their education, can work with teachers in a productive "bargain" to raise, rather than lower, the expectations for learning in a school. Within these schools, individual and collective groups of teachers had claimed or created institutional space for relational teaching, teaching which honored personal knowledge, children's experiences and their cultures, and which named those forces outside school that education must address (poverty, racism, ceilings on girls' futures, indifference—most evident in the absent resources, and even fear of "these children," as seen in the chain-link fences around only "their" schools). The prescribed curriculum, increasingly aligned with high-stakes tests, threatened the integrity of what was being taught. The checklist, the imposing of these "reforms" from centralized points of a hierarchy that identified "teachers" as the problem, undermined the possibilities for this model of teaching to be sustained when even to survive in the system required teachers and students to play games of compliance and resistance.

Staying in such a system was wearing. Yet, several teachers said that their decision not to leave immediately was based on what they saw of new hires. They had noted that new teachers (being hired into their magnet programs by central administrators, rather than by magnet coordinators or through recruitment by colleagues) seemed to be chosen because they conformed readily to standardization. The magnet teachers did not want to cede their schools to people who had so little understanding of what the children needed or what they could become.

Many other strong teachers did leave under this increasingly controlling system. As the next chapter will show, more are leaving as the curriculum controls begun under the proficiency system did grow into an increasingly "aligned" system of controls over content, assessment of children, assessment of teachers, and, ultimately, evaluation of schools. The reforms of the 1980s laid the groundwork for this "aligned" system in which each level of schooling is assessed according to its degree of compliance and conformity to a rigidly prescribed curriculum and testing system devised at a distance from the children.

The big system was not "nuked." Instead it increased in size, budget, and power. The design of assessment "instruments," the design of the consulting and training systems needed to inform administrators and teachers about the new systems, the increasingly expensive contracts for student testing and for materials to align curriculum with those tests—all of these increased the power of the central bureaucracy over the schools. The policy bombs from House Bill 72 and its correlated local policies fell on the quality and credibility of teaching and learning at the school level. Not even the magnet schools, the "best" schools, were protected from their damaging blows. The educational costs of the collateral damage have been high, and they have been borne by teachers and students.

Chapter 7

The Educational Costs of Standardization

The town's head librarian loved to encourage the children of his small, isolated farming community to read. He frequently went to the local school to read to the children. Most recently, he had been reading to a class of "at-risk" eighth graders—students who had been held back two or more years in school. They loved his reading and his choices of books. He reports feeling very frustrated: the department chair has told him not to come any more to read to the students—they are too busy preparing for their TAAS test.

—unsolicited correspondence

Three in a row? No, No, No!
[Three answers 'b' in a row? No, No, No!]

—one of several cheers taught to students at their daily pep rallies on test-taking strategies for the TAAS test

I would like to think of teachers moving the young into their own interpretations of their lives and their lived worlds, opening wider and wider perspectives as they do so . . . I would like to see teachers tapping the spectrum of intelligences, encouraging multiple readings of written texts and readings of the world.

—Maxine Greene
"In Search of a Critical Pedagogy"

My initial analyses of the negative effects of the Perot-era reforms on teaching and learning focused on the relationships between classroom practice and bureaucratic structures. The effects of the centralized controls over curriculum and teaching were so damaging, so limiting to the curricular content, and so de-skilling of teaching, that they seemed contrary to their own intent. They appeared to be *contradictory*. That is, in the name of improving education, Perot had inadvertently strengthened that very part of the system he had described as a barrier to educational quality—the bureaucracy (McNeil 1988a, 1994). The cycle of lowering expectations seen arising out of the informal relations between teaching and the controlling goals of schools in the *Contradictions of Control* schools, was under the Perot reforms, cast into official state policy. The early analysis of the school-level effects of centralized systems of education has been invaluable in bringing to light the ways standardization affects specific curricular content, particular children, and the capacities of their teachers to engage them in substantive learning. It has provided an unprecedented tracing of the origins and effects of standardizing policies from the state level, and the business forces pressuring state politics, through the local bureaucracy, and into actual classrooms. From this system-to-classroom analysis we can see without question the power of standardization to reduce the quality and quantity of what is learned in schools.

Institutionalizing Standardization

The long-term effects of these policies are even more damaging and more important to understand. An examination of the current system of standardization, borne of the Perot era, reveals that once institutionalized, *standardization widens educational inequalities and masks historical and persistent inequities. Standardization shifts both the control of schools and the official language of educational policy into a technical mode intended to divorce the public from the governance of public schools.* Each of these bears close examination because the effects are directly opposite the claims of "equity" and "higher standards" made by advocates of educational standardization.

The Perot reforms initiated the linking of teacher assessment to student test scores. "Performance" assessments, begun under Perot, will be shown to have a devastating effect on children's access to a substantive education when teachers and administrators are forced to choose between providing a meaningful education and raising test scores to assure their salary raises and contract renewals.

The Perot-era reforms inspired the creation and adoption of local, and then state-level, test-driven curricula. Current classroom practice reveals that aligning curricula to state tests narrows and trivializes what can be taught and that this narrowing and trivializing is most common in those schools where students have traditionally scored low on standardized tests—the schools of poor and minority children.

A further legacy of the 1980s reforms is the substitution of the language of accounting for other forms of discourse by which citizens and educators have traditionally discussed and debated what is to be taught, who will be served by schools, how school resources will be allocated, and who shall govern schools. Incipient in the reforms that hit the magnet schools were the pieces—the accounting language and the standardization, the disdain for teachers and the distance from communities—of the current comprehensive Texas Accountability System. As could be anticipated by the early effects of the test-driven curricula on the magnet schools, the current system of testing and performance accounting has made test-driven curricula the proxy for education in many schools. In describing this system of aligned controls, one testing expert has said repeatedly, "The consequences of the TAAS test for Black and Hispanic students are clearly criminal from an educational point of view. It remains to be seen whether they are criminal under the U.S. Constitution."[1]

Standardization, as it becomes institutionalized in these ways, falls hardest on those who historically have not done well on standardized tests. As a result, centralized standardization *creates inequities*, widening the gap between the education provided to poor and minority youth and that to which middle-class children have access. In addition, standardization is used to support management systems that in fact *mask persistent inequities*. Finally, the linking of cost-accounting to standardized management systems limits public discourse on the nature and purpose of education, *diminishing the role of the public in public education*. What appear on the surface to be a set of tests of children's learning are, upon closer examination, a fundamental realignment of the power relations governing education (Apple 1995). As examples from schools will show, the inequities, the divorce from public discourse, and even the decline in the quality of teaching and learning are not aberrations or malfunctions in the system, but *the logical consequences of the system when it is working*.

This chapter demonstrates the ways that standardization under the TAAS system of testing harms curriculum and teaching today in many of the same ways the Perot-era reforms reduced or jeopardized teaching and learning in the magnet schools. The test-driven curricula and teacher appraisal system from that legislation, as we have seen, reduced (or threatened to reduce) the quality, quantity, and the credibility of school knowledge and split classroom knowledge from teachers' best personal and professional knowledge. Furthermore, those centralized, standardized policies created, or attempted to impose, a generic curriculum that silenced the voices, the cultures, and the experiences of children. They undermined the teachers' and students' co-construction of curriculum when they entered into a productive bargain to make their schools authentic places of learning. These harmful classroom effects will be seen, under the TAAS system of testing, to be more resistant to teachers' capacity to work around them and to mitigate their effects on their students because of their link to administrator pay.

These extreme forms of educational standardization harm both the curriculum and the cultures of schooling in all the state's public schools. Their effects are not neutral on White, middle-class, and other privileged children. But they will be seen to fall disproportionately on the poorest children, children who historically have not scored high on standardized tests. There is an addition effect even more disturbing for the future capacity of public education to provide a meaningful education to all children. That is the power of the technical language of cost-accounting and management "accountability" to impede, or seriously jeopardize, the capacity for citizens—for parents, communities, and education professionals—to bring this "accountability" system to account. Its narrow and technical language excludes critique that employs nontechnical language: critique based on democratic values, children's development, and equity.

Testing as Accounting

The centralized testing policies begun under the Perot reforms continued as a succession of state-mandated, standardized computer-scored tests of individual students.[2] Throughout the 1980s the state introduced various state tests of children's school performance, beginning with tests of basic skills (TABS), followed by a test of slightly higher academic skills (TEAMS). It was the TAAS test, legislated in 1990, however, that linked the testing of students to what has come to be termed an "accountability" system (Heubert and Hauser 1999; Texas Education Agency [TEA] 1998). That is, students' scores on the TAAS test, aggregated by school building, are used as indicators of principals' and teachers' job "performance." The rhetoric of the test is that it is improving education (TEA 1998); the reality, as we will see, is that there is increasing evidence that the TAAS testing system harms children's learning and that it particularly limits the quality of education available to poor and minority children.

The logic of the TAAS system recalls that of the legislated reforms of the 1980s: the sense that public schools are failing is attributed to weaknesses in teachers. A small but vocal sector of businessmen has refused to support funding for schools, statewide and in the larger cities in particular, unless they see that the personnel in schools are being held "accountable" for their "performance" (McAdams 1998). The unit of accountability is to be the individual school; the currency of accountability is to be the aggregation of student test scores in each school, with special attention to the percentage passing a cut score to be set by the state. The state is to hold districts "accountable" according to their overall pass rates; the districts, in turn, hold schools and the personnel in them accountable for the average pass rates of their students. Schools' ratings, by test scores, are published in full-page spreads in the states' newspapers, under a star rating system reminiscent of restaurant guides. Whether schools are "exemplary," "acceptable," or unacceptable is determined almost entirely by the single indicator: the pass rate on the TAAS.[3]

"Accountability" is operationalized in two ways that become damaging to instructional quality. First, tenure for principals, particularly in the largest urban district (where the magnet schools are located), has been replaced by a "performance contract." Principals no longer have tenure, but work under a two-year contract. Contract renewal, building assignment, and annual salary bonuses are, under the terms of the performance contract, contingent on the passing rate on the TAAS in each principal's school.[4] With the fate of the principal based not on the overall health of the school's educational program, but on a single set of indicators, the principal becomes the building-level compliance officer for teaching to the TAAS.

Second, in the newspaper ratings, and in the state rankings of the schools, student scores are disaggregated by race and ethnicity. Schools are unable to advance in the ranking system unless the scores of minority children, as well as Anglos, "improve" from year to year. This disaggregating of scores gives the appearance that the system is sensitive to diversity and committed to improving minority children's education. This reporting, however, actually exacerbates growing inequities, because the push to raise the minority scores leads to a focus on the test to the exclusion of many other forms of education. Increasingly common is the substitution of commercial test-prep materials in place of traditional curricula and instructional activities for these students.

There is little reliable longitudinal data on TAAS scores because the state has changed several times the subjects and grades to be tested, the pass rates, and the benchmark years for testing, making comparability and longitudinal

analysis problematic. There are considerable claims, however, by the state education agency, the districts, and the governor's office, that the TAAS is "improving education" and even that is has rescued public education in the state.
Reports based merely on movement in TAAS scores are used to support claims
that Texas is one of the few states where "student achievement" is improving.
Apparent upward movement in test scores is cited as justification for using the
tests for increasingly high-stakes decisions regarding individual children's education. (At present, for example, all students must pass the tenth grade TAAS in
order to graduate, regardless of the number of credits a student has earned and
regardless of the grades earned in those courses. Legislation effective in the near
future makes passing a new eleventh-grade test the graduation bar and a third-
grade reading test the hurdle for promotion to fourth grade.) There is, however,
a growing body of data that taken together point to the damaging effects that
lie behind both "high" and "low" scores. These effects are not visible in the individual students' scores, the aggregate school scores, the star ratings of schools,
nor the performance rewards that accrue to principals. They are the effects
experienced by the children and their teachers. They include reducing the
actual amount of what is taught. The effects also include transforming content
into a format that, like the proficiency curricula imposed on the magnet schools
in the 1980s, is testable by computer-scored standardized tests, regardless of the
appropriateness of that transformation for the epistemologies of the subject or
for the ways children learn. These effects, which split school knowledge from
the knowledge base of teachers just as the proficiencies attempted to do, will be
seen to occur in both the subjects that are currently tested under the TAAS system and those which are presently not being tested.

Curriculum as Test Prep: Subjects That Are Tested

In many urban schools, particularly those whose students are predominantly
poor and minority, the TAAS system of testing reduces both the quality of
what is taught and the quantity of what is taught because commercial test-
prep materials are substituted for the regular curriculum. Reading skills, writing, and math are currently the subjects being tested. Because the principal's
pay (and job contract) and the school's reputation depend on the school's
scores, in those schools where students have traditionally not tested well on
standardized tests, the regular curriculum in these subjects is frequently set
aside in order that students can prepare for the test.

Common sense would suggest that if a teacher followed a traditional curriculum, even using the state's textbook, the teaching of regular lessons would

be preparation for success on the test. If students were able to do math problems, explain math concepts, and apply math skills in the regular sequence of lessons, then it should follow that they would do well on the test.

The tests, however, are not necessarily consistent with traditional teaching and learning. First, they are multiple-choice; they call for selecting among given answers. Second, they call for accurately darkening a circle beside the selected answer, without making stray marks on the paper.

In minority schools, in the urban school district where the magnet schools are located and in many schools across the state, substantial class time is spent practicing bubbling in answers and learning to recognize "distractor" (obviously incorrect) answers. Students are drilled on such strategies as the one in the pep rally cheer quoted at the beginning of this chapter: if you see you have answered "b" three times in a row, you know ("no, no, no") that at least one of those answers is likely to be wrong, because the maker of a test would not be likely to construct three questions in a row with the same answer-indicator. (The basis for such advice comes from the publishers of test-prep materials, many of whom send consultants into schools—for a substantial price—to help plan pep rallies, to "train" teachers to use the TAAS-prep kits, and to ease the substitution of their TAAS-prep materials for the curriculum in classrooms where teachers stubbornly resist.)

Under the proficiency system of test-driven curricula, the magnet teachers retained some discretion over how to "teach" to the proficiencies. They could teach the proficiency-numbered curricula (as the district directed them to do). They could ignore the proficiency curricula and hope that their students would do well on the proficiency tests by virtue of having learned from the lessons the teacher had developed and taught. Or, we have seen, they could try to juggle the two. This juggling became important when they saw that the proficiency format so trivialized and fragmented course content that the "knowledge" represented was too far removed from the substance of the curriculum the teachers wanted their students to learn. In addition, the testing by selecting among provided responses negated the teachers' desires that their students construct meaning, that they come to understandings, and that they connect course content with their prior knowledge.

The teachers who taught "double-entry" lessons included just enough from the proficiency curricula to assure that their students knew, or could recognize, the information in the format they would encounter it on the test. And they taught from their authentic curriculum so that their students would know, and come to have a deep understanding of, the richer knowledge of the course.

Teachers, even those who know their subjects and their students well, have much less latitude when their principals purchase test-prep materials to be used in lieu of the regular curriculum. The decision to use such materials forces teachers to set aside their own best knowledge of their subject in order to drill their students on information whose primary (and often sole) usefulness is its likely inclusion on the test. Examples of this splitting of personal and professional knowledge, and the requirement to do so, abound.[5] A particular example reveals not only how test-prep "teaching" diminishes the role of the teacher but also how it distances course content from the cultures of the students.

One teacher, a graduate of an Ivy League college, with a master's degree at another select college, had spent considerable time and money assembling a rich collection of historical and literary works of importance in Latino culture. She had sought titles especially related to the American Southwest for her classes at a Latino high school. Her building of a classroom resource collection was extremely important given the schools' lack of a library and its lean instructional budget. Her students responded to her initiative with a real enthusiasm to study and learn. She was dismayed to see, upon returning one day from lunch, that the books for her week's lessons had been set aside. In the center of her desk was a stack of test-prep booklets with a teacher's guide and a note saying "use these instead of your regular curriculum until after the TAAS." The TAAS test date was three months away. (The prep materials bore the logo "Guerilla TAAS," as in making war on the TAAS test; the booklet covers were military-camouflage colors; the Guerilla TAAS consultants came to the school in camouflage gear to do a TAAS pep rally for the students and faculty.) This teacher reported that her principal, a person dedicated to these students and to helping them pass the TAAS in order to graduate, had spent almost $20,000, virtually the entire instructional budget for the year, on these materials. The cost was merely one problem. Inside the booklets for "reading" were single-page activities, with brief reading selections followed by TAAS-type answer choices. These students who had been analyzing the poetry of Gary Soto and exploring the generational themes in *Bless Me Ultima* had to set aside this intellectual work to spend more than half of every class period working through the TAAS-prep booklet.

The imposition throughout the entire school of TAAS-prep as a substitute curriculum recast the role of teachers, making them into people needing outside consultants to tell them (and "pep them up for") ways to raise test scores. That these commercial materials were imposed proscribed the capacity of the teacher to resist. They also made it difficult for teachers to make accommodations at the margins, to try to hold onto the more substantive curriculum and cultural connections the magnet teachers for the most part had managed under the proficiency system to do.

The limiting of the role of the teacher in shaping or negotiating the course content and the means of assessment causes problems beyond deciding what to teach. When their students' learning is represented by the narrow indicators of a test like the TAAS, the teachers lose the capacity to bring into the discussion of the school program their knowledge of what children are learning. Teachers in urban schools say that to raise questions about the TAAS and about artificial test prep is characterized as being against minority students' chance to get high test scores. Or it is portrayed as "not being a team player." The test scores generated by centralized, standardized tests like the TAAS, and by the test-prep materials which prepare them for those tests, are not reliable indicators of learning. It is here where the effects on low-performing students, particularly minority students, begin to skew the possibilities for their access to a richer education.

At this school and other minority high schools, where TAAS-prep is replacing the curriculum, teachers report that even though many more students are passing TAAS "reading," few of their students are actually readers. Few of them can use reading for assignments in literature, science, or history classes; few of them choose to read; few of them can make meaning of literature or connect writing and discussing to reading. In schools where TAAS reading scores are going *up*, there is little or no will to address this gap. First, so much publicity surrounds the rising scores, and the principals' and superintendents' bonuses are contingent on that rise, that the problem of nonreaders is silenced. Second, with the problem silenced, there can be no leverage to add the resources, change the teaching, or invite discussion about the sources of the problem. In fact, the opposite occurs: the rise in scores is used to justify even more TAAS-prep, even more pep rallies, even more substituting of test-based programs for the regular curriculum.

Advocates of TAAS might argue that passing the reading skills section of TAAS is better than not being able to read at all. However, there is first of all no evidence that these students "cannot read at all." Second, teachers are reporting that the kind of test prep frequently done to raise test scores may actually hamper students' ability to learn to read for meaning outside the test setting. In fact, students report that in the drills and on the TAAS reading section, they frequently mark answers without *reading* the sample of text. They merely match key words in an answer choice with key words in the text. The defining of "reading" as captured on the test ignores a broad and sophisticated research base on the teaching of reading and on children's development as language learners. When teachers are able to draw on this professional knowledge base, what they see there does not lead them to testing formats like TAAS for help with their children's reading.

Teachers' knowledge of their subjects and of children's development as learners within a particular subject domain—particularly in key areas like reading—are compromised by the increasing reliance on teaching only to the format of the state test. The magnet science teachers saw the proficiencies as artificially fragmenting the processes of scientific thinking and of scientific phenomena into items to be recognized (among multiple choices) rather than understood. Similarly many reading teachers are finding that the teaching of reading in the early grades is being hampered by the overemphasis of test-prep requirements.

Elementary teachers have expressed the concern that extensive prep for the reading section of TAAS actually undermines children's ability to read sustained passages. The prep materials in reading, again purchased by principals eager to protect their performance contract or perhaps to help children pass the test, feature brief passages. After reading a passage, students are to answer practice questions ("Which of the following is the main idea?" "Which of the following would not make a good title for this paragraph?" "Which of the following was described as '. . . .'?"). The selected passage is not something they will see again; it is not even linked to the subsequent practice passage.

Students who practice these reading exercises day after day for months (many principals have teachers begin TAAS-prep in September, and do not let them revert to the "regular" curriculum until after the TAAS test in March) show a decreased ability to read longer works. A sixth-grade teacher who had selected a fourth-grade Newbery Award book for her class, thinking all the students could read and understand it, found that after reading for a few minutes the students stopped. They were accustomed to reading very brief, disjointed passages; they had difficulty carrying over information from the first chapter to a later one.[6] Discussions with other upper elementary and middle school teachers confirm that students accustomed to TAAS-prep, rather than literature, may be internalizing the format of reading skills tests but not the habits needed to read for meaning.

The teaching of "writing," also a subject tested by TAAS, has been reduced in many schools to daily practice of the essay form being tested that year. A

teacher who is African American and always alert to good educational opportunities for her sons was very pleased that her second son would be able to
have the same excellent fourth-grade teacher under whom her oldest son had
thrived. She was not prepared for the TAAS-based transformation of the
fourth grade in the intervening years. She said that although the principal and
teacher remained the same, the entire fourth-grade curriculum had been
replaced by TAAS-prep. Writing had become daily practice in "the persuasive
essay," consisting of five five-sentence paragraphs, a form which clearly quali-
fies as "school knowledge" in the most limited sense. What students had to say
in these essays was of virtually no importance; conforming to the form was the
requirement, and the students practiced every day. This mother knew that in
Anglo schools, while there was some abuse of teaching through TAAS-prep,
most of the children were nevertheless learning to tailor their writing to their
subjects, write in different voices and formats to different audiences, write to
stretch their vocabularies.

A principal of a middle- to upper-middle-class elementary school
explained to an audience at a school reform conference that her teachers had
heard that teachers at other schools were having their students practice the
five-paragraph essay every day. They were concerned to hear that it had
become the only form of writing done that year in their school. This principal, under much less pressure to contrive passing rates for her students on
the TAAS, worked with her teachers to include the TAAS as one of many
"audiences" when they teach students to develop voice and a sense of audience in their writing. Similarly, several high school teachers have told of discussions they had with their students about TAAS writing exam. After
learning more about TAAS, the students decided to think of the audience for
their TAAS writing test as "bureaucrats sitting in little offices, waiting to
count sentences and paragraphs." Ms. Williams at the Pathfinder school had
used "The Examiner" poem as a vehicle for helping students analyze the
school policies that were affecting their learning. These teachers, not
required to do only TAAS prep (usually in high-performing schools), are in
a similar way trying to make the test the subject of critical inquiry. This is
not typical in low-performing schools where teachers and principals are
using pep rallies and incentive prizes to get students to "buy in" to these
forms of evaluation.

A casualty of the proficiency system and the teacher appraisal checklist on
the magnet schools was the strong sense of mutual trust and credibility the
teachers and students had developed around their shared knowledge. The

younger children growing up with TAAS-prep may not always know (unless they compare with friends in private schools or have an older sibling whose learning was more substantive) how TAAS-prep reading and writing differ from good instruction. Older children, however, are not without skepticism that this system of testing is altering what they and their teachers jointly regard as important learning. Elaine, an eighth grader, knows firsthand the artificiality of "TAAS writing." In a previous grade, she won the citywide short story writing award conferred by the local chapter of the National Council of Teachers of English. This spring she received notice that she failed to pass the eighth-grade writing section of the TAAS because she "failed to provide sufficient supporting detail." Elaine and her teacher both know that she is known in her school as a writer. What distinguishes her writing is its rich detail. They could speculate that perhaps the scanning of her TAAS writing missed, by its haste or its rigid format, the elaborative and "supporting" detail that characterizes her writing. The TAAS, and not the quality of her writing nor the English teachers' judgment, lost credibility for her and for her parents as an indicator of her writing skills.[7]

An eighth-grade class in a predominantly poor, Latino middle school demonstrated pointedly the intellectual subtraction resulting from the TAAS system of testing when the emphasis is on raising minority scores. In mid-September a group of community visitors stepped into Mr. Sanchez's class just as he was covering the blackboard with rules for semicolon usage. Using semicolons in writing seemed a useful and worthy lesson for eighth graders working on their writing, so at first the visitors watched without comment. While the students were copying the semicolon rules, the teacher explained: "We are having to do grammar until after the TAAS. I'm so excited—this year we have a whole nine weeks after the TAAS to do eighth-grade English. I always do Shakespeare with my students. And I have many stories that they love to read. Last year we didn't have much time, but this year I will have a whole nine weeks." The visitors were just then realizing the import of his words: he was to do TAAS prep from September until March, and then "teach eighth-grade English" only in the remaining nine weeks. And the teacher was made to feel grateful for all nine of those weeks. He had opted to participate in the de-skilling the magnet teachers had avoided; he explained that it was the will of the principal that they get the scores up and that everyone in the school was feeling the pressure. He knew that by focusing on the TAAS alone, his students would be getting far less than the eighth-grade curriculum studied by students in schools where the student demographics (middle class, predominantly

White) would carry the scores, and they would be learning even less than his own students in the years before TAAS.

Under the proficiency system, the mathematics teachers had struggled to hold onto their goals for students to learn to apply mathematical concepts and operations in the face of increasingly computational mathematics. They also chafed under the test format that asked students to choose among given answers, permitting students essentially to be able to guess an answer without ever working through the thought processes the question would imply in a learning situation. The content was also highly sequential under the proficiency system, undercutting the teachers' desires that their students bring a variety of mathematics skills together to work on problems, rather than mastering them in an artificial sequence. Under the TAAS system of testing, these problems—of divorcing course content from the best thinking in mathematics education persisted. In addition, the rigid test sequence is causing teachers to bracket knowledge of the kinds of learning activities their own students need to enhance their mathematical understandings. For example, teachers who have worked with the frameworks and theories of the National Council of Teachers of Mathematics guidelines for math instruction increasingly teach students varied and divergent approaches to mathematical problems and proofs and help them learn to write out how they worked through a solution.

Under the TAAS-prep system, the teaching of mathematics, the third subject currently tested, is also highly truncated. TAAS tests math by having students choose among four or five possible answers. They are not asked to explain their answers, so if students have alternative ways of working a problem, their reasoning is not made visible on the test. Nor are their reasons for selecting "correct" answers. Being able to conceptualize in mathematics, being able to envision a solution and select among possible approaches, being able to articulate the reasoning behind an answer—none of these is tested by TAAS. TAAS tests computational accuracy and familiarity with basic operations. The reductive mathematics on the test is not adequate preparation for courses in more advanced mathematics. The TAAS-prep booklets, which emphasize test-taking strategies over mathematical reasoning, again create a gap between the content learned by poor and minority students in schools investing in TAAS-prep kits and the students in well-provisioned schools. In these latter schools, principals assume students will pass because of their family background and their having attended "good" schools in lower grades. They therefore support the teaching of the regular academic curriculum without substantial risk that to do so might "lower" the TAAS scores.

Curriculum as Test-Prep: Subjects
Not Tested by TAAS

If a teacher wants to avoid TAAS prep and focus on the students and the curriculum, then it would seem that the answer would be to teach a subject not yet tested by TAAS. At the Pathfinder school, Ms. Bartlett claimed a space for teaching complex biology topics by shifting some of her teaching out from under the controls of the proficiency system. She created elective courses and independent study seminars around such units of study as ecology and habitats (enabling her to integrate concepts and topics that were fragmented and sequenced separately under the proficiencies). She taught a biochemistry elective (using her knowledge gained from the medical school mentorship and crossing traditional subject boundaries) and in some semesters, marine biology. Under the TAAS system of testing, teachers report that there are fewer and fewer venues in which they can do authentic teaching, even though officially only three subjects—math, reading, and writing—are tested. In poor and minority schools, especially, teaching untested subjects such as art, science, or social studies is not exempt from the pressures of TAAS prep. An art teacher with a reputation for engaging her Latino students in serious studio work, and for exciting students about being in school, was required to suspend the teaching of art in order to drill her students daily in TAAS grammar. By the time the grammar drills were completed, there was no time to set up for art projects. Her students were doubly losing: their treatment of grammar was artificial, aimed at correctness within the multiple-choice format of the test, rather than at fluency in their own writing; and they were denied an opportunity to develop their sense of color and design in art.

A history teacher in an underresourced Latino high school worked with his colleagues to create a history curriculum that would maintain authentic content and yet incorporate some of the skills their students would need to do well on the TAAS; they included the writing of essays on historical topics and attention to reading skills. They had at first been given permission to create this on their own but later were told that they needed to set aside the teaching of history entirely in order to "cooperate with the rest of the faculty" in getting students to pass the TAAS. This history teacher's assignment was to drill his students every day on math, a subject outside his field of expertise.

Science teachers who have spent a year in the Rice University Center for Education Model Science Lab (located in an urban middle school) updating their science knowledge and upgrading their capacity for laboratory-based teaching enter the program with the consent of their principals to implement what they have learned when they return to their schools. Many of these teachers have discovered on returning to their home schools that they are required, for as much as two to four months of the school year, to suspend the teaching of science in order to drill students on TAAS math. Again, their students in these urban schools are doubly penalized, first for losing out on the science that their peers in suburban schools are learning. Second, they are penalized by having to spend extra periods on low-level, disjointed math drills—math divorced from both the applications and the conceptual understandings they will need if they are to hold their own later in upper-level math classes with middle-class students. It is unlikely that the middle-class students have been doing "math" from commercial test-prep booklets, rather than from math books, manipulatives, calculators, computers, and peer study groups. The TAAS, then, lowers the quality and quantity of even subjects not being tested in those schools where students have traditionally not tested well, the students who are poor and the minority.

From the losses in subjects being tested to the suspension of subjects not yet tested, it is clear that in any given year there may be weeks or even months of academic losses for these students whose principal's bonus, or even the principal's employment contract, depends on upward movement in student test scores. When the newspapers report "improvement" in the scores, the figures are taken at face value. There has been little public questioning into the dynamics producing these scores. The opportunity costs for minority students who are in effect being used to ratchet up administrator pay loom large. Those, too, were students of potential and promise, whose earlier schooling had not provided the background they should have going into secondary school but who, if taught a substantive curriculum, were able to develop into competent, even inspired, students. What is happening to and with the *students* under the test-prep system—and to curriculum content —is completely absent from consideration under an accounting system that uses only one set of indicators on which to base administrative and economic decisions in schools.

The TAAS as a Management System

The critique of standardization is often countered with the accusation that to be against standardization is to be against "standards." It is interesting that the Texas Accountability System, and its central element, the TAAS test, is almost never discussed in terms of academics or in terms of standards. The discussion in the policy arena and press releases (and school ratings) is couched in terms of "accountability," not academics. The TAAS as an accountability system has its immediate roots in the teacher appraisal systems implemented during the Perot era. At the state level, the appraisal system was demanded by business interests who opposed teacher raises without some mechanism for "quality control." At the district level, the proficiency system of test-driven curricula was, in the words of one of its planners, a way for principals "to be able to fire teachers" without extensive paperwork or the threat of lawsuits; test scores of the teacher's students would provide objective evidence of teacher failure or performance.

Under the new accountability system, the pressure to raise scores causes principals in poor and minority schools to divert the school's scarce resources into materials, activities, conferences, staff development days, consultants, and packages aimed at prep for the state test rather than at high academic quality. Increasingly, principals are paying for expensive test-prep materials, consultants to motivate teachers and students to work on TAAS (pep rallies, weekend lock-ins for test prep just before the test, motivational speakers), and expenditures for management conferences on compliance with administering and securing the TAAS. It is the schools that already have the scarcest resources, the schools that have historically been underfunded in this district and others, that are using those scarce resources to pay for materials and activities, that have no educational benefit beyond producing TAAS scores. Some of these are the neighborhood schools the magnet students have left behind because of their weak academic programs.

The district had a decade before imposed on them a proficiency system to try to raise their test scores but had failed to invest in resources that would enhance the substance of their academic programs. The attempt to manipulate the measurement outcomes without substantially addressing the issues of academic quality (and resource inequity) had left those schools as academically impoverished as ever. Their continued history of low test scores now makes them vulnerable to TAAS-prep as a substitute for real teaching and learning. This vulnerability is the price they have paid for being in a district that once again is trying to raise test scores independent of a commitment to redressing resource inequities. It is trying to raise test scores independent of attention to issues of academic content and instructional resources. It is ironic, then, that the stated need for TAAS testing—that is, the low levels of education of many of the schools in the state—arises in part from past attempts to address a history of weak public education by measuring outcomes, rather than improving teaching and learning. The measurement systems have not improved teaching and learning, but they have confirmed, however inadvertently, by continued low scores, the inadequacies of measurement systems to improve children's education. Policymakers whose political interest lies in the perpetuation of these systems and administrators whose rewards are now tied to them miss the effects of the system in perpetuating poor quality education and instead call for more investment in techniques to ratchet up the scores.

The pressure to raise TAAS scores to show evidence of effective school management is increasingly usurping not only scarce instructional dollars but also the avenues of conversation and policy discourse within the organizational hierarchies of schools and districts. A collective sense of responsibility for all the children (in Arthur Miller's words, "all my sons") is undermined by a competitive ranking of schools (by stars and words like "exemplary" or "acceptable") and by differential rewards to administrators at various levels. A competition is established that, according to a number of teachers, makes teacher collaboration across schools difficult if the principal or area superintendent fosters that competition. A lead math teacher was returning to her school, a Latino high school, after a year of consulting with other schools. She requested that her planning period (her nonteaching hour) be scheduled at the end of the day or over the noon hour so that she could leave several times a month to continue to serve as a mentor and math resource teacher to the math faculty of another traditionally underresourced minority school. Her principal's response was immediate: "Maybe we don't *want* their scores going up."

By the same token, many principals report that the superintendents of their geographic areas devote most principals' meetings and memos within those jurisdictions to TAAS-related issues. These are not discussions of academic quality, but advice on how to get scores up, what prep materials to use, how to get teachers and parents "on board," what pressures are coming from central office. A pattern that is pervasive, although more prevalent among historically low-scoring schools, is that these midlevel superintendents limit discussion of school plans and programs to those they see as directly affecting TAAS. (To the extent this pattern is less dominating of school programs in higher-scoring areas, the capacity of those already stronger schools to continue to build academic programs while poor schools are focusing on TAAS further widens the gap between them and, in a vicious cycle, puts further pressure on the low-performing schools to focus on TAAS.)

In those schools and districts where the schools' TAAS scores are tied to incentive pay for teachers and principals, or where TAAS-linked performance contracts have replaced administrator tenure, there is a greater tendency to displace the academic curriculum with test-prep materials and activities. And among these schools, where this displacement is taking place, those whose students are poor and minority are by far more likely to focus resources on the TAAS, to the detriment of other teaching.

Accountability as Pedagogy

The power of the magnet schools to widen students' intellectual horizons, to spark their curiosities and deepen their understandings came in the relationships between teachers and students around an authentic curriculum. Ms. Bartlett, the biology teacher at Pathfinder, exemplified the extraordinary efforts magnet teachers would exert to offer their students many ways of learning, investigating, and understanding. Every biology lesson in her course incorporated demonstration labs, lectures, films, computer simulations, model-making (often from found materials), experimental labs, reading, taking notes, writing up lab notes, asking questions, and submitting to oral quizzes and written exams. In each new study, some of these activities would be required of all students; others would be elected by students according to the ways they best learned or the skills they most needed to master. The learning included individual mastery as well as social construction of understandings. And Ms. Bartlett reworked the lessons every year trying to make them fit her students so they, many of whom were new to active science learning, could find their strengths as learners.

The TAAS system of testing, by contrast, crowds out most forms of learning, particularly in schools whose students are poor and minority. Teachers report having to omit or severely decrease extended reading assignments, analytical writing, research papers, role play (recall the night Thoreau spent in jail), student-led discussions, speaking activities, oral histories, multimedia activities, science experiments, library hours. They have been seen having to curtail or omit extended problem solving by students, in-depth discussions, approaches that end up with oblique perspectives because they are not seen as contributing directly to passing rates on the TAAS. In many schools where students have historically done poorly on standardized tests, principals require teachers to spend class time on TAAS prep materials instead of the regular curriculum; these losses in those cases occur by default. In other cases, teachers have absorbed without being directly told that the only thing valued in the school is the number of students passing the TAAS, and they narrow their own pedagogy lest students learn "too much" or learn to "think too much" for the TAAS. (Just as Mr. Drew cautioned his students not to think too much when they took the proficiency test, teachers aiming for TAAS scores remind students not to use their "complex minds" but to use their "TAAS minds" when they practice for TAAS.)

The use of class time for TAAS prep raises another issue related to theories of learning. When most of the class period every day for weeks is spent in drill for the tests, much of that time is spent in reading sample questions and trying to select among the provided answers. Two serious problems immediately come to light. The first is that the curriculum, as experienced by students, is "received knowledge." They are to select among provided answers, not offer their own responses. The second in terms of developmental learning is the continual exposure to wrong answers. During test-prep time, three-fourths of the material (if four possible answers are provided) is erroneous. It is meant to be excluded, discarded, forgotten; these are the "wrong" answers. The opportunity cost is great; again, students in schools doing test-prep rather than school are spending enormous amounts of time and mental energy on material they are *intended to forget,* further widening the gap between these students and their peers in more privileged schools.

The narrowing of the forms of learning is blatant in some schools. Valenzuela reports that in a large, traditional, integrated high school, where most middle-class students pass the TAAS but many minority students do not, the school has instituted "local credit" classes for TAAS prep (McNeil and Valenzuela 2000). "TAAS English" and "TAAS Math" do not count toward graduation credit. They take an hour of the student's school day but have no merit beyond TAAS-prep. Students know these are not real courses; the content is watered down and fragmented, arranged to fit the upcoming test rather than to bridge students into college-preparatory levels of these subjects. A cruel irony is that if they do pass the TAAS in October (the high school administration of the test), it is too late by then to transfer into a regular academic class, so they have that wasted hour for the rest of the semester. Many will skip school rather than participate in the waste. Valenzuela adds that Anglo and middle-class students in this school overwhelmingly pass the TAAS. They then go on with their regular schooling, while those who do not do well on the TAAS (mostly the minority students) are pulled out of regular schooling for an even weaker curriculum.

The use of TAAS-prep materials, particularly those commercial materials with no value beyond their potential to aid in passing this one test, is damaging enough when it displaces the regular curriculum over weeks or months of a school year. What we are beginning to see, however, is the effect of this substitute-curriculum over many years of a child's school experience. If year after year, minority children are subjected to test-prep activities and materials in lieu of the regular curriculum experienced by middle-class and suburban students, then the system will be exacerbating the academic weaknesses in these children. The system itself will be engendering a *cumulative deficit*[8] in these children's knowledge and in their knowledge of what it is possible to learn. If the librarian is not allowed to read to the children *because they have to get ready for the TAAS test,* then how will they know what they are missing?

When test-prep becomes pedagogy, there are other losses as well. A key question in the critical scholarship on education is the issue of whose knowledge becomes school knowledge? Whose interests are served by the knowledge that becomes the school curriculum (Apple 1995; McNeil 1986; Sharp and Green 1975; and others)? From the proficiency test-driven curricula to the state-enforced TAAS system of testing, it is clear that a standardized curriculum becomes no one's knowledge. It is so generic that it does not involve the mind of the learner, it rarely involves the mind of the teacher, and it sits somewhere in the institution untouched by the varieties of people who inhabit those institutions.

The first answer to the question of "whose knowledge," then, is "no one's." Students learn best when they construct their own knowledge (Cohen et al. 1993; Gardner 1991; Wiske 1998), a task made nearly impossible when information is so far removed from their connections to it. Standardization and technical renderings drain the human content from the information being conveyed and mastered. That being said, there are additional losses for minority children, whose cultures are even more noticeably absent from the content of standardized schooling. The magnet teachers managed to invite student voices into the classroom, not as mere respondents to teacher lectures or questions, but as contributors to the curriculum, to the socially constructed knowledge by which all, including the teacher, learned. A technical curriculum, designed to be testable by "objective" measures and represented by numerical indicators, does more than omit the diverse cultural content of the students' lived experiences. It structures out the possibilities that such content can enter into the curriculum. A technical test-driven curriculum closes out the stories children bring to school. Inherent in those stories are their cultures, home languages, perceptions of the world, questions, and special ways of knowing that may reflect a cultural difference or may just be a mark of their own individuality. Teachers tell us that the five-paragraph essay may offer practice in indenting, but it does not invite the writer's voice.

They tell us of having to omit literature, including the literature representative of their children's cultures (and in many classrooms this means a United Nations of cultures), in order for their students to practice reading and choosing answers for brief, unimportant, and entirely unmemorable passages. They tell of having to drop the art projects or group activities that in the past had linked the "regular" content to the children's cultures and interests. Under a regimented test-driven curriculum, particularly one that focuses on a highly reductive set of skills, the admissible "ways of knowing" are narrow, prescribed, and depersonalized.

The TAAS *scores* do not capture the nature of these losses. As mentioned above, many students who pass the reading section of TAAS are, in fact, nonreaders. Their schools enjoy the publicity of the rising scores, then have to search the following year for ways to help their students learn to read (without alerting the central administration or the public to their predicament). By the same token, many minority youth have skills and academic accomplishments not represented by their performance on the TAAS. They are seen as deficient, as failing, as in need of remediation because their forms of learning do not coincide with the forms of testing. Many adults will excuse their own history of test scores with the dismissal, "I'm just not good at taking standardized tests." Yet, that commonsense understanding of individuals' potential mismatch with forms of testing does not extend into the policy arena. Minority children who do not pass TAAS are seen as "problems" or failures, frequently marginalized into classes for remediation.

Valenzuela has described "subtractive schooling" as schooling that distances students and convinces them that no one cares about them and their education. It gives the signal that, in return, the students themselves should not care, because to conform to a U.S. school is to risk losing one's cultural identity (Valenzuela 1999). A generic curriculum, constructed for its scorability by computers rather than its relation to children's learning, layers on another form of subtractive schooling, further distancing minority youth from the processes of schooling. This is never so starkly evident than when a Latino student, intimidated by the looming TAAS, which he has seen so many of his friends fail or drop out to avoid, says, "This isn't about us, is it? Doesn't the principal get a raise or something?"

The Poverty of Sameness

A persuasive rationale for the TAAS system of testing is that it is equalizing public education in this state. These claims are being reinforced by the disaggregation of scores by race and ethnicity for each school. No school is allowed "exemplary" status whose averages are carried by Anglo students alone; there has to be movement in the pass rate of Latinos and African Americans as well. The political benefits this disaggregation affords state officials, with glowing press across the nation for rising scores, are not necessarily experienced by minority students as educational benefits.

Minority parents understand that passing the TAAS is required for graduation. According to many teachers and principals, some of these parents believe that the TAAS is important for post–high school employment and college admissions. Others know that it carries no weight beyond high school exit and therefore try to focus their children's attention to preparation for the SAT or ACT college admissions tests. Among Latinos, there is approximately a 10 percent high school graduation rate among adults in the United States (9 percent in Texas; 11 percent in California); among families in which high school graduation is a high goal, passing the TAAS looms large. To get more Latinos to pass the tenth-grade TAAS, some schools, as has been mentioned, offer courses with no value other than TAAS prep. Others counsel students to leave school after ninth grade (or do not discourage those who might want to leave). *The school's scores will be higher if these students exit before taking the tenth-grade TAAS.*

There are a number of serious problems with deducing the quality of education from minority students' test scores. First, the passing rates for minorities represent only those who are still in school and those who are tested. There are estimates that the most recent pass rates for Latinos (almost 80 percent) is based on only 75 percent of the Latino students who began school in that age cohort. That is, if 25 percent of a class has dropped out and 75 percent remain, 80 percent of the remaining students is equal to a 60 percent pass rate for the students who should have made it to tenth grade with that class. (The districts frequently say that the missing students "transferred to another high school," but the numbers across the urban high schools show no counterbalancing increases at "other" schools; the other explanation, that "they went back to Mexico," is a false and cynical disclaimer of responsibility for these students' education.)

A principal explained a further connection between the accountability system and the apparent rise in minority test scores. His students are poor, mostly Latino; he has worked with his faculty to restructure his school, created school-to-work learning opportunities, hired dedicated and smart faculty, added sports attractive to neighborhood students, and involved many faculty in a number of programs to enhance their practice. His school is improving, the academic program is becoming stronger, and his students feel much more purposeful about their schooling. Still, the test scores at this school have not risen substantially. This is one of those principals who quotes his supervisor as saying, "Do not talk with me about these things you are doing at your school. None of them matters unless the TAAS scores go up. Your job is in jeopardy."

This principal had refused to turn the school over to TAAS drills because he was determined to make genuine improvements in his students' education (what some educational evaluation experts call "real gains"). His fellow principals told him that the lack of TAAS drills was not his only problem. His problem, they said, was that he was promoting his ninth graders to tenth grade if they earned their credits. Passing students who had earned their credits seemed quite normal. This principal, however, explained that he was told there would never be a level playing field among the high schools, that his "performance" contract would always be in jeopardy, because he insisted on promoting ninth graders who had earned their credits, *whether or not they were good test takers*. The other principals, in a widespread practice that went beyond a few isolated cases (according to this principal's discussions with them over many months), were looking into the testing records of all their ninth graders. Any who had done poorly on the eighth-grade TAAS, and who therefore might be expected to produce weak or even failing scores on the tenth-grade TAAS (the one needed for graduation), were retained for an additional ninth-grade year. The ninth-grade classes at many of the minority urban high schools in the state were becoming numerically half the high school's student population. They included the regular ninth graders, the students who had been held back in eighth grade for two years who now had to be promoted whether or not they were academically ready, and this new category—students who should have been promoted to tenth grade but were held back to give them another year's practice for the TAAS test. The principal who reported this pattern of manipulating of student promotions in order to inflate test scores had no place, no administrative venue, to report or discuss this issue. The only discussions being permitted within the bureaucracy were those that could be expressed in terms of the outcomes measures themselves, not the dynamics producing them.

The New Discrimination

The educational losses to minority students created by a centralized, standardized system of testing are many. What is taught, how they are taught, how their learning is assessed and represented in school records, what is omitted from their education—all these are factors that are invisible in the system of testing and in the accounting system reporting its results. Standardization of educational testing and content is creating a new kind of discrimination—one based not on a blatant stratification of knowledge access through tracking, but one which uses the appearance of sameness to mask persistent inequalities.

"These Children"

This masking shows up first in the words of well-meaning people who restratify expectations by their use of the language of "basics." The myth that standardization produces sameness, and therefore equity, is based on the notion that standardization "brings up the bottom." The idea is that everyone should get the fundamentals. First students have to "get the basics" before they can get to the "creative" or "interesting" part of the curriculum. Within this myth, any good teacher, or good school, will "go beyond the basics" to provide a creative, interesting education.

There is increasing evidence that this use of "basics" is being applied to conceptions of minority children as "other people's children" (Delpit 1995). If "these" children are somehow different from "our" children (who are getting the regular curriculum), then they should be grateful for an education that provides them for the first time with the basics. The "creative" and "advanced" part of schooling is contingent upon "the basics," or so the logic goes. Evidence in classrooms points out several flaws in the constructing of curriculum around "these" students' basic needs.

First, as the magnet schools have shown, students learn "the basics" when they have significant, purposeful instructional activities, when they have models of thinking to emulate, when they can see how new skills can be applied at the next level. The magnet teachers (heirs to Dewey and others) engaged students' minds so that they could learn both the "basics" and the ideas and knowledge that cannot be sequenced in a linear fashion because they are part of an organic whole. Yet, a great deal of the official pride in the TAAS system is that "for the first time *these students* are getting the same education *our* students have been getting." The sameness is false, as we have seen. The myth is so strong that even some African Americans are buying into it, seeing challenges to standardization as denying their children access to the basics (Raspberry 1999).

That the political climate is becoming more permissive of this patronizing characterization of minority children was made graphically plain at an event in which Latino students would be demonstrating their learning mastery of packaged curricula that had been implemented in their historically low-performing schools. Each of the curricula represented a considerable investment including classroom materials, consultants to train the teachers to use the materials, tests to evaluate the students' performance on the materials, and other expenses related to the vendors of these programs. The curricular programs, in math and reading, were aimed at "the basics."

The Latino children, dressed in their Sunday best, filed in by grade level to demonstrate their skills in basic math operations. The activities were of high interest but of unknown long-term academic value, according to math educators and many teachers. The children's parents and teachers were seated in the large hall. Between the performances by groups of children, a White corporate executive, the event's master of ceremonies, would talk about the program. After one group of children exhibited their addition skills, he looked over the heads of the parents, to the [mostly White] corporate and community leaders standing around the room and said, "Isn't this great? Now, this may not be the math you would want for *your* children, but for *these* children—isn't this just great?" He was met with smiles and nods.

The pervasiveness of TAAS-prep as a substitute for the curriculum in poor and minority schools is legitimated by the tacit, rarely spoken (and mistaken) understanding that for "these children" repetitive practice in test-drill workbooks may be better than what they had before and is useful in raising the test scores of "these children."[9]

A Latina teacher in a San Antonio-area middle school testified in federal court (*G. I. Forum v. Texas Education Agency,* September 1999) on the harmful effects of the TAAS system of testing on the education she and her colleagues were able to provide to their students. She said that TAAS dominates faculty meetings. As an eighth-grade history teacher in recent years, she had found herself being required to alter the teaching of U.S. history in order to drill her students for the eighth-grade TAAS. Previously, she had engaged all her students in research projects, written papers, the study of primary source documents, role play, and debates. She said she had been able to motivate even the most reluctant history students at this Latino school to "get fired up" about learning history and to learn at a high level. And they had done well. In response to schoolwide pressure to raise the TAAS scores, she had to reduce history instruction for the lowest-scoring students. She reported that she was able to continue the more complex assignments only with her "high-scoring" students, substituting TAAS-prep in place of engaging history lessons for the other students. She testified that in the current school year, she had requested re-assignment, to teach seventh-grade Texas history, hoping to be able to teach *all* her students a rich history curriculum. With the eighth-grade TAAS a year away, she at first found more freedom to make complex assignments within the classroom. But this year a new emphasis pervaded the stratification of children throughout the school: the students a TAAS consultant termed the "bubble kids." Their scores formed a "bubble" just below the passing score.

This consultant was invited to help the faculty "raise the TAAS scores." Her strategy was literally aimed at raising the *aggregate* pass rate of the children in the building in order to raise the *school's* ratings. At the first faculty meeting of the year, she presented her simple, straightfoward strategy: aim preparation for the test at those students who had previously failed by only a few points. Aiming instruction and test preparation at *these* children, the "bubble kids," would be the most efficient way of raising the *school's* scores. The history teacher said that the consultant advised the faculty not to "waste their time" on the children who scored far below the "bubble kids"—those would never pass. The teacher concluded by saying that she feared her school was "nurturing drop-outs." If the lowest-scoring children were ignored in third, then fourth, then fifth grades, she feared they would not make it to tenth grade (the year of the graduation-exit-level TAAS). This teacher's experience encapsulates the extraordinary potential of teachers and children, the restratification of education access under this system, and the caughtness that prevents good people from acting on their own best knowledge when the dynamics behind the numbers go unexamined.[10]

Data are beginning to emerge that document the losses children are incurring. In a compelling analysis to be released in 2000, Walter Haney has analyzed graduation rates of cohorts of high school students from 1978 to the present. Using official data from the Texas Education Agency, Haney tracked ninth-grade cohorts to graduation. In 1978, more than 60 percent of Blacks and almost 60 percent of Latinos graduated—a gap of 15 percent below the average for Whites. By 1990, after four years of the Perot-era standardization reforms, graduation rates for Blacks, Latinos, and Whites *all dropped*. By 1990, according to Haney, *fewer than 50 percent* of all Black and Latino ninth graders made it to graduation. The gap between minorities and Whites was widening. By 1999, his data show that the White graduation rate has regained its 1978 level (around 75 percent). The graduation rate for Latinos and Blacks, however, has remained below 50 percent (Haney forthcoming).

Standardization may, through intensive test practice drills, "raise scores." But it has not enhanced children's learning. To those who would say that the graduation rate is dropping because the TAAS is "raising the bar," one must answer that to increase cut scores and make no investment to equalize educational resources is no reform. It is, rather, a creative new form of discrimination.

Any discussion of the education, and the learning capacities, of poor and minority children, must return to the magnet schools for a reminder of what children can do, even students from impoverished family backgrounds and uneven prior schooling, when a school district organizes schools toward giving them a rigorous, precollege education. The magnet schools showed what minority students can do when their teachers work with them to construct meaningful and productive learning experiences. The magnet schools demonstrated, and have continued to demonstrate without question, that students can learn, and to a high level and in racially and culturally diverse settings, when school knowledge is credible. They can learn when their teachers are encouraged to bring their best professional knowledge into the classrooms. They can thrive academically when students and teachers are both active participants in the learning process. The quality and authenticity of their education although threatened, was not destroyed by the test-driven proficiencies of the Perot era because that system, although intended to be highly controlling, was not so "aligned" administratively that it totally compromised teachers' professional discretion. Their teachers managed to find ways to assure that compliance with the standardizations did not entirely displace the authentic curriculum. They also worked to maintain their authority to build that curriculum around their students.

TAAS and the Magnets

It is interesting to see how the TAAS-system of testing has affected teaching and learning in the magnet schools themselves and how the role of those schools has shifted slightly in the production of test scores for this newer accountability system. Both of these contemporary TAAS effects relate to the magnets' complex role as schools for integration (for bringing diverse students together) and as schools that by their nature sharpened a two-tiered system of education through their focus on a college-prep education.

So long as the TAAS tests have been aimed at basic skills in reading, writing, and math, the magnet teachers have not had to compromise their course content under the current system to the extent that they did under the proficiencies. Because most of their students tend to do fairly well on standardized tests, they have not had to succumb to the pressure to substitute TAAS prep materials for their regular curriculum. Instead, their response to the TAAS has been reminiscent of Mr. Drew's taking time from his lively history classes to help his students practice "dumbing down their minds" for the proficiency tests. Among the core academic teachers in these magnet schools, their approach to the TAAS is closer to that of teachers in top academic tracks of traditional high schools: taking a few days (rather than months) to give practice tests, giving students strategies for simplifying their thinking, practicing weeding out distractor answers among the multiple choices. Generally they see TAAS prep as helping students step back from their most complex thinking in order not to second guess or engage in debate with the test-makers as they proceed through the questions. Magnet teachers of math generally advise their students to think "computationally" (as one teacher described), not conceptually. As another teacher told her class, "The maker of the test does not want your advice on the choice of formula or operation for solving the problem. He just wants to know what you think the right answer is. You are not the test-maker."

As a part of the system of schooling under the jurisdiction of the TAAS system of accountability (the test is not waivable, so not even these exceptional schools are exempt), the role of the magnet schools depends on their status as free-standing or schools-within-schools. Those schools that are free-standing (the arts school and MedIC), with their traditionally high scores, provide the district with positive numbers it can show when the district lists its "number of high-performing schools." The state education agency judges districts in part by the percentage of its schools that have a certain percentage of their students passing all three sections of TAAS. The freestanding magnets help increase this percentage because they are counted as separate schools.

The magnets like SET and Pathfinder, schools within larger schools, take on a role similar to their role in "desegregating" single-race schools. Under desegregation population counts, the placement of a magnet school within a larger school altered the racial ratio counts within the whole school, even if the magnet were a separate program. Carver High remained an all-black school in its neighborhood program, but appeared to be integrated because the racial demographics of the magnet students were counted into the student population of the entire school. (Teacher counts were similarly aggregated by building.) Under the TAAS accountability system, the scores of school-within-school magnets are used to help boost the averages of the *aggregate pass rates* within the whole schools. Their students' usual level of academic achievement and performance on standardized tests makes the magnets an asset within their buildings for purposes of enhancing the building-level scores. They thereby help boost administrator "performance" indicators all the way up the system. All they have had to do to sustain this level of test performance has been, as the teachers describe, to make sure that their students do not bring their sharpest minds, their best ideas, their most complex thinking into the TAAS test. Their accommodation up to this point, then, has been to prep their students for a reduced level of thinking and care not to make stray marks that the scoring machine might misread.

The magnet teachers are not, however, unconcerned about the TAAS and its effects on teaching and learning. They are seeing reduced skills among some of those incoming ninth graders who enter from schools where TAAS prep has taken the place a center role curriculum. And they know that within the next few years, additional subjects will be tested. These will include history and the sciences, fields where specific content as well as "skills" will be subject to the TAAS. Once these subjects come under TAAS, they anticipate that their teaching will be threatened in much the way it was under the proficiencies. The selection of content, the inclusion of diverse ways of knowing, the reflective component of their students' learning, the relevance of their lessons to their students' cultures and life experiences—all the things that have made their teaching successful for them and for their students' futures will be once again in jeopardy. A TAAS format is likely to transform all course content into reductive fragments of fact, into trivial unconnected pieces of information, into tightly sequences that do not permit stepping out of the sequence to pursue ideas that arise in class. Placing all subjects under the TAAS accountability system will, in the estimation of magnet teachers I have listened to on this issues, jeopardize the integrity of their subjects. It will cause them to have to set aside lessons that represent both a lifetime of learning and curriculum development and their most recent explorations of their subject. The proficiency tests were in themselves disrespectful of teacher knowledge, student experience, and the fundamental nature of the subject fields. But they were not a part of a tightly aligned system upon which administrator pay was based. They left some room for flexibility. The effects of the TAAS format of testing will be compounded both in harming the curriculum and in reducing opportunities for teacher resistance because of its role in the large system of accountability. The incentives and sanctions in that system are causing schools to turn curricula into simple prep for the TAAS.

At the forum that launched a major school-based reform initiative in the city, one of the most dedicated and successful English teachers in the city, a teacher whose Latino students proudly speak of themselves as "writers," spoke eloquently about the TAAS and its related controlling policies. She said, "Everything they are making us do takes us farther and farther away from the children." The teachers who have stayed in magnet schools, and those who transfer into them as the controlling environment in their previous schools increasingly narrows what they are permitted to do, anticipate no benefit for their students and for their teaching when these other subjects are added to the test. They and their colleagues who have dedicated years to improving the education of Latino and African American children repeatedly say that the testmakers do not know their children, their children's cultures, or the ways to successfully engage widely diverse groups of students in learning. Those who were in the public schools during the proficiency era worry that the content of all the subjects will be harmed by having them recast to fit TAAS—to fit a generic statewide curriculum and to fit the scoring format. Once again, teachers are talking about shifting into the shrinking list of subjects or program areas not encompassed by TAAS, moving to teach in private schools, or leaving teaching.

The use of the magnet schools as sources of passing scores, rather than as models for teaching and learning, is one of the cynical realities of a system of accountability that ignores extant models of good schooling and, in fact, that identifies schools and teachers across the board as "the problem." That the magnet schools would be used within the present system of standardized controls to reify discriminatory school practices (at the same time they are reversing past discrimination by providing their own minority students with rigorous education) is an extraordinarily perverse effect (to quote Art Wise) of the legislated reforms.

Masking Inequities

The TAAS system of testing restratifies access to knowledge in schools. It further harms the education of poor and minority youth by masking historical, persistent inequities. When the proficiency system of testing was implemented in the 1980s, two rationales were given. First, it would make the curriculum testable by "objective measures." Second, it would "assure that Algebra I at [poor, minority, northside high school] is the same as Algebra I at [suburban, middle- to upper-middle-class, mostly White high school]." It is true that the second high school carried a higher academic reputation, and it is probably true that what was studied as Algebra I at that school was far more rigorous than the course offered at the poorer, minority high school. But the proficiency tests, and the curricula they imposed, did not equalize the content, the teaching, nor what students learned in Algebra I at the two schools. The imposition of the proficiency curriculum carried with it no new resources for the historically underresourced schools. In fact, if the magnet schools' experience is in any way suggestive of the classes at the suburban school, probably required some lowering of the quality of Algebra I that school in order for it to accommodate to the test's reductive transformation of content. Sameness, absent massive investments at the underresourced school, is achieved by "leveling down" from the top, if at all.

The TAAS system of test-driven accountability masks the inequities that have for decades built unequal structures of schooling in this state. Test-score inflation, through concentrated test-prep, gives the impression that teaching and learning are improving in minority schools when in fact teaching and learning may have been severely compromised in the attempt to raise scores. The investment in expensive systems of testing, test design, test contracts and subcontracts, training of teachers and administrators to implement the tests, test security, realignment of curricula with tests, and the production of test-prep materials (Haney, Madaus, and Lyons 1993), serves a political function in centralizing control over education and linking public education to private commerce. But these expenditures do nothing to reverse the serious inequities that have widened over time in this district and across the state. In fact, the investment in the "accountability system," rather than in the schools, is a cynical masking, which under the screen of sameness obviates the need for new school-level investment. Even more cynical is the inverting of investments not to equalize resources but to reward those whose scores go up: the investment comes as a reward for compliance, not as a means to assure educational improvement prior to assessment.[11]

Scarce resources at the school and district level are being invested more in those materials and activities that will raise scores, than in curricula of lasting intellectual or practical value to students. Experience in the past five years, the period in which principal tenure has been traded for TAAS-based performance contracts, shows that it is the historically underresourced schools, with the greatest number of poor and minority students, that are shifting their already scarce resources into test-prep materials. There are middle-class schools and districts that spend time and money on test-prep materials. But educators and parents associated with these schools report that the expenditures of both time and money are much less than those in urban schools. TAAS-prep might be the focus of attention for the week or two preceding the test, but not for a whole semester preceding the test. And these schools' budgets are such that they can buy or produce some test review materials without having to forego other instructional resources.[12]

Jean Anyon writes compellingly in *Ghetto Schooling* (1997) about the "pauperization" of central city Newark—the starving of neighborhood resources in all areas of funding and public goods—as Whites left those parts of the city. The poverty of the people and institutions remaining was a result of this pauperization by alliances among more powerful political and economic interests. In much the same way, the stratifying of academic resources in the name of accountability compliance is a pauperizing, a making poorer, of many urban schools, compounding their academic insufficiencies because they are already academically weak and because there is little public will to address the sources of those weaknesses in the larger economic structure.

Accountability and the De-Democratizing of Education

The use of cost-accounting to hold down public investment in education and to remove educational practice from community governance has a long and discredited history, in England in the 1800s, in the United States during the factory efficiency days of the early 1900s, and in the "back to basics" movement of the 1970s (Martin, Overholt, and Urban 1976). Linking cost-accounting to its basis in political control, its advocate Lessinger (1970) speaks of cost-accounting as the means of assuring the "rights of taxpayers" to know the educational results of every dollar spent. According to Martin, Overholt, and Urban (1976, 35), each time cost-accounting is introduced into educational policy, there is a reluctance by the rich to pay for the education of the poor. The "poor" in late-nineteenth-century England and in the United States at the beginning and end of the twentieth century included large numbers of immigrants (35). In each case the educational considerations were subordinated to political and economic forces.

The introduction of the language of accountability during the Perot reforms and its emergence as the dominant language of educational policy in recent years is in fact more political than educational. It represents a shift in the locus of control over schools, a shift in the definition of public education, and distancing of the larger public from the governance of schools.

Accountability implies responsibility to a higher authority: being held to account for, being obligated to account to. Within this urban district and in the state, during the Perot reforms and at present, accountability is invoked to locate the problems of schooling at the level of the lowest employees, the teachers. The use of the word itself distracts from the historical inequities of funding, staff allocation, materials investment, and social support from the broader community. By implying a hierarchy, and a culpability at the bottom of the system, such calls for accountability by definition empower those who use the term. The presumption is that those who are calling for accountability feel they are in control and others (beneath them) have to answer to them. A common feint is to claim that "the public demands accountability," although in this educational context, when a public has tried to demand accountability, it has traditionally done so to try to make the top of the structures of schooling responsive to the particular school and community.[13]

Accountability in the Perot era came in the form of disjointed policies. The teacher appraisal system was meant to assure quality control in the classroom in exchange for Career Ladder salary increments. The appraisal checklist lasted for years; it retained its nuisance value but ultimately held little power to leverage compliance because soon after its implementation, the resources to fund the salary increments disappeared. The proficiency system tied curriculum to student tests and attempted to tie student tests to teacher pay, but widespread rejection of the system (and a new superintendent who saw its flaws) prevented its accomplishing its intended alignment between prescriptive policies and employee compliance. It failed as an educational measure and failed to deliver in its promise to give principals objective evidence for firing teachers.

Under the current governor, George W. Bush, and his business advisors, the Texas Accountability System now in place carries forward the Perot era shift in authority that locates the expertise for education outside schools (and outside the educational system, in the business advisors). The current policies, like the earlier reforms, rely on numerical indicators as evidence of relative educational quality. They shift the authority for schooling away from local communities. And the current TAAS system extrapolates educator performance from student test scores. What Perot and the legislature were not able to accomplish in House Bill 72 was a closed system of accountability, a system that aligned all the elements, from students to curriculum to teachers to principal to school to district to state. The current accountability system encompasses all of these levels (and is designed over time to encompass all school subjects).

As a closed system, it has substituted the language of accounting for other forms of educational discourse. A system of education that reduces student learning to scores on a single state test (and uses those scores for such high-stakes decisions as grade promotion and graduation), structures out the possibility for discussing student learning in terms of cognitive and intellectual development, in terms of growth, in terms of social awareness and social conscience, in terms of social and emotional development. It is as if the "whole child" became a stick figure. Upper-level administrators who tell principals literally not to speak about their students or their programs except in terms of TAAS scores are participating in the delegitimating of students as children. They are participating, however unwittingly, in the excluding of human and cultural development when they silence discussion of the particular children of a school.

Further, as presently employed, the reduction of *students* to test scores has two contradictory but equally depersonalizing effects: the scores have both a highly individuated effect that ignores the social and collaborative aspects of learning. And yet in the reporting of scores, children are subsumed into depersonalized aggregates. Often these aggregates are meaningless. A 75 percent pass rate at a school this year may appear to be an improvement over a 66 percent pass rate at the same school last year, but in an urban setting there is no assurance that even half of these are the same children in two successive years.

The accountability system equally depersonalizes teachers, flattening any representation of their particular practice in the reporting of aggregate pass rates for their schools. The role of principal has been severely limited, with greater authority to allocate resources for activities aimed at raising test scores but with less discretionary power to undertake other kinds of work in the school or to have that work recognized.

The use of a language of accountability also takes the discussion of public schooling away from the normal language of families and communities. Parents feel they have to master a jargon to understand how their children are doing; teachers feel mystified by the mathematical formulas that can turn known weak schools into "exemplary" in the star ratings. Parents report feeling confused by their child's TAAS report sheet. "I have never felt so distant from my child's school." "I have an education and I can't read this. I can't figure out what they are saying about my kid. I can't imagine how a less educated parent must feel when they get these reports they send you."

Finally, "accountability" as a closed system admits no critique. Criticisms of the system that have any currency and that generate response are those regarding the technical components of the system: At what point should English-as-Second-Language children have to take the reading TAAS in

English? Are administrators erasing students' wrong answers and changing them to the correct answer to raise school scores? Are the test questions valid/culturally biased? Is the cut score for graduation set too high or too low?

Questions about technical tinkering are tolerated. And to all such questions, there is basically one answer: more controls. If there is lax security, then the test materials must be more tightly controlled. If scores are going up, then test prep must be working. If scores are slipping, then more test prep must be needed. There is no acknowledgment among officers of the district and state system that the real problems are not cheating by altering answer sheets. The real problem inherent in such a system of controls is that it severely undermines teaching and learning while masking problems within the institution.

The technical language of accountability silences those professionals who want to stay in public education because it takes away the legitimacy for any other, counterlanguage to shape school practice. This problem is exacerbated as a system becomes so "aligned" that professionals in the system are locked into compliance if they are to stay in the system.

Ironically, such a closed system also prevents those business people concerned about the low level of skills being taught and tested from having a forum for discussing employers' needs for a better educated workforce (Murnane and Levy 1996a). To see a high tech future, especially in entrepreneurial terms, and to tie education reform to it, there should be a call for curriculum aimed at the highest knowledge in every field. It should call for risk-taking, experimentation, visionary possibilities, and open-ended instructional purpose. Such a model of school reform should be based on highly skilled professional teachers, not teachers de-skilled by mandated test-prep booklets in place of a valid curriculum. Now that the effects of highly centralized standardizations have been seen to be so damaging to teaching and curriculum, it may be useful to review the economic origins of the Perot reforms. The choice of Perot to lead the blue ribbon advisory commission and the timing of the 1980s reforms grew not only out of a weakening of the traditional extractive economic base in the state, but also from a perception that future economic strength would come more from high technology industries than from oil and gas, that future wealth that would build much more slowly than the get-rich-quick days of booming oil and real estate, and that the increase in high technology and service industries would necessitate expansion of the "human capital" side of the economic equation. Citizens would need sophisticated education to create and manage the complex commercial and technological enterprises that would make Texas competitive in world markets. The reputation of public education in the state was not only woefully inadequate as a base for economic restructuring toward high-technology industries, but it was also perceived as a barrier to relocation by well-educated high-technology scientists, engineers, and managers the state needed to attract if it were to lure industries from other places. The intense push for reform in the 1980s came primarily from the business sector seeking highly educated, highly skilled employees and managers.

Yet the interrelations between economic structures and school policy have proven to be not all as simple as Ross Perot's advisory role in shaping an economic rationale for school reform. Once the legislation was passed and its general enabling language operationalized by the state agencies, the rationalizing processes of the bureaucracy attempted to neutralize the reform process. This eroded the potential to debate the schools' appropriate role in support of the economic status quo, or new directions for highly technological economic development, or empowerment of a generation of students traditionally cut out of expectations of economic participation. The language of educational quality as institutionalized in the Perot reforms, and later aligned in all layers of the bureaucracy through the TAAS test, bypasses substantive discussion of the content of a public education equal to the task of fostering economic and technological revolutions. Its language of cost accounting, drawn from an early twentieth-century model of industrial production, while a "business" metaphor, proves to be inadequate—even oppositional to—the new economic goals and their reliance on highly skilled workers. The cost-accounting model, which marginalizes teachers' best knowledge, children's development as learners, and the richest curricular content, is also undermining the very role for public schools that the larger business leadership had seen as an essential requisite for business support of schools: the assurance of a workforce capable of moving the state's economy from oil and gas to information and technology.

The educational costs of standardization, then, include not only the direct impact on teaching and learning, but also the high costs of compliance when compliance silences professional expertise, marginalizes ethical discourse, and diverts what could have been productive support from the business sector into defense of a model of schooling that, in the end, will not serve even those business interests well.

De-Democratizing Public Education

There is one further cost to education under a system of standardization: the threat to the democratic governance of schooling. The technical cost-accounting management systems already narrow public discourse and silence many of the constituencies of public education. The language of accountability already reduces those aspects of the educational system that can even be discussed. It takes questions on the role of schools, the development of children and the substance of education and turns them into technical questions best handled by the testing experts.

If the language of accountability comes to dominate public school policy, then it will eliminate the means by which the public—the parents and teachers and other citizens of a community—can challenge the system of accountability. We have already seen the harmful effects of a cost-accounting system on curriculum and teaching. We have seen its tendencies to create new forms of discrimination as its control mechanisms reward those administrators who shift resources into the means of compliance, rather than into educational resources, a pervasive pattern in minority schools with a history of low scores on standardized tests.

In *Legislated Learning*, Arthur Wise (1979) warned that attempts to legislate learning, to legislate teaching, frequently have "perverse effects." He was speaking of the kinds of perverse effects within schools that have been documented as occurring in the magnet schools under the proficiencies and in the poor and minority schools described here in their responses to the TAAS. The effects within schools and school systems may not be nearly so "perverse" as the effects within our system of democracy, as these attempts to legislate and control learning reduce the public's possibilities for retaining democratic governance of schools once the controls are in place. One reason for this is that an accountability-based control system, as a closed system, structures out possibilities for external critique.

A larger reason may not be the *result* of the adoption of an accountability system of education, but its *cause*. There is increasing evidence that these systems are being employed precisely because they do limit public access to the governance of schools and public discourse regarding the purposes of schooling. It is this basis in an attempt to wrest schools from democratic control that needs to round out the circle of analysis of this system-to-classroom examination of the effects of educational standardization.

Throughout our history of public schooling (Kaestle 1983; Kliebard 1986), democracy has been invoked as the fundamental underlying premise for public support of schools: the necessity for all citizens to be educated to be effective as citizens, the necessity for all citizens to be actors in the economic and cultural life of the nation, the necessity of the democratic government itself to have its people educated. Democracy has been both the real basis for extending an education to all children and, sadly, at times the cover story that masked our failure to provide such an education equitably. Even when that provision was inequitable, it carried such slogans as "separate but equal," rather than deny the democratic basis for the structures of schooling. In the present policy climate, that need to invoke democracy—even as a cover story—is being set aside by those who are attempting to recast schools into a publicly funded but essentially private enterprise. The ways the accountability language is displacing democratic discourse have their origins this larger picture.

Where Perot, in his initial foray, located the problems of schooling within the bureaucracy, and the district created the proficiency system to counter perceived weaknesses in teachers, the accountability system that has come out of those earlier policies locates the problem in the democratic governance of schooling. The other problems of education, including weaknesses in teachers, would diminish if the right people were in charge of schools.

It is in examining the shift in the locus of control over schools that the use of the accountability language begins to make some sense. "Accountability" is not about saving taxpayer dollars; nor is it about tightening the management system so that all the employees in the system are held to account. Accountability, as it is emerging in this state and in this district, is increasingly the symbolic language of political control by people who want to turn public schools over to private interests. The former president of the urban district's school board has published a paper on "lessons learned" from his time on the board of this district (McAdams 1998). In the introduction and again in the conclusion, he states, "Urban school reform is almost impossible because urban schools are under direct democratic control" (1).

The conclusion that "democratic control" is the problem with urban schools is built on a reversal of "the public" and "special interests." "Special interests" in common parlance has meant groups that lobbied Congress or other legislative bodies on behalf of a particular ideology or legislative agenda—the National Rifle Association, the American Dairy Association, and the Chamber of Commerce are examples. They would advocate their single, "special" interest as distinct from interests shared by more generalized populations. In McAdams's view, "special interests" are teachers, educators' professional organizations, parent groups, minority board members representing their districts' interests, and any other group not allied with the "business leaders." He would put public education in the hands of the business leaders (where he acknowledges it resides de facto in this city) and use a system of accountability to make sure school employees do what they are told by this group to do. Until elected boards can be eliminated and replaced with corporate boards, he recommends granting as many school charters as possible, contracting with public and private agencies to run schools—essentially shifting the educational system out from under the publicly elected board.[14]

Lest this scenario sound too local to be significant for purposes of analyzing the growing reliance nationally on the language of accountability to restructure schooling, Paul Vallas, Chief Executive Officer of the Chicago Public Schools, made a televised speech to the National Conference of Governors in March 1999 in which he expressed essentially the same message: appoint a board of corporate executives "so there will be no special interests on the board." That board should bring in a few experts to tell the school people what their work should be, "set the standards," and then "hold them accountable" (Vallas 1999).

Throughout U.S. history, the rhetoric of democratic schooling has often been invoked even when our communities did not provide schooling for all children. In the current realignment of education and democracy, the invoking of the symbolic language of democracy seems to be much less necessary, even at a symbolic level. This became clear in a meeting of local educators and representatives of philanthropic foundations gathered to complete plans for a local affiliation with a national school reform movement. The mission of that movement was to reform urban schools by improving teaching inside the schools and by fostering much more direct and involved community participation in the communities surrounding the schools. A key education advisor to Governor Bush, a businessman who was not a part of the planning of the reform initiative, insisted on meeting with the group to explain how the reform would "have to be set up." He had been described as one of the architects and chief advocates of the Texas Accountability System. He came specifically to speak against the plans for the new reforming schools organization to include, as planned, a community council. Such a council would be made up of parents, representatives of community-based organizations, clergy, arts and health leaders, and as one planner envisioned, "people who are wise about children." The community council's role would be to open up lines of communication regarding educational issues (in this city of highly centralized school districts). It would help bring together groups of parents and people in the neighborhoods around reforming schools so that schools could become reconnected to their physical neighborhoods. Most important, it would help foster a much more diverse set of voices on behalf of children and schools.

Governor Bush's education advisor spoke emphatically: "You can't have this community council. And you definitely can't give them any authority, like getting to select the schools that will be funded. [He paused.] *Now, I'm not against democracy, per se. But when it comes to education, it just won't work.* What you need in education is a power board—of business executives—the right people in the community—then your board brings in a few experts and the experts will advise them on the plan. And then when you have your plan, you call the Black ministers in and tell them what you want them to do."[15]

The Danger of Normalization

With pressures to silence citizen and parent voices in setting both educational visions and policies, with the conscious use of technical systems of standardization and accountability to limit public participation in education, there is a sense that surely this is not what is happening. Surely these standardized reforms are just one more wave of "school improvement" remedies that will disappear if teachers and parents remain patient.

The effectiveness of these reforms in silencing dissent lies in part in the de-identification of individuals with social groups that have a shared history from which to voice a critique. In part the capacity for silencing opposition is to be found in the barriers inherent in a self-contained system that permits critique aimed at fine-tuning the mechanism but does not permit critique that challenges its premises. The co-optation of the use of the word "reform" by these centralized systems is itself a way that this normalizing is constructed. In addition, there is a normalizing effect that takes hold when a policy, even a highly flawed one, persists beyond those who initially questioned and resisted its implementation.

The magnet teachers were all too aware of the negative effects of the proficiencies on their teaching. They vividly recalled and held onto models of teaching they felt to be more authentic, more meaningful to their students, more credible when held up to the light of the world outside schools. They knew the standardized proficiency system held within it no such credibility.

The current accountability system has been implemented slowly and in stages. First as state tests that held almost no consequence for students, then as state tests that held moderate consequences for students (recorded in their records but not used for high-stakes decisions). Now the system uses students' scores for the evaluation of teachers, principals, schools, and even districts. Students who have been in school for the past ten years (the life span of the TAAS) think this is what school is. Teachers who have taught for fewer than ten years, and who have not come in from another state, assume outcomes testing to be a sad but "inevitable" feature of schooling. Principals will speak in private against the TAAS system of testing, but few reject the attraction of thousands of dollars of cash bonus promised for raising scores. Teachers and principals who hope to have long careers in public education in the state rarely speak publicly against the testing system or its premises, although in private conversations they may rage against its effects on their work and on their students. An extraordinary culture of intimidation accompanies such a system, reminiscent more of the old Soviet system than an institution inherited from Jefferson and Dewey.

The incremental normalizing of a system, the casual use of its language in conversations about education, can silence critique and can stifle the potential to pose countermodels, to envision alternative possibilities. That is the insidious power of an accountability system, to sound just enough like common-sense language that it is not recognized as a language meant to reinforce unequal power relations.

The power of the teaching and learning seen in these magnet schools is the compelling evidence they provide of what teachers and students can accomplish when they are given the opportunity to do so. The specific organizational and structural resources implied in these schools' names turned out to be at times fragile or even absent. But these schools were settings where teachers and students, along with parents, developed a shared commitment to a rigorous and equitable education. Where that commitment was permitted (even if not always adequately provisioned) to thrive, urban students proved to be eager and competent learners—not "these children," to be set apart and given a lesser education. Their teachers learned and grew in their work in ways they would not have done under standardized, de-skilling controls.

Among teachers, principals, and parents there is a growing awareness that standardizing teaching and testing is counterproductive. Participating in these practices goes against their common sense about what children need. That teachers and principals are participating in these practices shows the controlling effects of large-scale bureaucracy. What we have is many good people caught in a bad system.

We should not need further exemplars to affirm public confidence in the capacities of children of all races and home circumstances to be able to achieve at high levels. Nor should we need further evidence that teachers can continue to learn.[16] The language of accountability denigrates children and teachers. By contrast, these magnet classrooms provide a compelling case for re-examining the latent strengths in our children and schools and for looking at the damaging effects behind the technical labels and indicators before embracing "accountability" as a panacea. There is such danger that accountability systems will mask existing inequities and structure out the possibilities for authentic teaching and learning that we have to ask in every case *what* is being held to account, and to whom, and on whose behalf?

Standardization and Power

The educational costs of standardization are high. Standardization, when used as the tool of accountability in a highly centralized, aligned system, masks and thereby perpetuates inequalities by its misleading indicators and aggregations and by directing resources toward maintenance of the accountability system rather than toward relieving the inequities. Standardization in the schools analyzed here sets up a specialized language, which acts as a barrier between democratic publics and the institutions of schooling. This system, which has proven to be so damaging to the social construction of knowledge in classrooms, threatens to weaken the social contract by which education strengthens democratic governance.

This analysis might be less compelling if the problems of educational standardization documented here were malfunctions of the system, if they were glitches or problems to be fine-tuned and ironed out. It is critical to note that the effects of the Texas Accountability System, in de-skilling teachers, restratifying access to education, and, in incipient ways, de-democratizing education, are not flaws in the system. *They are the logical consequences of the system when it is working.* It is the purpose of the accountability system to render education into a technical enterprise, one that is less owned by the public and less hampered by the inefficiencies of democratic debate. And one of its intended purposes may be to limit the education of the least powerful among our young people. We know that it is a result; we hope it is an unintended consequence and not a deliberate one.

If our scholarship is to serve a public purpose, than we must be alert as witnesses. We must be awake to the shifting power relations that threaten to define a quality education as the province of a few and the governance of that education as residing in the hands of even fewer. Scholarship that examines the working out of unequal power relations from their origins through the systems of schooling, to the consequences for the children is essential at this time of redefinitions of education and of democracy.

We, as a people and as education professionals, have never known more about how children develop and learn. We have never known more about cognition and the brain and the effects of caring and community on children's growth and development. We have never had greater access to our rich cultural heritage in the arts, literature, history, the sciences, mathematics, astronomy, athletic performance, the world's languages, the geography of distant places, the functioning of our own cells. We have never had more to offer our children. How then do systems arise that narrow the possibilities for children's learning, which perpetuate old discriminations and create new ways of walling off this rich heritage from our poorest children? How can we accept as normal the structures of schooling that diminish the role of parents and communities in defining the purposes of education? We must embrace those ways of teaching and of organizing schools that encourage teachers to bring their best knowledge into the classroom. We must create curricula and learning environments that affirm all children's capacities to learn along with the diversity of children as an inherent *strength* of our educational enterprise. And we must pursue scholarship that, in the words of Maxine Greene, "encourages multiple readings of the world" and that continues to try to interpret not only the processes of schooling but who ultimately bears the costs.

Notes

Chapter 1: Standardization, Defensive Teaching, and the Problems of Control

1. A note on methodology: this study began as an analysis of the factors shaping curriculum in schools whose organizational and administrative structures were designed to support, rather than control, teaching and learning. For that analysis, daily observations in classrooms over the course of at least a semester in each school formed the primary data on curriculum and teaching. Interviews with teachers, students, administrators, and parents, and historical research into the schools and their programs, were conducted formally and informally at strategic points before, during, and following classroom observations. Interviews with central office administrators in the offices of curriculum, gifted-and-talented programs, magnet services, and evaluation and research provided key information on the administrative and legal contexts of the magnet schools during their formation and in the years leading up to and inclusive of the time of the study.

Once the state-mandated reforms under House Bill 72 and related state education agency directives began to affect the schools, subsequent investigation was made into the role of the SCOPE committee, Perot's use of advisors, state implementation of the legislation, and the offices and structures through which these policies were implemented within the school district. Reviews of legislative and committee documents, correspondence, initial evaluation reports, administrative documents, and related materials from a wide range of observers and participants in the state-level reforms and district implementation were essential to the understanding of not only the content of the reforms but also the rationale being used at each level to justify their implementation. Interviews with several key shapers of these policies, both from outside and from within SCOPE and the state government, were extremely helpful in tracking how decisions were being made, and the assumptions of schooling on which they were based. (None of these sources was available to or known to the teachers being observed, who were receiving the directives as rules emanating from a higher but undesignated level in the bureaucracy.) Copies of district and state standardized tests and test-driven curricula and teacher assessment instruments from a number of years were examined. The schools have been followed for several years following the initial implementation of the curriculum directives and teacher assessment instrument, through the successive state test-driven programs, which have followed from the proficiencies, with site visits to the schools, periodic interviews with teachers and administrators, and information gathered through a wide association with these schools.

The contemporary legacy of these early standardizations (especially in chapter 7) is analyzed here on the basis of extensive work with urban teachers and administrators through the teacher enhancement programs of the Rice University Center for Education, school visits and observations, analysis of TAAS-related materials from the state and the testing companies, interviews with teachers, conversations with a wide range of teachers and administrators, parents, and students, regarding the impact of the TAAS on classrooms, press coverage and district administrative bulletins related to the TAAS, and a variety of other formal and informal sources.

To counter any tendency to generalize from an in-depth but relatively small data sample, or from individual occurrences, several correctives were built into the research. First, any outlier occurrences, for which there was not a pattern beyond those occurrences, were not deemed as "data" for the purpose of the overall analysis. (Individual occurrences held significance in themselves, but are not reported in this analysis unless they indicate a *pattern of teaching* and *of the effects of standardization* that go beyond that any one occurrence.) There is no reliance on "horror stories" for this analysis, in other words, or exceptional events. Second, at each step of data collection and interim analysis, counter examples to trends in the data have been actively sought. For example, when it became apparent that biology teachers were having to eliminate many of their lessons, particularly those that integrated biological concepts around hands-on phenomena such as student-built marine aquaria or a natural habitat, interviews were scheduled with biology teachers at other schools to determine whether this problem was specific to the magnet schools, or even these teachers, or whether these curricular deletions were widespread.

Also, counter interpretations were investigated; for example, if a teacher was having to delete a portion of the curriculum, further research was conducted to see if factors other than the prescriptive testing had had an effect, perhaps a less visible effect.

The search for counter examples and counter interpretations is significant because this analysis is not a mere listing of problems or "unintended consequences" of an otherwise sanguine set of policies. As discussed in chapter 7, the negative effects of the standardizing policies have been their primary effects on classrooms and teaching, and their effects on the locus of control over schooling have become visible as, in fact, intended consequences, not circumstantial by-products.

2. This perspective has been reiterated by proponents of state testing, and the Texas Accountability System specifically, in public meetings and private discussions at which this researcher was present.

Chapter 2: Magnet Schools: "The Best Schools Money Can't Buy"

1. The magnet schools were established to address a long history of racial inequalities in the schools. They were created as the school district's response to a federal court order to desegregate by race. The district, school by school, was monitored for the schools' changing rations of student population by race. Racial categories of students and teachers, therefore, are central to both the district's and the students' understandings of one role of the magnet schools, to help desegregate this highly segregated district. The terms used in this book to designate the students and teachers by race are drawn from the common local usage of the participants and also from designations used by the school district. "Black" rather than "African American" is used more frequently in this book because the teachers, students, and parents who participated in this research study used "Black" to describe themselves, their families, neighborhoods, and schools. While "African American" is also in local usage, particularly in formal discussions of culture or policy, "Black" was used more commonly, especially self-referentially among

Blacks in both the observations and conversations as well as formal interviews in this study.

In this city where Hispanics now outnumber any other single cultural group in the schools, their origins vary, as do their self-referent cultural labels. "Hispanic" was not only more common among students and teachers; it has been the official legal category in the monitoring of the desegregation plan. "Mexican Americans" include the descendants of immigrants from Mexico (who are also termed "Mexicans" by themselves and others), as well as the descendants of the original and continuous occupants of this land, which was part of Mexico before it was Texas. (Interestingly, many of the descendants of these pre-Texas Mexican nationals also speak of themselves very proudly as "Mexicans," not "Mexican Americans.") "Latino" and "Hispanic" refer collectively in the schools and in the city to persons of Spanish-speaking heritage, including Mexican Americans and the many Salvadorans, Nicaraguans, and other immigrants from Central and South America. (It should be noted that unlike eastern seaboard cities, this city has few Cuban immigrants or Puerto Ricans.) "Latino" is currently in wider usage, but was rarely used by the people of Mexican and Latin American heritage in this book.

Whites are referred to by people in these schools as "White" or "Anglo," but rarely "Caucasian." From living and conducting research in the Midwest, I was accustomed to hearing many Whites self-identify by ethnic or national origin, even if their forebears had immigrated from a "home country" several generations ago. My neighbors, and the teachers I observed, talked of being "Norwegian," "Finnish," "Swedish," "German," or "Irish." In the southwestern state, however, where this research was conducted, neither in informal conversation nor in their formal self-identification as research subjects did many "White" teachers or students add a qualifier such as country of family origin, religion, or ethnicity. The lack of a social differentiation may stem, in part, from the newness of this part of the country and from the fact that most "White" people here came from another part of the United States, not from Europe; or that across the South and Southwest, most European immigrants were English or Scotch-Irish and thus did not bring non-English languages and customs that set them apart from "mainstream" culture. My use of "White," then, reflects local usage and not an ignoring of people's cultural distinctions. (For an excellent discussion of the construction of social diversity within and among groups, see Tyack 1993.)

Unlike California, where Asians and Pacific Islanders are designated by origins of country or ethnicity, in the official racial counts for desegregation purposes in this Texas city, Asians are counted in the student and teacher populations in the same category as Whites. (This is because they were not as a group plaintiffs in the lawsuit suing to redress discrimination in the schools, as were Blacks and Hispanics.)

These terminologies demonstrate the particular and local constructions of race and ethnicity as embodying known and little-known histories, hierarchies, and the interplay of self-referential labels and the labels that come from institutions and labeling by "others."

Every attempt has been made throughout this analysis to capture the language of the participants and to be most respectful of those words people use to describe themselves and their own cultural identities. One unfortunate term which is used in the book quite reluctantly is the word "minority" to describe the children of color in these schools. The word derives partly from the history of White majority in the school district, rather than the numerical ratios at the time of the school observations (or today). At the time of the study, no one group had a numerical majority in the schools; today, Latino children comprise more than 50 percent of the district's school population, with Blacks around 36 percent and Whites and Asians together at about 11 percent. Notwithstanding these demographic shifts, Feagin and Feagin (1996) cogently argue that the term "minority" is better understood as a political concept since differences in power are what characterize relations between dominant and subordinate groups in society. The continued use of "minority" in this community after the numeric basis for the word is long past supports their assertion that "minority" is a term of subordination, not arithmetic. Hence, rather than reifying a language of dominance, this terminology persists in the book because it persists in the school experiences documented here. It was not only used by people of all races in these schools to refer to Black and Latinos, but its usage herein records the institutional and relational realities in the schools imbedded in the term and in its move from a legal and numeric designation to a part of the accepted and unreflective language of common discourse in this multiracial but unequal community. It was claimed in a positive way by those teachers and others trying to redress past inequalities (as in "creating opportunities for minority students to go to college") as well as used as a marginalizing label by those who unthinkingly or not ascribed "minority" status to students they thought of as other than mainstream.

2. Any regular high school whose program is not primarily shaped by a centralized regulatory system could have served as a research site, as could such schools as Central Park East Secondary School in New York or other schools that have structural and organizational support outside a hierarchical regulatory system.

3. Houston did not have a substantial Mexican population until just after 1900; its "race relations" had been more of a Black-White issue characteristic of a southern city. For a powerful analysis of the transformation of the Mexican community in this city from its origins as a cohesive city-within-a-city of small-business owners and educated business professionals with on-going ties to commerce and government in Mexico, to its marginalization as a community of "others" in a White city, see Rodriguez (1993, 101–127). Rodriguez's analysis of the construction of *Latinos* as an underclass (ironically, as city services began to be extended into their neighborhoods) illumines the view of some Hispanics that desegregation could not serve their children's interests if it were built on a "subtractive" (Valenzuela's term) definition of what it means to be a Mexican, to be a Hispanic.

4. The dominance of a small group of "business leaders" continues to the present according to Don McAdams, who in his paper, "Lessons from [Urban School District]," describes one superintendent who fell out of favor when he proposed a budget to the school board without waiting to be told by the business leaders what that budget should be. "When it came to school taxes, the superintendent traditionally sought the advice of the business leaders first and then proposed to the board what the business leaders recommended. In [this city], power was diffused, but business leaders were the primary power brokers."

5. Kliebard (1986) provides a compelling history of the political and cultural struggles that have been fought with public school curriculum as both the arena of conflict and as the product of shifting political forces.

6. Among the few positive distinctions recalled by many who were parties of interest during this period were the momentary coalescing of a liberal political block at key times on the school board or among multiracial groups of organized parents, and the fact that the local desegregation efforts never included outright violence.

7. Vietnamese families came in large numbers after U.S. war with Vietnam ended in 1975; there are substantial Chinese, Korean, and Vietnamese communities as well as smaller numbers of Laotians, Thais, Japanese, and others.

8. In addition to the court stipulation that Mexican American children should be deemed "White" so that their reassignment to previously all-Black schools could then be considered "integrated," Asians too in this district are counted as "White" for desegregation purposes. In the case of Asians, it was their separateness from the lawsuits, whose plaintiffs were Mexican American and African American, and their small numbers at the time the desegregation plans were created, that left them by default in the "White" count. This differs from practice in California and other states that identify Asians (and subgroups of Asians and

Pacific Islanders) as having their own racial and cultural identity for consideration in admissions and other policy areas.

9. Names of schools, students, administrators, and teachers have been changed because from the outset I promised them anonymity. Accounts of interviews, classroom lectures, and discussions are as near verbatim representations as possible. Details of a few events or people have been slightly altered to protect identities while conveying as accurately as possible the significance of the original.

10. The first magnet schools to be established were so successful in drawing students from neighborhood schools that many schools came to propose internal "magnet" programs that would help keep their students at their home school. For example, a regular high school whose students were transferring to the School for Science, Engineering and Technology might apply to the district to become a "computer magnet."

11. Racial diversity is a high priority with the faculties, and race continued to be a consideration for admissions until it was challenged in the late 1990s by White students' families with the backing of a national anti-affirmative action political group.

12. The district's report to the court six years later documented that the number of "ethnically isolated schools" had dropped from 121 in 1974–1975 to 109 in 1981–1982, with 54.9 percent of the district's students in racially isolated schools in the baseline year, compared to 45.4 percent in 1981–1982. The report says that the "objective" to provide free transportation to all magnet students "was met," and that the overall makeup of the magnet school student population was 38.1 percent Black, 28.7 percent Hispanic, and 33.2 percent White. The report mentions that more than 23,800 students were enrolled in magnet programs, with "a total of 82,078 students . . . affected directly or indirectly by magnet school programs." This latter figure includes those students in "regular" schools whose school buildings showed in the statistics as desegregated even if the students, fac-

ulty, and classes in the magnet program were entirely separate from the regular school.

13. In one year in the early 1990s the figure was $60,000 per year, primarily to fund partial salaries for medical college outreach staff who have administrative roles in the school and to contribute symbolically for the students' rotations through labs and clinics (though the particular researchers and clinics do not directly benefit from this payment).

Chapter 3: Breaking the Cycle: The Pathfinder School

1. Elementary Pathfinder promotional brochure to prospective students and their parents (no date). "Pathfinder" is a pseudonym for the magnet schools based on theories of gifted-and-talented education.

2. Accelerated Schools is an organization founded by Henry Levin to bring communities and school faculties together to improve schools, with special attention to the children who are not thriving academically. Central to the Accelerated School model is direct parent engagement in task forces to identify problems in the schools, to work with teachers and administrators on specific school improvement programs, and a strong commitment to the school as rooted in democratic community. Accelerated Schools can be described as a movement, according to Levin, with structures for community/parent engagement than a prescriptive recipe for school programs. According to Henry Levin, by the late 1990s, Accelerated Schools included more than one-thousand schools affiliates.

3. The high school that rejected the Pathfinder magnet is presently a fully integrated school with an African American majority although its immediate neighborhood is predominantly White. Many of the families in the proximal area have grown children, no children in the household, or children in private schools.

4. This information was supplied by the principal in an interview and also by a central office administrator and parents who recall these events.

5. The principal provided this information in an interview. He remained for many years the principal of this school and a strong advocate of magnet programs. When, at seemingly regular intervals, new superintendents or newly elected school board members decided to make closing magnet schools their issue, this principal backed parents and teachers in their support of the benefits of the magnet education.

6. This information is found in Appendix A, page 1, Allen High School 1988.

7. Recent community organizing around pressure to strengthen several traditionally Hispanic high schools shows evidence that Hispanic families in this city are very interested in their children's education and want a good education for their daughters as well as for their sons. But the pressure to have their schools improved has remained focused on their neighborhood schools; the Pathfinder high school in a faraway African American neighborhood was not a strong draw for Hispanic students. According to a former coordinator of the Pathfinder program, their numbers in this program have remained at 13–15 percent, even though at the present time Hispanics are slightly more than half of the total district student population. The school has worked hard to attract students from all cultures, and both the teachers and students expressed strong preference to be in such a diverse environment.

The counting of Asians as "White" because they were not party to the original desegregation lawsuits further confuses the racial issue, because they contributed to the cultural diversity of the school but did not add to its official diversity *counts*. In fact, few Asian or Asian American students chose Pathfinder, opting instead for the honors programs, particularly Advanced Placement, in their neighborhood high school if they remained in public schools.

8. The district reports to the federal courts provided broad outlines for school programs pursuant to desegregation compliance, according to personnel who worked in the district's research and evaluation office during the early years of desegregation.

9. "The Cell" is a board game for teaching cell nutrition and enzyme functions, produced by Carolina Biological, Burlington, North Carolina.

10. AIDS guidelines for blood contact were not in force in these schools at this time although the local medical centers were sites of extensive research and treatment for HIV and AIDS-related illnesses. The teacher pointed out that an experiment such as this one would not be permitted under guidelines in force today without stringent controls in a professional medical laboratory setting.

11. These comments and this pervasive pattern of verbally expressed attitudes have emerged, while faculty and student researchers were studying other phenomena. The comments have surfaced in field journal after field journal even though they have not been directly looked for or in any way solicited (by such questions, for example, as "Do students do their homework?" or "Which students read the assignments?"). This pattern of direct expression by teachers of their low expectations for students is ubiquitous except in honors and Advanced Placement classes, where field observers report the pattern to be absent or much less prevalent.

Chapter 4: The School for Science, Engineering, and Technology: A Different Kind of Bargain

1. The history of desegregation in this city, as in cities across the nation, is a history of struggle, contestation, risk, compromise, hope, myth, and misperceptions. As was discussed in the second chapter, the decision to create magnet schools was championed as alleviating the need for forced cross-town busing; challenged as creating an elitist, two-tiered system of education; and hailed for creating havens for those teachers, children, and families who wanted to assure that desegregation and educational quality were explicitly linked. The magnet schools embody multiple narratives: educational, legal, racial, cultural, economic, personal, and professional.

2. Interview with a former teacher and leading school reform educator who gradu-

ated from Carver High about the time faculty and student "crossover" transfers were being enacted as a part of desegregation of the city's schools (1970–1971).

3. An interview with the magnet program coordinator is the source of this information.

4. It is no exaggeration to say that information regarding college admissions procedures and college entrance requirements is highly stratified in this large urban district. High schools with large White and middle-class populations are more likely to have honors and Advanced Placement programs, are more likely to have college counselors with close ties to the networks of college admissions offices, are more likely to host annual "College Nights" at which college admissions officers and other university representatives host information sessions regarding their institutions. Some of the Black and Latino high schools send fewer than 10 percent of their graduates to higher education (that is, 10 percent of those who remain after 25–40 percent drop out). A stark example of this stratified system of information and access came to light when through a corporate scholarship program, graduates of a Latino high school who met certain criteria were awarded scholarships to a local public university. According to the director of the scholarship program, the first year the scholarships were awarded, the recipients arrived on the opening day of the university to begin attending classes. The university had no record of them. These new graduates had not known that they would have to make applications, nor did they know what an application would entail. The corporate sponsors had assumed the high school counselors and the seniors' families would have guided them through the application process, as is true for middle-class and more typically White high school students. The failure to inform students early in their secondary school years about academic requirements for college admissions and about the timing of these requirements is a persistent problem across this urban district. The pervasiveness of the stratifying (by race and by family income in particular) of the information regarding post–high school opportunities has been validated over the years by the personal

observation of the author, by conversations and interviews with upperclassmen and recent graduates, and by teacher education student observation journals from high school field experiences. The magnet school as a "pipeline" to college becomes more understandable in light of these figures and these experiences.

5. A student in the Rice University Master of Arts in Teaching Program recorded these observations as a part of a required ethnographic component of a course on urban secondary schools; this information was provided by a school administrator.

6. The stratification of precollege advising by race includes more than White teachers' and counselors' withholding advising from students of color. There are many perceived and actual cultural barriers at work in the matter of connecting students (and families) to the information they need. An example is the situation of a very bright Latina, whose parents had emigrated from a war-torn country to secure safe futures for their children, who set her sights on a career in architecture. She had been advised by family friends to take precollege mathematics courses every year and to let her school counselor and teachers know that she wanted to be prepared to apply to colleges. This student earned solid grades and rose to leadership positions in several school clubs. She thought she was proceeding toward a college-preparatory diploma. What puzzled her was that each time she went by the counselors' offices to update her resume on the college advising computers, she was told that the counselors were too busy or that the wait time for a computer was too long. She was always advised to return another day. She was not distressed because she thought she was taking the appropriate courses and earning good grades. Her mother reported that it was not until a number of the other senior girls began, in the two months before graduation, to receive notice of college admissions and scholarships that this girl discovered that all year the counselors had been working with certain students to submit their college applications and financial aid forms. Those students, and the counselors, were Black. There may have been Black students underserved by these counselors as well,

but for this Latina and her family, the only visible barrier to her acceptance to college was the cultural barrier between herself and the 90 percent of the students who were Black. She had thought that graduation was such a major milestone, that it was the proper focus for her senior year. She was of the understanding that the time to apply to colleges would be after she graduated. That she had never been included in any advising sessions around college applications (despite a ranking high in her senior class) became clear when she was asked her grade point average. She replied, "Three and a half." She had never been included in precollege advising meetings to hear the currency of college admissions; she had never heard anyone say "three-point-five." With stories like these prevalent among many of the high schools, it is understandable that parents, particularly parents without much formal education, would seek out a magnet school with connections to college admissions officers, even if it meant their child's leaving the physical and cultural security of the home neighborhood.

7. Interviews were conducted with a broad range of the SET students, including students of every grade level and racial group, both girls and boys, students struggling to succeed and those for whom this highly technical school was almost easy. Students who were highly engaged and enthusiastic were interviewed, as were students who missed their home school, felt at sea academically, or seemed in some way distant from their classes and classmates. In addition, the interviewees encompassed the range of students highly committed to future studies and careers in engineering and technological fields to those with no special interest in those fields, and many variations in between. These interviews were supplemented by many hours of conversations with students and by listening to their casual conversations with teachers and with each other.

8. The librarian generously provided more than one interview to convey this information.

9. The finding that many students in highly selective high schools had never read a book for school prior to entering high school is on the surface not credible. Yet, students at all of the schools studied, three of the city's six most highly regarded academic programs, volunteered this information to their teachers or in interviews for this study. The reliance on state-adopted anthologies and other collections of excerpts had typified the English curriculum in most of their schools in the lower grades. "Never read a whole book" also implies a lack of reading in courses such as history and science classes, and second-language courses as well.

The context for this finding includes not only teachers and classrooms but also the general lack of provisioning of books throughout the district. The Pathfinder teachers frequently described their library as "empty"; a prominent Latino high school had no library, not even a room for books; and an elementary principal reports that the district has fewer than ten books per child (far beyond the recommendations of national library association recommendations of thirty to fifty books per child). As this book was being prepared for publication, the local newspaper reported that unlike the private schools, the public schools (with two exceptions) do not require summer reading of their students. The district's spokesperson stated that [this district] does not require summer reading because "there are not enough books in the city's libraries for its 50,000 high school students." Both the city and county have branch libraries throughout the community; whether they have "enough books" is not the issue. The issue illustrated here is that scarcity—of resources, of serious assignments, of opportunities to learn—is not seen as cause for action in a district whose students are more than 87 percent "minority."

10. The lack of adequate paper for photocopying is in some ways universal; teachers could always use more paper. However, in this district, it is not typical for schools to run out of photocopying paper in the third quarter of the school year. At some schools, teachers are physically handed their allotment of paper for the year in September and told that if they run out they will have to buy more themselves. At one Latino high school, students in the Rice University Teacher Education Program observed that a teacher routinely gave tests that covered only one-half of an 8-1/2 x 11" page of paper. Her explanation was both proud and

apologetic: by using only one-half of a side of paper for a quiz or exam, and by using both sides of the paper, she could make one page of paper per student last for four exams. Such ingenuity under stress is not unique to these schools or this district; it illustrates the too-typical level of provisioning in those schools where parents have neither the time nor means to host fund-raising carnivals or to be dunned for "dues" to cover basic school expenses. The university student observers noted that the format, rather than the teacher's pedagogical theories of what the students should have learned and how they should be able to represent that learning, dictated the kinds of tests she could give.

11. According to magnet coordinators, the school has never had funding to systematically track its graduates; informal contacts however seem to support a pattern of success and a high graduation rate, although most will graduate in a field other than engineering and technology. However, with the increasing importance of computers, even that is variable.

Chapter 5: "We've Got to Nuke This Educational System"

1. A portion of this paper was published as "The Politics of Texas School Reform," in *The Politics of Education Yearbook* (McNeil 1987b). Ross Perot made this statement to the experts gathered to brief him on their recommendations for the legislative package on school reform. Michael Kirst reported hearing this firsthand in that meeting; it has also been widely cited in the press.

2. Senate Bill 1, passed in 1990, provided for decentralization of the Texas public school system. While this would seem to overturn the provisions enacted under House Bill 72, in fact, it helped cement the centralization through its mandate of state testing. Senate Bill 1 decentralized most functions of schooling from the state agency and state board of education to the district central offices (not the schools) across the state. An intent of the bill was to relieve districts of micromanagement by the state, while holding the primary power at the state level through the student outcomes tests (to be discussed in chapter 7), which cannot be

waived. "Decentralization" and the requirement to have site-based decision-making committees made up of parents and teachers as well as administrators decentralized only the responsibility for the day-to-day running of schools; it did not decentralize the resources, nor did it decentralize the authority. In fact, decentralization as a policy has created a cover story for the increased centralization brought about by standardization.

3. This information was provided by State Representative Scott Hochberg of the Texas House of Representatives, Legislative District 132, in a personal interview in 1995.

4. See note 2 in "The Politics of Texas School Reform" (McNeil 1987b).

5. Interview at Stanford University with Michael Kirst, Professor of Education and Business Administration at Stanford University and Director, Policy Analysis for California Education, May 1994.

Chapter 6: Collateral Damage

1. *Collateral Damage* is a term used by the military to indicate damage inflicted on unintended targets in the course of military attacks on intended targets. People ("civilians") and the places of ordinary life (homes, churches and synagogues, shops, museums), when hit by bombs aimed at official military targets (munitions factories, military command centers, tanks, planes, and "troops") are, in the era of "bloodless warfare," *collateral damage:* "We have been very sensitive to collateral damage in the Baghdad area and I think the best source of how careful we have been is listening to the CNN reporters who were watching it unfold. . . we were very concerned about the collateral damage, making sure no innocent civilians were killed or injured, and we were very sensitive to cultural and religious sites in the area." U.S. General Colin Powell, responding to press inquiries regarding the U.S. bombing of Baghdad, as reported in the January 18, 1991, *New York Times*, A9.

2. As recorded in *Wings of Eagles*, by Ken Follett when employees of his corporation Electronic Data Systems, were held hostage in

Iran, Perot circumvented governmental and diplomatic channels and sent his own helicopters in to rescue them. The rescue was successful.

3. Some of the examples and analytical concepts in this chapter have been discussed in preliminary analyses previously published in "Exit, Voice and Community," "Teacher Culture and Standardization," and "Contradictions of Control Part 3: Contradictions of Reform," and in the "Educational Costs of Standardization."

4. Interview with staff person from district's research and evaluation office, and confirming interviews with high-level central office curriculum supervisors.

5. Interview with research and evaluation staff person who was a close observer of the design of the district's proficiency system of test-driven curriculum.

6. Interviews with central office personnel involved in creating a test-driven curriculum system for monitoring teacher performance.

7. This language dominated the central administration personnel's explanations of the logic behind the proficiencies.

8. There has been considerable press surrounding the increase of Texas students' scores on the National Assessment Educational Progress. However, testing experts have advised that test-prep on one test can create increases on related tests. According to Al Kauffman of the Mexican American Legal Defense Fund, there is an overlap of more than 50 percent between TAAS and NAEP coverage. In addition, test-prep can show short-term peaks in test scores that are not indicative of long-term learning gains. The *drop* in minority graduation rates since the implementation of the Perot reforms is a more reliable indication of actual student experiences in this state's educational system (see Haney, note 1, ch. 7).

Chapter 7: The Educational Costs of Standardization

1. Professor Walter Haney of the Boston College Center for the Study of Testing,

Evaluation, and Educational Policy (CSTEEP), after his review and analysis of state and "expert" statistical reports on TAAS scores in Texas school districts and after conducting his own independent research on TAAS and its effects on minority youth.

2. The data that informs this section also forms the basis for part of the analysis in Linda McNeil and Angela Valenzuela's "The Harmful Impact of the TAAS System of Testing in Texas: Beneath the Accountability Rhetoric," to be published by Century Foundation, 2000, in conjunction with the Harvard Civil Rights Project, "Proceedings of the Conference on the Effects of High Stakes Testing on Minority Youth," New York, Teachers College of Columbia University, December 4, 1998.

3 . The man who invented the star-rating system stated at a conference at the University of Houston in 1997 that he came up with the idea after he and his wife left a fine restaurant. A star-rating system had guided them to a fine dinner. He said he wondered aloud why schools couldn't be known by such an easy guide.

In addition to TAAS scores, the ratings also include such factors as attendance rates and dropout rates. The latter are highly suspect: one major urban district boasts lowering its dropout rate from "6.2 percent" to "3.6 percent." The same district graduates fewer than two-thirds of each year's entering freshman classes—far less in Latino and African American schools. Principals report that though the star-rating system in the newspaper includes these other data, in fact, the TAAS is the number their districts pay attention to.

4. The bonuses, according to McAdams (1998) and conversations with principals can range from 10–15 percent; one administrator put the average principal's bonus for TAAS increases at $7,500 in 1999.

5. Walter Haney surveyed Texas teachers of English and math, inviting them to write open-ended comments telling the researchers anything they felt the researcher should know about the TAAS. Their answers overwhelmingly spoke of the TAAS as frequently requiring them to go against their best professional judgment.

6. Discussions with other upper elementary and middle school teachers confirm that students accustomed to TAAS-prep, rather than literature, may be internalizing the *format* of reading skills tests but not the *habits* needed to read for meaning.

In addition, students report being taught to select answer choices by matching key words in the question to key words in the supplied answers without reading the passage at all.

The effects of the TAAS model of reading (and tests of reading skills) become especially egregious in the teaching of young children. George W. Bush, the present governor of the state, successfully pushed the legislature to pass legislation requiring the use of a passing score on the third-grade reading section of TAAS as the ticket to promotion to fourth grade. "All children reading by third grade" sounds like a worthy goal until the actions marked by the slogan are revealed. The pressure to have all children *passing the TAAS reading by third grade* is causing many principals to insist that *kindergarten* (age 5) and first grade students spend a part of each school day learning to bubble in small empty circles, learning, even before they can read, to stay inside the lines on an answer sheet. Many teachers of young children are exiting to private preschools and kindergartens rather than substitute TAAS prep for what they believe to be developmentally based introduction to language learning and prereading skills.

7. This gifted young writer has given me permission to include her story here.

8. I am in debt to my colleague Angela Valenzuela whose consideration of this long-term effect led to the conceptualizing of the *production* of cumulative deficits in minority students' education. That deficits in the the education offered to children and the learning they do are both cumulative and insitutionally produced stands in contrast to notions that somehow the children themselves are deficient, and has been the charcterization in much "deficit-based" education, which treats minority children as deficient or deprived for lacking White culture.

9. Professor Larry Cuban, of Stanford University, provided a response to the initial presentations of these findings in the "Moral and Historical Implications for Prescriptive Teaching" symposium of the American Educational Research Association Annual Meeting in San Diego in 1998. Cuban inquired whether this research fit the category of "the study of *unintended negative* consequences" of a policy. If so, he stated that that research tradition required first an examination of the *intended positive* consequences of the policy. Although I did not construe this study to be in the tradition he described, his question prompted a reexamination of the question of whether there had been positive consequences of TAAS that were not visible to me. To pursue this question, I raised the issue with dozens of teachers and a number of administrators during the year following the San Diego meetings.

Administrators, if they felt they were being interviewed, answered with test score results (positive or negative); in more informal conversation they discussed the pressures on them to produce test scores. Teachers tended to consider the question naive, uninformed, or "unfriendly." Their answers led me to an ever-greater understanding of many of the negative effects on reading and writing described in this chapter.

The two most positive responses not provided by central administrators or state officials regarding the effects of TAAS on teaching and learning are these: a largely Latino community in South Texas saw its children's low TAAS scores as evidence the state had neglected the school system by claiming it as "satisfactory." This community successfully lobbied the state for additional funds. The other example came from a middle school teacher. She replied, "Yes, there *has* been a positive effect at our school from the TAAS. There were some ESL kids who are now being taught *math*. They were getting almost no math instruction before." She paused and added, "but it's not real math, it's just TAAS math. It's not the math you'd want for *your* kids."

I am grateful to Larry Cuban for his probing the issue of positive effects. My school-level investigations have shown isolated, individual positive effects, but overwhelmingly generalized and widespread negative effects.

10. This teacher was a fact witness for the plaintiffs in the lawsuit *G. I. Forum, Image de Tejas, et al. v. Texas Education Agency, et al.* on

the harmful effects of the tenth-grade TAAS graduation requirement on minority youth in Texas public schools. U.S. Federal District Court, San Antonio, 1999.

11. For a powerful conceptualization of the creation and maintaining of inequality in a racially divided city, see the section on the *"pauperization* of Newark, 1945–1960" in *Ghetto Schooling* (Anyon 1998a).

12. It should be noted that whereas these schools describe their student demographics as "carrying the scores," the tri-racially integrated urban middle school, with a large percentage of children on free and reduced lunch, had the highest pass rate of any integrated middle school and did so with no TAAS-prep. The teachers there teach their students a curriculum that is traditional in its subjects and innovative in pedagogy; their students are engaged in learning. Imbedded in that learning are skills and information they can apply to TAAS. But they are never taught "to the TAAS." Students of all three races and immigrant groups go on from this school to successfully complete high school.

13. I have witnessed this dynamic in the central office of the district: when parents in the wealthier neighborhoods call the central office to complain about a problem or offer a suggestion, this is seen as "community involvement" and "parent participation." When students or parents from the city's predominantly Latino community try to set up meetings to get the district to supply books or enough teachers to provide every child with a class and classroom or to relieve overcrowding, it has been described as "we've got trouble on the East End." Teachers and parents know that "accountability" is highly variable.

14. A telling example of research that illuminates the increasing ambiguity of the line between the public and the private in public education is "International Business Machinations: A Case Study of Corporate Involvement in Local Educational Reform," (Mickelson 1999). Mickelson documents the role of IBM in urban redevelopment in Charlotte, North Carolina. The corporation

regarded as *theirs* the school under development and assumed they could claim a large percent of its student slots for its corporate employees. Most notable is the fact that corporate leaders expressed surprise that the community and school board were unwilling to view the school as a divisible private good, rather than a democratically controlled public institution.

15. A meeting of the leadership team of the planning of a multi-million-dollar local initiative affiliated with a national foundation grant for school reform. The community council remained in the plan. As the organization moved from its core planning board to a full board, and staff were hired, various events ensued that prevented the creation of a community council. The mission of the initiative is being carried out by its board, its staff, and a broad network of participating schools whose innovative reforms are helping to restructure schools and improve teaching. The central business leadership, as described by Feagin (1988) and McAdams (1998) remain the most powerful voices in educational policy in the region.

16. That teachers can learn, and can have their practice transformed by their learning, is evidenced in the hundreds of teachers who have participated in the teacher enhancement and school reform programs of the Rice University Center for Education. Each of these programs provides an innovative orgnization structure in which teachers can, over an extended period of time, update their subject matter knowledge, learn new pedagogies, learn to center their teaching on children's development, and, as a result, teach for meaning and understanding. Many of these teachers beign with limited or outdated knowledge; others are well-grounded in their subjects but seek new ways to teach effectively in culturally diverse schools. By investing directly in teachers' learning, and by creating open-ended possibilities for them to create curriculum, we at the Center have helped demonstrate, in partnership with several urban districts, the capacity for teachers to teach authentically when they are given support to do so.

Bibliography

===

"A Decade of School Finance Reform." (1994). *Intercultural Development Research Association Newsletter*, August.

"A New Accountability System for Texas Public Schools." (1993). Vol. 1, Educational Economic Policy Center, State of Texas, report prepared by faculty of the College of Education at Texas A&M, the LBJ School of Public Affairs at UT-Austin, and the College of Business Management of the University of Houston, with the staff of the Center.

Adler, Bill, and Bill Adler, Jr. (1994). *Ross Perot: An American Maverick Speaks Out.* New York: Citadel Press.

Allen High School. (undated). "Pathfinder Program."

Allen High School. (1988). "Magnet School Final Audit for 1987–88."

American Educational Research Association. (1995). *The Hidden Consequences of a National Curriculum.* Washington, D. C.

Anyon, Jean. (1997a). *Ghetto Schooling: A Political Economy of Urban Educational Reform.* New York and London: Teachers College Press.

Anyon, Jean. (1997b). "The Social Context of Educational Reform." In William Ayers and Janet L. Miller (eds.), *A Light in Dark Times: Maxine Greene and the Unfinished Conversa-tion.* New York: Teachers College Press.

Apple, Michael W. (1979). *Ideology and Curriculum.* London: Routledge & Kegan Paul.

Apple, Michael W. (1986). *Teachers and Texts: A Political Economy of Class and Gender Relations in Education.* New York and London: Routledge & Kegan Paul.

Apple, Michael W. (1991). "The Culture and Commerce of the Textbook." In Michael W. Apple and Linda K. Christian-Smith (eds.), *The Politics of the Textbook.* New York and London: Routledge.

Apple, Michael W. (1992). *Education and Power.* Boston and London: Routledge & Kegan Paul.

Apple, Michael W. (1993). *Official Knowledge: Democratic Education in a Conservative Age.* New York: Routledge.

Apple, Michael W. (1995). *Education and Power,* 2d ed. New York: Routledge.

Apple, Michael W. (1996). *Cultural Politics and Education.* New York and London: Teachers College Press.

Apple, Michael W. (1998). "Teaching and Technology: The Hidden Effects of Computers on Teachers and Students." In Landon E. Beyer and Michael W. Apple (eds.), *The Curriculum: Problems, Politics, and Possibilities,* 2d ed. Albany: State University of New York Press.

Apple, Michael W. (1999). *Power, Meaning, and Identity.* New York: Peter Lang.

Apple, Michael W. (2000). *Official Knowledge: Democratic Education in a Conservative Age,* 2d ed. New York: Routledge.

Apple, Michael W., and James A. Beane. (1995). *Democratic Schools.* Washington, D. C. : Association for Supervision and Curriculum Development.

Apple, Michael W., and James A. Beane. (1999). *Democratic Schools: Lessons from the*

Chalk Face. Buckingham, Eng.: Open University Press.

Apple, Michael W., and Linda K. Christian-Smith (eds.) (1991). *The Politics of the Textbook.* New York and London: Routledge.

Apple, Michael W., and Susan Jungck. (1998). "'You Don't Have to be a Teacher to Teach This Unit': Teaching, Technology, and Control in the Classroom." In Hank Bromley and Michael W. Apple (eds.), *Education/Technology/Power: Educational Computing as Social Practice.* Albany: State University of New York Press.

Apple, Michael W., and Anita Oliver. (1998). "Becoming Right: Education and the Formation of Conservative Movements." In Dennis Carlson and Michael W. Apple (eds.), *Power/Knowledge/Pedagogy: The Meaning of Democratic Education in Unsettling Times.* Boulder: Westview Press.

Archbald, Douglas A., and Andrew C. Porter. (1994). "Curriculum Control and Teachers' Perceptions of Autonomy and Satisfaction." *Educational Evaluation and Policy Analysis* 6, no. 1 (spring).

Ayers, William, and Janet L. Miller (eds.) (1997). *A Light in Dark Times: Maxine Greene and the Unfinished Conversation.* New York: Teachers College Press.

Banks, James A. (1994). *Multiethnic Education: Theory and Practice,* 3d ed. Boston: Allyn and Bacon.

Barnet, Ann B., and Richard J. Barnet. (1998). *The Youngest Minds: Parenting and Genes in the Development of Intellect and Emotion.* New York: Simon & Schuster.

Bartolome, Lilia I. (1994). "Beyond the Methods Fetish: Toward a Humanizing Pedagogy." *Harvard Educational Review* 64: 173–94.

Bernal, Jesse. (1994). "Highlights of the Education Bill Passed by the 68th Texas Legislature, Second Called Session, June 4– July 2, 1994." *Intercultural Development Research Association Newsletter* (August).

Beyer, Landon E. (1998). "Schooling for Democracy: What Kind?" In Landon E. Beyer and Michael W. Apple (eds.), *The Curriculum: Problems, Politics, and Possibilities,* 2d ed. Albany: State University of New York Press.

Beyer, Landon E., and Michael W. Apple (eds.) (1998a). *The Curriculum: Problems,*

Politics, and Possibilities, 2d ed. Albany: State University of New York Press.

Beyer, Landon E., and Michael W. Apple. (1998b). "Values and Politics in the Curriculum." In Landon E. Beyer and Michael W. Apple (eds.), *The Curriculum: Problems, Politics, and Possibilities,* 2d ed. Albany: State University of New York Press.

Bissinger, H. G. (1991). *Friday Night Lights: A Town, a Team, and a Dream.* New York: Harper Collins.

Boyer, Ernest L. (1983). *High School: A Report on Secondary Education in America.* New York: Harper & Row, The Carnegie Foundation for the Advancement of Teaching.

Braverman, Harry. (1974). *Labor and Monopoly Capital.* New York: Monthly Review Press.

Bromley, Hank. (1998). "Introduction: Data-driven Democracy? Social Assessment of Educational Computing." In Hank Bromley and Michael W. Apple (eds.), *Education/Technology/Power: Educational Computing as a Social Practice.* Albany: State University of New York Press.

Bruner, Jerome. (1990). *Acts of Meaning.* Cambridge and London: Harvard University Press.

Callahan, Raymond. (1962). *Education and the Cult of Efficiency.* Chicago: University of Chicago Press.

Carleton, Don E. (1985). *Red Scare! Right-wing Hysteria, Fifties Fanaticism, and their Legacy in Texas.* Austin: Texas Monthly Press.

Carlson, Dennis, and Michael W. Apple (eds.) (1998). *Power/Knowledge/Pedagogy: The Meaning of Democratic Education in Unsettling Times.* Boulder: Westview Press.

Carson, C.C., R. M. Huelskamp, and T. D. Woodall. (1993). "Perspectives on Education in America: An Annotated Briefing." *Journal of Educational Research* 86, no. 5: May–June, from a report by the Strategic Studies Center, Sandia National Laboratories, Albuquerque, New Mexico, April 1992.

Casey, Daniel, Terry Heller, Michael Kirst, Shannon Schumacker, and Billy D. Walker. (1994). "Good Governance and Accountability," Texas Association of School Boards, *Journal of Texas Public Education,* vol. 2, winter.

Casey, Kathryn. (1985). "Report Card on Reform: No Pass, No Play—One Year Later." *Houston City Magazine*, August, 59.

Celis, William, III. (1994). "40 Years after *Brown*, Segregation Persists," *The New York Times*, May 18, A1, B8.

Celis, William, III. (1994). "New Education Legislation Defines Federal Role in Nation's Classrooms," *New York Times*, March 30, B7.

Clandinin, D. Jean, and F. Michael Connelly. (1996). "Teachers' Professional Knowledge Landscapes: Teacher Stories—Stories of Teachers—School Stories—Stories of School." *Educational Researcher*, 19, no. 5: 2–14.

Clarke, John, and Janet Newman. (1997). *The Managerial State*. Thousand Oaks, Calif.: Sage.

Cochran-Smith, Marilyn. (1991). "Learning to Teach Against the Grain." In *Harvard Educational Review* 61, no. 3: 279–310, August.

Cohen, David K., and Deborah Loewenberg Ball. (1990). "Policy and Practice: An Overview," *Educational Evaluation and Policy Analysis* 12, no. 3: 233–239.

Cohen, David, Milbrey W. McLaughlin, and Joan E. Talbert (eds.) (1993). *Teaching for Understanding*. San Francisco: Jossey-Bass.

Craig, Cheryl J. (1998). "The Influence of Context on One Teacher's Interpretive Knowledge of Team Teaching." *Teaching and Teacher Education* 14, no. 4.

Craig, Cheryl J. (1999). "Life on the Professional Knowledge Landscape: Living the Image of 'Principal as Rebel.'" In F. M. Connelly and D. J. Clandinin (eds.), *Shaping a Professional Identity: Stories of Educational Practice*. New York: Teachers College Press.

Cuban, L., and David Tyack. (1995). *Tinkering toward Utopia: A Century of Public School Reform*. Cambridge and London: Harvard University Press.

Danter, H., and J. Madrigal. (1988). "The Texas Teacher Appraisal System: Neither Valid nor Reliable," a paper presented at the Annual Meeting of the Southwest Educational Research Association, San Antonio, Texas.

Darling-Hammond, Linda, and Barnett Berry. (1988). *The Evolution of Teacher Policy*. Philadelphia: Center for Policy Research in Education.

Darling-Hammond, Linda, Arthur E. Wise, and Stephen P. Klein. (1995). *A License to Teach: Building a Profession for 21st Century Schools*. Boulder: Westview Press.

Darling-Hammond, Linda. (1996). *What Matters Most: Teaching for America's Future*, report of the National Commission on Teaching and America's Future, Washington, D.C.

Darling-Hammond, Linda. (1997). "Education for Democracy." In William Ayers and Janet L. Miller (eds.), *A Light in Dark Times: Maxine Greene and the Unfinished Conversation*. New York: Teachers College Press.

Darling-Hammond, Linda. (1997). *The Right to Learn: A Blueprint for Creating Schools that Work*. San Francisco: Jossey-Bass.

De Leon, Arnoldo. (1989). *Ethnicity in the Sunbelt: A History of Mexican Americans in Houston*. Houston: Mexican American Studies Monograph Series No. 7.

DeVillar, Robert A. (1994). "The Rhetoric and Practice of Cultural Diversity in U.S. Schools: Socialization, Resocialization, and Quality Schooling." In Robert A. DeVillar, Christian J. Faltis, and James P. Cummins (eds.), *Cultural Diversity in Schools: From Rhetoric to Practice*. Albany: State University of New York Press.

Delpit, Lisa. (1995). *Other People's Children: Cultural Conflict in the Classroom*. New York: The New Press.

Duckworth, Eleanor. (1987). *"The Having of Wonderful Ideas" and other Essays on Teaching and Learning*. New York: Teachers College Press.

Edgewood Independent School District, et al. v. William N. Kirby, et al., in the Supreme Court of Texas, No. D-0378, 1990.

Egerton, John. (1994). *Speak Now Against the Day: The Generation Before the Civil Rights Movement in the South*. New York: Alfred A. Knopf.

Eisner, Elliot W. (1994). *Cognition and Curriculum Reconsidered*, 2d ed. New York: Teachers College Press.

"English, Language Arts: K–12 Curriculum Framework," (draft) 1983. Presented to State Board of Education by Texas Education Association for first reading.

Evaluator Interview. (1986). Research and Evaluation administrator, [urban] district, March 21.

Feagin, Joe R. (1988). *Free Enterprise City: Houston in Political-Economic Perspective.* New Brunswick and London: Rutgers University Press.

Feagin, Joe R., and Clairece Booher Feagin. (1996). *Racial and Ethnic Relations.* Englewood Cliffs, N.J.: Prentice Hall.

Featherstone, Joseph. (1971). *Schools Where Children Learn.* New York: Liveright Publishing.

Fife, Brian L. (1992). *Desegregation in American Schools: Comparative Intervention Strategies.* New York: Praeger Publishers.

Fine, Michelle (1991). *Framing Dropouts: Notes on the Politics of an Urban Public High School.* Albany: State University of New York Press.

Foley, Douglas E. (1990). *Learning in Capitalist Culture: Deep in the Heart of Tejas.* Philadelphia: University of Philadelphia Press.

Follett, Ken. (1986). *On Wings of Eagles.* New York: NAL/Dutton.

Fordham, S., and J. Ogbu. (1986). "Black Student's School Success: Coping with the Burden of 'Acting White'." *Urban Review* 18: (176–206).

Frank, Nancy. (1991). Letter to Michael Kirst, Kirst Perot file, Stanford University.

French, Thomas. (1993). *South of Heaven: Welcome to High School at the End of the Twentieth Century.* New York: Pocket Books.

Freire, Paulo. (1970). *Pedagogy of the Oppressed.* Translated by Myra Bergman Ramos. New York: Seabury.

Freire, Paulo. (1985). *The Politics of Education: Culture, Power and Liberation.* Translated by Donaldo Macedo. South Hadley, Mass.: Bergin and Garvey.

Freire, Paulo. (1995). *A Pedagogy of Hope.* New York: Continuum.

Fuller, Bruce, and Richard F. Elmore (eds.) (1996). *Who Chooses? Who Loses? Culture, Institutions, and the Unequal Effects of School Choice.* New York: Teachers College Press.

Gardner, Howard. (1991). *The Unschooled Mind: How Children Think and How Schools Should Teach.* New York: Basic Books.

Gardner, Howard. (1993). *Multiple Intelligences: The Theory in Practice.* New York: Basic Books.

Giroux, Henry A. (1983). *Critical Theory and Educational Practice.* Geelong, Victoria, Australia: Deakin University Press.

Giroux, Henry A. (1996). *Pedagogy and the Politics of Hope.* Boulder: Westview Press.

Giroux, Henry, and Peter McLaren (eds.) (1989). *Critical Pedagogy, the State, and Cultural Struggle.* Albany: State University of New York Press.

Goodlad, John. (1983). *A Place Called School.* New York: McGraw-Hill.

Gore, Elain Clift. (1998). "[Urban] High School for the Performing and Visual Arts: A History of the First 20 Years, 1971–1997." A dissertation at the University of Texas at Austin. Unpublished. August 1998.

"Governor Sticks His Head Out—and Wins." (1984). *Dallas Morning News,* July 8.

Governor's Task Force on Public Education, Final Report. (1990). "The Path to a Quality Education for All Texas Students," Feb. 27, transmittal letter signed by Charles Miller of Houston, chair.

Greene, Maxine. (1978). *Landscapes of Learning.* New York: Teachers College Press.

Greene, Maxine. (1985). "Public Education and the Public Space." *Kettering Review* (fall): 55–60.

Greene, Maxine. (1986). "In Search of a Critical Pedagogy." *Harvard Education Review* 56: 427–441.

Greider, William. (1997). *One World, Ready or Not: The Manic Logic of Global Capitalism.* New York: Simon and Schuster.

Grubb, W. Norton. (1985). "The Initial Effects of House Bill 72 on Texas Public Schools: The Challenges of Equity and Effectiveness." Austin: LBJ School Policy Research Project Report No. 70.

Gutierrez, Kris, and J. Larson. (1994). "Language Borders: Recitation as Hegemonic Discourse." In *International Journal of Educational Reform* 3, no. 1: 22–36.

Gutierrez, K., J. Larson, and B. Kreuter. (1995). "Cultural Tensions in the Classroom: The Value of the Subjugated Perspective." In *Urban Education* 29, no. 4: 410–42.

Gutierrez, K., B. Rymes, and J. Larson. (1995). "Script, Counterscript, and Underlife in the Classroom: *James Brown v. the Board of Education.*" *Harvard Educational Review* 65, no. 3: 445–71.

Habermas, Jurgen. (1973). *Legitimation Crisis.* Boston: Beacon Press.

Haney, Walter, George F. Madaus, and Robert Lyons. (1993). *The Fractured Marketplace for Standardized Testing*. Boston and London: Kluwer Academic Publishers.

Haney, Walter. (forthcoming). Unpublished analysis of a teacher survey on the impact of the TAAS test on teaching and learning, conducted May, 1999.

Harcombe, Elnora. (2000). *Dare to Learn: Science Teachers Accept the Challenge*. New York: Teachers College Press.

Heath, Shirley Brice, and Milbrey McLaughlin. (1993). *Identity and Inner-City Youth: Beyond Ethnicity and Gender*. New York and London: Teachers College Press.

Heubert, Jay P., and Robert M. Hauser (eds.) (1999). *High Stakes: Testing for Tracking, Promotion, and Graduation*. Committee on Appropriate Test Use, Board on Testing and Assessment, Commission on Behavioral and Social Sciences and Education, and National Research Council. Washington, D.C.: National Academy Press.

Hobby, Jr., W. P., and B. D. Walker. (1991). "Legislative reform of the Texas Public School Finance System, 1973–1991." *Harvard Journal on Legislation* 28: 379–94.

Hochberg, Scott. (1995). Personal interview, State Representative, Legislative District 132, Texas House of Representative, with author.

Hodgkinson, Harold L. (1986). "Texas: The State and Its Educational System." The Institute for Educational Leadership, Inc., December.

Horwitz, Tony. (1991). *Baghdad Without a Map: And Other Misadventures in Arabia*. New York: NAL/Dutton.

Howe, Harold, III. (1993). *Thinking about Our Kids: An Agenda for American Education*. New York: Free Press.

Hurtado, Aida, Patricia Gurin, and Timothy Peng. (1994). "Social Identities—A Framework for Studying the Adaptations of Immigrants and Ethnics: The Adaptations of Mexicans in the United States." *Social Problems* 41, no. 1: 129–51.

Irvine, Jacqueline Jordan. (1990). *Black Students and School Failure: Policies, Practices, and Prescriptions*. Westport, Conn.: Greenwood Press.

Irvine, Jacqueline Jordan, and Michele Foster (eds.) (1996). *Growing up African American in Catholic Schools*. New York: Teachers College Press.

Isikoff, Michael, and David Von Drehle. (1992). "Perot-Schools Shootout: How Billionaire Outdrew Texas Establishment." *Washington Post*, June 28.

Jackson, Phillip W. (1992). *Untaught Lessons*. New York and London: Teachers College Press.

Kaestle, Carl F. (1983). *Pillars of the Republic: Common Schools and American Society, 1780–1860*. New York: Hill and Wang.

Kirst, Michael. (1990). "Senate Bill 1, 1990: School Finance," sample summary prepared for talk on June 22.

Kirst, Michael. (1992). "Texas Public Education Reform," Reading List 1, Sept. 1.

Kirst, Michael. (1994a). Personal interview with author, April.

Kirst, Michael. (1994b). Personal interview with author, May 24.

Kliebard, Herbert M. (1986). *The Struggle for an American Curriculum*. New York and London: Routledge.

Kliebard, Herbert M. (1992). *Forging the American Curriculum*. New York and London: Routledge.

Kliebard, Herbert. (1995). *The Struggle for the American Curriculum*, 2d ed. New York: Routledge.

Koppich, Julia. (1987). "Education Reform in the Lone Star State." University of California, Berkeley, May, unpublished paper.

Ladson-Billings, Gloria. (1994). *The Dreamkeepers: Successful Teachers of African American Children*. San Francisco: Jossey-Bass.

Ladson-Billings, Gloria. (1998a). "Toward a Theory of Culturally Relevant Pedagogy." In Landon E. Beyer and Michael W. Apple (eds.), *The Curriculum: Problems, Politics, and Possibilities*, 2d ed. Albany: State University of New York Press.

Ladson-Billings, Gloria. (1998b). "Who Will Survive America? Pedagogy as Cultural Preservation." In Dennis Carlson and Michael W. Apple (eds.), *Power/Knowledge/ Pedagogy: The Meaning of Democratic Education in Unsettling Times*. Boulder: Westview Press.

La Franchi, Howard. (1985). "Texans Not Sure Whether to Fine Tune or Scrap Education Reforms." *Christian Science Monitor*, Feb. 27, 5.

Lampert, Magdalene, and Merrie Blunk (eds.) (1998). *Talking Mathematics in School:*

Studies of Teaching and Learning.
Cambridge: Cambridge University Press.

Lauder, Hugh, and David Hughes. (1999). *Trading in Futures: Why Markets in Education Don't Work.* Philadelphia: Open University Press.

Legislative Education Board. (1991). "Comparison of Senate Bill 1 (current law) and Senate Bill 351," a report in the regular session, 72d legislature, May 31.

Lessinger, Leon M. (1970). *Every Kid a Winner: Accountability in Education.* New York: Simon and Schuster.

Lightfoot, Sara Lawrence. (1983). *The Good High School.* New York: Basic Books.

Lipsitz, George. (1995). "The Possessive Investment in Whiteness: Racialized Social Democracy and the 'White' Problem in American Studies." *American Quarterly* 47, no. 3: 369–87.

Little, Judith Warren. (1993). "Teachers' Professional Development and Education Reform." *Education Evaluation and Policy Analysis* 25, no. 3 (summer): 129–41.

"Long-range plan of the State Board of Education for Texas public School Education, 1986–1990." (1987). Submitted by the State Board of Education to the Texas Education Association, as required by law, January.

Longoria, Thomas, Jr. (1998). "School Politics in Houston: The Impact of Business Involvement." In Clarence N. Stone (ed.), *Changing Urban Education.* Lawrence: University Press of Kansas.

Lutz, Frank W. (1987). "Education politics in Texas." East Texas State University, paper presented at the Annual Meeting of the American Educational Research Association, Washington, D.C.

Lutz, Frank W., and Thomas W. Mize. (1989). "The Texas Teacher Appraisal System: Some Interesting Aspects." Monograph No. 6, East Texas State University Center for Policy Studies and Research in Elementary and Secondary Education, May.

MacLeod, Jay. (1987, 1995). *Ain't No Makin' It: Leveled Aspirations and Attainment in a Low-Income Neighborhood.* Boulder: Westview Press.

Mahoney, Leo Gerald. (1985). "The Changing Face of Public Education in Texas: The Personnel Administration Challenge." Laredo State University, paper presented at the Annual Meeting of the Association for

Public Policy Analysis and Management, Phoenix.

Marshall, J. Dan. (1991). "With a Little Help from Some Friends: Publishers, Protesters, and Texas Textbook Decisions." In Michael W. Apple and Linda K. Christian-Smith (eds.), *The Politics of the Textbook.* New York and London: Routledge.

Martin, Don T., George E. Overholt, and Wayne J. Urban. (1976). *Accountability in Education: A Critique.* Princeton, N.J.: Princeton Book Company.

Massell, Diane, and Susan Furhman with Michael Kirst, Odden Wohlstetter et al. (1994). "Ten Years of State Education Reform, 1983–1993: Overview with Four Case Studies." Consortium for Policy Research in Education, January.

Mathematics Curriculum Task Force. (1993). *Mathematics K–12 Curriculum.* Draft as presented to the Texas Education Agency, October.

Matute-Bianchi, María Eugenia. (1991). "Situational Ethnicity and Patterns of School Performance Among Immigrant and Nonimmigrant Mexican-descent Students." In Margaret A. Gibson and John U. Ogbu (eds.), *Minority Status and Schooling: A Comparative Study of Immigrant and Involuntary Minorities.* New York: Garland Publishing.

McAdams, Donald R. (1998). "Lessons from [Urban School District]." Preliminary draft, later published in Ravitch, Diane (ed.), *Brookings Papers on Educational Policy: 1999,* Washington, D.C.: Brookings Press.

McAdams, Donald R. (1999). "Problems of Managing a Big City School System." *Brookings Paper on Educational Policy,* Second Annual Conference on Educational Policy, May 18–19. Washington, D.C.: Brookings Institution Press.

McCarthy, Cameron. (1993). "Beyond the Poverty of Theory in Race Relations: Nonsynchrony and Social Difference in Education." In Lois Weis and Michelle Fine (eds.), *Beyond Silenced Voices: Class, Race, and Gender in the United States Schools.* Albany: State University of New York Press.

McLaren, Peter L. (1986). *Schooling as Ritual Performance.* London: Routledge & Kegan Paul.

McLaren, Peter L., and James M. Giarelli. (1995). *Critical Theory and Educational*

Research. Albany: State University of New York Press.

McLaren, Peter L., and Kris Gutierrez. (1998). "Global Politics and Local Antagonisms: Research and Practice as Dissent and Possibility." In Dennis Carlson and Michael W. Apple (eds.), *Power/Knowledge/Pedagogy: The Meaning of Democratic Education in Unsettling Times*. Boulder: Westview Press.

McNeil, Kenneth E. (1978). "Understanding Organizational Power: Building on the Weberian Legacy." *Administrative Science Quarterly* (March).

McNeil, Linda M. (1985a). "Standardized Proficiencies: A Counter-Productive Reform for Magnet Schools." A paper presented at the Annual Meeting of the American Educational Research Association.

McNeil, Linda M. (1985b). "Teacher Culture and the Irony of School Reform." In Philip G. Altbach, Gail P. Kelly, and Lois Weis (eds.), *Excellence in Education: Perspectives on Policy and Practice*. Buffalo, N.Y.: Prometheus Books.

McNeil, Linda M. (1986). *Contradictions of Control: School Structure and School Knowledge*. New York and London: Routledge.

McNeil, Linda M. (1987a). "Exit, Voice, and Community." *Educational Policy* (January).

McNeil, Linda M. (1987b). "The Politics of Texas School Reform," In Charles Kirchner and William Boyd (eds.), *Politics of Education Yearbook*, 199–216.

McNeil, Linda M. (1988a). "Contradictions of Control, Part 1: Administrators and Teachers," "Contradictions of Control, Part 2: Teachers, Students, and Curriculum," and "Contradictions of Control, Part 3: Contradictions of Reform." *Phi Delta Kappan*, January, February, and March.

McNeil, Linda M. (1988b). "Students and the Knowledge Base of Teachers," A Paper prepared for presentation at the "How Should We Educate Teachers?" session of the Annual Meeting of the American Educational Research Association, New Orleans.

McNeil, Linda M. (1988c). "Teacher Knowledge and the Organization of the School." A paper prepared for presentation at the "School Organization and Climate" session of the Annual Meeting of the American Educational Research Association, New Orleans.

McNeil, Linda M. (1994). "Local Initiatives and a National Curriculum." In Elliot Eisner (ed.), *The Hidden Consequences of a National Curriculum*. Washington, D.C.: American Educational Research Association.

McNeil, Linda M. (1998). "Educational Costs of Standardization." A paper presented at the Annual Meeting of the American Education Research Association in the symposium "Moral and Historical Reflections on Prescriptive Teaching."

McNeil, Linda M., and Angela Valenzuela. (2000). "The Harmful Impact of the TAAS System of Testing in Texas: Beneath the Accountability Rhetoric." In Mindy Kornhaber, Gary Orfield, and Michal Kurlaender (eds.), a volume (as yet untitled) on the effects of high-stakes testing on minority youth.

Mehan, Hugh, Lea Hubbard, and Irene Villanueva. (1994). "Forming Academic Identities: Accommodation Without Assimilation Among Involuntary Minorities." *Anthropology and Education Quarterly* 25, no. 2: 91–117.

Meier, Deborah. (1995). *The Power of Their Ideas: Lessons for America from a Small School in Harlem*. Boston: Beacon Press.

Mentor, Ian, Yolande Muschamp, Peter Nichols, Jenny Ozga, with Andrew Pollard. (1997). *Work and Identity in the Primary School*. Philadelphia: Open University Press.

Metz, Mary. (1983). "Faculty Culture: A Case Study." A paper presented at the Annual Meeting of the American Sociological Association, San Antonio, August.

Metz, Mary. (1984). "The Life Course of Magnet Schools: Organizational and Political Influences." *Harvard Education Review* 85, no. 3 (spring).

Metz, Mary. (1986). *Different by Design*. New York and London: Routledge.

Metz, Mary. (1988). "The American High School: A Universal Drama Amid Disparate Experience." National Center for Effective Secondary Schools, Wisconsin Center for Education Research, a paper presented at the 1988 Annual Meeting of the American Educational Research Association, New Orleans.

Mickelson, Roslyn Arlin. (1999). "International Business Machinations: A

Case Study of Corporate Involvement in Local Educational Reform." *Teachers College Record* 100, no. 3 (spring): 476–512.

Miller, Arthur. (1951). *All My Sons.* New York: Dramatists Play Service, Inc.

Moffett, James. (1994). "On to the Past: Wrong-Headed School Reform." *Phi Delta Kappan* (April): 585–90.

Muellar, Van D., and Mary P. McKeown. (1986). *The Fiscal, Legal, and Political Aspects of State Reform of Elementary and Secondary Education,* sixth annual yearbook of the American Education Finance Association. Cambridge, Mass.: Ballinger Publishing.

Muller, Henry, and Richard Woodbury. (1992). An interview with Ross Perot. *Time,* May 25, 27–31.

Murnane, Richard J., and Frank Levy. (1996a). *Teaching the New Basic Skills: Principles for Educating Children to Thrive in a Changing Economy.* New York: The Free Press.

Murnane, Richard J., and Frank Levy. (1996b). "What General Motors Can Teach U.S. Schools About the Proper Role of Markets in Education Reform," *Phi Delta Kappan* (October): 109–14.

National Commission on Excellence in Education. (1983). "A Nation at Risk: The Imperative for Educational Reform: A Report to the Nation and the Secretary of Education, United States Department of Education," Washington, D.C.: The Commission: Superintendent of Documents, U.S. GPO distributor.

National Commission on Teaching and America's Future, Summary Report. (1996). "What Matters Most: Teaching for America's Future." New York.

Neufeld, Barbara (1985). "Organization in Action: High School Teachers' Efforts to Influence Their Work." A paper presented at the Annual Meeting of the American Educational Research Association, Chicago.

Newmann, Fred M., Walter G. Secada, and Gary G. Wehlage. (1995). *A Guide to Authentic Instruction and Assessment: Vision, Standards, and Scoring.* Madison, Wis.: Center for Education Research.

Nieto, Sonia. (1994). "Lessons from Students on Creating a Chance to Dream." *Harvard Educational Review* 64, no. 4 (winter): 392–426.

Nieto, Sonia. (1997). "On becoming American: An Exploratory Essay." In William Ayers and Janet L. Miller (eds.), *A Light in Dark Times: Maxine Greene and the Unfinished Conversation.* New York: Teachers College Press.

Noddings, Nel. (1984). *Caring: A Feminine Approach to Ethics and Moral Education.* Berkeley and Los Angeles: University of California Press.

Noddings, Nel. (1992). *The Challenge to Care in Schools: An Alternative Approach to Education.* New York: Teachers College Press.

Noddings, Nel. (1997). "Thinking about Standards." In *Phi Delta Kappan* 79 (November): 184.

Noffke, Susan E. (1998). "Multicultural Curricula: 'Whose Knowledge?' and Beyond." In Landon E. Beyer and Michael W. Apple (eds.), *The Curriculum: Problems, Politics, and Possibilities,* 2d ed. Albany: State University of New York Press.

O'Cadiz, Maria del Pilar, Pia Lindquist Wong, and Carlos Alberto Torres. (1998). *Education and Democracy: Paulo Freire, Social Movements, and Educational Reform in Sao Paulo.* Boulder: Westview Press.

Odden, Allan. (1988). "Readings and Research Findings on Special Topics." Compiled and prepared for the November 14–15 meeting of the Texas Select Committee on Education, October 26 version.

"Official Says Segregated Schools Have Done Better with Minorities." (1985). *Houston Chronicle,* May 12, sec.1, 40.

Ohanian, Susan. (1999). *One Size Fits Few: The Folly of Educational Standards.* Portsmouth, N.H.: Heinemann.

Olsen, Laurie. (1997). *Made in America: Immigrant Students in our Public Schools.* New York: New Press.

Orfield, Gary, Susan E. Eaton, and the Harvard Project on School Desegregation. (1996). *Dismantling Desegregation: The Quiet Reversal of Brown v. Board of Education.* New York: New Press.

Page, Reba. (1999). "The Uncertain Value of School Knowledge: Biology at Westridge High." In *Teachers College Record* 100, no. 3 (spring).

Pathfinder Elementary School. (undated). Admissions booklet.

Perrone, Vito. (1998). "Why Do We Need a Pedagogy of Understanding?" In Martha

Stone Wiske (ed.), *Teaching for Understanding: Linking Research with Practice*. San Francisco: Jossey-Bass.

Picus, Laurence O., and Linda Hertert. (1991). "Texas Case Study: Internal Working Document." Prepared for the CPRE Core Data Base, Evolution of State Education Policy, University of Southern California, Center for Research in Education Finance, Los Angeles, December.

Powell, Arthur, Eleanor Farrar, and David K. Cohen. (1985). *The Shopping Mall High School: Winners and Losers in the Educational Marketplace*. Boston: Houghton Mifflin.

Raspberry, William. (1999). "Classroom Riffs." *Houston Chronicle*, June 26.

Reyes, Raul. (1985). " 'Fine-tuned' Education Statute Clears Senate, Sent to House," *Houston Chronicle*, April 12, sec. 1, 22.

Rodriguez, Nestor P. (1993). "Economic Restructuring and Latino Growth in Houston." In Joan Moor and Raquel Pinderhughes (eds.), *In the Barrio: Latinos and the Underclass Debate*. New York: Russell Sage, 101–127

Rogers, Carl R. (1969). *Freedom to Learn*. Columbus, Ohio: Charles E. Merrill Publishing Co.

Romo, Harriet D., and Toni Falbo. (1996). *Latino High School Graduation: Defying the Odds*. Austin: University of Texas Press.

Rose, Mike. (1995). *Possible Lives: The Promise of Public Education in America*. New York: Penguin Books.

Rossell, Christine H. (1990). *The Carrot or the Stick for School Desegregation Policy: Magnet Schools or Forced Busing*. Philadelphia: Temple University Press.

San Miguel, Guadalupe, Jr. (1987). "*Let All of Them Take Heed*": *Mexican Americans and the Campaign for Educational Equality in Texas, 1910-1980*. Austin: University of Texas Press.

San Miguel, Guadalupe, Jr. (2000). "*Brown, Brown, We're Not White, We're Brown*": *Identity and Activism in Chicano School Reform in Houston, Texas, 1965–1980*. College Station: Texas A&M University Press.

Sarason, Seymour B. (1971). *The Culture of School and the Problem of Change*. Boston: Allyn and Bacon.

Sarason, Seymour B. (1990). *The Predictable Failure of Educational Reform*. San Francisco: Jossey-Bass.

Sarason, Seymour B. (1996). *Revisiting the Culture of School and the Problem of Change*. New York and London: Teachers College Press.

Sass, Ronald. (1993). "Thinking in Science." Unpublished draft of a monograph prepared for the College Board.

Schifter, Deborah, Catherine Tworney Fosnot, and Deborah Loewenberg Ball. (1992). *Reconstructing Mathematics Education: Stories of Teachers Meeting the Challenge of Reform*. New York: Teachers College Press.

"Science Objectives and Measurement Specifications: Tested at Grade 8," Texas Assessment of Academic Skills 1990–1995, Texas Education Agency, Division of Instructional Outcomes Assessment, fall 1992.

Sedlak, Michael W., Christopher W. Wheeler, Diana C. Pullin, and Philip A. Cusick. (1986). *Selling Students Short: Classroom Bargains and Academic Reform in the American High School*. New York and London: Teachers College Press.

Selby, Gardner. (1994). "Who's Running Our Schools?" *Houston Post*, A-43, 48.

Select Committee on Public Education (Texas) (SCOPE). (1984). Report of the Finance Subcommittee, May, enacted as Texas House Bill 72.

"Settlement Agreement." (1984). *Delores Ross, et al. vs. Houston Independent School District, et al.* U. S. District Court, Houston, September 10.

Shapiro, Walter. (1992). "President Perot?" *Time*, May 25, 27-31.

Sharp, Rachel, and Anthony Green, with assistance of Jacqueline Lewis. (1975). *Education and Social Control: A Study in Progressive Primary Education*. London and Boston: Routledge & Kegan Paul.

Shepard, Lorrie A., and Amelia E. Kreitzer. (1987). "The Texas Teacher Test." *Education Researcher* (August–September).

Shulman, Lee. (1987). "Knowledge and Teaching: Foundations of the New Reform." *Harvard Education Review*, 57, no. 1 (February): 1–22.

Sirotnik, Kenneth A. (1998). "What Goes on in Classrooms? Is this the Way We Want It?" In Landon E. Beyer and Michael W. Apple (eds.), *The Curriculum: Problems,*

Politics, and Possibilities, 2d ed. Albany: State University of New York Press.

Sizer, Theodore R. (1984). *Horace's Compromise: The Dilemma of the American High School.* Boston: Houghton Mifflin.

Smith, Stephen Samuel. (1998). "Education and Regime Change in Charlotte." In Clarence N. Stone (ed.), *Changing Urban Education.* Lawrence: University Press of Kansas.

Stahl, Cathy, Barbara Steakley, John Zapata, and W. Norton Grubb. (1984). "Moving toward Equity: The Effects of House Bill 72 on School Expenditure in Texas." *Public Affairs Comment* 21, no. 4 (summer).

Starkey, Brigid A. (1998). "Using Computers to Connect Across Cultural Divides." In Hank Bromley and Michael W. Apple (eds.), *Education/Technology/Power: Educational Computing as Social Practice.* Albany: State University of New York Press.

Steinberg, Laurence D. (1996). *Beyond the Classroom: Why School Reform has Failed and What Parents Need to Do.* New York: Simon & Schuster.

Stone, Clarence N. (ed.) (1998). *Changing Urban Education.* Lawrence: University Press of Kansas.

Stone, Clarence N. (1998). "Civic Capacity and Urban School Reform." In Clarence N. Stone (ed.), *Changing Urban Education,* Lawrence: University Press of Kansas.

Strain, Sherry. (1985). "School Finance Reform in Texas: Process on the Equity Front." Department of Education Administration, presented at the Annual Meeting of the American Educational Finance Association, Phoenix, April 13.

Streibel, Michael J. (1998). "A Critical Analysis of Three Approaches to the Use of Computers in Education." In Landon E. Beyer and Michael W. Apple (eds.), *The Curriculum: Problems, Politics, and Possibilities,* 2d ed. Albany: State University of New York Press.

Suarez-Orozco, Marcelo M. (1991). "Hispanic Immigrant Adaptation to Schooling." In Margaret A. Gibson and John U. Ogbu (eds.), *Minority Status and Schooling: A Comparative Study of Immigrant and Involuntary Minorities.* New York: Garland Publishing.

Suskind, Ron. (1998). *A Hope in the Unseen: An American Odyssey from the Inner City to the Ivy League.* New York: Broadway Books.

Tatum, Beverly. (1997). *"Why are All the Black Kids Sitting Together in the Cafeteria?" and Other Conversations about Race.* New York: Basic Books.

Texas Education Agency. (1985). "Texas Teacher Administrator Assessment System," (instruction booklet). Austin, Texas.

Texas Education Agency. (1990). "Training guide for recertification of appraisers: Texas Teacher Appraisal System." Austin, Texas.

Texas Education Agency. (1998). "Education Commissioner Proposes Changes to Testing, Accountability Programs." Austin, Texas.

Texas Observer. (1999). News note [untitled], June.

Texas Senate Bill 1. (1990). Published by Texas Legislative Service.

Texas Senate Bill 1 Summary. (1990). "Senate Bill 1 Includes School Funding, Public Education Reforms." *School Board Association Newsletter.* Texas Association of School Boards.

Texas State Board of Education. (1987). "Long-range Plan of the State Board of Education for Texas Public School Education, 1986–1990 to the Texas Education Agency." January.

"The Path to a Quality Education for all Texas Students: Final Report of the Governor's Task Force on Public Education." (1990). Charles Miller, chair.

Thornton, Stephen J. (1985). "How Do Teachers' Intentions Influence What Teachers Actually Teach and What Students Experience?" A paper presented at the 1985 Annual Meeting of the American Educational Research Association, Chicago.

Timar, Thomas B. (1988). "Managing Educational Excellence: State Strategies to Reform Schools." In Thomas B. Timar and David L. Kirp (eds.), *Managing Educational Excellence.* London and New York: Taylor & Francis.

Toch, Thomas. (1991). *In the Name of Excellence: The Struggle to Reform the Nation's Schools, Why It's Failing, and What Should Be Done.* New York and Oxford: Oxford University Press.

Tyack, David B. (1993). "Constructing Difference: Historical Reflections on Schooling and Social Diversity." In *Teachers College Record* 95.

Tyack, David, and Larry Cuban. (1995). *Tinkering toward Utopia: A Century of*

Public School Reform. Cambridge and London: Harvard University Press.

[Urban] Independent School District. (undated). "Magnet Schools: Enrichment Education." An overview of all magnet programs in the city district.

[Urban] Independent School District. (1985). "Honors courses: the International Baccalaureate, the honors program, the Pathfinder program, grades 9–12," curriculum bulletin no. 85CBM5, item number 33.0538, prepared under the direction of the General Educational Services Division.

[Urban] Independent School District. (1985). "[U]ISD Report: Special Edition." Report on administrative reorganization, with a special message from the superintendent.

Valenzuela, Angela. (1999). *Subtractive Schooling: U.S.-Mexican Youth and the Politics of Caring*. Albany: State University of New York Press.

Vallas, Paul. (1999). Address to the National Conference of Governors, C-Span broadcast, March.

Versetgen, Deborah A. (1985). "The Lawmakers Respond: Texas Education Finance Reform (part I): Funding Formulas." A paper presented at the Annual Meeting of the American Education Finance Association, Phoenix, April.

Veselka, Marvin. (undated). "Educator Recertification Testing in Texas: Big State, Big Challenges." Unpublished paper.

Walker, Billy D. (1990). "Highlights of Senate Bill 1 (finance)." Texas Center for Educational Research, Huntsville.

Walker, Billy D. (1991). "The District Court and Edgewood III: Promethean Interpretation or Procrustean Bed?" Unpublished paper.

Wallace, Sally. (1994). "How Successful is [the School for Science, Engineering and Technology] at Preparing Its Students for a Career in Engineering?" An unpublished paper prepared for the course on the secondary school in the Master of Arts in Teaching program of Rice University, December.

Wells, M. Cyrene. (1996). *Literacies Lost: When Students Move from a Progressive Middle School to a Traditional High School*. New York and London: Teachers College Press.

Whitty, Geoff. (1998). "Citizens or Consumers? Continuity and Change in Contemporary Education Policy." In Dennis Carlson and Michael W. Apple (eds.), *Power/Knowledge/Pedagogy: The Meaning of Democratic Education in Unsettling Times*. Boulder: Westview Press.

Whitty, Geoff, Sally Power, and David Halpin. (1998). *Devolution and Choice in Education*. Philadelphia: Open University Press.

Willis, Paul E. (1977). *Learning to Labor*. Westmead, Eng.: Saxon House.

Wise, Arthur, and Linda Darling-Hammond, with Barnett Berry and Stephen P. Klein. (1987). *Licensing Teachers: Design for a Teaching Profession*. Center for the Study of Teaching Professions, RAND corporation.

Wise, Arthur. (1979). *Legislated Learning: The Bureaucratization of the American Classroom*. Berkeley and Los Angeles: University of California Press.

Wiske, Martha Stone (ed.) (1998). *Teaching for Understanding: Linking Research with Practice*. San Francisco: Jossey-Bass.

Wood, George H. (1998). "Democracy and the Curriculum." In Landon E. Beyer and Michael W. Apple (eds.), *The Curriculum: Problems, Politics, and Possibilities*, 2d ed. Albany: State University of New York Press.

Wrigley, Julia. (1982). *Class Politics and Public Schools: Chicago, 1900–1950*. New Brunswick, N.J.: Rutgers University Press.

Yalow, Elanna S. (1986). "Tempest in a TECAT." A paper presented at the Annual Meeting of the American Educational Research Association, San Francisco, April 16–20.

Index